# CIO Wisdom II

## HARRIS KERN'S ENTERPRISE COMPUTING INSTITUTE

▶ IT Architecture Toolkit
*Jane A. Carbone*

▶ Software Development: Building Reliable Systems
*Marc Hamilton*

▶ High Availability: Design, Techniques, and Processes
*Michael Hawkins, Floyd Piedad*

▶ Data Warehousing: Architecture and Implementation
*Mark Humphries, Michael W. Hawkins, Michelle C. Dy*

▶ IT Organization: Building a Worldclass Infrastructure
*Harris Kern, Stuart D. Galup, Guy Nemiro*

▶ Building Professional Services: The Sirens' Song
*Thomas E. Lah, Steve O'Connor, Mitchel Peterson*

▶ CIO Wisdom: Best Practices from Silicon Valley
*Dean Lane, Change Technology Solutions, Inc.,
and Members of the Silicon Valley Community of Practice*

▶ IT Automation: The Quest for Lights Out
*Howie Lyke with Debra Cottone*

▶ Managing IT as an Investment: Partnering for Success
*Ken Moskowitz, Harris Kern*

▶ Web-Based Infrastructures: A 4D Framework
*Sanmay Mukhopadhyay, Cooper Smith with Mayra Muniz*

▶ IT Systems Management
*Rich Schiesser*

▶ Technology Strategies
*Cooper Smith*

▶ IT Services: Costs, Metrics, Benchmarking, and Marketing
*Anthony F. Tardugno, Thomas R. DiPasquale, Robert E. Matthews*

▶ IT Problem Management
Gary Walker

ENTERPRISE COMPUTING SERIES

# CIO Wisdom II

## More Best Practices

**Phillip A. Laplante and Thomas Costello**

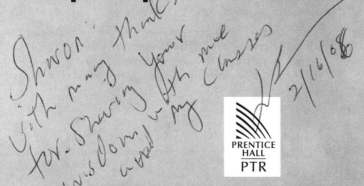

PRENTICE
HALL
PTR

Upper Saddle River, NJ • Boston • Indianapolis • San Francisco
New York • Toronto • Montreal • London • Munich • Paris • Madrid
• Capetown • Sydney • Tokyo • Singapore • Mexico City

Many of the designations used by manufacturers and sellers to distinguish their products are claimed as trademarks. Where those designations appear in this book, and the publisher was aware of a trademark claim, the designations have been printed with initial capital letters or in all capitals.

The authors and publisher have taken care in the preparation of this book, but make no expressed or implied warranty of any kind and assume no responsibility for errors or omissions. No liability is assumed for incidental or consequential damages in connection with or arising out of the use of the information or programs contained herein.

The publisher offers excellent discounts on this book when ordered in quantity for bulk purchases or special sales, which may include electronic versions and/or custom covers and content particular to your business, training goals, marketing focus, and branding interests. For more information, please contact:

U. S. Corporate and Government Sales
(800) 382-3419
corpsales@pearsontechgroup.com

For sales outside the U. S., please contact:

International Sales
international@pearsoned.com

Visit us on the Web: www.phptr.com

Library of Congress Cataloging-in-Publication Data

Laplante, Phillip A.
  CIO wisdom II : more best practices / Phil Laplante, Tom Costello.
     p. cm.
  Includes bibliographical references.
  ISBN 0-13-185589-1
 1.  Chief information officers. 2.  Information technology—Management.
3.  Information resources management. 4.  Management.  I. Costello, Tom. II. Title.
  HD30.2.L35 2005
  658.4'038--dc22

                                                                2005020503

Pearson Education, Inc.
Rights and Contracts Department
One Lake Street
Upper Saddle River, NJ 07458

ISBN 0-13-185589-1

Text printed in the United States on recycled paper at R.R. Donnelley in Crawfordsville, Indiana.
First printing, November, 2005

*To understand the pressure you would be under to write a dedication for a book, visualize yourself trying to name the person or persons who most shaped you into what you are today. Go ahead, take a moment...and then realize that this person will be reading it along with the hundreds of other people you know who don't see their name here. Not so much fun, huh?*

*At one point, we were emailing each other over this dilemma. In the midst of a short burst of humor, Phil suggested dedicating this book to our wives, kids, dogs, or some combination thereof. While we got a great laugh out of the prospect of limiting it to our pets so as not to offend any humans, it is clear that our families (dogs included) are the key to everything we are and do. While we all allow work to consume our time, we ultimately are doing all we can for our families and loved ones.*

*So, with that, we dedicate this book to all of our families: Phil's family, Tom's family, and your family...and to the balance we need to maintain to do both work and life well!*

# Contents

**Chapter 2**

# Scope of the CIO                                                  13
### By Thomas Costello

**Chapter 3**

# It's All About the Marketing                                      29
### By Autumn Bayles

**Chapter 4**

# Creating a Community of Practice for CIOs                         35
### By Phillip A. Laplante

SECTION 2  HARDWARE AND SOFTWARE TECHNOLOGY

**Chapter 7**

## Information Management: What's Next?                            89
*By John Wollman*

**Chapter 8**

## Enterprise Integration: Methods and Technologies            107
*By Min-Jung Yoo, Raghvinder S. Sangwan, and Robin G. Qiu*

## Section 3 Internal Forces

## SECTION 5   EXTERNAL FORCES

**Chapter 18**

## Open Source: Time for a Plan     271
*By Thomas Costello*

**Chapter 19**

## IT Governance: Toward a Unified Framework Linked to and Driven by Corporate Governance     283
*By David Pultorak*

**Chapter 22**

## Navigating the IT Procurement and Outsourcing Process     359
*By Francis X. Taney, Jr.*

## Index     401

# Preface

This sequel to the best-selling *CIO Wisdom* brings together expert contributions from members, speakers, and friends of the *CIO Institute*, a Greater Philadelphia Metro Area-based community of practice for CIOs. A complete description and history of this group can be found in Chapter 4, "Creating a Community of Practice for CIOs."

Inspired by the public meetings and private discussions of this elite group of thought leaders, this book covers many areas of interest to CIOs, IT professionals, and business leaders. Featuring new coverage of essential topics found in the original *CIO Wisdom*, as well several new topics, this book should be considered complementary to the *CIO Wisdom*, and we encourage you to read that book as well.

## ▶ Book Organization

One of the greatest challenges of any book is determining how to best structure and/or categorize the thoughts and chapters into a flow that is both meaningful and efficient for the reader. That challenge is compounded in this work by the vast array of contributors, writing styles, and intentions of the authors providing the chapters that comprise this text. Further, we wanted to ensure that this collection of material was evenly distributed across a set of timely focus areas. As a result, the chapters have been grouped into the following five major categories:

1. **What Makes a CIO Tick?**—The personal drivers and pressures facing the CIO.
2. **Hardware and Software Technology**—Nuts and bolts topics facing the enterprise.
3. **Internal Forces**—The internal pressure and value of the CIO.
4. **Information Architecture**—The mechanics and interconnection of the IT organization with the enterprise.
5. **External Forces**—Various pressures, technologies, and compliance opportunities/challenges facing the IT organization.

Although each author contributed his or her own thoughts without prompting or guidance, the threads that appear between the various works weave into something interesting. While you may cherry-pick your favorite topics and hop around between chapters, connections will appear around every turn. Every CIO has his own way of clustering his view of technology and business—the section grouping in this book is just one way to help you find a starting point for your learning experience. The following paragraphs describe the rationale behind each section.

# ▶ What Makes a CIO Tick?

Ever since the dotcom bust and the corporate financial reporting scandals of the late 1990s and early 2000s, dramatic changes have been taking place to the internal and external environment in which the CIO operates. This, in turn, has forced CIOs to reevaluate who they are, how they should set their priorities, and how best to react to the dynamic forces of change. In the wake of the Sarbanes-Oxley legislation and the mandated increased board oversight of operations, many CIOs struggle under the intense scrutiny. As the IT operation seeks to maintain its role in the organization, or perhaps gain more influence and respect at the executive table, how the CIO is viewed and how he[1] thinks is ever important.

In this section we look at the unique role of and try to understand what drives the CIO.

Chapter 1, "The Changing Role of the CIO," by Phil Laplante and Don Bain, first appeared as an article of the same name in the IEEE's respected magazine, *IT Professional*. It is reprinted here with permission. In this chapter they examine Nicholas Carr's hypothesis that the role of IT in the organization no longer matters because it offers no competitive advantage. In fact, because a company can only be at a disadvantage if its IT functions poorly, IT is a commodity. Phil and Don examine Carr's thesis from the perspective of CIO functional roles, reporting structures, and career risk.

In Chapter 2, "Scope of the CIO," Tom Costello, a long-time industry insider, looks at the evolution of the CIO and the environment around him along several broad dimensions, including organizational structure, governance, mission, and function. Tom argues that the role of the CIO has changed over the last 20 years, but that in some ways, it has remained the same. While the old checklist style of IT management may still work at some levels, a well-constructed IT plan may prove to be useful for both the operations of the IT department, as well as a roadmap for the career development of the CIO. Finally, the elements and purpose by which such a plan can be constructed are covered.

In Chapter 3, "It's All About Marketing," Autumn Bayles, gives us one perspective on the role of CIO: that of the CIO as "salesperson." We've heard time and again from our member CIOs of the importance of being able to influence colleagues, subordinates, superiors, and especially board members through persuasion (or, marketing, as she puts it), and Autumn addresses her enlightenment in this regard. This is the only chapter written in the first person but we didn't want to change it to third person because it's really a delightful glimpse into the life of one of our Superstar CIOs.

---

1. Throughout the text we use "he" or "him" most of the time when referring to the generic person. We find this less awkward than the use of "he/she" or "s/he" or "him/her." But in all cases, of course, we mean the generic person male or female.

In Chapter 4, "Creating a Community of Practice for CIOs," Phil Laplante describes the origins and evolution of the Philadelphia Metropolitan Area CIO community of practice, the CIO Institute. It provides the setting from which this book evolved and provides a glimpse at the dynamics and creation of this high-powered group. Some of the situations and issues described here should prove of value to those starting or nurturing a similar community of practice for CIOs or any C-level community, for that matter.

## ▶ Hardware and Software Technology

While it is true that many CIOs did not come up through the technical ranks (often through finance or operations) and even the most technical CIOs frequently delegate the most minute details of the technical aspects of the job to subordinates, a CIO must be techno-savvy. In this section we look at a selection of the hardware and software technology issues that the CIO must face. In particular, the convergence and integration of hardware and software within the physical operations—security, operations, and supply chain—is noteworthy in each chapter.

In Chapter 5, "Securing the IT Facility," Joel Richman and Paul Nowak look at a frequently overlooked aspect of the IT function—interfacing with the systems that control the physical security of the facility and its employees. Indeed, many CIOs are being tasked with overseeing some aspects of physical security as these systems become increasingly more complex and networked. In some cases, the CIO works in conjunction with a Chief Security Officer (CSO). Whatever the case, the CIO needs to be as aware of facility access control, fire protection and notification, and human identification as he is of firewalls and antispam filters.

Next, David Frigeri looks at the importance of network throughput measurement and improvement of data communications in Chapter 6, "Running Business-Critical Applications Over the Internet: 'The Middle Mile.'" In particular, he discusses why simply increasing bandwidth is not enough to alleviate congestion—you must also understand the underlying communications protocols and how they behave under stress. As he notes, taking advantage of the Internet is a matter of accomplishing two strategic objectives: assessing where the organization or the application is today and determining what the future requirements will be. David also addresses three reoccurring performance challenges: navigating through the Internet via the Border Gateway Protocol (BGP), TCP throughput, and resolving LAN–WAN mismatch. The CIO needs to take a structured approach via a situational analysis to ensure the underlying infrastructure is measurable, available, and performing (M.A.P.) to the requirements of the application. David offers extensive advice and case studies in this regard.

In Chapter 7, "Information Management: What's Next?" John Wollman focuses on the evolution of information management and the business and technology ramifications as organizations co-evolve with technology. To establish context, the chapter begins with a focus on the underlying technology of an information management value chain. Next, a novel Corporate Performance Management (CPM) model is described. This model is proffered as the business driver that requires organizations to increase the value-added information as it flows up through the management hierarchy to adequately measure, monitor, and respond to changes in the business climate.

In Chapter 8, "Enterprise Integration: Methods and Technologies," Min-Jin Yoo, Raghu Sangwan, and Robin Qiu, three friends from academia with extensive industrial experience, provide a high-level (and remarkably nonacademic) overview of enterprise integration. This chapter is a great primer on integration methodologies and enabling technologies and provides good background material for some of the later chapters, particularly those in Section 4, "Information Architecture." More importantly, their discussion is platform independent. Of particular note are their discussions on the very hot technologies of service oriented architectures, Web Services, and the sharing of business logic across applications.

Radio frequency identification or RFID is an important emerging technology that is not without controversy. In Chapter 9, "Toward Collaborative Supply Chains Using RFID" our friends Robin Qiu and Raghu Sangwan describe how rich, collaborative supply changes can be built using this emerging technology. While they don't go into the electronic implementation of RFID or the economic issues—that would be beyond the scope of this text—they address the more important issue of how to design and implement a product tracking and information system that enables the real-time visibility of products as they move through the supply chain. And they provide a usable architecture that is scalable, industry and platform independent, and that uses commonly available hardware and software.

Finally in Chapter 10, "Real-Time, Mission-Critical Business Intelligence: Lessons from the Military and Intelligence Community," renowned author and consultant, and CIO Institute member Alan Simon draws upon his experience as a bona fide air force intelligence officer to show how techniques from that domain can be applied to business intelligence. It's a neat chapter. While he introduces basic concepts of business intelligence and corrects some common misconceptions, he also provides an interesting glimpse at how real-time decision making is done in the military. The parallels between the decision-making needs of the Strategic Air Command and business are fascinating.

# ▶ Internal Forces

The CIO is a juggler—while in one hand he must deal with ever-changing hardware and software platforms, in another hand he must serve and satisfy his internal constituents. Then he has to find a way to manage the numerous, sometimes conflicting constraints of the external environment in a third, nonexistent hand. In this section we turn from hardware and software issues to look at the internal forces that confront the CIO. This is a short collection of chapters because many of the other internal influences are dealt with elsewhere; for example, the decision to outsource or not and IT portfolio planning are discussed in the next section. Moreover, many of the internal forces affecting the role of the CIO were covered in Section 1, "What Makes a CIO Tick?" But there are a number of additional internal issues that needed to be covered.

In particular the following chapters focus more precisely on the value proposition of the CIO function; that is, we address the question, What must a CIO deliver to the organization? The answer to this question involves the financial and business advantages that the IT function provides to a business (despite that Nicholas Carr might disagree that IT provides any value!).

In Chapter 11, "Software Return on Investment (ROI)," for example, Phil looks at various models for evaluating the cost of IT as well as the different mechanisms for representing IT as an investment. Besides covering the traditional accounting issues of whether software is an investment or an expense, this chapter examines the alignment of ROI calculations with organizational metrics. The chapter concludes with a mathematical review of many traditional cost justification techniques. If you hate math, you can just skip the final section (although we recommend that you don't).

Chapter 12, "Starting with the Users," by Melissa (Mickey) Skelton and Gerard Gallucci, (with the U.S. State Department at the time of this writing, now with the United Nations), examines the issue of how CIOs can become disconnected from their user clients and how important it is to remain connected. Their discussion is reminiscent of the quality function deployment (QFD) technique (representing the "voice of the customer"), which is widely used in manufacturing and has been adapted to software development as a means for capturing user requirements and ensuring satisfaction throughout the software production process. In any case, Mickey and Gerard describe what the CIO should do to ensure that technology is user-driven without becoming beholden to the users. Their approach includes involving the setting of expectations properly, engaging users early and often, and maintaining control.

What good is IT if it doesn't produce a process improvement? An organization should not spend even one dollar on IT if it is not clear how a business process will be improved and if it doesn't reasonably expect a return on that dollar. In Chapter 13, "Business Process Improvement," Peter Kraynak provides a simple yet effective framework for improving a business process of any kind and shows the relationship to business case development. Peter argues that the most effective approach to process improvement is through the use of Six Sigma, along with its roadmap of DMAIC. Adopting this discipline will guarantee the achievement of a positive ROI and will enable you to do your job properly as a CIO. In addition to being a primer on the topic of Six Sigma and DMAIC, the chapter answers the following questions: What does a CIO need to know about business process? What is Six Sigma, and why is it so effective? and Why should a CIO utilize a Six Sigma approach? The chapter includes a case study.

# ▶ Information Architecture

With the rapid changes in language, protocols, and standards, tools defining robust information architectures are of supreme importance to the CIO. But the architecture does more than isolate the enterprise from these rapid changes in technology—it must insulate the organization for environmental changes such as government regulations, competitive pressures, and market conditions for the product and for labor. In this section we look at approaches for protecting the organization and adapting to these changes.

A version of Chapter 14, "The Five Ws of IT Outsourcing," was derived from a roundtable discussion of the CIO Institute and first appeared in *IT Professional* as "The Who, What, Why, Where, and When of IT Outsourcing." It is reprinted here with permission. In this offering, members of the CIO Institute describe the nature of IT outsource and the main drivers in the decision to outsource or not. They then describe several rubrics for the outsourcing decision.

In Chapter 15, "Outsourced Environments," Raghu Sangwan looks in detail at the perils inherent in outsourced projects, such as time zone differences, time dynamics, and tool compatibility. This chapter is a natural follow up to the previous one. After describing the inherent difficulties of outsourced development, he provides management techniques for mitigating these challenges; these include focusing on monitoring and control through the use of appropriate metrics. The resultant set of best practices can be used in virtually any outsourced environment.

Enterprise information architectures (EIA) may easily be one of the more used and misused terms in our industry, and Tom Costello takes his turn at boiling the key elements and history into a primer on EIA. With a combination of observations and "how to," Chapter 16, "Enterprise Information Architecture," provides an overview of the value of an EIA and how this document fits into the array of tools every CIO needs to efficiently and effectively chart the course for aligning the vast tangle of IT with the business needs of the enterprise.

In Chapter 17, "Adaptive and Aware: Strategy, Architecture, and IT Leadership in an Age of Commoditization," Rob Kelley presents a sweeping tour de force that, at once, places the evolution of IT into the context of other kinds of technology revolutions and describes how IT leaders can respond to this revolution and protect against the next one. The key lies in the structure of the IT organization, how well it shifts paradigms to operate in the new world, and how intelligently it allocates resources and selects its business partners. Indeed, the nature of the IT organization has evolved from the bastion of monks with mysterious powers that no one else understood to a brotherhood of diplomat-accountants. Rob suggests that the configuration of the IT organization's strategy, resources, and business intelligence to form a learning organization (our term, not his) is critical to its survival.

# ▶ External Forces

If this book were considered to be a kind of SWOT (strengths, weaknesses, opportunities, and threats) analysis, the first section would be focused on CIO strengths and the last section on threats (the opportunities and weaknesses are threaded throughout all of the chapters. In particular, we look at the various external threats, drivers, constituencies, and stakeholders with which the CIO must contend. These include use of open source software, tools, and standards; conformance to open and closed standards; compliance with laws and best practices; and dealing with the threat or eventuality of litigation.

In Chapter 18, "Open Source: Time for a Plan,"[2] Tom Costello updates and expands on a work previously published by *Technology Times*, the bimonthly newspaper of the Eastern Technology Council. Elements of the original article are reused with permission. This chapter provides a brief update on the world's view of Open Source compared with the narrower use within the United States. This chapter includes some definitions and background material to familiarize you with Open Source, and then takes a broader look at the drivers and challenges facing the market at large. Though not a "how to" of Open Source, this chapter will broaden your thinking on the need for an Open Source plan for your enterprise.

---

2. Tom Costello, "Familiar with Open Source? You Should Be," *Technology Times*, August 2003.

In Chapter 19, "IT Governance: Toward a Unified Framework Linked to and Driven by Corporate Governance," Dave Pultorak takes a look at IT governance from a unique perspective. He starts by providing a theoretical framework for corporate governance. He then looks at three dimensions: ensuring that the corporation meets regulatory requirements, ensuring that the corporation achieves performance objectives, and paying appropriate attention to relevant stakeholders. Along the way Dave provides a whirlwind tour of most of the relevant standards or models to which many CIOs are held or that are used as frameworks for management and decision making (e.g., CMMI, ISO 9000, Six Sigma, TQM, ITIL). Finally, he offers an IT governance checklist that can be used for a rapid assessment of your organization's IT governance health.

Municipal, county, state, and federal government entities are increasingly relying on email and Web-enabled facilities to improve service, increase information flow, and in some cases reduce costs. But governments don't and can't always work like private enterprises. In Chapter 20, "E-Government," Dianah Neff, CIO of the City of Philadelphia, one of the most e-savvy cities, provides a great perspective on this topic. Dianah provides best practices, lessons learned, and important information on setting and meeting strategic goals and objectives, governance, technology issues, and communications, and outreach. This information is particularly useful to any government or nongovernment entity that is considering an initiative to deploy customer-centric e-services.

The job of the CIO includes the function of risk manager, and religiously following the rules is the best way to mitigate risk. In Chapter 21, "Compliance," John Supplee tackles the sticky issue of complying with the ever-shifting sands of governmental regulations that can hamstring an IT operation, raise the stakes of any problems encountered, and give the board fits. John knows what he is talking about, having navigated the many regulations of the SEC, Federal Reserve Bank, and more. John takes the perspective of a small to mid-sized company CIO—the large companies have teams of compliance people to work with IT.

Finally, Frank Taney's Chapter 22, "Navigating the IT Procurement and Outsourcing Process," represents a kind of reality check for the IT industry. In a way, he frightens us into realizing that we ought to be more careful about the way we negotiate contracts, make promises, and inadvertently set expectations. If you follow Frank's advice, you'll stay out of the kind of trouble that every CIO dreads—costly and distracting litigation, arbitration, or mediation. Nothing is worse for a business than to have to waste resources defending poor decision making, management, or project execution. The best remedy is prevention.

We have seen Frank present this material in person, and we wanted all of our readers to have the benefit of his counsel. This chapter is the next best thing to actually visiting with him.

## ▶ Book Development Process

CIOs are very busy people. Therefore, when we undertook to recruit them to write chapters for this book, we knew we had a challenge on our hands. But we were surprised at how many CIOs had something to say and felt compelled to put it in writing. While we certainly did not expect that every CIO who offered to write a chapter could ultimately find the time to deliver, we were surprised at how many came through. Nonetheless, we ensured that this book would be comprehensive and protected ourselves against the inevitable disruption by overlapping assignments. We felt that if duplications of material did occur, this could be handled in the editing. Moreover, providing more than one perspective on the same issue would be beneficial. Nonetheless, you'll notice very little duplication in these chapters.

After assigning chapters to potential authors, or rather, as they were self-assigned, we constantly monitored progress and provided advice and encouragement to our authors.

Any endeavor of this sort—trying to coordinate the activity of many important and busy people—takes a great deal of effort. Fortunately, the technology of email helps a tremendously.

After we received all of the chapters, we undertook the process of editing them. We did not impose heavy editorial restrictions on the contributors because we wanted to preserve the authors' original voices. Therefore, each chapter is uniquely original, varying in length, writing style, and most importantly, perspective. We did not want to destroy any of the contributors' intent with heavy-handed editing, and so the chapters remain largely as diverse as the contributors themselves.

Finally, after we had compiled and edited the chapters, we sent the compilation out to each of the authors and to other CIOs and experts for review. We then incorporated their comments into the final draft. This draft went into production process for copy editing and formatting. Finally, the edited and formatted draft was sent to each of the authors for one last check before going into production. The result is the book you hold in your hands, and we are very proud of it.

## ▶ Disclaimers

No product or service mentioned in this book is endorsed, nor are any claims made about the capabilities of such product or service.

All trademarks are copyrighted to their respective owners.

# Acknowledgments

First and foremost, we must acknowledge our colleagues and friends who contributed chapters. They came through with great work and showed tremendous patience with our constant harassment for more, more, and still more. These contributors are listed, along with their biographical sketches, at the end of the book.

We must also thank Rob McCord, Chairman, and Dianne Strunk, CEO, of the Eastern Technology Council, a business advocacy organization in the Greater Philadelphia Metro Area, for helping to create and nurture the CIO Institute. Without their vision and contribution of resources, the CIO Institute would have never existed, and therefore, neither would this book.

We also want to thank the administration and staff of the Eastern Technology Council for providing logistical and moral support for all of the CIO Institute events. In particular, we single out Karen Evans for her outstanding work in recruiting members and sponsors, and Karen Carr for her tireless work in planning and seeing through the flawless execution of all of the CIO Institute's events. Other members of the Eastern Technology Council who have worked hard behind the scenes to make everything run smoothly include Melissa Delicci, Kim Demchik, Ida Marie Higgins, Laurie Rhoades, and Carol Thompson Hartpence. Thank you, ladies, for all your great work.

Gianna Alicea, Research Analyst, Upstreme, Inc., provided significant editorial and logistical assistance in the preparation of the manuscript. We want to thank her for helping keep things running so smoothly in the development of this work.

Many sponsors have provided substantial financial resources, speakers, and venues for the CIO Institute's programs and have thus been a driving force in its evolution and have had an indirect but significant impact on the input to this text. While this is not the place for a name-by-name listing of these sponsors, we want to collectively acknowledge them for their past, ongoing, and future support.

Of course, the members of the CIO Institute have had a great deal of influence in shaping the destiny of this community of practice and, in turn, this book. In particular, we want to recognize our advisory board, who's members may be considered expert consultants to this volume:

Dianah Neff
Chief Information Officer
City of Philadelphia

Kenneth Weirman
Chief Information Officer
Keystone Foods Corporation

John Supplee
VP, Information Technology
Haverford Trust

David Fenske
Isaac L. Auerbach Professor and Dean
College of Information Science and Technology, Drexel University

David Monahan
General Manager
Microsoft Corporation

Thomas Costello
President & CEO
Upstreme, Inc.

John Carrow
CIO
Unisys Corporation

The following individuals participated in one or more of the CIO roundtables mentioned in various chapters of this book. Although we deliberately omit their affiliations to "protect the innocent," we want to thank them individually for their contributions.

| | |
|---|---|
| Don Bain | Chris Martin |
| Sudi Bindiganavile | Neil McCarthy |
| Choukran Borak | Jim Mercante |
| Jeff Cepull | Susan Millstein |
| Chris DiFonzo | Michael Moore |
| Paul Evers | Colin Neill |
| Suzann Fairlie | Claudia Piccirilli |
| David Fenske | Scott Plichta |
| Tim Fisher | Tom Reidy |
| Dave Gillespie | Joel Richman |
| Sanjay Khatani | Peter Rugg |
| Robert Knecht | Ivan Ruzic |
| Joe Kokinda | Larry Strawley |
| Peter Kraynak | Calvin Sun |
| Mark Landon | John Supplee |
| Kunle Malomo | Bryn Thomas |

A number of our members, experts, and other CIOs reviewed various portions of the text. Their comments proved invaluable in improving the readability and focus of the text, and we wish to collectively thank them.

Finally, we want to thank our series editor, Harris Kern, and acquisitions editor, Greg Doench, for their inspiration and guidance during the development of this project, and the production staff at Prentice Hall, in particular Kerry Reardon, Kristy Hart, and Carol Lallier for their expertise in preparing the final manuscript.

# About the Authors

## ▶ Phil Laplante

Dr. Phil Laplante is Associate Professor of Software Engineering at Penn State University and the founder and director of the CIO Institute, a three-year old community of practice for CIOs in the Greater Philadelphia Metro Area. He is also the CTO of the Eastern Technology Council, a business development organization for the Greater Philadelphia Metropolitan Area. Prior to coming to Penn State, he was a senior academic administrator at several other colleges and universities.

In addition to his academic career, Dr. Laplante spent almost eight years as a software engineer, project manager, and director of a software consulting firm. He has authored or edited 20 books and more than 140 other papers and articles and is a highly sought mentor and coach for CEOs and CIOs.

Dr. Laplante received his BS, M.Eng., and PhD in computer science, electrical engineering, and computer science, respectively, from Stevens Institute of Technology, and an MBA from the University of Colorado.

# ▶ Tom Costello

As the CEO of UpStreme, Mr. Costello currently provides technical and business consulting to corporate CxOs, boards of directors, venture capital firms, angels, and investment bankers in the evaluation, planning, and implementation of technologies to meet strategic and tactical business needs. Mr. Costello has advised both private and public sector organizations ranging from the U.S. Department of State and established top Fortune 500 organizations to early-stage/prefunded startups.

Mr. Costello's 20-year career has spanned the universe of computing challenges and solutions. He has formerly held positions with such firms as Cambridge Technology Partners as director of IT Strategy and Planning, CoreTech Consulting Group as Director of Management Services, U.S. Healthcare as Director of Development, AssetTRADE as both COO and CTO, the QVC Television Network, Shared Medical Systems, and GMIS.

Mr. Costello earned a BS in management information systems from the Indiana University of Pennsylvania, where he is currently a member of the Eberly College of Business Advisory Council.

# ▶ Don Bain

Don assists executives and corporations in creating business value with technology. Active in the entrepreneurial and venture communities, he serves on the board of Robin Hood Ventures. While a management consulting partner at Ernst & Young, he specialized in enterprise systems and supply chain management. Especially notable was his work in leading practices for achieving business success with enterprise software.

Don was president of Setpoint Europe, a software and project services firm serving the process industries. He has executive experience in the Americas, Europe, and Asia. Don earned an electrical engineering degree from Stanford University and completed the Management Program at Rice University.

# ▶ Autumn Bayles

Autumn Bayles is the CIO of Tasty Baking Company (TBC: NYSE) headquartered in Philadelphia, Pennsylvania. Prior to joining Tasty Baking Company, Bayles was a managing principal consultant with IBM Business Consulting Services, pre-merger PricewaterhouseCoopers Consulting. Bayles also served as a technology consultant for Safeguard Scientifics and director of consulting for Destiny Websolutions.

Autumn received a BS in industrial engineering from Lehigh University and an MBA from the Wharton School of the University of Pennsylvania. She serves on the boards of Junior Achievement, Girl Scouts of SE PA, Society of Information Management, and the Forum of Executive Women.

# ▶ Sudi Bindiganavile

Sudi Bindiganavile is Director of Information Services at Primavera Systems, Inc., in Bala Cynwyd, Pennsylvania.

# ▶ David Frigeri

As Director of Technical Services, David oversees the Technical Consultant and Professional Services teams for Internap Network Services. Internap Network Services Corporation is the leader in route control technology and Internet optimization professional services. In the role of Director of Technical Services, David is accountable for the integrity of the network design and IP solutions implemented for the customer. David is also the co-chairman of the FCC Network Reliability Interoperability Council Subcommittee on Public Data Network Best Practices. The IEEE has recognized David for his significant contribution for advancing the quality, reliability, and security of the international communications industry. David graduated from Hobart College and has attended the Massachusetts Institute of Technology Sloan School of Management Executive Program.

# ▶ Gerard M. Gallucci

Gerard M. Gallucci is a member of the Senior Foreign Service serving as Director of eDiplomacy in the State Department. Over the past 25 years, he has served as Charge'd'Affaires of the U.S. Embassy in Khartoum and in Brasilia and at the National Security Council as Director for Inter-American Affairs.

Gallucci was Assistant Professorial Lecturer in Media and Public Affairs at the School of Media and Public Affairs, George Washington University, in 2003. Prior to government service, Gallucci was Assistant Professor of Political Science, West Virginia Wesleyan College, and Assistant Professor of Political Science, University of Arkansas at Little Rock. Gallucci was born in 1951 in Jersey City, New Jersey. He received a PhD from the University of Pittsburgh in 1978 and a BA at Rutgers University in 1973.

# ▶ Robert T. Kelley

Robert T. Kelley is a Founding Partner of LiquidHub, a systems integrator and technology consultancy serving clients globally in Life Sciences, Financial Services, Retail, High Tech, and other industries. Prior to starting LiquidHub, Dr. Kelley served as Partner and Vice-president at Broadreach Consulting, where he began and led a national Internet and eBusiness practice, as IT Manager for Right Management Consultants, a global human resources consulting firm, and as a consultant for various large enterprises. Dr. Kelley received his BS in mechanical engineering from the University of Missouri-Rolla, and his Masters and Doctorate degrees from Indiana University, where he investigated the cultural implications of virtual reality.

# Peter Kraynak

Peter Kraynak is the owner and managing director of Info724 Ltd. (www.info724.com), which provides middle market companies with its expertise in business process, IT strategy, and implementation to leverage a better return on IT investment. Mr. Kraynak has 17 years of professional IT and business experience, including strength in leadership and facilitation, IT strategic planning, project management, and business process improvement. He has served as an Adjunct Professor for Drexel University's MBA Program, and has earned the PMP Certification for competency in Project Management. Mr. Kraynak completed the Wharton MBA program in 1992 for Strategy and Finance, and previously was a professional management and technology consultant in the systems development group at Coopers & Lybrand in Philadelphia. He is a Board member of the CIO Institute.

# Mark Landon

Cofounder and CTO of Educational Directories Unlimited, Inc., Mark Landon has played a leading role in the creation and design of all EDUs products and services since the company's inception. Currently he oversees systems, development, and the technology direction for the organization. As such he is committed to finding innovative solutions that continue to help the company maintain its edge in a volatile and challenging industry. He is also active in the study-abroad field, a member of NAFSA, the Association of International Educators, and a regular presenter at NAFSA events.

# Dianah Neff

Dianah L. Neff is the CIO for the City of Philadelphia. Appointed by Mayor Street in May 2001, she is also a member of the Mayor's Cabinet. Ms. Neff is recognized for her vision in long-range systems planning and her work in developing innovative systems. Prior to working in government, she had 14 years experience in the private sector working for high-tech software and hardware firms in Silicon Valley.

As CIO, Ms. Neff is currently leading Wireless Philadelphia. This initiative of Mayor Street is designed to strengthen the City's economy and transform Philadelphia's neighborhoods through the creation of a metro-scale wireless environment serving all of the city.

# ▶ Paul Nowak

Paul Nowak has been in the electronic security business for over 12 years, starting as an installation technician. For the last seven years he has been in the Information Technology department of SST, working on customer integration needs as well as heading the IT department that focuses on SST's internal network and systems. A veteran of the U.S. Army Paratroopers, Paul has an Associates degree in electronics, an MCSE, is certified on many security-related products, and is finishing his Bachelors degree at St. Joseph's University.

# ▶ Dave Pultorak

David Pultorak is president of Fox IT (http://us.foxit.net), a global IT management consulting and training firm, and founder of Pultorak & Associates (www.pultorak.com), which specializes in business process improvement. A recognized authority in IT and process management, David has devoted 19 years to helping organizations better manage IT for business value. Mr. Pultorak holds a Masters degree from the University of Pennsylvania in IT and organizational science, and is a founding member of the University's Center for Organizational Dynamics. His most recent book is *The Definitive Guide to IT Management for the Adaptive Enterprise* (Realtime Publishers 2004) with Kevin Behr.

# Robin Qiu

Robin G. Qiu received MS and BS degrees from Beijing Institute of Technology, Beijing, China, and a PhD in industrial engineering with focus on control and information systems and a PhD (minor) in computer science from the Pennsylvania State University, University Park, in 1996. He is currently with Department of Information Science at the Pennsylvania State University. He has had about 80 articles published or presented in international journals or conferences. Dr. Qiu's research interests include issues on instant/automatic information retrievals (IIR/Auto-IR), component-based software, distributed computing, control and management of manufacturing systems, service operations, service process engineering, and enterprise information integration. Dr. Qiu has organized and chaired numerous international conferences. Dr. Qiu is the Editor-in-Chief for *International Journal of Services Operations and Informatics* and an Associate Editor for *IEEE Transactions on System, Man and Cybernetics*.

# Joel Richman

Joel Richman Jr. draws on over 18 years in the electronic security industry. One of the original cofounders of Security Services and Technologies, he held positions in all operation facets, including CIO and Executive VP of Corporate Services, a position he currently occupies. Joel's responsibilities range from merger and acquisition integration, security architecture, and deployment of systems to organizational planning and execution. Based in Norristown, Pennsylvania, Joel has spearheaded the technical growth of SST and is directly responsible for all IS resources throughout the United States for SST.

# Raghu Sangwan

Dr. Sangwan is an Assistant Professor of Information Science in the School of Graduate Professional Studies at the Pennsylvania State University. His research interests include analysis, design, and development of large-scale object-oriented distributed systems; their communication, connectivity, portability, security, and interoperability; and automated approaches to assessment of their quality. Prior to joining Penn State University, he worked as a lead architect for Siemens on geographically distributed development projects building information systems for large integrated health networks. He still serves as a consulting technical staff member for Siemens Corporate Research in Princeton, New Jersey, investigating approaches to managing global software development projects. He holds a PhD in computer and information sciences from Temple University in Philadelphia.

# ▶ Alan Simon

Alan Simon is the global Vice President of Business Objects' Data Warehousing Services and Solutions Practice. He is the author of 27 books, including *Data Warehousing For Dummies* and *90 Days to the Data Mart*. Alan was a monthly columnist for *Database Programming & Design* in the late 1990s. He specializes in business intelligence strategy and architecture and has worked with clients such as Quaker Oats, McDonald's, Pfizer, PNC Bank, and various governmental organizations.

# ▶ Pawan Singh

Dr. Pawan Singh is president of Quantum Performance Solutions in Bethlehem, Pennsylvania.

# ▶ Melissa Skelton

Melissa "Mickey" Skelton is an independent consultant currently working with the U.S. Department of State to craft and implement knowledge management strategies and practices. Prior to her work at the Department, Skelton was a project manager at the American Productivity and Quality Center in Houston, Texas, conducting studies in and writing articles about benchmarking and best practices. She has also worked as a consultant with Ernst & Young Management Consulting (now CGE&Y) and American Management Systems (now CGI-AMS). Skelton holds an MBA from the University of Texas, and a BA in Political Science from Bucknell University.

# ▶ John Supplee

John S. Supplee, Vice President of Information Technology, joined The Haverford Trust Company in 1998 to manage the computer systems and technology areas of the company. For ten years prior to joining The Haverford Trust Company, John applied his computer networking expertise within the financial arena. In 1997, he became a Microsoft Certified Systems Engineer. He currently sits on the Advisory Board for the CIO Institute of the Eastern Technology Council. John graduated from West Chester University with a BS in accounting and received his Masters of Science in information science from Pennsylvania State University.

# ▶ Frank Taney

Francis X. Taney, Jr. is a trial lawyer and commercial litigator who focuses on commercial litigation in a number of substantive areas, including information technology, antitrust, intellectual property, and construction litigation. Frank also represents vendors and purchasers of IT products and services in IT-related transactions, and counsels his clients on ways to avoid or minimize disputes arising from these transactions. He speaks and writes frequently on legal issues affecting IT. Frank is a shareholder in the Philadelphia law firm of Buchanan Ingersoll PC, and the chairman of the firm's IT litigation practice group. He can be reached at taneyfx@bipc.com.

# ▶ John Wollman

John Wollman is Executive Vice President and CTO of Alliance Consulting, a premiere IT Consultancy. Mr. Wollman is responsible for Alliance Consulting's vision and go-to-market strategy, manages Alliance's Vertical Industry and Business-Driven Solutions practices, develops strategic initiatives, and works with many leading clients.

An 18-year veteran in the IT industry, Mr. Wollman has held executive level positions in services and product companies, including PLATINUM Technology, Whittman-Hart, and Accenture.

# ▶ Min-Jung Yoo

Min-Jung Yoo is an Assistant Professor of Computer Science at the University of Lausanne, the Faculty of Economics and Business administration (Ecole des Hautes Etudes Commerciales). Min's research interests include multi-agent systems, application integration and interoperability, Semantic Web, and Web Services. She focuses on the application of multi-agent systems and other Web-based technologies to practical enterprise information systems and e-learning as well. She obtained a PhD in computer science from the University of Paris 6 (Pierre et Marie Curie) in 1999.

# The Changing Role of the CIO[1]

*Phillip A. Laplante and Don M. Bain*

## ▶ Introduction

In May 2003, Nicolas Carr published "IT Doesn't Matter" in the *Harvard Business Review*, arguing that information technologies have become a commodity rather than a source of competitive advantage. He also suggested that companies would be well served to manage IT using strategies of minimum cost and carefully managed risk (Carr 2003). Carr set off a firestorm. Some pundits cited the article as capturing the spirit of a contemporary backlash, which has resulted in diminished mandate and budgets for IT. Others rebuked Carr, claiming that IT-enabled transformational and business innovation opportunities are increasing and within reach given only the necessary increase in will and resources.

---

1. ©2005 IEEE. Reprinted with permission from Phillip A. Laplante and Don M. Bain, "The Changing Role of the CIO: Why IT Still Matters." *IT Professional*, May/June 2005.

In the fallout of Carr's article, some intrepid CIOs are skillfully navigating the maelstrom and winning more responsibility and influence. Other CIOs are embattled to save their budgets and their seat at the executive table. This chapter explores the role of the CIO and addresses a number of related issues, such as changing responsibilities, goals, expectations, and risks.

Much of this chapter was derived from a moderated panel discussion held in May 2004 involving several members of the CIO Institute, a community of practice based in Southeastern Pennsylvania. Although the meeting from which these observations were derived was open, we choose to keep the identities of the participants anonymous. Therefore, the quotes attributed herein are apocryphal or paraphrased. The sentiments expressed by the participants, however, are real.

## ▶ Challenges for the CIO

Whether the title is chief information officer (CIO), chief technology officer (CTO), vice president or director of information systems (or vice president of "anything technical"), the job is vital and difficult.[2] CIOs deal with sophisticated technical issues such as rapidly changing software packages, platforms, and standards. They face the challenge of leading and earning the respect of a diverse technical staff. They oversee the operations of systems on which business, revenues, and profits are dependent and, in some cases, impossible to achieve without. Then, there is the management of relationships with executive administration, internal customers, a board of directors, and other stakeholders.

Cash and Pearlson observed that those holding the CIO title have widely ranging positions in the organizational chart and varying job responsibilities. But they specifically identified four CIO job types: corporate CIO for operations, corporate CIO for functional leadership, business unit CIO, and regional CIO (Cash 2004).

---

2. Throughout we use "CIO" to mean any person with the duties of a CIO-like executive regardless of title.

Consider the difference, for example, between a CIO operating at the corporate level in a large multinational corporation—whose main responsibility is to oversee the budget, ensure standards compliance, and coordinate the activities of her direct reports—and the functional CIO of a small, $50 million per year information services company—who might even have to go hands-on when a major system crashes. The duties of these CIOs differ from those of a CIO of the consumer products division of a major electronics company, or from those of the CIO responsible for the Asia-Pacific region for an automotive manufacturer. The duties differ still from the CIO of a 100-person consulting company.

Regardless of position in the organizational chart or formal job description, Cash and Pearlson identified five primary roles of the CIO (Figure 1.1).

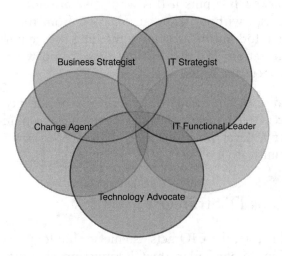

**Figure 1.1** Five primary roles of the CIO.
*Source:* James I. Cash and Keri E. Pearlson, "The Future CIO," *Information Week*, Special Anniversary Report, 2004.

These roles include business strategist, IT strategist, change agent, technology advocate, and functional leader. Challenges are found in each (Cash 2004).

## CIO as Business Strategist

According to Donald Tapscott, perhaps Carr's most vocal critic, the role of the CIO is to find the best practices of the business. In a global economy, however, the differences in best business practices are shrinking (Tapscott 2004). The challenge for the CIO, then, is to find these best business practices while at the same time finding increased benefits, continued cost reductions, or, somehow, all of these advantages. And the improvements have to be implemented fast, before inevitable competitive pressures degrade advantage into mediocrity and commodity status observed by Carr.

One approach to business strategy optimization is to plan initiatives that help shape business processes, not simply automate existing processes—especially if the processes are not working. One of our community's CIOs puts it this way: "We are not putting up new business processes without some automation from the outset. Competency to design for automation is something we require throughout our IT organization. We then deploy these competencies into other business and operating units."

Because of the need for the CIO to be deeply involved in business process reengineering, some companies combine the CIO role with other C-level positions rich with process ownership, such as chief administrative officer.

## CIO as IT Strategist

In this role, the CIO acts as chief technology evangelist for the organization. In particular, the CIO must provide the answer to fundamental questions and then sell the viability of the solution. Key IT strategic questions include: Which standard platform should we use? Do we use open source software or not? Do we build or buy? Do we use a single, integrated solution and risk vendor lock-in, or do we take a heterogeneous approach and risk creating a stovepipe architecture? And so on.

The CIO may be involved in major shareholder initiatives and certainly IT vendor contract negotiations. An often unavoidable side effect of these dealings is shareholder or contract disputes. Because legal and shareholders issues can significantly drain corporate resources, managing the incumbent risks are a major part of the CIOs strategic dashboard. No CIO wants to find himself on a witness stand in a business court.

## CIO as Change Agent

In providing IT support for any aspect of an organization, the choices are to buy off-the-shelf solutions, build a software solution from scratch, or change the organization so that no new IT resources are needed. But most organizations resist change. It is here, in particular, where the CIO can act as a change agent by demonstrating the cost-benefit analysis of the build, buy, or change decision.

No company would think about rolling out a new initiative without including IT from the beginning. Therefore, the CIO has a great deal of opportunity to influence change in the organization apart from that which is directly IT related. Consider this reported success story from one chief executive officer (CEO), "We were trying to deploy standards in our systems and support processes—trying to harmonize our infrastructure. Now we really do have just one email system, one desktop, more use of enterprise applications, and fewer one-offs. Our CIO has done a good job of showing us how."

## CIO as Technology Advocate

A CIO also has to help the organization to intelligently deploy technology. This might involve evangelizing a new platform, product, or standard. It might involve setting up a skills training program to help the organization retool. Or, it might be simply attracting and retaining top-notch technical talent.

Many might think that CIOs only think about putting in big systems and supporting them. But IT organizations also have to provide desktop support and help desk services. And depending on the size of the company, the CIO may be closely involved in these activities too.

The notion that the CIO has to be a great technologist is, however, a myth. The CIO needs to be an excellent leader and have some technical prowess, for sure. But it is naïve to think that the CIO must be as technically competent as each and every member of her organization. Often, CIOs are criticized by those at the lower levels of the IT organization for being less than technically adequate (sometimes fairly, sometimes unfairly). But frankly, people, financial, and organizational skills are far more valuable to the CIO than any kind of technical proficiency.

## CIO as Functional Leader

CIOs are, after all, managers. They have to hire, evaluate, promote, and fire staff. They have to motivate their organizations and defend the actions of individual staff members.

CIOs are also project planners and resource managers and will get blamed first when projects run over schedule or over budget (but do not always receive credit when they don't run over). Saying no to rogue initiatives and identifying and removing underground processes is also an important role of a functional leader.

Many excellent functional leaders use the "management by walking around" principle. Under this principle, the CIO is fully aware of what is going on within the business process chain by regular interaction with all levels of staff (and not hiding in a mahogany-paneled office).

Consider this sentiment from one of our CIOs: "Achievement of benefits is as important as ever and as rare as ever. Given the need for continued cost reductions, we are still focused on process improvement and associated headcount reductions. Skills in how to do this are ever important. Our IT organization has to engage with our process owners to get this done. We have been hurt by the fact that we have had some turnover since our big initiatives prior to year 2000. And of course, the consultants are gone. But the office of the CIO and IT organization are the place where we expect that knowledge to be retained and redeployed."

# ▶ CIO Reporting Relationships

The late 1990s saw an increase in the number of CIOs directly reporting to the chief executive officer. Has that trend reversed? In one survey conducted by *CIO Magazine*, it seems that the CIO is reporting to the CEO less often (CIO 2004).

In fact, from a high of 51 percent in 2002, only 40 percent of CIOs report directly to CEOs in 2004, according to the survey (Figure 1.2).

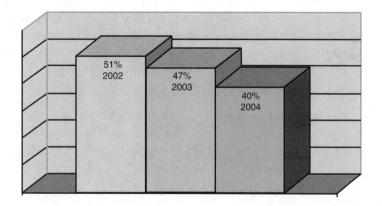

**Figure 1.2** Percentage of CIOs reporting to CEOs.
*Source:* CIO Research Column, *CIO*, October 1, 2004, page 74.

But the change in the reporting structure trend might be a function of company size. For example, in another survey, CIOs of small companies (less than $1 billion revenues) reported to the CEO 55 percent of the time, but in large companies only 41 percent of the time. In a different survey, the CIO reported to the CEO 60 percent of the time in very large (more than $5 billion revenues) (*CFO* 2004). Thus, the reduction in CIOs reporting to CEOs might have something to do with industry consolidation or the shakeout of smaller companies after the dotcom bust.

What do CIOs think about whom they should report to? Our community of practice expressed three different views: First, CIOs should report to the CEO; second, CIOs should report to someone other than the CEO, typically the chief financial officer (CFO) or chief operating officer (COO); and third, it doesn't matter to whom the CIO reports.

The case for the CIO reporting to the CEO seems to be based upon equalizing the responsibility of the CIO with the level of authority needed to fulfill that responsibility. That is, if the CIO is providing sufficient value, then the CIO should report to the CEO. This is an advantage to the IT organization because the ability to influence the strategic IT direction is greater if the CIO reports to the CEO.

The case for the CIO reporting to someone other than the CEO is based on financial accountability to shareholders. Consider this comment from one CIO: "Accounting scandals and the subsequent Sarbanes-Oxley legislation tell us that for the CIO to be at the C-level, it is all about risk and trust. It is not that we have decreased the role of the CIO. Rather, we count so much on the CFO to protect our corporation. It just seems natural, now more than ever, for our IT function to report in through the CFO."

The case for "it doesn't matter" to whom the CIO reports is simple— a title isn't as important as the chemistry between the CIO and his boss. Most CIOs would rather not report to the CEO if they don't have a good relationship.

Now consider what role the CIO should play in corporate governance and how this role can be reconciled with other day-to-day activities. Some corporate board members believe that the CIO should report in dotted line fashion to an IT subcommittee of the board of directors, in addition to a direct reporting line to the CEO or CFO. This situation is similar to a CFO also reporting to a board audit committee. Indeed, some CIOs have engineered such a governance body to help ensure alignment between corporate strategy and IT investment decisions. There needs to be an approval process for most large IT projects anyway, and the ability to pitch to the board can be critical for gaining support for the CIO's initiatives. Having more interaction with the board increases the influence and stature of the CIO overall.

But many CIOs view that situation as undesirable because of the potential for a board committee to micromanage the CIO's activities and budget. Our community's CIOs believe that boards have the duty to weigh in on the strategic decisions before them and leave the professionals to manage without undue interference. In other words, they don't want a board committee making decisions around them.

# ▶ CIO Career Risk

The position of CIO is inherently risky because the stakes are high, budgets are substantial, and stakeholder tolerance for failure is low. Furthermore, many CIOs face additional risks because their systems produce data used for public reporting and compliance, subject to regulations and oversight by international, federal, state, and local agencies. CIOs in the financial, pharmaceutical, medical, and many other industries, for example, must deal with the SEC, FCC, the Federal Reserve Bank, FDA, and other industry-specific regulatory agencies. Each of these agencies has arduous reporting requirements, paperwork, audits, and the ability to hold rule breakers accountable. Every time a new IT system is brought on line or modified, the risks of compromising any regulatory compliance or reporting to one these watchdog agencies need to be considered.

Another risk for the CIO arises from the need to establish trust with stakeholders. If the CIO, for example, pads the schedule and budget in order not to overrun, eventually, this might be found out. If her predictions are too aggressive, however, then costly overruns might occur. Either way, she loses credibility. And consider this trust breaker for the CIO: the year 2000 problem caused the expenditure of huge amounts of money from IT budgets to avoid business disruption. Yet, because there were no cataclysms, in retrospect many have criticized the huge expenditures and prophecies of doom. This sequence of events has been used as an excuse to diminish the strategic importance of IT.

Here's what one senior IT executive of a major corporation thinks: "I feel sorry for our CIO. You know, we never did learn how to properly specify our needs and requirements for IT. Even when the development group was sitting down the hall, we couldn't really get it right. Along comes this offer to do development for $18 an hour in India—which is $100 less than our internal cost. So of course the executives pressure the CIO to take the offer and give back budget. Poor soul did—now he has to go to India regularly and, no way of hiding it—our gap in specifications skills is going to come out. I do have dibs on his chair before they clean out his office."

With the increase in expectations, has the career risk for the typical CIO increased? Is there a shortage of people who want to become CIO? Perhaps not. Consider this comment from one CIO: "For me, career risk is diminished. We have a need to execute better, faster, cheaper, and I am the biggest, most consistent contributor in this regard. We now have better alignment with our business units and our IT functions. In fact, it is truly embedded in all that we do." And another IT executive of a different company notes, "Technology is here to stay. We would never start a new undertaking without it. IT threats to our company have increased. In our company, the CIO is leading our defense."

## ▶ Conclusions

The implication of Carr's article for CIOs is "spend less, do not lead, and manage risk." If this becomes a mantra, a period of IT malaise will ensue with CIOs going "underground" in the corporation. There will be less fuel, less spark—less chance for an idea to combust into a growth-driving innovation that drives our companies, our economy, and puts some fun back in the profession. And the reverberations through our economic system may be felt for many years. Our appeal to CIOs, then, is this: set aside some budget, bring your zeal to bear on carefully nurturing whatever opportunity your environment can muster—make something happen!

Finally, a footnote on Nicholas Carr. He apologized for having said, "IT management should become boring." But he has a new book coming out: *Does IT Matter?* In the book, the message is the same as his controversial paper (Carr 2004). And so the debate will continue for some time.

# ▶ References

Carr, N., 2003. "IT Doesn't Matter." *Harvard Business Review*, 81(5), May.

Carr, N., 2004. *IT Doesn't Matter*. Harvard Business School Press.

Cash, J. I., and K. E. Pearlson, 2004. "The Future CIO." *Information Week*, Special Anniversary Report.

CFO Research Column, 2004. *CFO-IT*. Summer.

CIO Research Column, 2004. *CIO*, October 1.

Tapscott, D., 2004. "The Engine That Drives Success." *CIO*, May 1.

# Scope of the CIO

*Thomas Costello*

Where have the "good old days" gone? If you have been a CIO over the past decade, you probably remember the time when you had whopping signature authority, when tech-light CxOs[1] looked to you for wisdom and direction, when the board expected you to turn the ship at a moment's notice to tackle the latest technology for the business to remain competitive. Depending upon your particular situation, those may have been either the good times or the dark ages.

One thing is certain: the scope of the CIO has changed, and not all of it is related to technology. While we continue on the march to sell our "business acumen" and strengthen our ties to the boardroom, we have been equally challenged to manage more with less. The nature of the global economy has caused current CIOs to become masters of portfolio management, a skill which, once learned, will pay dividends in the competitive landscape in the near future. In addition to the usual internal and external pressures every CIO has faced along the way, we now find ourselves working in new realms such as Sarbanes-Oxley and more.

---

1. By "CxO" we mean any Chief corporate Officer such as Chief Financial, Chief Executive, or Chief Operating Officers.

It is clear the role of the CIO continues to experience evolution and change. Whether you are presently a CIO or aspiring to be a CIO in the future, the key to your individual success and that of your business will be to properly define the required skills and master as many of them as possible *before* you're tasked to exercise them. Just as important, you need to remain vigilant to the ongoing changes in your role and learn to adapt and continue your learning.

# ▶ Today's CIO

If you think technology has changed a lot in the last 20 years, look at what has happened to the role of the CIO. Though our industry is still quite young (relative to other business functions like accounting and manufacturing), we have seen CIOs evolve from something akin to a "corporate plumber" to the navigator for entire corporations. We've moved from being responsible for running wires and giving visibility to accounting data in huge mainframes to simultaneously virtually connecting data and devices of an entire enterprise and driving core business planning.

We have more data, more devices, more applications, and the boundaries have spanned far outside of the four walls of our corporate domain. Financials aren't just for budgeting anymore. Security isn't just for servers—and disaster recovery doesn't equal risk mitigation. We are as much therapists and politicians as we are technicians. If we compare checklists of the CIO of 1985 with the checklists of 2005, we see a lot of similarities—and a vast array of changes.

## Organization

From the CIO down into the IT shop, most organizations typically appear the same as they have for the past 20 years with only minor exceptions. You'll find infrastructure, security, analysts, development, package integration experts, DBAs, project management offices, and more grouped in various clusters. These clusters are probably not very dissimilar to the structure of an IT shop of the 1980s. The biggest change you'll find is that nearly every firm now operates IT in some form of matrix management. It is a necessity of the leaner IT staffing, and it had a make-or-break effect on the effectiveness of the entire team—both operationally and from a morale perspective. Any CIO who came up through the ranks in a hierarchical and silo-ed organization has been forced to make a leap and learn the ins and outs of the dynamics of this management style.

From the CIO up, the organizational attachment of the CIO has shifted fairly dramatically over the years. In the "old days," it was not uncommon to see IT connected with the COO. Technology had a direct impact on the ability of the organization to function (whether it was manufacturing, retail, banking, etc.), and operations wanted its hand on the pulse and the throat of IT. For a brief period, many CIOs actually broke the barrier and reported directly to CEOs, and they started to make inroads with direct board interaction. This was especially true of tech-centric or aggressive growth firms looking to technology as a driver and not a support team.

In the past several years, the combined pressures of the Enron and Worldcomm scandals and the fallout of the dotcom era have caused a vast array of CIOs to move under CFOs—and along with that shift has come a drastic reduction in signature authority. Many CIOs report that this new reporting structure has caused two major dilemmas: first, increased lag in the agility and responsiveness of IT due to protracted financial reviews of all spending, and second, a more "penny wise pound foolish" stance on IT budgets that is hampering long-term capability of IT to respond to future business needs.

CIOs must now be prepared to speak in completely different terms, prepare and sell ideas in a completely different way, and learn the politics of working with and around CFOs. And, yes, work "around" does mean "circumvent"—an above-board technique that must be learned to promote ideas without conflict or reprisal. Many in our industry would use the term "CIO as the salesmen" when speaking of these skills.

Along with this new reporting structure, the post-Enron world has introduced a new (and permanent) requirement to the CIO realm—Sarbanes-Oxley. The CFO to whom most CIOs now report is ultimately accountable for the financial surety of the corporate environment—a point of which they will remind you each year as the annual statement and 10K is about to roll out with their signature on it.

Enterprises must now be prepared to shine the light into their entire environment and explain, defend, and adapt the veracity of any and all access and transactions—with the CIO being the mapmaker and sherpa on these expeditions.

## Culture

There is little doubt that IT has flowed along with the cultural changes happening in enterprises around the globe. While we quickly focus on things like dress codes and the presence of ping-pong tables as evidence of our progress, more dramatic changes are in progress and require the monitoring and support of CIOs.

In the broader context of the enterprise, diversity and conflict management continue to be areas of focus for human resources. While in the United States diversity is perceived as an issue of race, global enterprises will be quick to point out that it is a gender issue as well. Conflict management is not the same as conflict avoidance. Many organizations strive to focus their efforts and energy on eliminating conflict in their organizations. Balanced organizations recognize that conflict resolution (including anonymous reporting, mediation, peer review, etc.) is the key to a productive workforce, and they employ various tools and techniques to quickly solve issues and correct systemic deficiencies.

As increasingly more enterprises continue to explore outsourcing of a complete array of business functions (including and beyond IT), CIOs should be aware of and manage the interaction between their staff, vendors, partners, and customers.

From a training perspective, most IT shops tend to ensure that the staff is properly prepared for the present and future challenges of the team. The greatest output is typically achieved by firms that ensure training includes a balance of tactical skills (coding, project management, infrastructure, etc.) coupled with education on critical thinking and problem solving.

CIOs ultimately own the responsibility to foster the growth of their staff and create learning institutions that will ultimately yield a strong, balanced workforce. The ultimate byproduct of that effort should be a stable and ever-improving succession of talent for the enterprise.

# The Governance Within

For clarity, while "organization" tends to describe how we are grouped and clustered (physically, logically), governance outlines *how decisions are made*. When IT was perceived as simply "plumbing" for the enterprise, it was pretty simple to determine the extent of governance for the CIO. Most nontechnical executives didn't understand IT, didn't want to understand it—they only wanted it to work. As the scope of IT has grown to meet the ever-changing challenges facing the business, so too has the awareness, understanding, capability, and expectations of nontechnical business leaders. These changes have created a friction between IT and nearly every part of the business.

Every IT executive I know can describe numerous occasions when a business leader has spawned a technology initiative without the knowledge, involvement, or blessing of IT. The vast percentage of these stories do not have happy endings for either the business or IT. Worse yet, these stories typically aren't followed by any corrective policy or procedure to prevent repeats.

Unfortunately, most enterprises are not very adept or nimble when it comes to evaluating and changing governance. This statement is not limited to their view of IT—most firms are generally slow to recognize the need for change, and changes to spheres of influence are hard to sell unless the change includes "more" of something.

There is no silver bullet when it comes to IT governance. CIOs must adapt their personal goals to meet the dynamics of the organization, industry influences, and the business personalities of the organization.

# Governance: Outward Facing

As part of the wave of outsourcing that continues to sweep through organizations, many executives (again, not limited to IT) are falling prey to a dangerous trend. Many firms that turn to outsourcing providers have already learned their lessons regarding service level agreements: be clear on expectations. Many years ago, a very wise CIO told me that he would never outsource something he didn't completely understand—because it would put him at a great disadvantage when creating the SLA and still delivering to his business users.

The lesson that doesn't appear to have sunk in, however, is that out-sourcing does not absolve the CIO of responsibility! Too many in our industry have equated outsourcing with abdication. I am not implying that CIOs are doing so maliciously. CIOs are signing contracts that don't realistically address the world in which they do and will function.

I suggest that a dependency is created when a CIO attempts to structure an outsourcing arrangement for something that is not fully or properly defined (either in business or technology terms). A CIO in this circumstance will look to the provider as an expert and rely on that provider's delivery capability to solve the stated problem.

The greater error of outsourcing contracts is how they address the problems of today *and tomorrow*. Unfortunately, CIOs are failing to construct agreements that contemplate their changing landscape. For those CIOs who do recognize that there will be change but can't define or quantify the change, they again look to the vendor for a solution. From the vendor perspective, pricing for that kind of uncertainty would result in some amount of up-pricing to accommodate the unknown. CIOs must be skilled at reviewing and comparing these pricing alternatives when selecting outsourcing vendors. No one is well served for getting a great deal on a bad outcome.

# ▶ Categorizing

All of the CIOs I know have their own way of clustering their work into categories in an effort to better track their world. First-time CIOs tend to create lists that are heavily imbalanced in favor of their background (infrastructure, software, business, etc.) with stubs inserted for areas in which they lack expertise. In most cases, these lists tend to lack critical components that the first-time CIO just doesn't see coming, or they remain blank in areas that the CIO fears to enter (e.g., budgets). Experienced CIOs typically have a method of organizing that is more aligned with their measures and/or deliverables. Specifically, you'll see a list that separates repetitive, ongoing tasks from major projects—with the major projects aligned with some form of corporate measurement (e.g., bonuses, balanced scorecard, or other corporate goal setting).

In fairness, there are many CIOs who have neither type of list. They are talented people who tackle their day-to-day issues and achieve great things for their organizations. These people will argue that they have an approach and will flaunt a variety of documents to prove it. I would not argue that this approach can be useful, but I would argue that it is neither easily adaptable nor scalable to fit the enterprises this CIO will move through in his or her career.

At this very moment, the readers of this text have self-selected themselves into two categories: people who now want to see a checklist and a very few CIOs who are picturing something bigger. I hate to disappoint the majority, but you need to produce something that is more like a technology plan than a checklist—and stick to it. Rather than focusing on a specific script for the plan, the key to it will be creating categories that look at the present and future; provide enough detail to articulate cost, time, and investment; and, most importantly, portray a balance across the IT deliverables that meets the business goals. For each CIO and each environment, this document will have a slightly different table of contents, but its purpose and use should be the same.

# ▶ The IT Plan

## The Mission: "Destination"

I've seen a variety of ways to construct a good plan, but all the best have a very solid connection with the business mission. This is not a paragraph that repeats the corporate mantra. Balanced scorecards or other mechanisms that outline the corporate initiatives and measures of success are key. They are "the destination" on the map you'll be following.

Many organizations that lack the "compass" provided by stating the organizational targets simply repeat an annual blitz of needs-list comparisons. These firms usually end up with two deliverables: a budget and a project list. By the end of the first quarter, both the plan and the budget are usually well off target. Most companies will not reflect back on or reconcile the plan and budget until the next annual planning cycle. This is the result of plans that rarely include slack to address as-yet unknown or unexpected requirements, and the correlated budgets never have cash reserves to address these ad hoc needs. If you must follow this path, forcing discussion on these two points will yield greatly improved efficiency. However, the ability of this process to ensure the optimum path to the corporate goals is directly linked to the accuracy (or luck) of initiative selection.

How you connect the dot between where the organization is (requiring an honest assessment of your situation and capabilities) and the destination outlined by the outcomes/measures mechanism will be the path that the corporation will follow. If done correctly, each functional area of the enterprise will have a guide to follow, and the plan becomes the document from which all discussions should start.

The CIO role should be an active participant in the creation and approval of these initiatives and measures. The CIO must come to the table prepared to articulate either the effort required to move to the desired outcome or the research required to describe and quantify that effort. To accurately depict the effort and costs, the CIO must work closely with the business users to articulate the needs (as outlined in other chapters in this book).

And here lies the greatest challenge to all of senior management in nearly every organization—the biggest, most common, and destructive error of all—don't just focus on the achievements within a single year: think long-term strategy. So many organizations are caught so tightly in the web of annual budgeting that their actions and measures are limited to that same 12 month-window. A healthcare-related firm in the Philadelphia area used a unique budgeting/planning process that seemed quite effective: 18-month vision, 12-month budget, 6-month signature approval, with a 6-month review cycle to ensure they were always vectoring in the right direction. If you remain focused in the narrow 12-month view, you'll be locked into achieving the simple and never achieve great things that require long-term planning and investment.

## For Whom

No matter how small the organization, few CIOs can accomplish this feat without the aid of their staff and a continuous monitoring of the pulse of their users. I've seen a variety of ways of constructing a good plan, but all of the best include a solid focus on the constituents of IT, both internal and external. The manner in which this is captured varies widely, but for the sake of a usable plan this list should be concise and should clearly connect the constituent with one (or more) of the stated goals. Don't forget to include yourself on this list. Every IT has a fair number of operational and growth initiatives that are for the ongoing health of the firm, and they can't get lost or absorbed and should be clearly stated in the plan.

Stacking these constituents in some order based on ROI, number of initiatives, or dollars invested can yield startling reactions from nontechnical executives. I have seen a very well-done version of a plan presented to a senior executive team and the resulting discussion from visually seeing the list ordered by ROI and then by investment.

First, this allows the CIO to clearly accept and reject initiative requests on the basis of a corporatewide criteria—alignment with corporate goals. Second, it forces the dialog to occur between the business leaders with the focus on relative value to the enterprise. I am certain there are CIOs reading this who have done this exact process and vividly recall the joy in watching the business leaders negotiate and thrash through the process without the CIO bearing the brunt of the pain.

## How Much

The CIO (and all other CxOs) will ultimately create a budget to deliver the stated objectives and initiatives. Much of this will be in the form of estimating well in advance and during the planning process. Few if any CIOs gain the precision necessary to finalize a budget during the process, but the budget is always locked. As noted earlier, it is imperative that some amount of slack is built into the process to address ad hoc" needs, not project overrun. As part of the CFO-speak, this is a key distinction.

CIOs should ensure that this ad hoc number be contemplated, debated, and included very early in the budget process. Not all CFOs will find this an acceptable approach, but reviews of prior budget spending will help justify the need and provide a means to quantify the size of that allocation. Once this ad hoc amount is set and agreed upon, the CIO becomes responsible for drawing the line between aligned-and-approved projects and those that are not.

# ▶ What You Do For Others: The Approved Portfolio

The review and ultimate approval or rejection of projects and initiatives and categorization of the outcome are critical to the well-being of IT and the CIO for the coming budget year. It is imperative that projects be categorized into buckets. A sample of possible classifications could include the following:

- Approved for current year with budget
- Approved for current year pending clarification (clear mission alignment)
- Hold for current budget year pending clarification
- Hold for future budget year(s)
- Rejected—lack of alignment
- Rejected—poor ROI or other budgetary reasons
- Rejected—other

CIOs must be cautious to not allow the ad hoc bucket to be consumed by projects that hit the reject pile. Nor should the ad hoc be used for project overrun. If these distinctions are followed and planned-and-approved projects are done on time and on budget, the ad hoc bucket will be available when an urgent business need surfaces.

Now that the script has been written, the CIO has some of the key elements necessary for a document that becomes the basis for all dialog between IT and business users (as well as within IT). The CIO is responsible for ensuring that all initiatives by his staff are regularly reviewed against this plan. Larger organizations tend to rely on the project management office (PMO) to perform this monitoring with some form of reporting or dashboard provided to executive leadership for status. Most PMOs tend to ensure that the projects are proceeding as approved and are mechanically functioning properly (on time, on budget) but should be extended to monitor compliance with the objectives and scope stated in the alignment portion plan.

# How You'll Do It

Now that you have outlined whom you're addressing and the manner in which you'll tackle the approved business initiatives, you have to turn your attention to describing how you'll do it.

Your plan can be categorized in any structure that allows you to visualize and guide your team. Categorizing your plan on the basis of your organization structure will present a great task-based outline for your team leaders to follow but tends to lack the horizontal connectivity between your teams. Some of the best alternatives to define your organization allow you to visually depict it as well.

As an example, I've seen one technique that organized everything in the CIO's domain in a structure like Maslow's Hierarchy of Needs (see Figure 2.1), a pyramid showing the core survival functions at the base of the diagram (power, servers, network connectivity, etc.) as minimum requirements, followed by functioning (core applications critical to the business), followed by operating (the array of tools necessary for the ongoing and regular operations of the enterprise), and finally by peak (stretch functions or tools that are either experimental or differentiate the operations and may ultimately transition down into the pyramid). Ultimately, the diagram

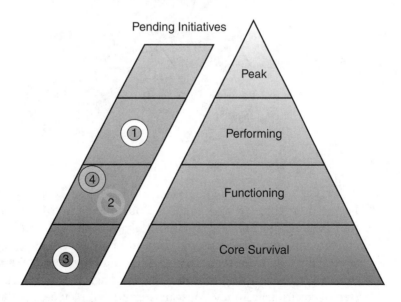

**Figure 2.1** IT plan pyramid of needs.

also included unfunded and/or unapproved strategic issues relating to future requirements (some business driven, some purely IT driven) mapped beside the pyramid to show their importance. This approach allowed for easy explanation of IT to other nontechnical managers, gave the CIO a structured approach to meet and discuss status with his staff, and provided a great tool to focus energy, effort, and budget.

Another visually driven model is a connection of three loops stacked in the shape of a triangle dividing the organization into three key functional areas: strategic leadership, business operations, and business support (see Figure 2.2). Each of the major systems were mapped into one of the three areas. The center where all three loops converged (or overlapped) was reserved for monitoring efforts, including PMO, balanced scorecard–performance reporting, and other decision support efforts. Again, the diagram was a useful tool in noting where energy, risk, budget, and resources were being dedicated. Ongoing and future initiatives were mapped in different colors to show status.

**Figure 2.2** IT plan: three loops.

I've seen attempts to map detailed constituents onto these diagrams, and they become quite cluttered with little value added. If you're forced to get constituents into this visual, you should consider creating a separate version of the document for each role, showing only their applications of need or interest. If you produce these mirror diagrams, there will be the extra step of ensuring accuracy, consistency, and completeness of the applications list to ensure you didn't omit something in the cloning process.

While these diagrams provide a concise macrolevel view, they lack the detail components found in an enterprise information architecture (EAI). There is a clear connection and progression between the IT plan and the EIA. While the IT plan is meant to provide an overview of constituents, efforts, and direction, the EIA is a more exhaustive depiction of these things, plus inventories of processes, services, data, the environment, and more. The two should be used in concert to ensure that any requests of IT are evaluated on both the adherence to the corporate and IT direction (IT plan) as well as the effort necessary to connect and accomplish with the existing and proposed state of the EIA.

## Who Will Do It

The next step is to add plans showing the connectivity of business initiatives to functional teams and the matrix manner of those connections. You can then articulate how the teams (IT and more) are to address and support each initiative, and it makes visualizing their tasks much clearer. The trick is to then designate team leaders to document their efforts, and validate your resources, skills, and the timelines. Though much of this was done at the macro level during the leadership approval process, this is where the details must be exhaustively worked out.

The product of this next level of detail should be a resourcing plan that maps how existing resources will be utilized (including any training or skill recrafting required), how new resources will be identified and added (including new employees, contractors, outsourced vendors, etc.), and project timelines that contemplate the preparedness and availability of the required resources.

# ▶ Risk Analysis

Most IT plans tend to run out of steam at this point. While documents that include this level of detail are quite useful (and certainly more than most organizations currently use), there is one more step that will greatly enhance the value of the IT plan: a risk analysis.

Perhaps the greatest challenge of any plan is recognizing and dealing with risk. In order to minimize the pain associated with this step, it is important to immediately separate risk by two key factors: likelihood and impact. Using either factor without the other is simply dangerous. No one wants to be responsible for missing that "one in ten thousand" chance that happened to cost a million dollars when it happened. The art at this step is ensuring that the list of risks is balanced—not too conservative and not "the sky is falling." The resulting list of risks can be sorted in any number of ways, including a combined score of the two scales (with or without weightings).

As with any good problem solving, there is a vast difference between recognition and response. Very few if any organizations can afford the cost of eliminating all of the risks that have been articulated. Now that your plan has defined the possible risks and filtered for likelihood and impact, it is time to move onto "response."

Split the risks into those that should be mitigated from those that must be eliminated. Review these lists and identify key "review points" and "flares" that will signal the possible risk is materializing. The "must eliminate" list should result in action plans and be incorporated into the timeline, budget, and resource plan. These checkpoints and corrective actions should be worked into the timeline for each effort and overtly stated in the IT plan.

## ▶ What Makes Your Plan Great

Now that you've strategically decided what you'll do, survived the approval process, and have described tactically what and how you'll get the job done, you have to turn your attention to the broad array of things you need to handle that are beyond the list of projects and initiatives. This portion of your plan should include all of the considerations mentioned earlier in this chapter and more—including items such as staff development, HR issues, and succession planning.

The last element necessary for any good plan is the measurement of outcomes. If your organization is utilizing balanced scorecard or similar tools, you'll probably have corporate metrics defined as part of that process. While those are useful at the enterprise level, you'll still need to create departmental, team, and individual metrics. These metrics should be closely tied to the IT plan to ensure alignment of the corporate goals down to the individual. Be sure to set a rewards system that quantifies the outcomes for efforts that come up a little short, those that meet stated goals, and those that exceed stated goals. These rewards should be consistent across all efforts.

No matter how well you've done on constructing this plan, you already know that it is destined for changes. You need to review this plan with your internal leadership on a regular basis. You need to adapt the plan with new pressures and levels that will pop up in our field and your industry. Most importantly, you should ensure that the measures you put into this plan are being tracked and that progress is being achieved.

# ▶ Drawing It All Together

If you produce this plan and follow the steps outlined, it should be the mirror of your role and the map for your future. It defines the scope of your role and shows you the areas of growth for you and your team. You should be able to look at this document and see the tactical and strategic nature of your job, the hard and soft skills required of you and your staff, and the map of how you're moving in concert with your firm. You should also be able to monitor the progress of your team.

Can any one document do all of these things? I would ask, how can you do them without it?

# It's All About the Marketing

*Autumn Bayles*

I used to think that technical prowess, analytical capability, and project management expertise were the skills that turned the best technical resources, in time, into the best technology managers and executives. Unfortunately, I was off target on that one, and I didn't even realize it until I was in the technology management ranks and missing a critical skill.

My epiphany came to me suddenly in the middle of marketing class while obtaining my MBA. I had struggled for a while with management situations that were foreign to me, yearning for the "golden" years of quantitative and analytical technical challenges that bent eventually to disciplined and logical effort. Funny, but people somehow didn't work or respond the same way that computers did.

I had already gotten the clue that there were nontechnical skills I needed to learn and use in my everyday work, but I was clumsy in my adaptation of them. But it crystallized in my mind that day when it dawned on me that the marketing skills I was learning to apply to fictional business customers were the same that would apply to my customer, the company I worked for. It seemed so obvious, and for those of you who weren't challenged like me in learning some of these things, it may have been obvious to you from the start of your career. Some of you are probably thinking right now that I must have been the worst manager ever. I certainly felt that way, so don't feel guilty thinking it.

But for those who may be in that situation where I was and interested in what I'm talking about, trust me in that marketing is the most important skill you can have as a technology executive.

So what is marketing? In my definition, it is an art, a way to present your subject matter in a way to achieve your goal with your intended audience. In my MBA class they taught us how to sell a product to a target market. That's no different than selling your idea, your solution, or your project to decision makers, peers, staff, and partners or vendors. Some of you may be thinking, um . . . that sounds an awful lot like just plain old selling. Well (and I'm applying a little marketing here myself), I prefer to use the term marketing because to me, that implies a nonthreatening way to influence, while selling is a more overt approach. I guess I see marketing as enjoyable to all parties, while sales has mixed reviews depending on the experience.

Why do I call it an art? Because it isn't easy to simply pick up and do in our industry, especially with the backgrounds that technology types usually have. It isn't logical like writing a line of code or researching the newest technology. It requires knowledge of some basic concepts that you must then determine how best to apply and tweak to use in different situations. Sincerity is the key—you can't say or do things you don't mean or things that require a noticeable effort to produce. And as you start to use more marketing in your work, you'll notice that most of the other successful executives you work with do it too. They'll become more comfortable with you because you are more familiar to them in terms of the way they work—you're not just the techno-geek who talks about things they don't understand.

So where do you start? Here are a few simple steps to get you rolling on marketing an idea or working to influence someone to support you in an important decision.

- *Identify the "market."* You have to identify your target market— who you are attempting to influence. This can be the steering committee to whom you are presenting your solution, your team member whom you want to work on a certain project but who may not be keen on it for the moment, or the peer who isn't quite sure what to make of you. If you don't know specifically who you are attempting to get buy-in from, take time to figure it out.

- *Understand who you are talking to.* You have to understand what your target market is about. What is this person or group of people thinking, and what is important to them? What knowledge do they already have on the subject? You must think about how they will perceive what you are about to say and make sure that you communicate with that in mind to achieve the end result you are looking for.

  If you get technical with a nontechnical person, he will shut you out. If you talk down to someone who has expertise, she will be offended that you are being condescending to her. You must find the right balance between technical and business perspectives. If someone cares about sales and nothing else, position your topic on how it positively affects sales. You must communicate to your subjects in language they understand and with words that are interesting to their particular situation. Otherwise, your message will not be heard or will not be effective. I can't emphasize this concept enough.

- *Toss the golden rule.* Throw out the golden rule—treating others as you would want to be treated is great if you were talking to yourself. But you aren't—you are talking to someone who is not you and is probably very often not *like* you. So you have to understand the other person first, and then open your mouth. There are a lot of great books on the topic of different personalities and what makes them tick, so read one. I used to wonder why one of my lower performers didn't seem to respond to the same techniques that my boss used to motivate me. Then I realized he wasn't me, and he had different priorities than mine and could not have cared less about the incentives I was trying to use.

- *Figure out what you are trying to say.* Now that you've got your audience down and know what makes their blood flow, what are you trying to say? Determine a clear, simple message that conveys your objective and what you want agreement on. Practice in your mind so the concept is natural to you and can be said with different words in different ways. Gather supporting details that back up your message to use if you need them. Nothing speaks better than facts, so use them but don't overwhelm. Keep it clear, clean, powerful.

- *Know when to say it.* Timing is another critical component. If there is a big meeting coming up to decide which option to choose, don't wait until the meeting to attempt to influence others to your position. Surprises and new information right before a decision needs to be made are never good. Prime the pump ahead of time by talking to key decision makers, communicating your message, and telling it to each one in a different way that makes sense and is important to them. Then, when you need their support, you already have them lined up.

- *Get them to say it for you.* The holy grail of marketing is getting your customer to come to the conclusion you want her to reach without your directly coming out and saying it. You can achieve this by laying out your case to lead to the desired conclusion, using facts and credible supporting evidence from third parties. If someone truly believes what he is saying—and is not being prompted—it is much more powerful to others when they hear it. This doesn't mean you can't share your opinion, but use it carefully. If someone is challenged on why he supports your idea, having only one person's opinion as a reason is not a very strong argument. And if things go awry, the idea will become simply your opinion rather than an independently made decision that is supported by others. Good marketers will lead people down their chosen path by using the same facts and other credible evidence that led them to want to propose the idea in the first place, and their audience will come to their own conclusions that match the desired outcome.

- *Don't forget to listen too!* While marketing, it is also crucial to listen because this is a key part of effective communication. Listening gives you an opportunity to learn something about how your audience is feeling, and you may want to tweak your message on the basis of their feedback. Listening also lets your audience members know that you care about what they think and that you will consider what they say and take appropriate action. After all, you want people to listen to you, so you should listen to them with the same respect and attention that you are looking to attain in your own communications.

There are a few other marketing concepts that are not specifically related to attempting to obtain buy-in to an idea but are extremely useful to the technology executive.

- *Silence is not golden.* Telling people something is better than letting them make things up on their own. If you are having a problem, tell the user community about it right away. I had an argument once with one of my staff over whether you should wait to communicate an issue until after the problem is solved. After listening to some of the explanations of what the problem was, some of which were pretty interesting but not acceptable, I realized it is better to have stakeholders hear the news, good or bad, from you—and to hear the truth about what is going on.

- With this approach, you control the message. If something bad is happening, you want the users to hear the truth but also to have faith in that you are working on the problem and plan to take care of it. Market accordingly. You are putting a message out there that conveys what you want your target audience to hear, that reassures them that someone is at the controls, and that also provides facts on the issue.

- *Advertise.* Another important piece of marketing is the importance of advertising. Just like a product, you need to advertise the partnership your technology group is in with your company. Communications from IT are all too often around problems or project statuses. Use a little marketing by highlighting accomplishments that the business stakeholders wouldn't know about unless you tell them. Give your people awards. Show the stakeholders all the good things that are going on for them. You don't want to go over the top to seem obnoxious or to be continually patting yourself on the back, but letting people know is just plain good marketing.

I have found these simple marketing concepts to be invaluable to me in my role as a technology executive. Recognizing that people are unique and need to be communicated to differently was a real eye-opener for me. It's all about the message and how you deliver it, and practice makes perfect. It takes time to become a natural marketer, so don't rush yourself. Just get acquainted with the ideas, and in time, marketing skills just start to flow naturally.

# 4

# Creating a Community of Practice for CIOs

*Phillip A. Laplante*

## ▶ Introduction

A community of practice (CoP) can be described as "a group of people who are brought together by a desire to learn more about a common class of problems, opportunities, and their possible solution" (Lane 2003). One such example is the Silicon Valley's CIO group described in this book's predecessor, *CIO Wisdom*. The CIO Institute is another CoP for senior IT professionals in the Greater Philadelphia Metropolitan Area.

In this chapter we review the history, mission, and operational details of the CIO Institute. It is hoped that this description will help to archive the group's history, illustrate best practices, and provide guidance to others who seek to build a similar CoP.

# ▶ History of CIO Institute

The CIO Institute was formed in January 2002 as a subsidiary group of the nonprofit Eastern Technology Council, which focuses on supporting business in the Greater Philadelphia Metropolitan Area. With nearly one thousand member companies, the Eastern Technology Council (http://www.techcouncil.org) helps its members make contact with each other through participation in a broad variety of events, publications, and innovative services. Most Technology Council members use the Council to form vital money-making relationships or to take advantage of Council-negotiated discounts.

In 2001 there were few social and educational groups in the Philadelphia metropolitan area for presidents and CEOs. There was one such group for CIOs, but it was national in scope, and its center of gravity was far from the region. Moreover, the group had been described as "stuffy" and "boring" by some. When Technology Council executives Rob McCord (chair of the board), Dianne Strunk (CEO), and Phil Laplante (CTO) conceived of the CIO Institute, the intent was to build a CoP that would be unique. The goal was to build a CoP that emulated the Technology Council's mission to provide contacts and capital to its members and to deliver the latest information in an entertaining and agile format.

In late 2001 the CIO Institute was born with the explicit objectives to

- create a focal point and raise awareness of regional IT expertise;
- discuss the latest technologies, trends, government initiatives, and other relevant topics;
- offer technological and managerial resources to its members;
- act as a nexus to stimulate technological competencies through education, dialogue, and mentoring; and
- connect members through regular communications via email, a Web presence, and Eastern Technology Council's widely read newspaper, *Technology Times*.

Another objective of the Institute was to help it members to better educate and communicate with other executives.

By January 2002, the go-ahead for the CIO Institute had been given and a business plan was drawn up. Marketing materials were developed and a preliminary interest survey was administered to Eastern Technology Council members. The results of the survey provided a group of prospective members as well as a set of potential program topics. Subsequently, recruitment of charter members and the advisory board began.

By May 2002, the first program on Wireless CRM was delivered to an attendance of about 25 prospective members, from which an initial class of eight was recruited. Publication of the remainder of the 2002 program and aggressive recruitment led to the subsequent growth of the CIO Institute, described later in this chapter.

# ▶ Community Description

One of the guiding principles of the CIO Institute is that it focuses on the needs of its members. The community also respects the value of its members' time. This principle means explicitly avoiding "informational" meetings that are thinly veiled vendor sales pitches. In fact, the CoP generally does not focus its programs on a specific product, but rather on a "band" of technology, such as wireless computing or security, or on a business topic of importance to the CIO, such as outsourcing or software return on investment (ROI).

CIO Institute meetings include technology forums led by world-class speakers, moderated roundtable discussions, and social events. A Web site and electronic newsletter are used for additional communications between members. There are also occasional planning and advisory board meetings. The next sections briefly describe all of these meetings and associated artifacts.

## Technology Forums

Technology forums bring the best and brightest minds to discuss the latest technologies, trends, government initiatives, and other topics that are of importance to a CIO. These meetings are designed to enhance technological competencies in a convenient format. The forums are topical presentations by visiting world-class technologists. Sales pitches are strictly forbidden, though sponsors are allowed to distribute some materials at the end of the program. Meetings generally start either at 8:30 a.m. or noon and last about two hours.

Typical forums of this type have included High Speed Wireless, Data Warehousing, Web Services, and Security Certification.

## CIO Roundtables

Introduced to the CIO Institute in 2003, these moderated discussions cover various topics of timely importance to a CIO. The forums also provide CIOs with "away" time to keep up with the latest technology advances and to learn from each other's experiences. Led by a moderator (often a CIO Institute member) who is expert in the topic of discussion, the members are given questions ahead of time to allow time for thoughtful consideration. Members can also post additional questions and advance comments to the CoP Web site.

Typical roundtables have focused on the changing role of the CIO, software ROI, and computer use policies. To illustrate the scope of discussion, the questions used for the roundtable on the changing role of the CIO are shown in Table 4.1.

The group does not follow Robert's Rules of Order because it was discovered that an informal format is much more conducive to learning and building working relationships. These forum events have proven to be highly successful, and attendee ratings for these events are consistently high.

## Web Site

The CIO Institute's Web site is concise and full of useful information to its members. One significant feature is a white paper library, which is an archive for past presentations (in PowerPoint format) as well as white papers written by our membership. The calendar of events is listed, and members can sign up for events through the site (Figure 4.1).

**Table 4.1** Questions for CIO Institute Roundtable on the Changing Role of the CIO

| |
|---|
| 1. What process do you use in developing your budget? Zero based? Wish list? Top down? Bottom up? |
| 2. What does your budget look like? Do you set aside $x$% for maintenance contracts, $y$% for hardware, $z$% for software purchases, then go from there? Is there a common proportionality between your budgets? |
| 3. What level of involvement do your subordinates have in the development of your budgets? |
| 4. Which of the following methods do you use for IT capital budget formation (showing value), and when do you use them? <br> • ROI <br> • payback method <br> • cost benefit ratio <br> • profitability index <br> • IRR <br> • net present value |
| 5. When do you start preparing your budget? How long does it take to prepare your budget? How could your budget development process be improved? |
| 6. Does your organization have a formal "IT project evaluation criteria," and what is it? How do you use it to write and evaluate your budgets? |
| 7. How do you plan staffing needs? How do you justify additional staff and defend existing ones? |
| 8. Are you expecting to staff up or down this year? What about outsourcing? Does that go into your budget or a "contracted services" budget that is outside of your control? |
| 9. What is the process that you must go through in your organization in gaining approval for your operational and capital budget? Is it an annual process or more frequent? At what level must approval be given? What are the greatest obstacles you face? |
| 10. How good are your budgets? How do you track expenditures, and who is watching you? |
| 11. How do you account for contingencies in your budgets? Do you use padding? Is there an explicit contingency fund, or do you have to go back for more if an "emergency" occurs? |
| 12. If you could have anything you wanted with respect to budgeting (a tool, a technique, a practice, etc.), what would you wish for? How realistic is it? |
| 13. What are questions to your colleagues on how they handle budgeting? |

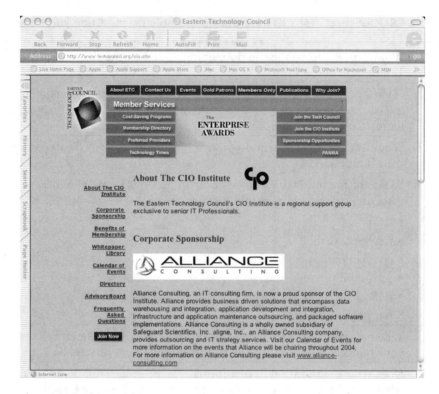

**Figure 4.1** CIO Institute Web site screenshot.

A directory of member companies is listed, but not names of individual members or contact information. Confidentiality is preserved to save our members from unwanted solicitation. The advisory board members are listed, however, with their permission, but contact information is not posted. Other information on the site includes details of current corporate sponsors, a brief history of the CIO Institute, and membership information.

## E-Newsletter

Prepared by the CTO of the Technology Council, a monthly electronic newsletter provides information and communication to members as well as announcements and product updates. A listserver is maintained to facilitate adding or deleting members from the list and for anonymous distribution.

# Program History

In 2002 the CIO Institute's program was based on forum events only. These forums included Wireless CRM; IT Strategy for Delaware; IT: Strategic Direction of PA; Business Process Reengineering; Philadelphia's Strategic IT Initiative; and Computer Security (the ISO 17799 Standard).

In 2003 the roundtable events were added. Forum events for that year included Audio Visual/Computing Conversion, High-Speed Wireless, Data Warehousing, Web Services, Enterprise Collaborative Computing, E-Government, Advanced Encryption Standard, and Managing IT as a Business. Roundtable events were held in the following topics: IT outsourcing, hiring and evaluating IT professionals, open source, use policies and monitoring, and software ROI.

In 2004 the program schedule was wide ranging and explored technical, financial, governance, and human resource topics, and the number of events was significantly increased. These events included the following forums:

- .Net and Web Architectures
- The ITSM Reference Model
- Building the Ideal IT Organization
- Real-time Customer Data Integration and Information
- The Data Center Dilemma: Buy vs. Build
- Business Intelligence
- Data Integration
- IT Procurement and Outsourcing
- Aligning the IT Organization and Process with Business Goals
- Running Business Critical Applications over the WAN
- Business Intelligence
- Regulatory Compliance

The following roundtables were held: The Changing role of the CIO, Budgeting, and RFID. Two planning meetings were held, and a social event—a well-attended and received two-year anniversary cigar and whiskey party—was also added.

Figure 4.2 provides a visualization of the growth in number of events and evolution of event types. For example, in 2002 there were seven talks by guest speakers and one planning meeting. In 2003 the round-table meetings were added, and there were five of them along with nine speaker meetings and one planning meeting. In 2004 there were 14 speaker meetings, three roundtables, and two planning meetings

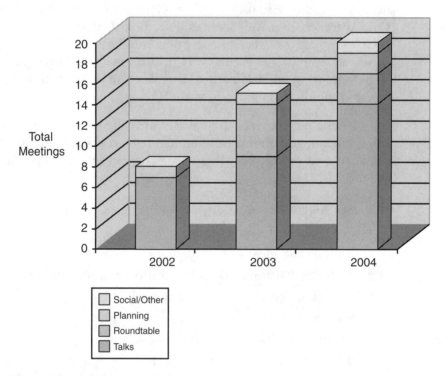

**Figure 4.2** Distribution of event types over the life of the CIO Institute.

The CIO Institute is also affiliated with other regional IT activities, particularly as a major contributor to the annual Philadelphia Information Technology Exposition & Conference (ITEC) show, which showcases the latest in IT technologies and trends. In addition, members regularly participate in the Eastern Technology Council's black tie awards dinner, the Enterprise Awards.

# ▶ Member Profile

The CIO Institute's members are drawn from Fortune 500 companies, companies of 50 or fewer, nonprofit organizations, and government entities in Southeastern Pennsylvania, Northern Delaware, and Southwestern New Jersey. Prospective members must be very senior IT professionals. Members are recruited either by referrals, self-nomination, or prospecting by the CIO Institute's CTO and Technology Council staff. Members are invited to join after review of their application materials by the CTO of the Technology Council and in consultation with advisory board members and Technology Council staff. By policy, the CoP specifically excludes sales executives or others who are clearly infiltrating the group simply to sell to its members. This policy is vigorously enforced.

Typical member titles include CIO, CTO, CEO, vice president and directors (of information systems MIS/telecommunications, information services, technical services, information technology), chief software architect, general manager, president, regional manager, executive vice president, and dean of information technology.

Despite that the last three years have provided a very challenging business environment, the CIO Institute has grown quickly (Figure 4.3). From an initial "class" of eight members, after two and one-half years, it now boasts nearly 50 members—an average growth rate of about 100 percent per year. This growth seems to be leveling off to just about 40 percent per year, which seems healthy. With new signs of economic recovery and an always relevant program, the membership is expected to continue to grow.

While the CoP doesn't publicize its membership list, its members are by no means anonymous. Members are able to obtain contact information for one another through the events, through a printed paper directory, and through a searchable Web-based directory.

Many members are with Fortune 500 companies such as Unisys and Lockheed, as well as smaller and even boutique firms, where the CIO is a main driver of the business. In addition, the CoP members have been involved in several other professional and scholarly conferences relating to IT, and many members have published in practitioner and scholarly publications, some of which are excerpted in this book.

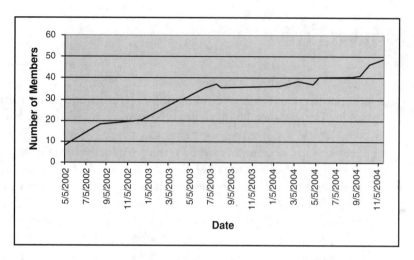

**Figure 4.3** Membership growth since the CIO Institute's inception in May 2002.

# ▶ Operational Details

The CIO Institute draws upon the support staff of the Eastern Technology Council to deal with the logistics of membership enrollment, event planning, publications, and so on. The CTO of the Eastern Technology Council is the de facto "leader" of the CIO Institute. His responsibility involves preparation of the technical program, moderation of discussions, and recruiting members, and he provides the overall leadership and vision for the Institute. This is a part-time position but requires a great deal of engagement.

An advisory board of current members provides advice and relevancy and a sense of opportunism that drives the Institute's program. Members are appointed on an ad hoc basis upon referral from an existing advisory board member or the CTO.

Program quality is a primary operational concern. For example, after each event is held, a paper survey of attendees is conducted and the results immediately analyzed to control for quality of the event, speaker, and venue. A sample evaluation form is shown in Figure 4.4.

## EVALUATION

Title of Event - "IT Procurement and Outsourcing Pitfalls for CIO's: A Trial Lawyer's Perspective"
Date - 6/3/04
*Please complete the following questions by circling your responses.*

| | Poor | | Acceptable | | Excellent |
|---|---|---|---|---|---|
| 1. Did the content (subject matter) Meet with your expectations? | 1 | 2 | 3 | 4 | 5 |

2. How would you rate the speaker(s), (clarity, effectiveness, knowledge, responsiveness, etc):

| | | | | | |
|---|---|---|---|---|---|
| a. Frank Taney | 1 | 2 | 3 | 4 | 5 |

Buchanan Ingersoll, PC          Comments: _____

_____

3. Ideas for future speakers and/or topics?

_____

4. Comments/recommendations of any kind regarding this event, future events, and/or Technology Council services:

_____

_____

5. I think the following companies would be interested in attending these events and/or joining the Council:

_____

_____

6. Would you like to hear about the discounts and customized services provided by Technology Council Preferred providers? If yes, please check areas of interest:

❑ telecommunications          ❑ health benefits
❑ cellular services          ❑ 401k management/creation
❑ real estate          ❑ Internet access
❑ long distance & local access

7. Please check:
❑ I would like to receive the Council's newspaper, *The Technology Times*
I am interested in advertising in the Technology Council's related publications
❑ *The Technology Times*          ❑ Annual Membership directory
❑ I am interested in Sponsoring an Event

Type

8. What prompted you to come to this event (interest in topics, networking, and/or other interests)?

_____

_____

9. If you have developed a business relationship with another council memeber:
❑ I will contact Lori Rhoades at lrhoades@techcouncil.org to share my story.
❑ Please have Lori call or email me for my business success story at _____

10. Name: _____ Title: _____

Company: _____

Description (size, # of employees, revenues, type of business): _____

Address: _____

City: _____ State: _____ Zip: _____

Phone #: _____ Fax: _____

Website: _____

E-Mail: _____

**Figure 4.4** Sample evaluation instrument for a forum event on IT procurement and outsourcing.

Each year a survey of the entire membership is distributed via email, and the results are used to determine program needs. One of the first annual surveys conducted is reproduced in Table 4.2.

**Table 4.2** Typical Annual Survey Form

| |
|---|
| Who would you like to hear present (name of individual/company)? |
| What do you envision as the future mission of the Institute? |
| When are good days for you to meet? |
| When is a good time of day for you to meet (morn breakfast, afternoon lunch, evening dinner, cocktails only, etc.)? |
| Do you have a geographic preference (city, suburbs, office building, school, etc.)? |
| Do you have anyone you would like to refer to the Institute? |
| Are you a member of any similar organization(s)? |
| What attracted you to the Institute? |
| Would you like to sponsor either a roundtable or presentation (financial investment, marketing opportunity)? |
| Would you like to host either a roundtable or presentation (includes space, food/beverage)? |
| Are you interested in any special outings? Any hobbies in which other members can participate (golfing, boating, wine tasting, etc.)? |

The financial model for the CIO Institute has evolved over time. As previously noted, the CoP is embedded in a not-for-profit entity. Therefore, the revenue goal is to cover the CoP's operational costs.

Initially, it was planned that the revenues for the CoP be entirely based on membership dues (which are several hundred dollars per member per year). It was expected that some of the operational costs for the meetings (food and venue, for example) and the salaries for the staff support would be substantially covered by these revenues. However, over time it was realized that sponsorship monies could further offset some of these costs as well as provide for enhanced programming (e.g., speaker fees), better venues, and resources for social events. This was the case in the second year of its existence in which the CIO Institute was able to engage major event sponsors. In addition, some of the members have hosted events at their sites and provided food and refreshments at no cost to the CIO Institute. Finally, the CoP has been seeking a large annual sponsor to help further upgrade the program and to reduce the need to go "hat-in-hand" to recruit further sponsors. In summary, the CoP will continue to operate with its revenue coming from membership fees and external sponsors.

# ▶ Analysis of Success

It would be too easy to declare the CIO Institute a success simply on the basis of its growth rate, particularly during a challenging economic period. However, CoP researcher Etienne Wenger and colleagues have articulated seven principles for successful CoPs (Wenger 2002):

1. Design for evolution.
2. Open a dialogue between inside and outside.
3. Invite different levels of participation.
4. Develop public and private spaces.
5. Focus on value.
6. Combine familiarity and excitement.
7. Create a rhythm for the community.

It is worthwhile, therefore, to briefly analyze the CIO Institute with respect to these seven dimensions.

- *Design for evolution.* This principle means that the organization adapts to meet the needs of its members, responds to opportunities for partnerships, and maintains the interests of the community. Unlike many traditional organizations, CoPs can be agile so that they can adapt to engage their members. Clearly, the CIO Institute has been able to adapt in this manner and will continue to do so.

- *Open a dialogue between inside and outside.* This guideline implies that the leader of the community must be good at identifying the key members and listening to them. The CTO of the CIO Institute embraces this principle. In addition, the CIO Institute relies on the advice of its advisory board, and a great deal of informal dialogue that really drives the community occurs behind the scenes.

- *Invite different levels of participation.* The best practices for a CoP suggest three different levels of participation; a small (10% to 15%) core group who participate in most activities, an active group (10% to 15%) who participate in many but not nearly all activities, and the peripheral group who rarely participate (Wenger 2002). Some members may move between these groups over time. Outside of these three groups is a community of interested stakeholders: suppliers, customers of members, and "intellectual neighbors." The CIO Institute roughly exhibits this distribution. Wenger notes that this is, in fact, a healthy distribution and that it is important not to "force" all members to be core or active members. Different members get from the organization what they need—no more and no less.

- *Develop public and private spaces.* A healthy CoP is not identified solely by its public events. Rather, it is also distinguished by the private interactions: the emails, phone calls, and one-on-one relationships that arise from affiliation with the community. When these behind-the-scenes relationships are strong, then the public interactions become that much richer. Although such personal interactions are not measurable performance indicators, anecdotal evidence suggests that the CIO Institute provides a foundation on which members can build relationships through business or other common interests..

- *Focus on value.* Every CoP needs to sponsor value-added events, meetings, and relationships that make membership worth the cost of time and money. This value package must evolve over time, but if members do not perceive value, then they will not stay. As one metric of value to the members, the CIO Institute has a member turnover of less than 20 percent per year, and several members have been involved since the organization's inception.

- *Combine familiarity and excitement.* It is imperative that the community combine elements of predictable programming with varied and exciting fare. For example, in the CIO Institute the regular programming is supplemented with a number of "unscheduled" events, which are usually hosted by other organizations but in which a special invitation to CIO Institute members has been extended.

- *Create a rhythm for the community.* A community of practice is distinguished by the relationships that develop and the pace or rhythm of the community's events. Wenger and colleagues also note that the rhythm of the community is the strongest indicator of its vitality. This rhythm is unique to each community and cannot be dictated. For example, in the beginning the CoP anticipated holding one public event per month. After about a year, it became clear that this was not enough because as members selected which events to attend, many attended only one or two. By the third year, the CoP was hosting almost two dozen events, but this seemed like too much because members were overwhelmed and enough critical mass could not be achieved for many of the events. It was finally determined that about 12 to 18 equally spaced public events are about right for our group. This frequency is expected to continue to change as the membership evolves.

# ▶ Future Directions

It was already noted that one of the hallmarks of a successful community is that it is designed for evolution. In keeping with a desire to continuously evolve, some events in next year's program will include a new twist. In particular, several meetings will be held at selected member sites with the hosts sharing their particular expertise.

Another proposed CoP enhancement is the CIO Advisor. This forum is intended to provide an opportunity for CIOs to receive advice from a group of selected peers who have "been there and done that." This is a confidential, moderated group of peers who share and gain practical knowledge and counsel on the challenges and opportunities they face with the client. Formed on an ongoing basis with four to six CIOs of comparable experience from noncompeting businesses and led by a staff moderator, each forum will be autonomous with respect to issues, location, meeting day and time, direction, and content. The agenda, objectives, and deliverables will be set by the participants.

Product debates are also being considered as an additional activity. In these events, vendors present competing products and answer technical questions. Members can question product claims in a "safe" environment, and vendors can reach a wide audience efficiently.

Some members have suggested the need for a Career Center, which would provide no-cost, confidential career advice to members. This would be neither a headhunting service nor a referral service. Simply put, the resources of the Institute would be used to connect members with those who can help them in their careers.

Finally, it has been suggested that a think-tank be established to provide research reports to the Institute members. These reports would contain important global, national, and regional information that will keep the membership better informed. These reports might include

- Market research and forecasting
- Technology research and forecasting
- Tracking of government actions and legislation that affect CIOs

The Institute could also provide customized research and consulting to members for a fee by establishing an indigenous research group. The additional revenues could then be used to subsidize additional events and services.

# ▶ Conclusion

The future is very promising for the Southeast Pennsylvania–only regional CIO community of practice. As it continues to evolve to serve its members and to grow, even more services and events can be provided to enhance the value of membership. The Eastern Technology Council has looked at the success of the group as a prototype for other CoPs, including one for CEOs, which has already been formed. In any case, perhaps other regions can use the experiences of this CIO Institute to pursue their own CoP.

# ▶ References

ETC (Eastern Technology Council) Web site, http://www.techcouncil.org. Last accessed 11/28/04.

Lane, D., Change Technology Solutions, Inc., and Members of the Silicon Valley Community of Practice, 2003. *CIO Wisdom*, Prentice Hall PTR.

Wenger, E., R. McDermott, and W. M. Snyder, 2002. "It Takes a Community," *CIO Online*, May 15. Available: http://www.cio.com/archive/051502/excerpt.html. Last accessed 11/21/04. (This is a reprinted excerpt from Wenger, McDermott, and Snyder, *Cultivating Communities of Practice*, Harvard Business School Press, 2002.)

# Securing the IT Facility

*Joel Richman Jr. and Paul Nowak*

Security has become a catch-all word to describe many diverse technologies and procedures. To an IT person, the idea of security is usually applied to data security and integrity. Network security, file integrity, and a secure database all fall into this category. To a security or facilities person, security is usually applied to perimeter, workplace, or any one of a number of systems that protect physical assets or employees. Both are correct views of security based on the views presented.

Another view is becoming more prevalent in corporate environments, which has led to the creation of a new executive post in some organizations, the chief security officer. This view toward security is one of the most comprehensive that an organization can take, that security is not limited to the front door or the firewall, but involves the entire business process. Often' some of the first questions that the CSO asks are, How secure is the network? and How secure is the facility? The CSO is often required to have a working understanding of the following areas:

- Access control systems and methodology
- Applications and systems development

- Business continuity planning
- Cryptography
- Law, investigation, and ethics
- Operations security
- Physical security
- Security architecture and models
- Security management practices
- Telecommunications, network, and Internet security

# ▶ Organizational Issues

A successful deployment of a security system must take into account the needs of the many departments that will be protected in the company. Although the facilities and security departments are the two most prominent owners of the security system, other departments are affected and should be a part in the deployment. Human resources needs access cards issued and activated, and when an employee is terminated, the card must either be returned or deactivated, sometimes immediately. The IT department needs to be involved because of the required network server installation, backup, and maintenance. There will also most likely be network-enabled security devices running on the network, and the IT department should have some understanding of the function of these devices (e.g., bandwidth requirements, static IP addresses). The cost savings to the customer of using the existing network infrastructure is significant. The cost of wire and the subsequent labor needed to install the wire can easily double the cost of a new security system. Also, by hardwiring the system directly back to a server, any flexibility of redundant system operations is eliminated.

Most vendors going into a customer's site to install a security system will try to involve IT immediately if they are not involved already. The most successful installations are those in which IT buys into the system and is integral in the selection. The CIO, or at least director of IT, has a good relationship with the director of security and ensures that the security server and system are compliant with any and all standards that were set up for the other servers running on the network. IT already has the skills necessary to perform backups on the security system and to work with the vendor so that any network-enabled devices can be installed and functional.

The convergence of IT and security is the main topic of conversation among many of the vendors and integrators in the security industry. Systems have developed into software- and database-intensive platforms, and almost every part of a system can run over the company's LAN/WAN architecture. Security systems have gone from being hardwired masses of electronics to a combination of specialized electronics modules and software. This has led to a shift in personnel who install the systems—away from the electronics technician alone and toward combinations of engineers, IT technicians, as well as electronics technicians. The systems have scaled up in their complexity, which now requires security vendors to have specialized IT technicians on staff. The system could have a digital video recorder, or DVR, with storage capacity well into the terabyte range. The system could also be an access-control system with a database taking direct personnel feed from an HR system and linking to the DVR as well.

While the systems have grown more complex, the job of securing the facility has remained unchanged. Many companies use third-party guard services to monitor facilities, and the systems that are being installed, although very complex on the back end, have an end-user interface that is simple and easy to use. These third-party guard services often do not understand exactly how the system works, so it is in the best interest of the customer's security to have at least one of the internal IT staff have a working understanding of how things are supposed to interact. The guard service that is monitoring the facility should not be expected to know if the system is functioning fully; that should be left to people more inclined to systems monitoring.

# ▶ The Two Aspects: Hardware and Software

Using hardware and software to secure your data center or facility can take a lot of research and time. The security industry has grown over the years to include software with every device, including simple alarm panels that report intrusion and fire to sophisticated networked software programs.

There are four main sections that should be included when thinking about securing a facility or data center: closed-circuit television (CCTV); card access; fire alarm; and heating, venting, and air conditioning (HVAC), or building controls. Today, all of the sections are interconnected through hardwire connections or software connections.

## CCTV

The video industry, or CCTV industry, is undergoing rapid change from the traditional analog television system to a totally new digital communications method over IP networks. With this rapid change are new enhancements and expanding applications in the CCTV world.

Most of today's digital CCTV businesses are designed utilizing DVR or NVR (network video recorder) technology, which is replacing the old TLR (time-lapse recorders) and VCRs in deployment today. DVRs and NVRs provide recording of high-quality compressed video and add the capability of remote monitoring over local and wide area networks.

This new digital revolution affects every aspect of the video security system—the wiring, the camera, the switching of the video, and the signal distribution. The IP-based CCTV solution offers better performance and a wider variety of system capabilities (see Figure 5.1).

CCTV cameras have also moved into the digital revolution, moving from the old technology of vidicon tubes to CCD (charged couple device) chip cameras. Cameras come with internal encoders to convert to digital or utilize an external encoder. The signal is then broadcast over a LAN/WAN for streaming video and recorded video.

Following are two scenarios comparing analog (TLRs and VCRs) and digital (DVRs and NVRs) IP-based CCTV recording.

- *The Analog User.* Mike is responsible for security at seven shoe stores and saved lots of money by using traditional time-lapse VCRs to record video. Each day, he has to have someone swap out the tapes. When an event does occur, he has to visit the site,

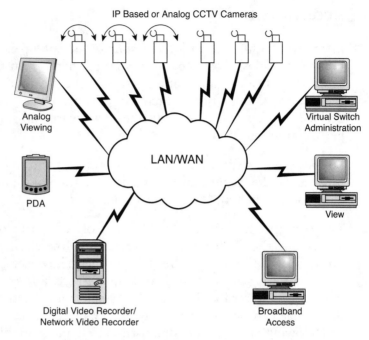

IP Based or Analog CCTV Cameras

Analog Viewing

PDA

LAN/WAN

Virtual Switch Administration

View

Digital Video Recorder/ Network Video Recorder

Broadband Access

**Figure 5.1** Simple IP CCTV diagram.

sometimes hours away, and retrieve the tape. He then takes hours to sequentially search the tape, which costs him time and money.

- *The Digital User.* Leanne is responsible for security at thirty shoe store locations. She recently invested in a powerful digital video system to manage her daily security information and operations. Leanne receives an alert at her office anytime an incident happens and takes just seconds to retrieve, review, and even share the information over the WAN.

Digital IP video saves time, delivers more reliable information, reduces operational costs (including travel and the cost of required dedicated resources), and leads to a quick payback. Digital video allows enterprises to transform an existing analog security and monitoring system into a business tool. Benefits include lowering operating and labor costs and the ability to manage and monitor numerous sites more efficiently.

# Access Control

In today's high-tech world, the simple task of opening a door has become complex. Access control is everywhere, from high schools to hospitals, offices to universities, petro-chemical plants to pharmaceuticals, network operation centers to prisons. Once access control is decided on, you must choose the best hardware and software for your particular application.

Businesses can deploy access-control products and associated systems because of the advancement of network topology and its universal adoption throughout the business community.

The security department usually controls all parts of the physical access, and the IT department must control the electronic intellectual property of the company. The IT department, however, is starting to get involved with access control to combine access across the enterprise into one single card and platform. A single authorization or identification badge can save the company money by reducing duplicate efforts and allowing one place of administration. It allows employees to access the facility, log onto the network, and gain access to different areas, all with one access-control badge Employee identification is also achieved by allowing a visual verification between the employee and their printed photograph. On the network, employees can utilize their access-control badge to provide token and PIN verification to intranets, VPN-encrypted tunnels, and protected company files.

The standard technologies of a card-access badge used by security in the past—wiegand, berrium ferrite, magnetic, and proximity—are slowly being replaced with smart cards and biometric devices. Smart cards, with an enhanced frequency of 13.56 MHz technology, allow for faster and more secure methods of data transfer. They become stored sets of information separate within the database, which are commonly referred to as "pages." These pages can be used for cashless vending machines, libraries, parking garages, personnel information, hand and facial biometrics, and more (Figure 5.2). There is now new value to the access-control badge: it is no longer solely for access control and identification. The smart card is used for a variety of applications throughout the enterprise.

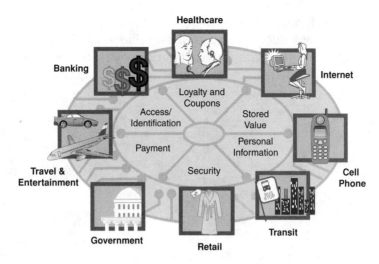

**Figure 5.2** Smart card options.

Biometrics along with smart cards expands the breadth and depth of access control products and systems. The ability to store information on a smart card and to change that data with read/write capabilities allows the user of the smart card to carry around their personal database. For example, a user can upload a fingerprint or a picture of their iris to the card, and with a single card read and a biometric device, verification can be obtained. This concept of layered security will allow companies to become compliant with their many physical and enterprise security requirements.

The use of an access control card after it is presented to a verification device needs to transfer the data to a data gathering panel. The method is typically sending binary data in a Wiegand format over copper wires to a panel to decode the data and provide verification. There are multiple data gathering panels in the security industry today. The decision to utilize a gathering panel is usually made with the software capabilities of the system in the forefront.

Access control software can come in many different operating systems to different server type systems. Open systems and non-proprietary systems are the preferred solution, providing IT friendly solutions that are network capable. Software development kits are readily available, which provide the open architecture necessary to develop and customize on many different levels. GUI's, utilities, and interfaces can be developed to interface with specific vertical markets, such as HR connections, ODBC linking, and third party vendor integration (Figure 5.3).

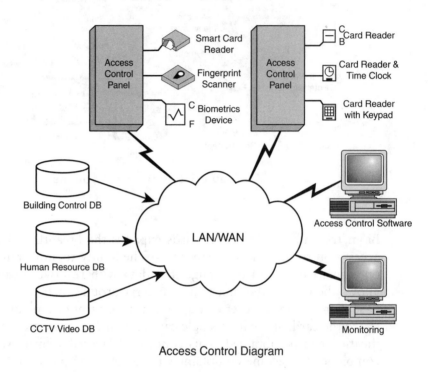

Access Control Diagram

**Figure 5.3** Access-control software architecture.

## Fire Alarm

There are many key issues to consider when installing and operating a fire alarm system in a data center. What kind of glass and frame system will provide a passive fire protection without any assistance? How does a water-based system compare with a clean-agent fire-suppression system?

Glass installed in a data center must allow light for security and visibility and offer fire protection. It needs to maintain a consistent temperature for the operation of computer equipment and must block heat, flames, and smoke. Glass and frames that are rated to block these environmental disasters must be utilized and installed properly.

Sprinkler systems, although effective, should be used only if required. A clean-agent fire-suppression system that extinguishes fires at the molecular level without reducing the oxygen supply of the protected area is recommended.

Ionization detector and photoelectric detector are the two types of smoke detectors that can be utilized in the fire protection system. Both are suitable for early warning of slowly developing fire conditions. In addition to these detectors, heat detectors and rate-of-rise detectors can also be used.

If you are seeking an additional detection layer, an incipient fire detection, or IFD, device can also be installed. The IFD detects the invisible byproducts of materials as they degrade during the precombustion stages of a fire. It actively and continuously samples air.

The IFD consists of five major components:

1. Small diameter PVC pipes to provide air transport
2. Filter to remove large dust particles
3. Actual examination of the air sample by an optical detector
4. Air pump that continuously moves air through the system.
5. Controller that interprets the detector's results.

Continuous sampling of the detector allows for more time to react between the first notification of an event and the actual fire. This will provide a manual intervention before the need for automatic suppression.

## HVAC, or Building Controls

Building controls and the growth of IT have resulted in the integration of access control, CCTV, and building automation. Security systems are sometimes thought of as one component of building automation. This integration includes the ability to have PC desktop control over temperature and lighting settings, zone-specific control for after-hours occupancy, and occupancy-based comfort for your facility or data center. For example, an access-control cardholder can present her card to the smart card reader, verify access, and turn on the heat and lights for the facility.

A digital sign, which is a display device used to present constantly changing, full-motion video, graphics, text, or animation, presents an opportunity to display building occupants on fire drills or security breaches. Signage messaging can be integrated with CCTV to show live video, and the access-control system can unlock doors or display maps for evacuation.

The integration of building controls in the security industry allows systems to be of great benefit in the control of their facilities. The widespread deployments of networks and open systems have made this connectivity possible.

# ▶ Best Practices: Procedures and Policies

Physical security is not the same as Internet or cyber security, but is certainly just as important. Physical entry into a building or a data center is a tremendous advantage for an attacker or thief. Appropriate procedures and policies must closely control the physical access to your most valuable assets.

Creating the appropriate policy should include the following:

- Piggy-back rules for access through controlled doorways
- Access control to all areas containing valuable assets
- Human guards
- Card readers with enhanced security (smart card readers and biometrics)
- Proper wearing of identification badges, possible color-coding of badges to perform visual checking
- Auditing of access to all areas
- Monthly testing of controls

Security procedures require a great deal of planning. Identifying the appropriate security procedures to protect the information and assets while providing the necessary level of access takes time and must be able to change at any given moment.

Security procedures start with identifying what it is that you want to protect and how much you want to protect it. You can then write your security procedure to implement the appropriate level of protection. A security procedure is the set of laws, practices, and rules that control how you protect your assets.

Security procedures for the level of protection you need can be written in two sections: resolution and implementation. Resolution is the decision that the executives review and approve the requirements. Implementation is for the managers who accomplish the requirements. A simple procedure that focuses on these two levels will be easier to implement than a 500-page detailed guideline.

Implementing the security procedure should be done by individual bulletins that are single-lined (e.g., access to the server room) and should include the resolution and implementation with enough detail to be testable. If it is kept small, is focused, and is assigned to the right department, the procedure can be an effective solution to protect the asset. It will also be easier to review the procedure and make any necessary changes.

# Running Business-Critical Applications Over the Internet: "The Middle Mile"

*David Frigeri*

## ▶ The Importance of the Network

How do we capitalize on the opportunity presented by the connected world while managing the challenges associated with the reliability of the Internet? In fact, many CIOs struggle to understand why new applications have not enjoyed all the promises of the Internet or have simply postponed the roll-outs.

Despite the known and unknown challenges, the Internet has become a critical component for companies with strategies of globalization, real-time enterprise, merger/acquisitions, and the introduction of new business models. Our everyday communications may be traversing the globe via the Internet without our even knowing who has access to them. The number of VoIP calls has increased from 150 million minutes in 1998 to 24.5 billion minutes through 2003. Today when major network issues occur, such as the Akamai outage of June 16, 2004, and the Vonage outage of August 2, 2004, it is front-page news.

# ▶ Evolutionary Phases of Internet Readiness

The CIO needs to recognize that the enterprise and the individual applications and initiatives within the enterprise will go through discrete phases depending on the expectations of the business. Before entering the discussion of the evolutionary phases, let's confirm we understand how the Internet is different from the networks with which most CIOs are familiar (Table 6.1).

**Table 6.1** Network and Internet Compared

| Traditional local and wide area networks | The Internet |
|---|---|
| Carrier controls both ends of the transmission | Carrier will control only a subset of the entire path |
| Circuit switching (pre-established path) | Internet TCP/IP (path determined hop by hop) |
| Closed applications | Open applications |
| Centralized system design | Distributed architecture (multiple companies, technologies, and market pressures) |
| Intelligence in the network | Intelligence at the edge |
| Several different and specialized networks | Single, converged, multipurpose connection to network of networks |

We can understand the evolutionary process of running mission-critical applications over the Internet as a progression through increasingly sophisticated phases. These phases represent the degree of integration of the Internet into the enterprise as well as the dependency of the enterprise on the Internet. The four phases are connect, collaborate, control, and complex. Because we discuss these phases in the context of the application, it is normal to see an enterprise residing in multiple phases simultaneously. As the application progresses through these phases, its dependency on the Internet and specifically on the health of the Internet becomes increasingly vital.

Initially, companies betting their business-critical applications over the Internet expected benefits such as increased employee productivity, improved access to information, and the ability to communicate seamlessly with partners anywhere in the world. We would say the primary objective was to "connect"—that is, to connect to customers, suppliers, employees, and partners. This usually involves simple applications such as email and file transfer protocol.

Once the connection has been made, the enterprise moves into the collaboration phase. The collaboration phase is also commonly referred to as digitization, such as for electronic form submittal and processing. The collaboration phase involves facilitating access to information, or in other words, collecting, processing, storing, mining, selling, and distributing information. In the collaboration phase, we see the real-time sharing of applications either within the enterprise or across enterprise boundaries. In the collaboration phase, the quality and reliability of the Internet plays an increasingly important role in the execution of business processes.

The control phase is characterized by the enterprise's ability to use the network to extend the sphere of control for management and governance. This includes the facilitation of product development, managing the sales force, enterprise resource planning, optimizing processes, and monitoring the supply chain. In the control phase, the enterprise is highly dependent on the Internet for the execution of business processes.

The complex phase spans the range from finding customers to conducting transactions to guaranteeing transactions to introducing whole new business models, such as search engine marketing, e-commerce, auction, real-time data streams, and VoIP. In the complex phase the whole business or a significant portion of the business will be severely impacted with broad exposure by performance degradation or downtime.

# Definition and Illustration of Phases

## Connect Phase

In the connect phase, we see the enterprise migrating from an inflexible, slow, and expensive private network to the public Internet (Figure 6.1). The enterprise is leveraging the speed, flexibility, and cost savings associated with the one-to-many nature of the public network infrastructure. The enterprise is quickly accessing basic information and communicating with other enterprises with only small incremental bandwidth costs.

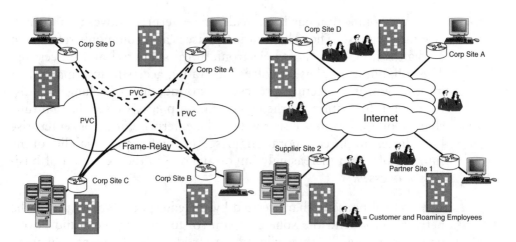

**Figure 6.1** The connect phase.

## Collaboration Phase

In the collaboration phase (Figure 6.2), the enterprise leverages the Internet to gain access to information both in data form and human form. Employees use the Internet for online brain storming sessions, interactive presentations, and access to corporate portals. The successful

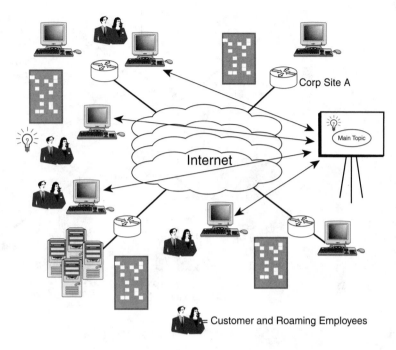

**Figure 6.2** The collaboration phase.

collaboration is dependent on the quality of the Internet to ensure unobstructed interaction.

## Control Phase

In this phase, we see an energy company that must transfer large geological surveys to corporate sites located in the far reaches of the earth (Figure 6.3). We can assume that these data files must be analyzed and certified before the next business unit can commence data processing. The enterprise is in the control phase because it unquestionably relies on the Internet to control workflow and optimize product development anywhere in the world. We also see the underlying transport within the Internet cloud can be anything, including satellite links.

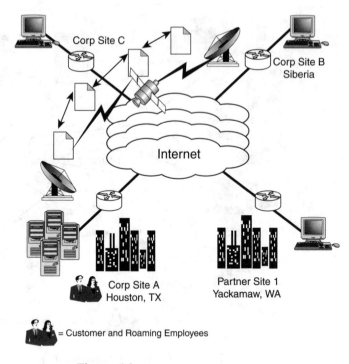

**Figure 6.3** The control phase.

*Complex Phase*

In the complex phase, the enterprise is running the backbone of the business across the Internet (Figure 6.4). The Internet drives an increase in productivity, revenue, and speed to market, and it drives costs out of the business. Some of these new business models are brokerage (marketplace exchange), infomediary and metamediary (incentive marketing), subscription (content), and utility (on-demand metered usage).

## Situation Analysis

After evaluating the preceding descriptions, you should be able to identify what phase you are currently in and gain a picture of the phase the enterprise should be moving to. By answering the following questions, you can build a baseline or launch point to evolve the underlying network architecture from the current phase to the next. Answering these questions is a priority because they go to the very heart of effective execution.

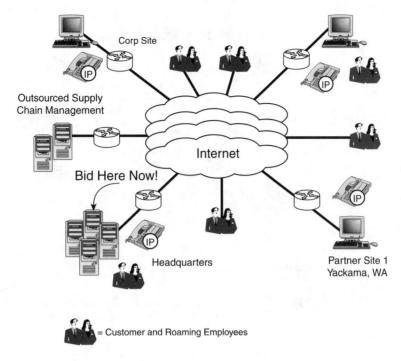

**Figure 6.4** The complex phase.

- What is your objective?
- Do you know the performance and availability requirements of your business-critical application?
- What is the nature of your traffic patterns?
- Is the key application database intensive?
- Do you control both ends of the transmission?
- Do you know how your Internet traffic is currently routed?
- Are your business-critical applications event driven?
- Are you in control of your bandwidth costs?
- Is your traffic growing? If yes, what application is driving the growth?
- Where are the destinations of interest?

Based on the on the answers to these questions, you should be able to create a pictorial illustrating the current environment and network topology (Figure 6.5).

**Figure 6.5** Pictorial situation analysis of a current operating environment and network topology.

# ▶ The Importance of Measurement

The Internet, from a business perspective, has represented many positives, including lower costs and increased flexibility and reach. The Internet comprises thousands of autonomous networks, creating a very fluid and dynamic environment in which any one network has limited influence and span of control. This complexity means the application is constrained by forces that are not easily identifiable or understood.

A frequently used moniker for the Internet is a cloud, rightfully so because it is so difficult to understand what is occurring inside of it. The most frequently used metrics for characterizing network performance across the Internet are latency, packet loss, availability, throughput, capacity, and jitter. Any enterprise interested in running the business over the Internet must have a means for measuring and thereby managing these metrics.

Although the following represents several iterations of each of these metrics, it is important from a CIO perspective to understand the major areas of measurement and management.

- **Network latency:** The time it takes for a packet to get from its source to its destination—in other words, the period of time a network component or human is frittering away the company's time—is called network latency.

- **Packet loss:** This metric represents the percentage of packets that will be lost out of 100 percent, particularly detrimental to applications such as VoIP.

- **Network availability:** Network availability is the percentage of time available for sending a packet to the Internet and receiving a response.

- **Throughput:** Closely related to availability and latency, throughput in its most basic form is the number of transactions per second; in the network we refer to it as the amount of data that arrives during a period of time. Later, we discuss why throughput may not match the actual data rate contracted.

- **Capacity:** Capacity is frequently characterized as the current utilization rate for a given amount of total available bandwidth. Capacity is a more sophisticated area of management than is usually recognized. The enterprise must consider time of day, traffic bursts, explosive growth, and performance-sensitive applications.

- **Jitter:** There are two commonly used definitions for jitter. The first is the variation in latency, and the second is interpacket arrival time. Jitter has become a very popular metric with the advent of VoIP and video conferencing.

## Common Measurement Tools

The most common tools used for measurement purposes, such as traceroute, PING, SNMP, and flow measurement, are relatively old and in some cases quite rudimentary. Traceroute and PING are the most popular means for path identification, packet loss, and round-trip time.

Traceroute is a utility that traces the network route between the local host computer and any other host computer connected to the Internet. The output of the traceroute utility, which is also called a traceroute, shows each hop (an Internet router or another host computer) between the two endpoints and the round-trip time it took for a packet to be bounced off of that hop. Despite their manual nature, traceroutes can be useful for locating network congestion and failures (Figure 6.6).

```
EnteranIP address or Hostname:
WWW.AMAZON.COM

RemoteHost: 216.52.65.164

 1  Vlan5.css-nts-r1.net.umd.edu (128.8.5.252) 0.545 ms
 2  Gi5-1.css-core-r1.net.umd.edu (128.8.0.9) 0.378 ms
 3  Gi3-2.css-fw-r1.net.umd.edu (128.8.0.82) 0.904 ms
 4  Gi2-1.css-max-r1.net.umd.edu (128.8.0.234) 0.411 ms
 5  umd-isp-clpk.maxgigapop.net (206.196.177.49) 0.439 ms
 6  dcne-so3-1-0.maxgigapop.net (206.196.178.45) 1.004 ms
 7  dca-edge-03.inet.qwest.net (65.114.173.1) 0.990 ms
 8  dca-core-02.inet.qwest.net (205.171.9.61) 0.783 ms
 9  dca-brdr-01.inet.qwest.net (205.171.9.54) 0.633 ms
10  so-1-3-1.pr1.iad1.us.above.net (208.184.233.33) 1.296 ms
11  so-2-0-0.cr1.iad1.us.above.net (64.125.28.138) 1.460 ms
12  so-3-0-0.mpr1.iad5.us.above.net (64.125.29.230) 1.240 ms
13  amazon-above.mpr1.iad5.us.mfnx.net.175.185.208.in-addr.arpa (208.185.175.66) 1.270 ms
```

**Figure 6.6** A sample traceroute.

PING is short for Packet Internet Groper, an Internet utility used to check the connection with another site. It repeatedly sends Internet Control Message Protocol (ICMP) echo requests of the remote site (attempts to bounce a signal off of the target) and shows you how long it took to complete the round trip each time (Figure 6.7). If you get no returns at all, the site is either down or unreachable. If only a portion of the signal is returned, it indicates some trouble with the connection that will slow down performance; this is the primary means for measuring packet loss.

Simple Network Management Protocol (SNMP) gathers statistical data about network traffic and the behavior of network components; SNMP uses management information bases (MIBs), which define what information is available from any manageable network device.

```
Trying ping from node 'Dallas, Tx, US' to 'NS1.PH1.PNAP.NET'
64 Bytes from 216.52.65.1: icmp_seq=0 time=44 msec
64 Bytes from 216.52.65.1: icmp_seq=1 time=41 msec

64 Bytes from 216.52.65.1: icmp_seq=2 time=42 msec
64 Bytes from 216.52.65.1: icmp_seq=3 time=41 msec
```

**Figure 6.7** Sample PING output.

Flow measurement provides information about who is using the network, what applications are used, when the network is utilized, and where traffic is going on the network.

# ▶ A Word on Service-Level Agreements

Now that we have become familiar with the common metrics and tools to measure the metrics, it is time to discuss the service-level agreement (SLA) and how it relates to running mission-critical applications over the WAN. An SLA can specify bandwidth availability, response times for routine and ad hoc queries, and response time for problem resolution (network down, machine failure, etc.). SLAs can be very general or extremely detailed and should include the steps to take in the event of a failure. Obviously, putting in place contractual obligations to meet predefined and pre-agreed-upon levels of service is smart business. The CIO should apply rigor when reviewing and negotiating an SLA with an Internet service provider (ISP). You need to see quantifiable data, time frames, and dollars; you need to work to take out all limitations and qualifiers. For example, many SLAs cover only the ISP's own network but not the vast majority of other networks that constitute the Internet. The vast majority of Internet traffic traverses, on average, three to four different networks. In effect, your ISP covers only a small portion of your overall Internet traffic. Also, make sure you understand clearly how the ISP gathers SLA metrics, what the thresholds are, and what the process is for recouping credits if the ISP violates a service-level metric.

# ▶ Design

As Karl Rauscher (executive director, Bell Labs Network Reliability & Security Office) stated, "Reliability is not something you can spray paint on when you want it. High reliability is achieved only through careful attention throughout the entire design, implementation, and operation stages." Complex systems, whether power grids, the space shuttle, or the Internet, are prone to small and catastrophic failures. The point is to prepare for the inevitable and provide your company with alternative means to continue to leverage the connected world even when something does go wrong. This is typically achieved by *multihoming*, or connecting to multiple ISPs. Multihoming ensures the fundamental reliability for continued access to the Internet, but what happens once the IP packet enters the Internet?

It is important to note that multiple connections to the Internet do not guarantee end-to-end redundancy throughout the Internet (Figure 6.8). This fact is where path diversity plays a very important role. Path diversity can be expressed as a percentage, the number of unique hops out of the total number of hops to the final destination.

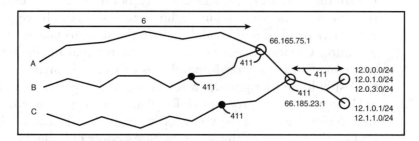

**Figure 6.8** Path diversity.

Path diversity can also be understood as degree of risk: the higher the percentage of demonstrated diversity to all interesting destinations, the lower the risk. To improve path diversity, the right combination of providers is as important as the quantity. Quality refers to how the ISP routes your traffic—you want to choose the ISP that routes your traffic over the highest percentage of unique router hops to achieve the highest degree of end-to-end path diversity. The Internet diversity report provides a graphical representation of the amount of diversity for all destinations (Figure 6.9). The percentage of diversity achieved to a given destination is the percentage of the total path length (in router hops) before the convergence point.

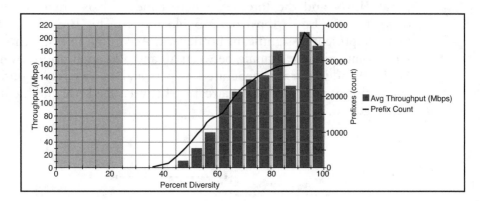

**Figure 6.9** Sample Internet path diversity report.

Figure 6.9 depicts a high degree of path diversity: the bar graphs are significantly shifted to the right. This means the paths are at least 60 percent diverse, and the majority are over 70 percent diverse.

# ▶ Most Common Performance Challenges

Surprising as it may seem, the Internet is still run by humans, and most major issues and outages can be traced back to human or procedural error. The major challenges to running applications with high performance requirements over the Internet, however, are more technical in nature. There are several technical challenges; we concentrate on LAN–WAN mismatch, Border Gateway Protocol (BGP), and Transport Control Protocol (TCP).

## LAN–WAN Mismatch

In 1997 the most common LAN port was 10 Mbps, and in less than 5 years 100 Mbps port was the norm. Before long, 1,000 Mbps will be the norm on corporate LANs. Meanwhile, the Internet utilizes OC48, OC192, and now even OC768.[1] The challenge occurs between the corporate LAN and the Internet, where bandwidth is often channeled down to T-1 (1.54 Mbps) or DS3 (45 mbps). This LAN–WAN mismatch represents a significant bottleneck. According to research firms, most companies are running between 50 and 300 applications over the WAN. By adding traffic generated by personal use, we find significant contention at the point of demarcation between the LAN and the Internet (Figure 6.10).

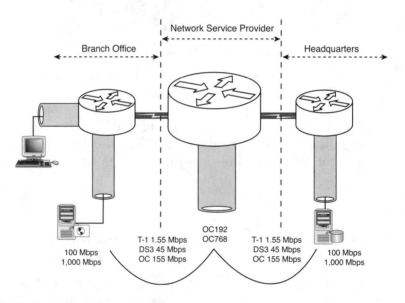

**Figure 6.10** Demarcation between the LAN and the Internet.

---

1. OC48, OC192, and OC768 are long-haul, fiber based backbone connections capable of transmitting data at 2.45, 10, and 40 gigabits per second, respectively.

# Border Gateway Protocol (BGP)

The BGP is the de facto routing protocol on the Internet that enables the communication and advertisement of locations between networks. It is the control mechanism for choosing paths through the Internet. The primary challenge associated with BGP is the inability for it to take latency and packet loss into consideration when selecting a path. BGP is only concerned with directing routers on how to route packets from one autonomous system to another. It does not consider events within a solitary network from a routing perspective or a performance perspective. The network engineer can manually tune the BGP attributes to more effectively control the distribution of traffic. This manual process has proven not to scale well due to the thousands of destinations and the continuous changes in the Internet routing table.

In Figure 6.11 we see BGP selecting the lower performing path of Link 2 because it has fewer "hops."

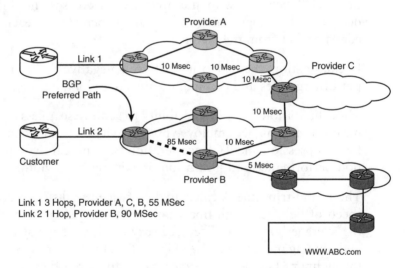

**Figure 6.11** Identifying the preferred path.

# Transport Control Protocol (TCP)

There still remains a limitation less associated with the network than with TCP, specifically TCP's slow start and congestion control. TCP's objective is to send packets into the network without reservation, then react to observable events that occur. TCP then attempts to adjust the "congestion window" based on those events. *TCP's congestion window controls the number of packets a TCP flow may have in the network at any time (RFC 2861).*

The congestion window has two significant aspects that impact throughput and therefore the performance of certain applications. TCP is very conservative in increasing the congestion window, meaning it sends more packets when the network is performing well. *Additive increases* means TCP will add only one packet for each successfully received acknowledgment from the recipient.

On the other hand, TCP is very sensitive to detected network congestion. TCP behaves with multiplicative decreases. In this case, TCP decreases the congestion window by 50 percent for each unacknowledged packet from the recipient.

In culmination, these algorithms have a negative effect on the throughput of large files and communications over long distances.

These limitations restrain the ability to achieve seamless global communications and higher employee productivity. Several technologies allow for compression and TCP acceleration to significantly improve application performance and utilization of existing bandwidth.

The round-trip time is calculated as twice the distance divided by the speed of light (through fiber) times the number of router hops, times the average hop delay. The necessary send, wait for acknowledgment, and send again sequence (see Figure 6.12) further restricts the effective throughput. The dealy is exacerbated for large files transmitted over long distances and leads to inconsistent performance and availability.

Studies have found that while productivity losses from full network outages for larger companies cost on average $1.5 million a year, productivity losses from service degradations are $3.5 million a year. It is not uncommon to find an enterprise suffering in excess of 5 percent packet loss for 5 to 10 percent of the time, which is the equivalent of

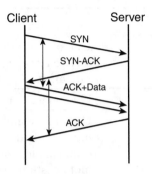

**Figure 6.12** Handshaking needed to complete a single transmission results in significant transimisison delay.

almost 2 weeks a year (4,320 minutes) when an application is unusable by each end user.

For example, a 10 Megabyte file under normal latency conditions should take 10 seconds to download; under severe situations, it could take 262 seconds or not arrive at all. Multiplying this idle time by the number of employees impacted, by the number of widgets produced or sold per unit of time, and by the length of the degradation, it is easy to understand how $3.5 million can be wasted per year through lost productivity.

# ▶ Case Study

In this case study, we take a before and after look at the network, understanding the requirements, challenges, and solutions. As we will discover, the requirements primarily involve performance and availability to maximize the potential value of VoIP. The company is entering the complex phase because it is looking to leverage the Internet strategically by using it to enter new markets, provide new value-add services, and drive down costs.

| Company | Travel, Inc. |
|---|---|
| Information | One of the country's largest independent, full-service travel agencies specializing in the corporate market |
| Initiative | IP Contact Center/VoIP |
| Objective | Coordinate multiple contact centers and agents into a unified and virtual contact center operation; enable remote workers to function in a more cost-effective manner; accelerate revenue via rapid entry into new markets through virtualization and introducing new services |
| Requirement | Establish high-speed and reliable links |
| Current configuration | Hundreds of agents in small offices and home offices interconnect via private frame-relay network using interfaces as small as 56K |
| Telecom cost before | Average per agent $1,500 |
| Telecom cost after | Average per agent $90 |

## Situation Analysis

Following are relevant questions to be asked before starting the design for the Travel, Inc., case study.

- What is your objective?
- Do you know the performance and availability requirements of your business-critical application?
- What is the nature of your traffic patterns?
- Do you control both ends of the transmission?
- Do you know how your Internet traffic is currently routed?
- Are your business-critical applications event driven?
- Are you in control of your bandwidth costs?
- Where are the destinations of interest?

The situation Travel, Inc., faces is illustrated in Figure 6.13.

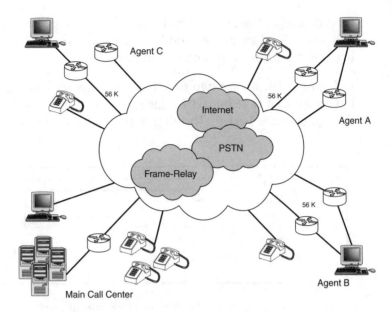

**Figure 6.13** Situation illustration for Travel, Inc.

We know that that the calls will be routed from one center to another, the performance of the network is critical, and the costs associated with routing must be low. The opportunity to control both ends of the transmission must be considered, although at this point the company does not know how packets are being routed through the network. We should assume that bandwidth requirements will increase due to an increase in the number and size of files, such as pictures, brochures, and customer profiles, being shared between sites.

Three primary domains must be addressed while transitioning from one phase to another: measure, availability, and performance—or, easier to remember, MAP.

The *measurement* domain in the context of this case study is extremely important because we are dealing with VoIP, and in order to effectively manage this application, we must be able to measure it. It may be surprising to learn that VoIP has relatively liberal thresholds for the latency, packet loss, and jitter due to the CODEC's (Compressor/Decompressor) ability to buffer incoming packets; However, it is very important to know when, where, and why the performance thresholds are being breached. For example, VoIP can sustain up to 100 ms latency and 1 percent packet loss, but when these ceilings are exceeded, the end user will hear a loud snapping sound or experience the awkwardness of talking over his or her communication partner.

In Figure 6.14, we see two of three paths are performing suboptimally, but because of the ability to measure, we can detect and shift traffic to the ISP with the best-performing path, depicted in yellow.

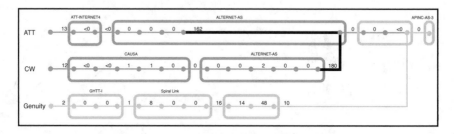

**Figure 6.14** Three suboptimal paths.

Gauging the degree of required *availability* is the foundation of the network. Looking out from the corporate site, every network element may need to be redundant, including the individual components within the network element (Figure 6.15).

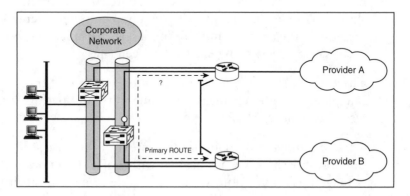

**Figure 6.15** Network redundancy.

To ensure long-term performance, we will take a multipronged approach by concentrating on the network layer and the transport layer. As described earlier, once we have taken the required steps to add diversity to improve availability, we must address the inherent weaknesses of the Internet. We can leverage the diverse connections to the Internet to improve the overall performance of our applications. Performance refers to the three primary metrics: latency (round-trip time), packet loss (retransmissions), and jitter (interpacket arrival time). A route-control device provides the ability to control traffic at the edge of the Internet by measuring the performance of each ISP and then automatically routing traffic onto the best-performing ISP (Figure 6.16). The logic is that the more ISPs to select from, the better the chance of finding the optimal path and therefore the more value created by route control.

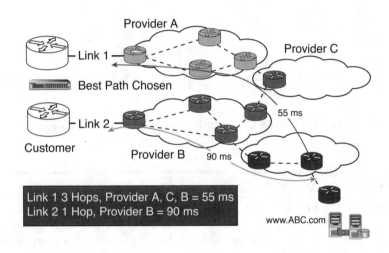

**Figure 6.16** Best performance may be found across several providers.

There are several technologies that allow for compression and TCP augmentation to significantly accelerate application performance and improve the utilization of existing bandwidth without upgrading. To address the potential throughput challenges associated with TCP, we implement TCP acceleration and compression technology. Another aspect to be addressed is the bandwidth limitations on the distant ends by migrating from small, fractional and 1.5 Mbps frame-relay circuits to higher capacity DSL (Figure 6.17).

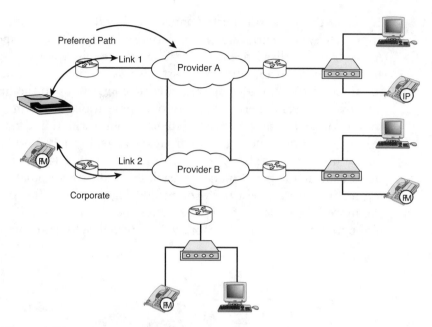

**Figure 6.17** Bandwidth limitations on the distant ends of the network.

In the following case study, you, as the CIO, will evaluate and recommend an approach for ABC Manufacturing.

| Company | ABC Manufacturing |
|---|---|
| Information | In over 60 countries, ABC Manufacturing is the leading custom manufacturer of tools for the construction industry, offering more than 25,000 products. Growth has been constrained due to the inability to rapidly deploy new products or fulfill sales orders requiring customization in a timely manner. Further, due to the high costs, frame-relay has proven too expensive to reach global markets. ABC Manufacturing wants to leverage the Internet to expand reach and improve responsiveness. The company currently uses the Internet for email, remote access for salespeople, and browsing (Figure 6.18). |
| Objective | Shift to a real-time, Internet-centric format for faster deployment of services to trading partners. |
| Requirements | Speed time to market and build network infrastructure to expand reach economically and support more sophisticated custom designs via CAD drawings. The desired end result is to move the entire business operations to the Internet. |

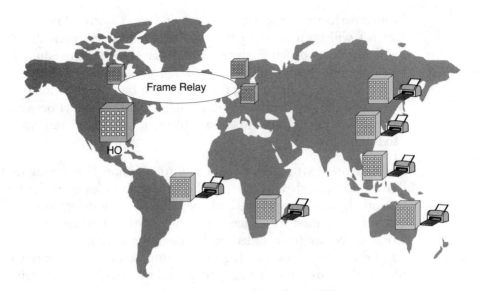

**Figure 6.18** ABC Manufacturing's global Internet needs.

Answer the following questions:

- What phase is the corporation currently in?
- What phase is it moving into?
- Do you know the performance and availability requirements of ABC's business-critical applications?
- What is the nature of ABC's traffic patterns?
- Does ABC control both ends of the transmission?
- Are ABC's business-critical applications event driven?
- Where are the destinations of interest?

## Discussion

In this situation, the company is potentially in a pre-context phase but may rapidly progress through the collaboration phase (custom designs) to the control phase (support supply chain) and eventually to the complex phase when ABC Manufacturing introduces new business models, such as auctions. As the CIO, you must understand and plan for the long-term potential the Internet represents.

From a performance perspective, moving from a private network to the Internet will require two priorities to be addressed immediately. The company must procure diverse ISP connections with redundant network components to fulfill the availability requirements of a 24/7 global operation. Equally important, there must be an automated means for measuring the performance and availability of the paths between ABC and customers and vendors—remember, if you can't measure it, you can't manage it.

There is one extra aspect to take into account: the throughput and latency associated with moving the huge CAD files over the Internet, potentially traversing thousands of miles. Fortunately, since ABC can control or at least influence both ends of the communication, a network device can be installed on the distant end to accelerate the transfer of these large files. In a high-tech manufacturing environment, these files could be as large as 1 Gigabyte, and the delay in transferring these files could significantly slow workflow.

Taking advantage of the Internet is a matter of accomplishing two strategic objectives: assessing where the organization or the application is today and predicting what the future requirements will be. There are three recurring challenges—BGP, TCP throughput, and LAN-WAN mismatch—and as the enterprise progresses through the phases, these challenges become increasingly acute. Therefore, the CIO needs to take a structured approach via a situational analysis to ensure the underlying infrastructure is measurable, available, and performing (MAP) to the requirements of the application. The Internet provides unprecedented opportunity for the CIO to enable the enterprise in new exciting ways. The Internet's frailties must be avoided, but by following the advice in this chapter, you are well on your way of making the Internet deliver on its promises.

# Information Management: What's Next?

*John Wollman*

## ▶ Introduction

This chapter focuses on the evolution of "information management" and the business and technology ramifications as organizations move forward from today's technology landscape to tomorrow's. The chapter begins with a focus on the technology underpinnings of an information management value chain (to provide context) and then describes corporate performance management (CPM) as the business driver that will require organizations to increase the information management "value-add" to adequately measure, monitor, and respond to changes in the business climate.

89

# ▶ Is Structured Data Management a Solved Problem?

Many practitioners in, and observers of, the data management space espouse that "structured data management" is a solved problem. That is to say, most companies have been successful in deploying data warehouses and data marts that enable them to better understand and manage their businesses.

This stands in stark contrast to not-too-many years ago when industry publications and analysts were consistently reporting the failure of small- and large-scale data warehouse projects. It's conceivable that data warehouse practitioners got dramatically better at defining requirements and designing better solutions, but it's more likely that:

- The infrastructural elements (the processors, storage, database management systems, data transformation and movement tools, BI tools, and analytic applications) improved to the point that even mediocre warehouse designs could be made to work and perform adequately. In particular, the dramatic decrease in the costs of storage space and processing power afford mediocre designers the ability to "throw hardware at the problem" and succeed where the same project would have likely failed a few years ago.
- The industry tackled smaller problems and declared victory. The major "enterprise modeling"–driven, multibusiness-unit data warehouse programs were halted and replaced with successful business-unit warehouse and data mart projects that offered dramatically less risk, politics, and cost.

Regardless of whether data warehouse practitioners have truly become craftsmen, or the tools have evolved to the point that a journeyman team can accomplish an acceptable result, most companies today have implemented some form of data warehouses or data marts that are in production and serving the business. Additionally, the vendor community is responding with analytic applications that reduce the time-to-market, risk, and (ideally, some of the) expense associated with data warehousing.

# ▶ Information Management Value Chain

It's clear that while most organizations are doing an increasingly better job of managing structured data and building data marts and warehouses that increase their ability to manage their businesses, most companies don't feel that they have the right information available at the right time, at the right level, and in the right format to make quality business decisions. This is especially true for executives ("business optimization managers") as opposed to "process managers" or "departmental/divisional managers" who have been the beneficiary in the advancement of structured data management capabilities.

As depicted in Figure 7.1, the ideal scenario is providing increasing value-add to information as the information progresses "upwards" in an organization.

- Beginning with execution-oriented, transactional (structured) data that is used to measure process efficiency and for tactical planning at the business or functional unit level, value is added by correlating structured and unstructured data from multiple departments and/or processes into management support tools

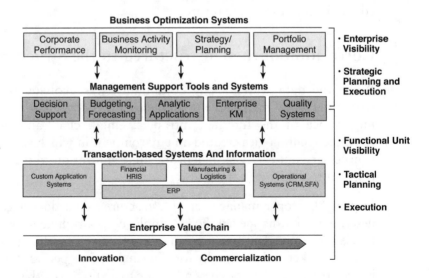

**Figure 7.1** Information management value chain.

(data warehouses and analytic applications) for strategic planning and execution.

- Further value is added to the information contained in the management support tools via cross-tool, cross-department and cross-functional unit correlation and the addition of supplemental structured and unstructured data from other internal and external sources to feed business optimization systems

# ▶ What's Next?

Assuming that you concur with the notions that

- structured data management is somewhat of a solved problem (at least at the departmental/data mart level), and
- there is benefit to increasing the level of value-add in the information management value chain as described above,

then the likely question you're asking is, What are the logical next areas of focus worth considering? Following are interdependent (and, in some cases, discrete) concepts that will be evolving (and be implemented en masse) in the near future.

## Correlation of the Unstructured to the Structured

While the data warehousing community was evolving to solve the structured data management challenge, the continual expansion in importance of the Internet, intranets, email, chat, and other Web-spawned technologies created an environment in which structured data is necessary but rarely sufficient for an organization to truly sense and respond to changes in the market.

In general, proper management of structured data does a good job of describing what happened. For example, even a rudimentary data warehouse can easily identify a drop in sales of a given product or solution in a given market and geography for a given past time period. The challenge is that structured data rarely is adequate to identify why (Figure 7.2). The reason for this is that clues to stimuli that caused a response that was

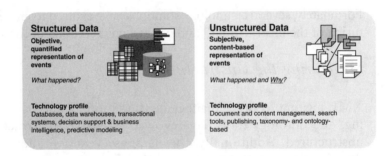

**Figure 7.2** Structured data versus unstructured data in determining what happened and why.

detected in structured data are typically available only in unstructured content (examples could include a competitor launching a promotion on its Web site, unexpected weather conditions, an announcement by the Fed, etc.).

Future business intelligence solutions and data management processes will evolve to support the intersection of structured data and unstructured content to enable companies to correlate the why to the what and make better decisions more rapidly (Figure 7.3).

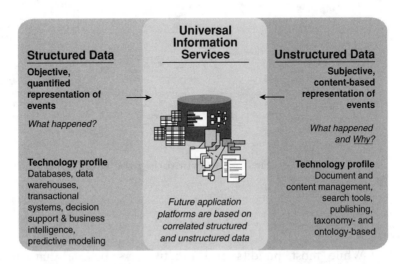

**Figure 7.3** Correlated structured and unstructured data.

Fortunately, several technology solutions have evolved to enable the "structuring of the unstructured" and/or the "unstructuring of the structured."

## Structuring the Unstructured

XML tagging, content management, taxonomy and/or content indexing, and ontology tools have evolved to enable the structuring of the unstructured. Additionally, the database vendors' adoption of XML documents as an object type and the ability to parse XML and automatically populate relational tables have removed much of the complexity of adding a level of structure to unstructured content and cross-correlating content to structured data.

The current challenge with this technique is the latency. Structured data can be rapidly extracted, transformed, and loaded with minimal human intervention (other than initially defining the business rules and coding the extract, transform, and load, or ETL scripts). Unstructured content (currently) typically requires some additional levels of human analysis or agreement prior to loading. Over time, as the tools increase in usage and stakeholders become more comfortable with taxonomies and unstructured content aggregation tools' ability to infer appropriate indexing, this latency will become comparable to structured data (Figure 7.4).

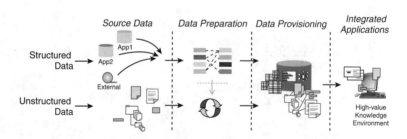

**Figure 7.4** Structuring the unstructured.

## Unstructuring the Structured

While most pundits and practitioners believe that structuring the unstructured is the likely fertile ground for enabling the business intelligence solutions of the future, it is quite possible that unstructuring the

Chapter **7** I Information Management: What's Next?

structured will become an equally viable strategy. Search technologies are quite adept at discerning patterns within unstructured content. Applying search technologies across unstructured realms and databases could provide a new class of future business intelligence tools. This may include some level of the "denormalization" of structured data into XML documents to improve performance and search efficacy (Figure 7.5).

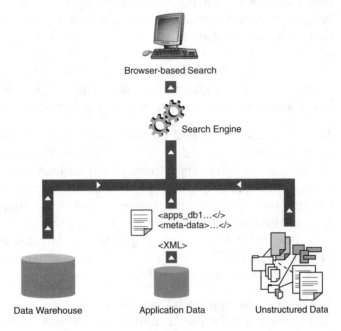

**Figure 7.5** Unstructuring the structured.

## Another Possibility: Data Structure Evolution

It's quite possible (in my opinion, probable, on the basis of pioneering work that Alliance Consulting is doing with two technology partners and clients under nondisclosure) that there will be a "next generation" in database technologies that are not based upon today's relational structures but that better support business intelligence applications that integrate structured data and unstructured content. These new database structures are more akin to neural networks and automatically (and in real time with enhanced compression) integrate structured data and unstructured content while inferring and creating sufficient structure for analytic applications and reporting.

# The Evolution of the Enterprise Model

During the late 1980s and early 1990s, there was a tremendous amount of activity around the notion of information engineering and the attempted development of "enterprise data models." Most of these efforts were unsuccessful because the problem of capturing the totality of a complex organization's information was daunting. Client/server became the next technology wave, favoring departmental or point solutions. The world of data warehousing followed a similar trajectory in which several enterprise data warehouse projects were spawned with limited success. Following this wave of massive, challenging, enterprise-level projects was a wave of smaller scale, departmental warehouse and mart projects that yielded much more successful results.

Today's landscape in most companies is dotted with several warehouses and marts that provide analytics for, or report upon, several aspects of the business. Given the current global economy, the scarcity of budget dollars to spread across departments, the heightened needs for profitability, the relatively inexpensive cost of processing power and storage, and the new rigors of modern corporate governance driven by Sarbanes-Oxley (and industry-specific regulations including Basel II, Patriot Act, 21 CFR Part 11, etc.), there is renewed interest in enterprise visibility to metrics, analytics, and reporting.

The "federated approach" to enterprise data warehousing can now enable the multiple, disparate data warehouses and marts to be integrated to form a corporate and/or global view (Figure 7.6). However, the approach requires the conformance of key enterprise dimensions (customer, product, supplier, vendor, agreement, parts, market, geography, etc.).

There will be a tremendous amount of activity in the short term for enterprises to establish master data management programs to create conformed dimensions. These programs will have a side CRM benefit of helping keep transactional systems in synch with regards to customer data. Following this wave of master data management programs will be a wave of federated, enterprise data warehouse projects.

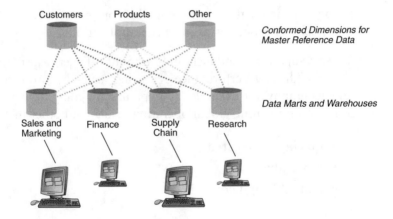

Figure 7.6 Federated approach.

## Increased Frequency, Reduced Latency

The velocity of business has increased dramatically, and there are no signs of this abating over time. The expected timeframe for sensing and responding to market dynamics has evolved in most industries from quarterly to monthly to weekly (and even down to daily, hourly, and to-the-minute for several industries). The acceptable latency associated with producing analytics must be continually reduced. At the same time, the associated frequency must be increased (and in many cases, analytics will need to be produced on demand).

Several organizations will be implementing new physical data structures to enable increasing the frequency, reducing the latency, and still providing adequate performance. Additional data structures will be implemented to support additional interactive analytics ("what if" analyses, pattern and scenario definitions, etc.) in lieu of static and ad hoc reporting.

## Increased Globalization

As more and more companies operate globally, they very rarely have consistent transactional, operational applications in place. Even where companies have standardized on an ERP package worldwide, there can be significant local variations in the configurations, application logic, and business processes around the applications.

These companies spend incredible amounts of energy just trying to get consistent high-level performance reporting (sales by product line, channel, and geography, for example). Companies are going to increasingly require a method for getting global operating results and other metrics that are

- quickly aggregated
- repeatable
- auditable and controlled

## Improved Information Delivery

Most organizations have established portals that provide users (mostly internal, often external) with access to libraries of (sometimes personalized) standard reports. Additionally, some analysts and managers are provided with the ability to leverage business intelligence tools to perform ad hoc analysis and drill downs. These self-service "pull" models have added value in providing the ability to access current information from a consistent place. However, the requirements are evolving as

- The proliferation of collaborative technologies in business-to-consumer and consumer-to-consumer realms (alerts, instant messaging, event-driven notifications, etc.) have raised expectations for business-to-employee and business-to-business realms.
- The sheer volume of standard reports is becoming daunting for many user communities and it is becoming increasingly difficult to find the nuggets of actionable information among a bevy of standard reports.
- Push technologies within business intelligence tools are becoming cheaper and increasingly robust and easier to implement and administer.
- Database technologies and business intelligence tool advances are enabling threshold- and milestone-based alerts with actionable information.

Many organizations are in proof-of-concept or early production usage of push technologies for disseminating actionable, personalized information based upon thresholds and milestones from their business intelligence applications. This will become the dominant form of information delivery (eclipsing business intelligence portals and pull metaphors).

It's worth noting that many business managers and field personnel are getting "flooded" with new reports and analyses coming from uncontrolled business intelligence environments. In some companies, it's conceivable that a user reviewing five sales analysis reports from different business units may see five different formats with different metrics, making it difficult to find patterns and manage the business effectively. The challenge with push technologies will be as much about consistency and predictability of quality of information as it is about improving the quality of the delivery.

# The Business Driving Force: Corporate Performance Management

The notion and role of "information management" within corporations is evolving from a tactical, transaction-integrity focus to a more strategic orientation associated with top- and bottom-line results and risk management. The driving forces behind this transformation (and the shift from data management to information management) include

- The inherent and intrinsic value of information from the business data consumers' perspectives.
- The need to improve the accuracy and frequency of information delivery to internal sources.
- The need to improve the accuracy and frequency of data delivery to external sources (driven by corporate responsibility legislation and other external forces).
- The complexity of aggregating data across business functions and processes.
- The maturity of database engines and management environments.

Accordingly, organizations are striving to increase the value-add in their information management value chains (as described previously) to improve the ability to "sense and respond" faster and more appropriately to external and internal stimuli while mitigating risk factors. However, the "target" of much of this activity will no longer be departments and individual process areas; the targets will be the broader business context and the executive suite. The focus on corporate performance management will lead to the evolution and deployment of the aforementioned "What's Next?" topics in information management.

## Corporate Performance Management

Corporate performance management (CPM) is one of the hottest trends in business intelligence today. While CPM can mean many things to many people, CPM generally relates to the approaches, processes, metrics, applications, and technologies for organizations to improve business performance and adherence to strategy and goals via proactive measurement and monitoring. In effect, CPM enables holistic sensing and responding to the organizational ecosystem (the market, internal processes and events, etc.).

Because most organizations have not created tremendous value-add in their information management value chains (beyond the beneficial departmental visibility to structured data aggregation), it is likely that most companies will struggle with implementing true, holistic CPM initiatives. In fact, most companies struggle with defining, measuring, and monitoring appropriate metrics at even the departmental level on a continuous basis with appropriate levels of buy-in. In accordance with the information management value chain, Alliance Consulting has defined a CPM maturity model to assist clients with improving their maturity in evolving toward enterprisewide CPM.

## CPM Maturity Model

A maturity model for CPM describes the evolution of a CPM program toward total enterprise visibility and a "horizontal culture" of accountability. Alliance's CPM maturity model plots various points against two axes: enterprise visibility/horizontal culture and platform and process maturity. The intent of the model is to capture cultural, process, measurement, and technology aspects of the CPM environment and program.

## Enterprise Visibility/Horizontal Culture

Enterprise visibility implies that the sensing and responding mechanisms, metrics, and processes for CPM are adopted throughout an enterprise, and horizontal culture implies that there is peer (and "cross-silo") management and control of CPM metrics and the response to what the metrics sense.

## Platform and Process Maturity

Platform and process maturity describe a continuum of automation for the aggregation, manipulation, analysis, and publication of CPM metrics. The continuum is from completely manual CPM processes to fully automated platforms and processes. The platform and process maturity correlates to the ability to increase the value-add in the information delivery value chain.

## CPM Maturity Model Plateaus

Plotting various points (without, beginning, established, improved, and optimal) against these two axes yields Figure 7.7.

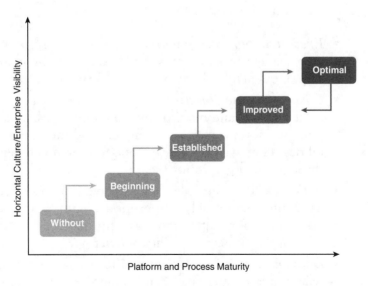

**Figure 7.7** CPM maturity model.

*Key Dimensions*

The five plateaus depicted on the CPM maturity model can be described against several key dimensions, including:

- Scope of visibility within the enterprise: How widely adopted is the CPM program?
- Depth of measurement: How deep within the organization are the metrics targeted (executive reports, critical processes, supporting processes, etc.)
- Periodicity.
- Strategy integration.
- Information systems integration.
- Adoption and acceptance.
- Sophistication of indicator models.

Table 7.1 provides an elaboration of these plateaus.

# Critical Success Factors

Regardless of the maturity level, there are consistent critical success factors for effective CPM:

- *Executive sponsorship with proactive leadership.* A performance management program must have executive buy-in and sponsorship. How involved are executives in the organization?
- *Clear corporate objectives.* A performance management program must measure and monitor the correct metrics, and employees (and business partners) must understand their roles and responsibilities. How well is strategy communicated and deployed through the organization?
- *Action culture.* Tangible results evolve from a performance management program only if appropriate actions are taken to capitalize on opportunities and correct problems. How effective is the culture for accountability and action?
- *Data and integration platform.* Effective decision making is highly reliant on accurate, timely, and comprehensive data. How accessible and insightful is the underlying data? How good are your data

**Table 7.1** Plateaus Mapped to Dimensions

| Plateau Dimension | Without | Beginning | Established | Improved | Optimal |
|---|---|---|---|---|---|
| Scope of Visibility | Ambiguous; each department has mechanisms | Departmental/divisional scope | Enterprise scope | Enterprise scope | Enterprise scope |
| Depth of Measurement | Executive information | Core key performance indicators (KPI) for some business processes and departments are defined | All high-level, critical processes are measured; KPIs for supporting processes are collected | All critical and supporting processes and some sub-processes are measured | |
| Periodicity | Various | Quarterly | Monthly | Monthly or more frequently for some metrics | On-demand plus monthly or more frequently for some metrics |
| Strategy Integration | Information is not integrated to strategy | Loosely coupled to corporate strategy | Tightly coupled to corporate strategy | Tightly integrated to corporate strategy with high degree of integration with planning processes | |
| IS Integration | Multiple measurement systems, personal spreadsheets—ambiguity | Performance data collected manually | A CPM (or executive information ) system is established as "system or record" for corporate performance; most metric data and KPIs are automatically collected/determined | CPM system of record supports drilldown to supporting data and analysis; measures are linked to underlying systems | High degree of integration with collaborative analytical applications; predictive modeling and AI for corrective action |
| Adoption and Acceptance | No visibility | Range of adoption and acceptance | High reliance and adoption by executive team | High reliance and adoption by management team | High reliance and adoption by the entire organization |
| Sophistication of Indicator Models | Various | Simple leading and trailing indicators and KPIs | Complex KPIs and indicator models but limited to single functional areas | Sophisticated, more accurate KPIs for cross-functional processes | Dynamic KPIs determined via pattern recognition |

warehousing and business intelligence skills? Is the infrastructure capable of handling low latency across the enterprise?

- *Data management process focus.* Evolving from a departmental focus to CPM requires consistent processes at the departmental level to enable an enterprise view with sufficient "trust." How consistently are data management best practices applied across departments? How well are the key dimensions (customer, product, item, etc.) understood and conformed?

## CPM as a Component of the Real-Time Enterprise

It's worth noting that CPM is, in and of itself, not the real end-game for business optimization. CPM provides strong sensing and monitoring capabilities but requires rapid response mechanisms to be fully effective. The confluence of globality and the need to respond with near-zero latency will create an environment where organizations must become much closer to the ideal of the real-time enterprise (RTE). The CPM initiatives of the next few years (which will be pervasive and ever-expanding) will provide the underpinnings for progressive organizations to sense and respond more rapidly. An organization that exhibits many of the traits of the "optimal" plateau needs only to add highly optimized and rapid (ideally, zero latency and automated) response mechanisms to be a true RTE. As such, CPM is a significant component of the RTE.

# ▶ What Should Leading IT Groups Be Doing Today?

## Establishing Maturity in Core Information Management Processes

Solving the technological challenges of structured data management and data warehouses has created a new problem: how to realize business benefit from the investment. There is some degree of business benefit that comes naturally from giving knowledge workers access to this newly integrated structured data (plus, of course, the tools to analyze it with). However, companies are realizing that once they have successfully built the infrastructure and applications, they need to put some degree of process and structure around the use and evolution of that capability so that usage translates into business benefit (not just random, hard-to-quantify "benefit" to the business, but solid measurable progress at meeting the company's strategic objectives). There are a lot of things that are "good" for the company in a generic sense but that do little to help the organization realize its strategic objectives. Given that those "good" activities are consuming nonrenewable resources (and thereby taking resources away from activities that might more directly support the strategic direction of the company), are they really so good? Perhaps part of the role of CPM is, in a sense, to focus analysis and measurement on the *right* good activities.

Additionally, the tools and analytic applications vendors have made their offerings significantly easier to use (and in some cases cheaper). This implies that business departments can procure them and can find them easy to use—or misuse. Misuse is exhibited frequently with departmental data marts where the cost of implementing one can be so inexpensive that they are sometimes implemented without IT involvement. The future landscape will be cluttered with the proliferation of less-expensive and easier to use tools for managing structured data, which will require a new set of organization-wide "ground rules" to promote their effective use. One wouldn't want to prevent some members of the organization from exploring and innovating, of course, but exploration on a mass scale is akin to confusion. A more optimal solution would be to focus the majority of data analysis and management on avenues that will support the organization's vision, objectives, and goals, still enabling some knowledge workers to go beyond this structure in attempts to find new business value and new paradigms, but the existence of the framework will bring needed order and discipline to what is (for many organizations) a chaotic process.

The key stakeholders for information management would do well to establish the "governance" models for centralized/decentralized information management, which could include the specification and management of

- Guiding principles
- Rules of engagement
- Funding/chargeback mechanisms
- Definition of success (and associated metrics)

- Key operational processes

The governance models are applied to several dimensions of information management (both structured and unstructured), including

- Requirements analysis
- Information delivery
- Data and content acquisition
- Data and content quality management
- Metadata management
- Technical architecture
- Ongoing data structure management

## Adopting a Federated Philosophy

Given the history of enterprise data warehousing, the inevitable proliferation of departmental and subject area marts, and unstructured content sources, and given the desire for increasingly higher level views of information aggregation, the desirability of a separate, physical enterprise model or fully populated enterprise data warehouse as a stand-alone entity is suspect. Rather, organizations are more likely to adopt a federated approach in which the "corporate assets" are the dimensions (customer, product, supplier, item, etc.) that are conformed to support usage by multiple departments and/or processes to enable an easier path to enterprise integration for CPM.

Adopting a federated philosophy entails creating governance structures, processes, and technical solutions for managing the creation, evolution, continuous improvement, and publication and dissemination of "master reference data" that is available to multiple applications via multiple invocation mechanisms (batch, real-time, near real-time, etc.). The notion of "exchange hubs" for conforming the key dimensions (the reference data) of customer, product, and so on, will become a prevalent method for keeping transactional applications, data warehouses, and third-party data in synch, facilitating a federated approach to data and content aggregation.

# Enterprise Integration: Methods and Technologies

*Min-Jung Yoo, Raghvinder S. Sangwan, and Robin G. Qiu*

## ▶ Introduction

Enterprise integration enables delivery of the right information to the right user in a timely manner, giving businesses a competitive edge in today's global manufacturing and services market. Effective and efficient information systems ensure informed decision making by the management of an enterprise, production of high-quality products on schedule, and delivery of satisfactory services to the customers. However, many existing information systems support only individual business units; they were developed and deployed using ad hoc rather than well-defined enterprise integration approaches, resulting in information silos that make data sharing and information integration difficult. Consequently, enterprises spend up to 35 to 40 percent of their information technology (IT) budgets annually on integrating these information silos. The vast technology landscape, numerous legacy applications, heterogeneous data sources, and changing business environments are also continuously adding complexities and challenges to enterprisewide integration projects. In general, the following issues are commonly and frequently confronted by the integration practitioners:

- **Complexity:** Corporate best practices capable of accommodating the needs of different cultures have been embodied in information systems through complex and dynamic business processes.
- **Diversity:** Operational and information needs have been diversified from department to department, facility to facility, and corporate to corporate.
- **Heterogeneity:** Information silos have been developed using different tools and methodologies, written in different programming languages, and run on different operating systems and communications networks.
- **Scalability:** An integrated system has to be scalable in terms of continuously delivering the expected information services when the system and supported business grow with time.
- **Agility:** An integrated system has to be flexible, responsive, and adaptable as market demands fluctuate and technologies advance.

This chapter discusses enterprise integration methods and corresponding enabling technologies to help overcome these challenges. First, data, object, and application levels of integration and supporting technologies are introduced. Next, workflow management–based and business process management–based integration computing paradigms are presented. Finally, service-oriented architecture and Web Services are discussed.

# ▶ Enterprise Integration Essentials

Practitioners have used a variety of techniques to integrate information silos in the past decades. In this section, three essential enterprise integration methods and corresponding technologies that have been widely applied to different integration projects are discussed. These include data-level integration, object-level integration, and application-level integration (Figure 8.1).

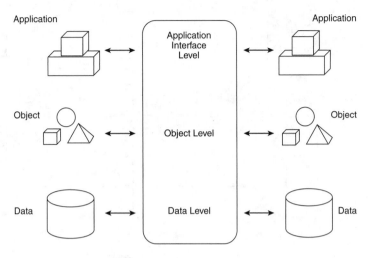

**Figure 8.1** Three common types of integration.

## Data-Level Integration

This type of integration aims at synchronizing data between different data sources among heterogeneous applications. The type of synchronized data can vary from a relatively small volume to a large-scale database. This type of integration can be further divided into two categories: common data transfer and database integration (Linthicum 2003).

Common data transfer typically involves information sharing among applications through text-based files. This approach is frequently applied to simple, short-term integration projects. Database integration attempts to interconnect databases, either by means of database-to-database integration or by constructing a federated database.

Database-to-database integration simply moves data between two or more databases using many of the database-oriented middleware. Database federating integrates multiple databases into a single, unified view by way of enabling a federated virtual database (Figure 8.2). Contrary to database-to-database integration that physically replicates or synchronizes data tables and elements, database federation constructs a single, virtual, and comprehensive view of all (potentially heterogeneous and geographically distributed) databases.

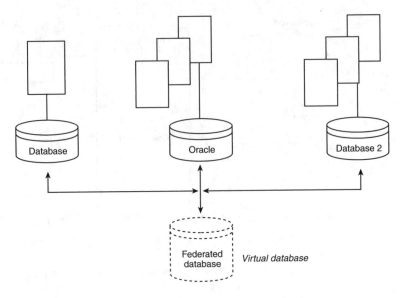

**Figure 8.2** Federated database integration.

## Object-Level Integration

Object-level integration focuses on synchronizing and sharing business rules and logics through direct interactions among objects within applications. This approach minimizes the impact on data sources because system integration occurs one level above the data sources. As a result, an enterprise can orchestrate business activities among applications, effectively synchronizing data across all applications. Object-level integration, however, is viable only when the integrated applications have privileges to access each other's business objects and implementation.

## Application-Level Integration

Application-level integration is also called application programming interface (API)–level integration and is used when applications have no access to the business objects and data sources of other applications. An application is packaged as a whole system, and instead of allowing users to have direct access to its internal algorithms and data, it provides a set of APIs to communicate with other applications. API-level integration has many advantages, such as preserving the application's data integrity, requiring no changes to the application itself during integration, and providing ease of use of new integration architecture and technologies.

# ▶ Enabling Technologies

This section discusses popular technologies that are widely used to achieve the kinds of integration discussed in the previous section.

## EDI (Electronic Data Interchange)

EDI (electronic data interchange) was originally developed in the mid-1970s and 1980s in order to reduce the procurement costs by minimizing delay and errors from suppliers. It has been in widespread use as a technique for conducting data-level integration between heterogeneous systems for both intra-enterprise and interenterprise applications. EDI is essentially a group of defined standard communication protocols for applications—for instance, ANSI X12 from the American National Standard Institute and EDIFACT (Electronic Data Interchange for Administration, Commerce, and Transport) from the United Nations (UN Economic Commission for Europe).

EDI messages contain distinct fields for each of the important pieces of information in a commercial transaction, such as transaction date, product purchased amount, and sender and recipient information (Laudon & Traver 2002). Since EDI was initially designed as a standard communication protocol for sharing business documents over a private communication network (Figure 8.3), it was typically customized for a specific industrial sector. As a result, an EDI used in one business domain will most likely not be able to communicate with one in a different business domain.

Recent advancements in telecommunication, networking, and computing technologies have made the Internet extremely popular. It has become an electronic means for conducting business, forcing integration practitioners to incorporate Internet technologies in EDI-based applications aimed at further improving their interoperability.

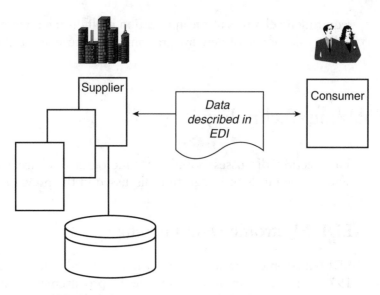

**Figure 8.3** EDI-based data-level integration.

## Data Warehouse

A data warehouse is an online analytical processing (OLAP) database that aggregates, in a single location, data on customers and business transactions from numerous online transaction processing (OLTP) databases for offline analysis aimed at improving business decision-making. Data warehousing focuses on the integration of information among databases for the purpose of providing consistent global data in an enterprise to enable business intelligence. Not only are the contents of databases extracted, transformed, cleansed, and aggregated, but also transactional log data are filtered and analyzed. The objective is to gather all data into one logical repository where it can be centrally and cost-effectively analyzed by managers without accessing the distributed enterprise's production systems and databases (Laudon & Traver 2002). Because this approach is mainly based on batch processing for aggregating data, it is not appropriate for real-time data synchronization among heterogeneous applications.

# XML

XML (Extensible Markup Language),[1] a language for describing structured documents and data, can be used for transmitting, validating, and interpreting data among applications. XML Schema Description Language (XSDL) is the language that enables one to define the structure of and the elements that make up a document or data. It is comparable to a database schema, which defines the column names and data types in database tables (Daconta et al. 2003). From an XML schema (or definition), multiple instance documents that conform to the schema can be created. DTDs (document type definitions) are a type of XML schema.

XML namespaces are a simple mechanism for creating globally unique names for the elements and attributes of the markup language used within an XML schema. This eliminates possible conflicts caused by using identical words to mean different things and therefore allows different markup languages to be mixed together without ambiguity. Unfortunately, at the moment, namespaces are not fully compatible with DTDs, but XSDL supports namespaces.

By agreeing on a standard XML schema or DTD, an organization can produce documents that can be transmitted, validated, and interpreted by any integrated application within heterogeneous environments. For business-to-customer (B2C) transactions, XML can be used on the client tier, transformed via XSLT[2] to any of the multiple presentation languages. It can also be used on the Web tier for integration.

Business-to-business (B2B) transactions have also been revolutionized through XML-based standards such as SOAP (Simple Object Access Protocol),[3] the purpose of which is to standardize the content structure of communication, and BizTalk[4] or ebXML,[5] which aim at standardizing the semantics of the content for particular business information exchange.

---

1. http://www.w3.org/XML
2. XSLT, Extensible Stylesheet Language Transformations, http://www.w3.org/TR/xslt
3. http://www.w3.org/TR/SOAP
4. http://BizTalk.org
5. http://www.ebxml.org/

SOAP provides a simple and lightweight mechanism for exchanging *structured* and *typed* information between peers in a decentralized, distributed environment using XML. It is discussed further in the section "Emerging Technologies for Business Processes Integration."

The goal of BizTalk.org is to provide an XML-based universal vocabulary to be used by businesses for describing all their processes for enterprise application integration and B2B document exchange.

ebXML is a standard set of specifications for collaborative B2B-based Web Services. The primary goal of ebXML is to facilitate a global electronic marketplace based on XML. It was pioneered by the United Nations Center for Trade Facilitation and Electronic Business (UN/CEFACT) and the Organization for Advancement of Structured Information Standards (OASIS) for the purpose of building an open framework in which business organizations can participate in a global electronic marketplace anytime, anywhere. ebXML includes

- ebXML Message Service (ebMS) specification for reliable messaging-based on SOAP
- ebXML Business Process Specification Schema (ebXML BPSS) to define business activities and describe relationships among partners in a collaboration
- ebXML Collaboration Protocol Profile and Agreement (ebXML CPP/A) to manage partner profile and agreements. This layer holds configuration information for partners' runtime systems and stores QOS (quality-of-service) information
- ebXML Registry/Repository to provide a powerful classification and storage mechanism for artifacts

There are several commercial products supporting numerous business vocabularies developed by RosettaNet,[6] OASIS,[7] and other organizations, which can serve as XML namespaces and be used with SOAP or ebXML.

---

6. http://www.rosettanet.org/

7. http://www.oasis-open.org/

# Component-Based Computing Technologies

An integrated application may comprise many different software components. These components may be written in various programming languages and deployed on different platforms on machines that are geographically distributed. Any framework for integrating such a suite of heterogeneous components must provide for:

- **Language Transparency:** Components must interoperate regardless of the programming language used for their implementation.
- **Platform Transparency:** Components must interoperate regardless of the operating system of the machines on which they are deployed.
- **Location Transparency:** Components must interoperate regardless of the location of the machines on which they are deployed.

The key is transparency; software engineers must be able develop and integrate these components with the same ease as they would if these components were written in the same language and deployed on a local machine running a single operating system. Many different models for integration have been proposed that achieve varying levels of transparency.

Sun Microsystems' Java Remote Method Invocation (RMI)[8] achieves platform and location transparency, but the components to be integrated must all be written in Java. Microsoft's Distributed Component Object Model (DCOM)[9] achieves language and location transparency, but the components to be integrated must all run on Microsoft's Windows operating system. Object Management Group's Common Object Request Broker Architecture (CORBA)[10] is the most general and provides language, platform, and location transparency. All of these frameworks insulate software engineers from the details of how components are located, how methods on remote components are invoked, and how the results of such method invocations are marshaled back to the initiator of the method invocation. This reduces the complexity of the application code that must be written.

---

8. http://java.sun.com

9. http://www.microsoft.com

10. http://www.omg.org

The primary drawback with RMI, DCOM, and CORBA is that RMI requests must go through the firewalls installed to secure an enterprise's computing infrastructure. Typically, these firewalls are configured to let through only those requests targeted for port 80, the port reserved for Web servers. Requests targeted for any other port are denied, and system administrators are reluctant to open ports other than 80 to outside traffic for security concerns. As a result, component integration technologies are moving toward a Web-centric model. Sun's J2EE and Microsoft's .NET platform now emphasize the use of Web Services as opposed to RMI and DCOM. Web Services are discussed in the section "Emerging Technologies for Business Processes Integration."

## Message-Oriented Middleware (MOM)

Message-oriented middleware, such as Sun's JMS (Java Message Service),[11] IBM MQSeries (now called WebSphere MQ),[12] and Microsoft's MSMQ (Microsoft Message Queuing),[13] is a queuing software that enables information exchange among information systems using a messaging protocol (Figure 8.4).

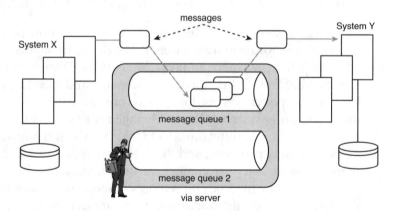

**Figure 8.4** System x and system y communicate through message queue 1, maintained by MQ server.

---

11. http://java.sun.com/products/jms/

12. http://www-306.ibm.com/software/integration/wmq/

13. http://www.microsoft.com/msmq/

The communication mechanism is point-to-point and asynchronous. Two applications are directly linked with the help of a simple pipe or communication line called a message queue. The asynchronous communication mechanism allows two applications to execute independently and communicate via message queues without any synchronization efforts. One of the many advantages of this communication model is that the middleware will not block the applications for its processing, and even if one of the applications on one machine is not available, the communicating application on another machine will continue to function and its message eventually will be delivered once the application it is communicating with becomes available.

Different MOM products offer general features, which are more or less equivalent. Some functions of Microsoft's MSMQ, for example, are

- **Guaranteed message delivery:** Messages can be stored on a disk-based queue and later forwarded in order to provide guaranteed delivery.
- **Message prioritization:** Message prioritization allows urgent or important messages to be sent before less important messages, so you can guarantee adequate response time for critical applications at the expense of less important applications.
- **Message backup and retrieve:** Message storage files, log files, transaction log files, and registry settings can be backed up and restored in case of computer failure.
- **Multiple distributions of messages:** Clients are able to send the same message to multiple recipient queues.

MOM is also very secure. The security feature in MSMQ, for instance, enables administrators to define privileges and access rights, such as who can send to a queue or receive from a queue, on a queue-by-queue and user-by-user basis. In some cases, it is possible to apply a type of encryption to messages for privacy, use digital signatures to verify message integrity, or digitally sign messages for nonrepudiation protection. There is little danger of messages being lost because of a routing process or system failure. These features often make MOM a quick solution to the integration of heterogeneous systems at the application level.

# Interface Processing and Java Connector Architecture

The approach to interface processing uses well-defined application interfaces in order to provide a unified interface of all internal application services. The objectives of interfacing can be unification of information, unification of services, or both (Linthicum 2003). Instead of conducting important modifications on source codes, an integration middleware based on interface processing provides a framework for linking heterogeneous applications.

As a kind of interface processing, Java Connector Architecture (JCA)[14] tries to solve the problem of heterogeneity between several types of enterprise information systems (EIS), including ERP systems, mainframe transaction processing, nonrelational database systems, and legacy applications not written in the Java programming language. Because JCA provides a standard interfacing architecture for heterogeneous applications, it is often compared to JDBC,[15] whose purpose is to give a unified interface of accessing to different types of relational databases.

If an application server vendor has extended its system to support the J2EE Connector architecture, it is assured of seamless connectivity to multiple EISs. Figure 8.5 illustrates the overall architecture of JCA with the serverside and clientside applications integration.

- **Resource Adapter:** A resource adapter is a type of software driver used by an application server or an application client to connect to an EIS.
- **System Contracts:** The role of system contracts is to keep all system-level mechanisms, such as transactions, security, and connection management, transparent from the application components. This allows application component providers to focus on the development of business logic without necessarily getting involved with the system-level details.
- **Common Client Interface (CCI):** CCI defines a standard client API for application components. It enables application components and enterprise application integration (EAI) frameworks to drive interactions across heterogeneous EISs using a common client API.

---

14. http://java.sun.com/j2ee/connector/

15. http://java.sun.com/products/JDBC/

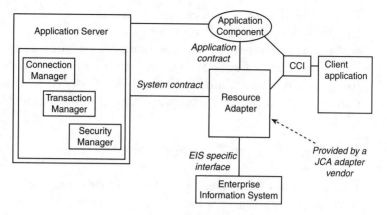

**Figure 8.5** JCA overview.

# ▶ Emerging Technologies for Business Processes Integration

Business process integration deals with building enterprisewide business processes incorporating existing applications into those processes. This approach is characterized by providing another layer of process management that resides on top of other applications. This layer supports the flow of information and control logic between existing processes that existing applications contain. Workflow management and business process management initiatives have been emerging as the two popular approaches, which are well technically supported by the service-oriented architecture technology.

## Workflow Management Systems

According to the Workflow Management Coalition (WFMC),[16] a workflow is "the automation of a business process, in whole or in part, during which documents, information, or tasks are passed from one participant to another for action, according to a set of procedural rules." The participants can be human, machines, or software systems. The automation of processes is achieved with the help of a software

---

16. http://www.wfmc.org

system called a *workflow engine*. A process controlled by a workflow engine is viewed as a collection of tasks executed by various resources within a value system comprising one or more integrating organization units. The reach of subprocesses within a workflow model can extend to interorganizational processes, and the model of workflow can contain not only automated processes but also human resources.

## Business Process Management Systems

Business process management (BPM)[17] emerges as a promising technology for integrating existing assets and future deployments through transforming the behavior of disparate and heterogeneous systems into standard and interoperable business process. BPM essentially provides a framework of applications to achieve effectively tracking and orchestrating business process through enterprise integration. Beyond the workflow concept, BPM not only allows automation of processes but also enables process self-management. Therefore, BPM systems position as the platform for the next generation of "process-aware" integrating applications, providing the agility needs for today's uncertain business environment.

## Service-Oriented Integration and Web Services

Technically, a common trend in the enterprise system evolution is the offering of collaborative services from an implementation perspective, using the Internet as the communication infrastructure and reusing existing applications. As mentioned in the introductory section of this chapter, companies are no longer satisfied with proprietary, static solutions to enterprise integration, which are a barrier against flexible or agile business in a rapidly changing business environment. By embracing open standards such as XML and Internet communication infrastructure, the enterprise integration horizon can be extended toward the organization of a virtual enterprise (Petri & Bussler 2003). Web Services exploit these open standards to achieve the desired service-oriented integration.

Service-oriented integration in general allows applications to share common business logic or methods. Not only is it important to share and

17. www.bpmi.org

stream information between applications, but service composition is also significant. The main purpose is therefore to give a unified service infrastructure, which is composed of several service applications (Figure 8.6). Users only see the composite form of a virtual service without dealing with the background details. By connecting to the composite service, a user can benefit from the various services offered by existing applications, which may offer the same services in a different context.

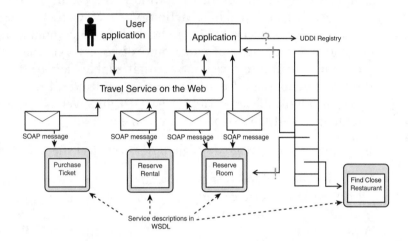

**Figure 8.6** Service-oriented integration.

Web Services are in fact software applications that can be discovered, described, and accessed via standard Web protocols based on XML over intranets, extranets, and the Internet. Web Services send data in XML format, and client applications can add style and formatting when they receive the data. The next section discusses the Web Services.

## What are Web Services?

W3C[18] defines a Web Service as "a software system identified by a URI, whose public interfaces and bindings are defined and described using XML. Its definition can be discovered by other software systems. These systems may then interact with the Web Services in a manner prescribed

---

18. http://www.w3.org/

by its definition, using XML-based messages conveyed by Internet protocols." The ultimate goal of such a service description is to make a program (software agent) capable of understanding the service characteristics and using the service (Petri & Bussler 2003).

The important components that enable Web Service technologies are SOAP, XML and XML namespaces, Web Service Description Language (WSDL), and Universal Description, Discovery and Integration (UDDI) (Zimmermann et al. 2003). Even though the use of SOAP and WSDL is not clearly mentioned in its definition by W3C, they are essential elements of Web Services. SOAP is the underlying communication protocol between requestor, provider, and discovery agencies. WSDL provides the formal interface contract that enables service discovery. The discovery agency level connection is a publish/find mechanism, used either at build time or at runtime; UDDI and Web Services Inspection Language (WSIL) are two of its implementations.

In the next section, we go through these essential elements of Web Services.

SOAP is the envelope syntax for sending and receiving XML messages with Web Services. According to W3C, it is "a lightweight protocol for exchange of information in a decentralized, distributed environment." A SOAP message in Web Services is composed of the following parts:

- SOAP envelope that wraps the message on the whole
- A description of how data is encoded
- A SOAP body that contains the application-specific message that the receiving application will understand

In order to know the application-specific details for talking to a Web Service, communication details are described with the help of WSDL,[19] which is an XML grammar. The W3C defines WSDL as "an XML format for describing network services as a set of endpoints operating on messages containing either document-oriented or procedure-oriented information." To know how to send messages to a particular Web Service, an application can look at the WSDL and dynamically construct SOAP messages. WSDL describes the operational information: where the service is located, what the service does, and how to invoke the service. Programmers and integrators do not have to understand WSDL

---

19. http://www.w3.org/TR/wsdl/

and SOAP to create Web Services. There are many toolkits provided with developing environments, such as J2EE and Microsoft .Net, which help create WSDL.

UDDI is the "yellow pages" for Web Services. Different business partners can register public information about their Web Services and types of services with UDDI, and applications can view information about these Web Services with UDDI. In general, UDDI provides the following information (Daconta et al. 2003):

- **Company Contact Information:** any kind of basic business contact information
- **Categorized Businesses by Standard Taxonomies:** the kind of information a service provides
- **Technical Information about Services that are Exposed:** business rules and instructions specifying how to invoke Web Services

ebXML, as discussed earlier, also provides a common way for businesses to quickly and dynamically perform business transactions based on common business practices. Businesses can do business transactions after they agree on trading arrangements. Contrary to UDDI, however, the ebXML registry contains domain-specific semantics for B2B.

## Web Services Architecture (WSA)

The purpose of the Web Services architecture is to organize software systems appearing in the Web Services definition. W3C defines two levels for the resulting architectures:[20]

- **Basic Architecture:** It defines the roles software systems can take in the WSA, the operations supported by them, and the related technology stacks.
- **Extended Architecture:** It adds extension points to the basic architecture through which various advanced requirements can be addressed.

The basic architecture is expected to support the following functions (Zimmerman et al. 2003):

---

20. http://www.w3.org/TR/ws-arch/

- Exchanging messages (Web Service invocations)
- Describing Web Services
- Publishing and discovering Web Services descriptions

The roles of each participant are as follows:

- *Service provider* publishes services to the discovery agency.
- *Service requestor* finds services in the discovery agency; this can happen at design time, which enables fixed binding, or at runtime, which guarantees dynamic binding.

The extended WSA includes advanced features such as additional message exchange partners, message attachments, reliable messages, message routing, asynchronous messaging, and request and response correlation (Zimmermann et al. 2003).

## Why Web Services for Enterprise Integration?

Web Services provide the following desirable features (Malks & Sum 2004):

- **Coarse Granularity:** Compared to object-based or component-based application integration, as in the case of DCOM or CORBA, the granularity of a Web Service is rather coarse, dealing with relatively high levels of abstraction.
- **Loose Coupling:** Service consumers and service providers know nothing about each other's underlying implementation. Web Services are platform and language independent.
- **Self-Describing:** Web Services provide standard descriptions of themselves. Those descriptions inform other systems of the details of the services, including ways to connect to them as well as their reliability characteristics and security parameters.

Furthermore, Web Services provide interoperability between heterogeneous businesses, guaranteeing low-cost and (relatively) fast integration for time-to-market products. The Web Services infrastructure is based on an open environment and dynamic integration of different applications. The Web Services standards are supported and implemented by many software providers providing off-the-shelf products that make it possible to leverage the work of existing applications and turn them into Web Services by using the standard Web Service protocols that everyone understands (Daconta et al. 2003).

# Summary

Businesses need timely dissemination of the right information to the right people to maintain a competitive edge in the global market economy. Efficient dissemination of information, however, requires that it be readily available. This is challenging because most systems within an enterprise are designed to support only individual business units, creating information silos. Integrating such systems to improve information availability gets even more difficult because these systems are inherently heterogeneous. Enterprise integration methods are designed to overcome some of these challenges. Traditionally, integration has been achieved at the data, object and application levels using technologies such as EDI, data warehouses, XML, SOAP, BizTalk, ebXML, Java RMI, DCOM, CORBA, MOM, and JCA. More recently, however, efforts have focused on coarser grained integration. Business process integration deals with defining enterprisewide business processes via composition of processes within existing applications using workflow management and business process management systems. Service-oriented integration allows exposing and sharing of business logic across applications through the use of Web Services technology.

# References

Daconta, M. C., L. J. Obrst, and K. T. Smith, 2003. *The Semantic Web: A Guide to the Future of XML, Web Services, and Knowledge Management*, Wiley.

Laudon, K. C., and C. G. Traver, 2002. *E-Commerce: Business Technology Society*, Addison-Wesley.

Linthicum, D. S., 2003. *Next Generation Application Integration: From simple information to Web Services*, Addison-Wesley Information Technology Series.

Malks, D., and M. Sum, 2004. Developing Web Services with ebXML and SOAP: An Overview, Technical paper for Webservice.org. Available: http://www.mywebservices.org/index.php/article/articleview/1015/1/24.

Petrie, C., and C. Bussler, 2003. "Service Agents and Virtual Enterprises: A Survey," *IEEE Internet Computing*, July/August 2003.

Zimmermann,O., M. Tomlinson, and S. Peuser, 2003. *Perspectives on Web Services: Adding SOAP, WSDL and IDDO to Real-World Projects*, Springer.

# Toward Collaborative Supply Chains Using RFID

*Robin G. Qiu and Raghvinder S. Sangwan*

Supply chain management (SCM) aims to enhance the whole value chain by orchestrating product engineering and management processes from suppliers to customers so that promised orders and services can be promptly and satisfactorily delivered. An SCM system essentially manages products along with their data and information when the products are physically delivered from one location to another on the supply chain. This chapter discusses how the emerging radio frequency identification (RFID) technology can actively participate in enabling collaborative supply chains for a competitive advantage. The main discussion in this chapter is the design and development of a product-tracking and information-retrieval system to enable the real-time visibility of products on the supply chain in support of effective collaborations among the participating enterprises.

# ▶ Introduction

In today's stringently competitive business market, enterprises rely on product performance, quality, and competitive price to fulfill customer orders, and they count on shorter lead times, satisfactory service, and better responsiveness to provide customers with high satisfaction. An SCM system plays a critical role in these business operations in an enterprise, which makes the enterprise capable of accommodating business fluctuations, enabling faster intra- and interenterprise information flow, and accordingly providing employees the precise and just-in-time information and assistance about jobs on hand.

The supply chain for an enterprise is a very complicated network, which typically includes multiple suppliers, facilities, warehouses, distributors, retailers, and many customers. A schematic view of a supply chain is illustrated in Figure 9.1. It essentially provides a means for rapid purchase and responsive order fulfillment. Pertinent information on product movement should be accurately delivered to proper users in a timely manner as the product moves from one location to another. Prudent use of data and information on the supply chain not only can improve productivity but also can reduce operational uncertainties (Muckstadt et al. 2001).

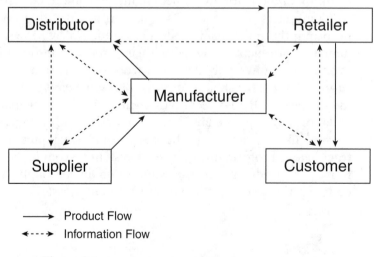

Figure 9.1 A schematic view of a supply chain.

The world is accelerating the process in digitalizing all the possible physical objects by taking advantage of advanced computing technologies so the conduct of businesses can be performed more cost effectively (ADIC 2003). In SCM, "some suppliers are pioneering efforts to develop new vendor management processes and systems that extend all the way to the retailer's shelf rather than to the distribution center" (Byrnes 2003). No matter what kind of SCM an enterprise has deployed, it is a trend for enterprises to evolve their SCM systems into fully collaborative systems in order to stay in competition. In a fully collaborative SCM system, the accurate and timely visibility of product movement, alert on a timely business operation, and instant and precise information on a business activity should be provided for all the privileged users on the whole supply chain from supplier's supplier to customer's customer (Ye & Qiu 2003).

However, participating enterprises on a supply chain usually execute different business practices and employ heterogeneous information systems, which usually complicate SCM integration and degrade SCM system performances as a whole. Nevertheless, integrations among the involved applications are mainly done using traditional point-to-point integration approaches. Since heterogeneous information silos are hardly integrated, the desirable visibility of product movement and precise information on business operations simply cannot be provided in a timely fashion when point-to-point integration approaches are applied (Alexander et al. 2002a, 2002b; Qiu 2002).

Recently, there is a renewed interest in using RFID technology for supply chain management. RFID purports an efficient inventory-tracking and warehouse management solution providing improved visibility of products in the supply chain at a low operational cost when compared to the prior solutions (Sarma 2004). More specifically, when the locality information of an individual product is embedded in its identity tag, the precise and pertinent information of the product can be instantly delivered to its user whenever needed (Qiu & Ye 2003). To ensure the expected real-time tracking and information services available on a collaborative supply chain, an effective product identification and tracking scheme is necessary, along with a context-aware, integration-ready, and responsive information-retrieval method (Qiu 2002; Qiu & Zhang 2003).

# ▶ What Is a Collaborative Supply Chain?

An effective SCM system should coordinate all the business activities among partners in a timely manner. However, the complexity and uncertainty of business operations and the cost of a sophisticated system with its supportive technologies make it difficult for an enterprise to deploy a fully collaborative SCM system at the early onset. Most enterprises usually take an evolutionary approach to structure relationships with customers and suppliers; they accordingly take the same path to deploy SCM systems. Byrnes (2003) articulates a view of a typical enterprise's evolving role in a supply chain: "The company starts as stable supplier, evolves into a reactive supplier, then an efficient reactive supplier, then an efficient proactive supplier, and finally becomes a 'revenue and margin driver.'"

By analyzing the degree of integrations on information, business practices, and corporate strategies, Muckstadt and colleagues (2001) summarize four types of SCM adopted or to be adopted in enterprises (Figure 9.2).

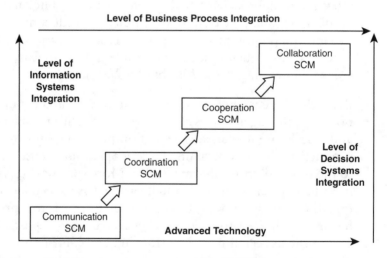

**Figure 9.2** The supply chain management evolution chart.
*Source:* (Adapted from Muckstadt, J., D. Murray, J. Rappold, and D. Collins, 2001, "Guidelines for Collaborative Supply Chain System Design and Operation." *Information Systems Frontiers*, 3(4), 427–453.)

- The communication type is built based on the most basic relationship model in a supply chain. Only the most critical operations and activities are informed of relevant partners on the supply chain. It requires the least integration of information, decision-making, and business process among all the participants on the supply chain.
- The coordination type allows certain information sharing on each other's operational data, such as inventory levels, production/service capacity, logistics policies, and customer demand. The increased visibility enables better forecasting for the conduct of businesses throughout the supply chain.
- The cooperation type further integrates all the partners' information systems, decision-making systems, and business processes with a potential of forming tactical partnerships. Participating partners aim at improving the business forecasting accuracy and mitigating the customer demand fluctuation and uncertainty.
- The collaboration type entails the best visibility of cross-enterprise business operations. It requires full integration of information systems, decision-making systems, and business processes across all the partners. A variety of strategic and tactical business plans must be formed and executed collaboratively by all the participants (Figure 9.3).

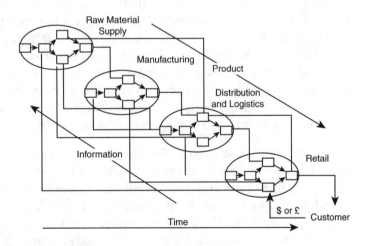

**Figure 9.3** System view of a collaborative supply chain.
*Source:* (Adapted from Muckstadt, J., D. Murray, J. Rappold, and D. Collins, 2001, "Guidelines for Collaborative Supply Chain System Design and Operation." *Information Systems Frontiers*, 3(4), 427–453.)

SCM systems essentially aim at improving product engineering and management processes throughout all the participating enterprises so that promises can be delivered in a timely fashion and customers' requests met satisfactorily. Entities that are engineered and managed can be either physical (e.g., home electronic appliances) or logical (e.g., software, online service, electronic payment). The physical entities, either individual or assembled, along with their information, have to travel concurrently throughout the supply chain. When entities travel from one enterprise to another, they can be packed in quantities. In this chapter, the term *product* is used to generally refer to a managed physical entity. Since product movement can be mathematically defined as tracings in graph theory, where nodes are locations and transitions are journey paths (Qiu & Joshi 1999), the effectiveness of an SCM system then becomes that there exist optimal and satisfactory traces on the supply chain when involved partners collaboratively execute businesses as desired.

## ▶ State-of-the-Art Product-Tracking Technologies

To have individual products identifiable, an identity is needed for each product. In practice, as an individual product is labeled by an identification code, it can be identified and tracked by a computer application or sometimes by a human being through some paperwork. The identification code usually is assigned using a proprietary identification scheme; as a result, the code is a proprietary number. The number is therefore of no meaning if not properly transformed in a different information system, such as an integrated and heterogeneous SCM system.

There are various standard identification schemes for types of products, such as the Universal Product Code (UPC) or so-called bar code, vehicle identification number (VIN), and International Standard Book Number (ISBN). One of the most successful identification schemes during the last two decades is the bar code. A bar code is created using a 12-digit numeric sequence scheme. Bar codes require "line-of-sight": they can be scanned only when a scanner can "see" them. When groceries are checked out, for example, a cashier has to scan the groceries one by one. If the bar code is ripped or soiled, or if it falls off, the bar code cannot be scanned (AIDC 2003). Apparently, tracking and identification systems based on bar codes technologies are not fully automatic; consequently, intensive and expensive labors become necessary. Nevertheless, a bar code tells only the manufacturer and product model, not the unique product item, which provides manufacturers with ambiguous visibility unless there is a proprietary identification scheme used to track individual items.

With the advances of semiconductor technologies, RFID has recently advanced substantially as a promising tagging technology (Bonsor 2003). An RFID transponder or tag (also called a smart label) can hold much richer information than can a bar code. More importantly, an RFID tag can be read-only or read-write. The data capacity of an RFID tag continues to increase, while the cost is dropping (Kambil & Brooks 2002; AIDC 2003). It is this data capacity that creates an opportunity of labeling any single item in the physical world, making it possible for a tagged product to be uniquely identifiable and trackable throughout the whole world. However, all currently existing RFID-based systems are proprietary (AIDC 2003). The MIT Auto-ID Center has been focusing on the standardization of the RFID technology. For instance, Electronic Product Code (EPC) is designed and developed for uniquely tagging an individual product, aiming at promoting the efficiency and effectiveness of identification and tracking systems (Brock 2001; Kambil & Brooks 2002; AIDC 2003).

Taking into consideration the ubiquitous application of bar codes, MIT Auto-ID Center works very closely with the Uniform Code Council and EAN International, the two core agencies that oversee international bar code standards (Brock 2001). Rather than replacing the existing bar codes, EPC is aimed at extending the capability of UPC and accordingly realizing better visibility of objects on the supply chain. The Auto-ID technology focuses mainly on the synergy of EPC and RFID technology for the future industry that could substantially transform industry value chains by providing manufacturers, retailers, and logistic providers with numerous benefits, such as "more responsive supply chain; increased revenue through fewer out-of-stock situations; lower inventory carrying and management costs; improved asset utilization" (Kambil & Brooks, 2002). More specifically, the Auto-ID technology will enhance the distribution operations and maximize the product availability for retailers (Alexander et al., 2002a, 2002b).

Typically, product information and relevant services nowadays can be accessed through an intranet- or Internet-based distributed software application (Figure 9.4). For example, when a UPC code is used for the identification of a product, a barcode scanner attached to a client computer scans the code. If a user needs to access the relevant information from a remote service provider, the application client has to get the IP address of the application server by looking up a database based on the read UPC code and searching a public directory service, or through a hard-coded direct mapping. If an EPC code is used for the identification of an individual product, a request to an object naming service (ONS) can be initiated to retrieve the corresponding server's IP address (Kambil & Brooks 2002). In general, the current approach requires a lookup of the servers' IP addresses using a server reference module; the lookup is typically solution-specific or proprietary (Qiu 2002).

The MIT Auto-ID Center claims, "By creating an open global network that can identify anything, anywhere, automatically, it [the center] seeks to give companies something that, until now, they have only dreamed of: near-perfect supply chain visibility" (AIDC 2003). However, few articles have systematically addressed the real-time visibility issues on supply chains.

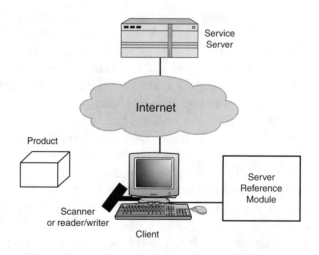

**Figure 9.4** A generic tracking system model.

# An Approach to the Real-Time Visibility of Product Movement on Supply Chains

Products, either individual or assembled along with their appropriate information, travel through a supply chain. An SCM system is mainly an application managing and controlling the movement aimed at maximizing the profits and satisfaction for all the participants throughout the chain. A mechanism to locate the moving products and have their proper information updated promptly is fundamental to enable the real-time visibility of product movement on a supply chain.

Context-aware information retrieval is receiving a lot of attention in the wearable computing community, where the content delivery requires high relevance and perception. As a user moves, his or her context is dynamically changing; it is extremely challenging to form an effective cognitive process, enable quick information filtering, and conduct fast context matching and reasoning such that prompt information retrievals can be meaningfully executed (Brown & Jones 2001; Harter et al. 2002; Lehikoinen & Suomela 2002; Marmasse & Schmandt 2002). In a product identification and tracking system, on the contrary, individual products, rather than users, move. As an individual product travels across the supply chain, different users might need different information to process different business operations. Apparently, the information retrieving on a supply chain confronts the same challenges as those in wearable computing. While complex context-trace technology using artificial sensors and contextual displays has been proposed for reasoning personal traces in a wearable computer (Rahlff et al. 2001), an RFID-based solution to product identification can be enabled, avoiding complicated reasoning processes (Brown & Jones 2001; Marmasse & Schmandt 2002; Rahlff et al. 2001).

If a product arrives at a new location, the product state can be classified. In other words, the product life cycle can be defined using multiple states. Therefore, for the simplified supply chain (Figure 9.1), for instance, states such as "supplier" (C1), "manufacturer" (C2), "distributor" (C3), "retailer" (C4), and "customer" (C5) can be defined. For a real application, each state could be continuously refined on the basis of defined workflow processes. A conceptual product context space is illustrated in Figure 9.5, where states can be defined on the basis of a

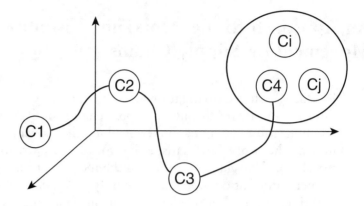

**Figure 9.5** Context trace in a geographic context space.

combination of a variety of classifications, such as workflow processes, user roles, and geographic locations (Qiu 2002). Note that traces can be redefined manually or through self-learning if the processes, locations, customers, or suppliers on the supply chain are changed.

By taking advantage of RFID technology, each product can be labeled by embedding an RFID tag in the product. The stored data in a tag can include the tagged product identity and trace information. The data can be overwritten as the item travels across the supply chain. For instance, the tag's content gets revised as products arrive at the gate of a facility; the status and location of in-transit products are monitored or updated if necessary (Figure 9.6). By taking advantage of the well-established

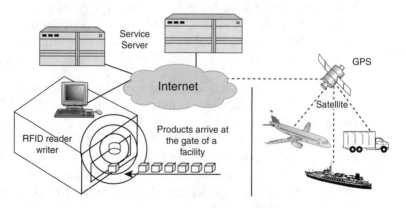

**Figure 9.6** Product tags are updated with new states.

Chapter **9** I Toward Collaborative Supply Chains Using RFID worldwide communication infrastructure, the updating process can be either automatically performed without any human intervention or initiated on demand with human intervention. A simplified protocol to update product states is shown in Figure 9.7.

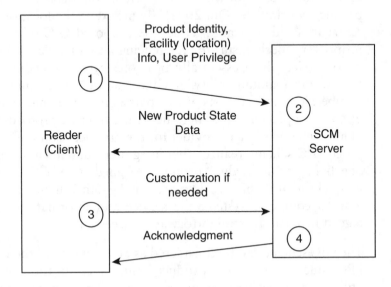

**Figure 9.7** Protocol for activating a new product state.

In addition, the world is building more integrated and dependent relationships between human beings and their living and working environments; it becomes natural that daily life counts on more reliable and least-effort digital information systems (Rhodes 2000). On one hand, an end user wants to use common computing devices, such as a desktop, personal digital assistance (PDA), or cellular phone, to promptly access the needed service; on the other hand, to minimize the cost of ownership, companies prefer information service systems that can utilize commonly deployed rather than solution-specific, industry-dependent, or proprietary infrastructures (Qiu 2002).

To have the proposed approach successfully implemented, a well-defined framework should be architected and supporting technologies investigated, identified, and created. A well-defined solution model should include at least the following: (1) a well-defined identification scheme, (2) a least-effort client solution, and (3) a systematic and responsive content delivery scheme and corresponding server application.

# Global Identification Code Scheme

By taking advantage of the well-deployed and widely adopted Internet, GL AgilityTech, Inc., has proposed an innovative identification scheme called global identification codes (GIC) for identifying and tracking products worldwide (Qiu 2002). By including the location of a service server in an identification code, the proposed GIC scheme eliminates proprietary mechanisms for referencing an individual product identification code, which essentially promotes system scalability, interoperability, and maintainability. A GIC is a code of a finite hexadecimal number; it mainly consists of two parts: one is the unique identification of a tagged product, and the other is the Internet protocol (IP) address of a designated service provider for the product. Consequently, the proposed GIC scheme realizes two integrated fundamental functions. On one hand, an individual product assigned with a GIC code can be uniquely identifiable worldwide; on the other hand, through a networked computer system, the service and information for the GIC-tagged item can be straightforwardly accessed.

The GIC scheme can be considered as an extension of the EPC when an EPC code is used as the product unique identification. An EPC code utilizes three separate numbers, one for a manufacturer identifier, another a product model number of the manufacturer, and the other the object serial number of the given product model made by the manufacturer. EPC makes possible the unique identification of any single object in the world (AIDC 2003).

For example, when an EPC is used as the object identifier, a GIC code can be defined as

```
02. 1206A66. 5D6710. 1A22476FC.IP. xxxxxx
8 bits.28 bits.24 bits.36 bits.IP.finite bits
Header.Enterprise.Product.Serial Number.IP Address.Other Parameters
```

in which the actual allocation of bits and the length of each part may be determined by the header information and can vary with applications (e.g., present and future standards) (Qiu 2002).

A generic implementation of the GIC scheme is illustrated through a service model shown in Figure 9.8 (Qiu 2002). An individual product is tagged with a GIC-based RFID tag. An RFID reader is mounted as a

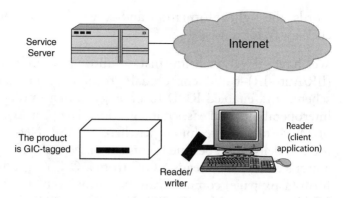

**Figure 9.8** A GIC-based tracking system model.

plug-and-play device in a computer system. An application (e.g., Internet browser) with a GIC software module parses the read data from the tag and directly requests the needed service or information from a given service provider based on the embedded IP. Apparently, no burdens are added on the user side; that is, no proprietary mechanism or application (e.g., hard-coded mapping, database search, directory service lookup, or ONS referencing) as discussed earlier is required.

## Design for a User Least-Effort System

A user could abstain from frequently using an information service system if it provides imprecise and overwhelming information (e.g., results from the Internet search), requires too much learning, and is not friendly to use. Undoubtedly, the provided service will not be satisfactory, resulting in, most likely, a negative impact on product sales.

Rhodes (2000) proposes an agent method of realizing just-in-time information retrieval (JITIR) in general software applications. He indicates three necessary features for JITIR—that it be proactive, nonintrusive yet accessible, and provide local context—that should be enabled in providing information retrieval services. From a user's perspective, when a product is labeled with an RFID tag containing a GIC code, the best practice will be to use a click of computer mouse to read the RFID tag, and the precise and pertinent information (not thousands of related links) will appear on the computer screen right away. In other words, the right information and service on a product is simply one click away for a user.

We have developed an instant/automatic information retrievals (IIR/Auto-IR)–based conceptual prototype using the proposed GIC scheme and enabled RFID technology taking into account the system interoperability and ease of integration. The prototype takes advantage of Microsoft .Net technology, where an ASP .Net–based Web form is used to deliver the pertinent content based on the request triggered by a user's click, which reads a GIC from a GIC-tagged product. The Web form (aspx page) communicates with the Web Services server through SOAP messages (Manes 2002; Ye & Qiu 2003). Figure 9.9 shows the IIR/Auto-IR service model of the proof-of-concept prototype. A customized button is inserted into a standard Internet Explorer (IE) browser. By doing so, the IE browser is enhanced with the RFID capability when an RFID reader is attached with the computer. As a result, when a user clicks the button, the enhanced IE reads a GIC code from a product item, sends a request automatically to the GIC-specified server, and displays the pertinent information as soon as the information arrives from the server.

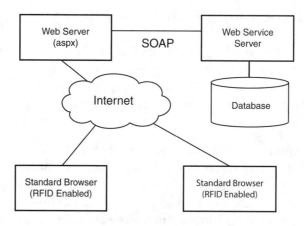

**Figure 9.9** The IIR system model using .Net.

## Design of a Responsive Information Server

To enable tracking the state of millions of individual products, the design and development of its Web server can be extremely difficult given the requirements of performance and high availability on a supply chain (Ye & Qiu 2003). Qiu and Zhang (2003) propose the following approach:

- Think of each product as being in one of a limited number of states.
- Construct a graph to represent all the states and transitions among the states. Call this a product context graph (i.e., defined context traces in a given context space).
- Based on which state the current product is in, decide what kind of information or service should be delivered to the user.
- Since the state graph may change over time, retire an old state only when no products are currently in that state.

Therefore, the key for designing a responsive Web server is to have an efficient mechanism for discovering state of the product based on the information in the HTTP request. When the state information of a product is piggybacked with its identification code in the RFID tag, the precise and pertinent service can be delivered in a very responsive manner due to avoiding complex server product searching, context reasoning and mapping, and information filtering. The piggyback approach, however, is not applicable for products that use read-only tags. Qiu and Zhang (2003) propose a binary search tree for reasoning and mapping product states when read-only tags are used.

# ▶ Conclusions

Today's market needs are highlighted by a greater variety of products that have to be delivered at low cost and high quality in order to be competitive. In the meantime, product life cycles are shortening, the time-to-market for new products is decreasing, and customers demand shorter lead times (the time between placement and delivery of an order), which require a better enterprise information system, such as

SCM (Muckstadt et al. 2001). Well-informed operational, tactical, and strategic decisions can only be made when perfect visibility of products can be provided in the future e-business environment. Using the proposed GIC scheme for product identification and information retrieval makes it possible for precise information or services on a GIC-tagged product to be instantly/automatically accessible, visible, and modifiable worldwide. The proposed approach uses commonly deployed rather than solution-specific, industry-dependent, or proprietary computer hardware and software for the majority of users on a supply chain. More investigations are needed in modeling the interactions among partners because the proposed GIC scheme is used to real-time identify and track individual products so all the business activities on the supply chain can be more effectively and efficiently synchronized in the real world (Pham et al. 2003).

In addition, as the prices of RFID tags and readers continue to drop, RFID devices will pervade in people's daily lives, warranting prevention of abuse of RFID-based systems (Stanford 2003). Security and privacy concerns, therefore, will become important research issues on a supply chain and will need further investigation if this emerging RFID technology is applied.

# ▶ References

Alexander, K., T. Gilliam, K. Gramling, M. Kindy, D. Moogimane, M. Schultz, and M. Woods, 2002a. Focus on the supply chain: Applying Auto-ID within the distribution center. *White Paper of MIT Auto-ID Center.*

Alexander, K., G. Birkhofer, K. Gramling, H. Kleinberger, S. Leng, D. Moogimane, and M. Woods, 2002b. Focus on retail: Applying Auto-ID to improve product availability at the retail shelf. *White Paper of MIT Auto-ID Center.*

Auto-ID Center (AIDC), 2003. Auto-ID center technology guide, http://www.autoidcenter.org.

Bonsor, K., 2003. How smart labels will work. http://www.howstuff-works.com/smart-label.htm, February.

Brock, A., 2001. The electronic product code (EPC): A naming scheme for physical objects. *White Paper of MIT Auto-ID Center.*

Brown, P., and G. Jones, 2001. "Context-Aware Retrieval: Exploring a New Environment for Information Retrieval and Information Filtering." *Personal and Ubiquitous Computing*, 5, 253–263.

Byrnes, J., 2003. "Supply Chain Management in a Wal-Mart World." *Harvard Business School*, August 4.

Iyengar, A., J. Challenger, D. Dais, and P. Dantzig, 2000. "High-performance Web Site Design Techniques." *IEEE Internet Computing*, 17–26, Mar./Apr.

Harter, A., A. Hopper, P. Steggles, A. Ward, and P. Webster, 2002. "The Anatomy of a Context-Aware Application." *Wireless Networks*, 8, 187–197.

Kambil, A., and J. Brooks, 2002. Auto-ID across the value chain: From dramatic potential to greater efficiency & profit. *White Paper of MIT Auto-ID Center.*

Lehikoinen, J., and R. Suomela, 2002. "Accessing Context in Wearable Computers." *Personal and Ubiquitous Computing*, 6, 64–74.

Manes, A., 2002. Introduction to Web Services. *White Paper of Systinet, Inc.*

Marmasse, N., and C. Schmandt, 2002. "A User-Centered Location Model." *Personal and Ubiquitous Computing*, 6, 318–321.

Mohapatra, P., and H. Chen, 2002. "WebGraph: A Framework for Managing and Improving Performance of Dynamic Web Content." *IEEE Journal on Selected Areas in Communications*, 20(7), 1414–1425.

Muckstadt, J., D. Murray, J. Rappold, and D. Collins, 2001. "Guidelines for Collaborative Supply Chain System Design and Operation." *Information Systems Frontiers*, 3(4), 427–453.

Nissen, M., 2001. "Agent-Based Supply Chain Integration." *Information Technology and Management*, 2, 289–312.

Pham, H., Y. Ye, and V. Nguyen, 2003. "Autonomous Mapping of e-Business Demands and Supplies via Invisible Internet Agents." *Electronic Commerce Research*, 3, 365–395.

Qiu, R., and S. Joshi, 1999. "A Structured Adaptive Supervisory Control Methodology for Modeling the Control of a Discrete Event Manufacturing System." *IEEE Transactions on Systems, Man, and Cybernetics, Part A: Systems and Humans*, 29(6), 573–586.

Qiu, R. 2002, Global identification code schema: an approach to instant/automatic information retrievals. *White Paper of GL AgilityTech, Inc.*, December.

Qiu, R., and Z. Zhang, 2003. Design of Enterprise Web Servers in Support of Instant Information Retrievals, *Proceedings of 2003 IEEE International Conference on Systems, Man and Cybernetics*, 2661–2666.

Qiu, R., and S. Ye, 2003. Design and Development of Instant/Automatic Information Retrieval Systems, *Proceedings of 2003 IEEE International Conference on Systems, Man and Cybernetics*, 2639–2644.

Rahlff, O., R. Rolfsen, and J. Herstad, 2001. "Using Personal Traces in Context Space: Towards Context Trace Technology." *Personal and Ubiquitous Computing*, 5, 50–53.

Rhodes, B., 2000. *Just-In-Time Information Retrieval*. Ph.D. Thesis, MIT, Cambridge, MA.

Sarma, S., (2004). "Integrating RFID." *ACM Queue*, 2(7), 50–57, October.

Stanford, V., 2003. "Pervasive Computing Goes the Last Hundred Feet with RFID Systems." *Pervasive Computing*, 9–14, April–June.

Ye, S., and R. Qiu, 2003. "Web Services Oriented Approach to High Availability of Product Information." *2003 International Conference of Industrial Engineering & Engineering Management*, Dec. 6–8, Shanghai, China.

# 10

# Real-Time, Mission-Critical Business Intelligence: Lessons from the Military and Intelligence Community

*Alan R. Simon*

## ▶ Introduction

For most organizations, the quest for *business intelligence* (BI) has been closely tied with early 1990s-style *data warehousing*: batch-oriented data flows from source systems into a single data warehouse from which individuals run reports and analyses of interest to their respective job functions.

Since the late 1990s, some "early adopter" organizations have dabbled in real-time business intelligence for parts of their respective enterprises, but the results have been decidedly mixed. On the one hand, end users now have access to critical pieces of data much more rapidly than before as a result of the real-time data flows, and—in theory at least—are now in a much better position to make critical business decisions in a more timely manner.

The reality, however, is that many of these real-time business intelligence environments do little else other than speed up the flow of data from the point of entry into the enterprise until available for reports and analysis—but with little or no actual benefit to decision making, business process monitoring and management, organizational productivity, and all the other laudable goals that drove their business intelligence initiatives in the first place.

Real-time, mission-critical business intelligence requires much more than simply real-time–enabling data flows between source systems and the target data warehouses and analytical environments. Indeed, an entirely new way of thinking about what an enterprise wants to achieve is required to help avoid the missteps and disappointments that so many others have encountered in their real-time business intelligence initiatives.

As it turns out, one needs only look toward the military and intelligence communities and the ways in which their command, control, communications, and intelligence ($C^3I$) or command, control, communications, computers, and intelligence ($C^4I$) systems are constructed. This chapter looks at best practices in creating a hybrid architecture in which the advantages of "classical" business intelligence environments are blended with those of $C^3I$ and $C^4I$ systems to provide a solid foundation for mission-critical business intelligence. It also looks beyond technology and architecture fusion at some key operations principles from military and intelligence systems that have rarely been part of commercial or civilian government business intelligence environments but, upon closer examination, should be key objectives of any mission-critical business intelligence initiative.

# ▶ Definitions

No doubt you have come across numerous definitions for the term *business intelligence*. The business intelligence definition I have always preferred and used goes as follows:

The pursuit of timely, actionable, high-value insight.

Each of three descriptors in the above phrase—timely, actionable, and high-value—is equally important regardless of what our specific objectives might be. If the sought-after insight isn't timely, it is of marginal use at best, perhaps even useless. Similarly, very timely *low-value* insight isn't likely to be of much use nor worth the cost of building a complex system, either.

Then we have the word in the middle—actionable—that provides a nice segue into the body of the material in this chapter. Anyone who has watched cable or network news in the past few years and followed the search for and capture of a particular deposed Iraqi dictator or the search for high-profile terrorists, or most anything else dealing with military matters and combat operations, has heard the phrase *actionable intelligence* used. The premise of actionable intelligence is exactly as the words themselves read: gathering intelligence not for the sake of the intelligence information itself but specifically to be able to take precise action based on that information and insight.

Therefore, as we proceed with looking at how to apply principles from the $C^3I$ and $C^4I$ realms to mission-critical business intelligence, it's important to keep the three phrases in my preferred definition in mind and, in particular, to remember that unless we plan to actually do something with the insight gained—that is, take action—and architect the environment to achieve and enable that goal, the result will likely be just one more exercise in futility.

## ▶ A Tale of Two Architectures

Figure 10.1 shows a high-level conceptual architecture diagram of the type you have most likely seen dozens, perhaps even hundreds, of times: a "classical" data warehousing/business intelligence environment built on a foundation of batch-based integration of information from multiple sources, with subsequent spin-off of portions of the newly consolidated and integrated data into more tightly focused *data marts*—geographically based in this particular example.

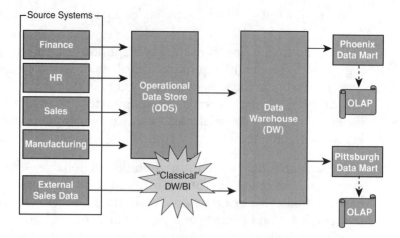

**Figure 10.1** "Classical" data warehousing and business intelligence high-level architecture.

Even though you might draw the conclusion from my dismissive remarks at the outset of this chapter that I see little or no value in business intelligence when implemented as shown in Figure 10.1, that conclusion would be an overstatement. In fact, this early 1990s approach to business intelligence does have its merits:

- The ability to integrate, consolidate, and organize very large volumes of data and to make that data readily available to a large number of users for analysis.
- The ability to summarize the data at multiple levels and for users, during their analysis, to drill down and drill up as desired to various levels of granularity as dictated by the needs of the moment.
- Equipping users with graphically oriented tools that are relatively easy to use—once users have been properly trained, of course.

At the same time, a look inside the classical approach to business intelligence shows some glaring weaknesses that have tripped up almost every business intelligence practitioner at one time or another:

- A lack of confidence in the results received from a particular report or analytical function: "Can I base a critical, bet-my-job decision on the answer the system is giving me?"

- A reliance on structured data—numbers, dates, and character strings—with inadequate linkage (or, more commonly, no linkage at all) to unstructured information found in compound documents and multimedia.

- A dominance of individual analysis with little or no collaborative—and when collaborative work processes do exist, they are almost always "kludged" together in a highly manual manner rather than on any kind of workflow or collaborative computing infrastructure.

- An operating model that essentially leaves users to their own devices and assumptions for linking the results of reports and analyses with their job functions rather than actively guiding their usage of the environment.

The approach many architects and planners have taken to date in the pursuit of real-time, mission-critical business intelligence has been to simply transition most or all of the batch data feeds to real-time replacements. But regardless of the specific technology used for the real-time data flows—message queuing; an enterprise application integration (EAI) tool; the real-time capabilities of a data warehousing extraction, transformation, and loading (ETL) tool; or even "brute force" database-stored procedures and triggers for database-to-database transfers—what most of those architects and planners wind up with is faster transfer and loading of data to the target database, but little or no help with the critical shortcomings listed previously.

To address these procedural and operating model shortcomings, we must look at the way the military and intelligence communities address their own mission-critical needs of air defense, missile attack warning, space defense, and intelligence-based combat operations. Figure 10.2 illustrates the high-level conceptual architecture common to many military and intelligence systems that are charged with a mission of warning and defense.

The architecture illustrated in Figure 10.2 is based not only on a foundation of "ultra-real-time" data transmission from sensors (e.g., satellites, radars, etc.) and similar sources into "the environment" but also on

- Determining if the just-received information denotes a threat or possible threat that must immediately be addressed.

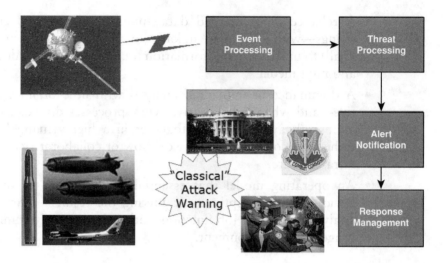

**Figure 10.2** C³I/C⁴I conceptual architecture for military warning and defense missions.

- Putting certain high-ranking authorities "on notice" that a threat determination is forthcoming and their response may or may not be required, depending on the outcome of that threat determination.

- "Forcing" all those involved in either monitoring automated functions or interjecting human decision making into the situation to follow their work processes to a conclusive determination and, if applicable, decisive action.

Still, many C³I and C⁴I systems have some shortcomings compared with the traditional business intelligence environments we looked at earlier:

- Data volumes tend to be "modest" rather than the multiterabytes of information increasingly found in data warehouses that support business intelligence functionality.

- Many C³I and C⁴I systems are built around "fixed-screen" user interfaces with little or no variability dynamically adjustable by users to specific needs of the moment.

- Data tends to be "flat" rather than dimensionally structured along multiple hierarchies with various levels of summarization, as would be found in the typical data warehouse.

- $C^3I$ and $C^4I$ environments that aren't hindered by the preceding shortcomings—typically those for the intelligence community rather than military attack warning and response systems—have their own issues, such as information overload.

In many ways, the strengths of data warehousing–based business intelligence are weaknesses in $C^3I$ and $C^4I$ systems, and vice versa. The question must then be asked: Is it possible to create a hybrid architecture that combines the best aspects of data warehousing–based business intelligence with those of $C^3I$ and $C^4I$ warning and defense systems? The answer: absolutely! Figure 10.3 shows the result.

The architecture illustrated in Figure 10.3 was specifically created for military and homeland security "business intelligence"–style functionality such as bioterrorism, law enforcement, and similar missions. It is, however, just as applicable to commercial and civilian government business intelligence that in those respective environments are absolutely mission critical. Essentially, almost any problem to which business

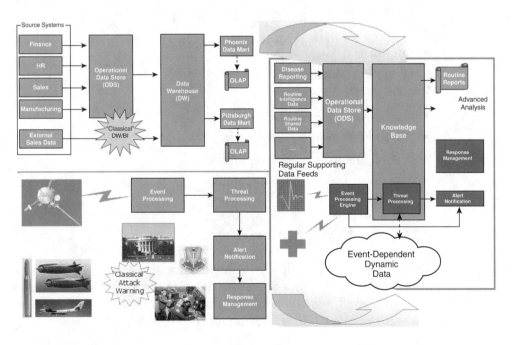

**Figure 10.3** Hybrid architecture suitable for real-time mission-critical business intelligence.

intelligence planners and strategists have applied real-time data flows in the pursuit of real-time business intelligence would likely be better served by the hybrid architecture shown here than by simply replacing batch data flows with real-time counterparts.

# ▶ Beyond Architecture: Key Principles

Achieving real-time, mission-critical business intelligence is more than a matter of fusing two different architectural approaches into a new one similar to that illustrated in Figure 10.3. When architecting the *operating model* of the environment, we must keep a number of key principles "front and center" (in the spirit of the military side of this discussion) and infuse most or all of them into the resulting system. These key principles are

- Events and event management
- Hypothesis formulation
- Correlation
- Interdiction
- Definitive conclusions
- Collaboration
- Outbound information flows
- Failsafe functionality replication
- Well-defined roles and responsibilities
- Planning for personnel succession

## Events and Event Management

Many mission-critical military or intelligence systems are built around the concept of *events*: an occurrence of some type that *must* be immediately addressed, with *potentially* (though not definitely) dire consequences for failing to do so. Examples of events include

- A missile launch picked up by a "first detection" sensor

- The sudden appearance of several unidentified aircraft on the perimeter of sovereign airspace
- A person under surveillance taking specific actions categorized as "significant"

The premise behind events is that they *must* be managed—that is, not "lost in the shuffle" or set aside to be picked up at some later point at which time it might be too late to take appropriate action. Further, the system components (communications links, protocols, screening and filtering software, etc.) dedicated to receiving and doing the initial pre-processing of events are architected and engineered to get the applicable information to some sort of threat processing (or equivalent) algorithms *as quickly as possible*.

Applying this concept to commercial or civilian government mission-critical business intelligence is very much a situational matter, with the types of events, how they're handled, and other properties being very much dictated by the specific mission(s) that are driving the development of the environment in the first place. The lesson that does pervade every single mission-critical business intelligence development effort, though, is that simply having a collection of real-time source-to-target data interfaces is *not* enough; the system must be architected and engineered to take full advantage of those real-time data flows in an almost fanatic pursuit of (referring back to my preferred definition of business intelligence) timely, actionable, high-value insight.

## Hypothesis Formulation

Traditional business intelligence environments typically deal in cold, hard facts: for example, last quarter's revenue produced by each salesperson in each of the company's regions with various levels of aggregation and "slicing" of information available upon demand; or, for a public sector organization such as a city-level public welfare department, a complete report of all disbursements organized and categorized by neighborhood cross-referenced with information drawn from state-level job-training programs.

$C^3I$ and $C^4I$ systems must also deal in cold, hard facts, but before those facts are determined, many of these systems formulate hypotheses on the basis of the first fragments of information. Consider a military system responsible for detecting intercontinental ballistic missile (ICBM) launches and determining whether or not that launch is a threat to the United States or its allies. As discussed next, making an "official" threat/no threat call may require the consolidation and correlation of many different data points from multiple sensors. However, upon the first detection of a launch, the system may make a "best guess"—that is, formulate and report a hypothesis—of whether or not the launch is likely to be a threat. The system may factor in data points such as the missile's initial trajectory; if it appears headed toward the other side's regular testing target zone, in the opposite direction of the U.S. mainland or the territory of an ally, then the initial hypothesis may be that the launch is likely to not be a threat.

Note, however, that the word *hypothesis* was selected for a reason. Just like in geometry, where an initial hypothesis is essentially little more than an educated guess until proven correct, a warning system's initial hypothesis is reported to the users, *but processing and tracking continues until the "proof" occurs.*

Applying this concept to real-time, mission-critical business intelligence, we might architect an environment in which a system not only receives real-time data inputs but passes the newly received data through a series of filters and algorithms looking for an early indication of a potential problem—not a definitive indication of a problem but rather a first hint that something *might* be amiss—and absolutely must be monitored closely until it can be determined with absolute certainty whether or not a problem actually does exist.

## Correlation

Most business intelligence environments provide a wealth of information to users, but within the portfolio of available reports and analyses, it is rare to find any two that work cooperatively with one another. Many reports may be available for supply chain performance and even more analyses available for customer satisfaction, but it is inevitably left up to the user to make the link between the two functionality areas and determine, for example, whether or not supply chain problems materially affect customer satisfaction and subsequent buying patterns.

In the military and intelligence world, however, *correlation* is often an integral part of a system's functionality and the underlying architecture. Consider the missile warning example. Suppose that several sensors are solely responsible for detecting launches, while other sensors are primarily responsible for detecting a missile's trajectory on the basis of factors such as altitude, direction, speed, and other data points. Essentially, a single missile launch may be detected by different sensors at different points in time.

A missile warning system must therefore correlate all of its data inputs using algorithms that are "aware" of the characteristics and missions of the sensors providing information into the system. The reason? It makes a big difference to folks such as four-star generals and the President of the United States whether a barrage of inputs actually indicate only one or two missiles that in fact aren't headed in our direction or erroneously (and potentially catastrophically) indicate that dozens of missiles are flying and nobody is quite sure in what direction they're headed.

Business intelligence strategists and planners should look for opportunities to correlate different portions of the overall base of information in the quest for high-value, actionable insight.

## Interdiction

Most business intelligence systems built around batch processing do provide insight to their users—after-the-fact, "tell me what *did* happen" insight. Too often, this insight is neither timely nor actionable, and the users can do little but plan workarounds, recovery plans, and other reactive steps.

In contrast, think about a warning system responsible for air defense. Detecting incoming enemy aircraft penetrating North American airspace is one thing; doing something about that penetration—sending intercept aircraft or preparing to launch air defense missiles—is typically called for in these situations. Detecting a potentially problematic situation isn't enough; what's called for is *interdicting* the situation by taking appropriate action in time to positively influence the outcome (for our side, at least).

How might interdiction be accomplished in a mission-critical business intelligence environment? Perhaps by triggering an automated feed of critical data into an enterprise's transactional systems for immediate action, or by persistently alerting and updating appropriate senior-level executives of the nature of the problem along with recommended solutions based on the system's knowledge base and embedded business rules.

## Definitive Conclusions

In the typical business intelligence environment, information is delivered to users in the forms of query results, reports, or through some other vehicle, and then it's often up to those information recipients to draw their own conclusions from the information they receive. Certainly, those users typically receive hard facts, as discussed earlier: actual sales dollar volume; performance by all the organization's sales people; changes in the market value of real estate property "owned" by a particular governmental or quasi-governmental organization; upward or downward trends in the number of problem properties on the roles of a government agency responsible for subsidized housing; and so on.

But despite the millions of discrete facts delivered every single day to millions of users of business intelligence systems, almost every one of those users would be hard pressed to answer, with absolute confidence, the following question: "So what does it all mean?"

Consider, in contrast, a military or intelligence system that relates to decision makers' definitive conclusions, such as:

- "Yes, a missile was launched from a particular site in Russia, but it *was* a test launch and is *not* a threat to the United States or its allies."

- "Yes, an unidentified aircraft suddenly appeared on the fringes of North American airspace, but based on further identifying data. it was determined that this aircraft was an international commercial flight that had gone off-course due to poor visibility and possible instrumentation failure—but regardless of the cause, it's not a threat."

- "(Person X) who has been under surveillance by the intelligence community for the past 18 months has been gathering documents of the type that indicate it is a virtual certainty she will try to enter the United States under a false identity and will try to do so within the next 15 days."

Mission-critical business intelligence environments often stop short of getting to the point where the facts they produce can be drawn together and, based on how those facts all fit in the context of one another, point to a definitive conclusion. Absent this final step, users often find themselves in "analysis paralysis": they *do* have all the information they need, but they are unable to perform the proper correlation and synthesis to get to the point where they are absolutely certain of what the situation is and what actions to take.

By equipping these environments with the procedural logic and other facilities to get to this final stage, the value of business intelligence environments will be far, far greater than we typically see today.

## Collaboration

Business intelligence environments can be lonely affairs despite being architected for hundreds or even thousands of users. Why? Because for the most part, a single user issues queries or information requests against this vast wealth of information, and the response comes back to that user—and nobody else.

Certainly, a user could email report results to a coworker with a message asking for that person's thoughts about the results, or even call that coworker over to his or her PC screen to discuss what the report is showing. But doing so is very much a reactive action, done only on the initiative of the first user. Should that user decide to "go it alone," there is no system-managed facility that would otherwise require that person to collaborate with anyone else, even if doing so would bring tremendous value to the analysis being undertaken.

In the $C^3I$ and $C^4I$ world, however, collaborative processing is usually built into the support systems as well as the work processes associated with that particular mission. Actually, "built into" is an understatement: collaboration is an integral, immutable aspect of these systems and their missions. Operators in the missile warning center in Cheyenne Mountain, Colorado, work in concert with other operators elsewhere in "The Mountain," who also work in concert with operators at other places: Offutt Air Force Base in Nebraska, the Pentagon, and so on. And somewhere in the chain are codified communications processes with generals and civilian command authorities, all of whom have a well-defined, well-rehearsed role in the mission.

In the commercial world, workflow engines and collaborative "groupware" have long been part of transactional applications such as insurance claims processing. Why not apply those principles from the transactional world—commercial or military—to analytical environments?

## Outbound Information Flows

Not to "pile on" the shortcomings of traditional business intelligence systems, but here's another one. The feeding of information from sources into a data warehouse or equivalent analytical environment is often an endpoint: that information that has undergone such rigorous quality assurance and been synthesized together is available for the users of that environment—but nobody else!

In contrast, consider a missile warning system that synthesizes data from numerous sensors and, even when nothing is happening (launchwise, thankfully!), regularly sends a status report to other critical links in the national defense system indicating such facts as the upstate and downstate of each sensor, number of protocol errors in the past 24 hours, and similar facts. Essentially, a system that integrates data from many different sources (sounds like a data warehouse, right?) turns around and acts as a source system to some other downstream consolidator of information.

Most everyone can think of dozens of examples in his or her organization where there is a tremendous desire—an unfulfilled desire—to automatically feed selected outputs from a particular business intelligence system to one or more environments elsewhere in the enterprise, to the benefit of everyone. Look for these opportunities; you won't be sorry.

## Failsafe Functionality Replication

One of the primary mantras of data warehousing has long been the quest for "a single version of the truth." A laudable goal, no doubt; but I would argue that the typical data warehouse is more likely to be a single version of *an answer*, and that answer might—or might not—be correct. A better approach, I've always felt, is to have *planned* redundancy of selected key data managed by several components in various source systems and analytical environments throughout the enterprise, with codified, formalized, *ever-present* QA procedures running in the infrastructure that compare totals that should be same, do spot checks of data values that should be identical, and so on.

Planned redundancy is a long-standing concept in the $C^3I$ and $C^4I$ world: multiple missile warning systems, multiple air defense systems, multiple intelligence systems. The secret, however, is that the redundancy must be not only planned but actively (and correctly) managed. Having multiple intelligence systems with overlapping "watch lists" that have conflicting data is extremely detrimental and potentially catastrophic.

Remember this theme—"controlled replication is good; uncontrolled duplication is bad"—and you won't go wrong.

## Well-Defined Roles and Responsibilities

So far, the good news/bad news points made have dealt in matters of technology and systems architecture. Beyond these obviously critical pieces of the puzzle, we must also look at the personnel side of mission-critical business intelligence. Unfortunately, many business intelligence environments are structured in the same manner as a 1970s or 1980s era class registration day at a 30,000-student public university—one big free-for-all in which lots of people line up for certain classes but other equally important classes are all but ignored.

Okay, maybe it's not the best analogy, but the point is this: without some order and discipline as to which users should work with which data, a very real risk exists that certain segments of the business intelligence environment will be overserved as a result of duplicate efforts by users in different organizations—or perhaps even the same organization—while other critical insights available go untapped because of the "role gap" situation.

As noted earlier, mission-critical military and intelligence systems are usually hallmarked by users working together collaboratively. However, it's more than just users working together: it's *how* they work together. The same principle should apply to business intelligence environments:

well-defined, precisely orchestrated roles and responsibilities for all involved to help ensure that the maximum value and insight is obtained from the synthesized data.

## Planning for Personnel Succession

One final point to make also deals with the user community of a business intelligence environment. Think about how many times a person disappears from an organization because of resignation, involuntary termination, job transfer, promotion, or some other reason, and the information that person used on a daily basis as part of his or her job suddenly is "lost" because that person's replacement doesn't work with the data the same way or doesn't understand the nuances of the data and what it all means.

In contrast, military missions are fundamentally grounded in a never-ending turnover of personnel. True, some roles are served by civilian employees who may stay in their roles for 10, 15, or 20 years, but for the most part, critical operations roles are filled by enlisted personnel and officers for periods of 1 to 3 years, with succession an absolute certainty.

Succession planning involves extensive training in all aspects of a job: the work processes, the information, the interrelationships, even what to do in various crisis situations. These facets are, in the military world, drilled into the very fabric of newcomers through rigid training and even formal certification.

Why not apply these same principles to mission-critical business intelligence environments? Newcomers should receive more than a user ID, a password, and a quick tour through the environment's online help facility. Planners and executives should assume that staff turnover *will* occur, and this must be factored into the environment to avoid compromising the mission. Again, it takes more than just data and how it's delivered to users to create a viable mission-critical business intelligence environment.

# ▶ Conclusions

At the time of this writing, we're about 15 years into the data warehousing/business intelligence "modern era" that began in the 1989 to 1990 timeframe. On the one hand, these disciplines have certainly proven themselves to be more than passing fads like so many now-faded technology "movements." Still, as noted at the outset of this chapter, too many of these environments do little other than produce a lot of reports but very little timely, actionable, high-value insight.

We can look toward the mission-critical systems run by the military and intelligence communities for some critical hints and assistance on how to take the next step in the business intelligence realm to enable the same degree of "mission-criticalness" (to coin a phrase) in how we use our terabytes of data for much more than most of us do today.

# 11

# Software Return on Investment (ROI)[1]

*Phillip A. Laplante*

With the grand scale and high cost of enterprise software systems and in the wake of the Sarbanes-Oxley legislation mandating corporate fiscal responsibility, the value of IT expenses are being more carefully scrutinized by CFOs, CEOs, and particularly governing boards. In response, CIOs are looking for ways to justify these costs as investments, or at least accurately portray them to CFOs and CEOs. But the IT industry does not have a good reputation for tracking and controlling its costs, nor is it always easy to attribute a benefit or return to software- and IT-related activities.

In this chapter we examine the nature of software ROI and the methods of its determination. In particular we seek to answer the following questions:

---

1. Much of this chapter is derived from a moderated panel discussion held in September 2003 involving members of the CIO Institute.

1. Is software an investment or an expense?
2. What is software ROI, and how is it defined?
3. How do we align ROI calculations and metrics?

The chapter concludes with a brief review of some of the financial calculations typically used to compute ROI. While this discussion may appear to be more of an accounting discourse than one on information technology, it underscores the fact that the best CIOs are very strongly grounded in financial management principles.

# ▶ Is Software an Investment or an Expense?[2]

Is software an investment or an expense? The answer, of course, is that it depends. For example, to the owner of a small car dealership, a customer information system mandated by the manufacturer might seem an outrageous expense, not an investment. On the other hand, if it can be demonstrated that this software can significantly increase sales volume, then the dealership owner might see that software as an enabling technology with a substantial ROI.

Generally accepted accounting principles,[3] or GAAP, as they are collectively known to CFOs, provide guidance on whether to treat software as an expense or an asset. But there is still a great deal of flexibility within these guidelines.

For example, CFOs would always record the purchase of a large ERP system as an asset to be depreciated on a 5-year schedule—the same as computer hardware. But the purchase of software licenses for a certain desktop application might be recorded as an expense depending on its purpose, terms of sale, and price.

---

2. I want to acknowledge discussions with my colleague, Dr. Andy Felo, Assistant Professor of Accounting, Penn State University, as contributing to this section.

3. Which are established by the Financial Accounting Standards Board (FASB). The FASB is an independent organization governed jointly by various professional accounting and management organizations.

On the other hand, most CIOs view software as an asset. Why? Because this viewpoint demonstrates the importance of the role of the CIO as one of adding value, not support. And it increases their capital budget, which means greater influence throughout the organization.

Whatever the case, expense or asset, justifying a software purchase as a business case is not just about "the numbers"—there is more to it than that. In determining the value of any IT investment, a holistic view must be taken. Indeed, many of the evaluation criteria for competing for the capital to make the purchase within an organization will likely come into play, such as alignment with the corporate mission and goals, relevance, priority, and so on.

Far too often, however, the decision making tends to go wrong when the "business case" is made to get the capital for the software purchase and then the business case is thrown away. As a result, the purported benefits of the software are not realized, and the perceived ROI for the software is diminished.

In other cases, the total cost of ownership (TCO) of the software is not correctly determined. TCO is more than the purchase price of the software—many senior executives don't realize this. Forgotten are the costs of deployment, hardware, training, integration, and so on. This ignorance of the non-purchase costs leads to disinterest in the use of the software once these costs are discovered. This scenario contributes to the reduction in the perceived ROI of the software, and a vicious cycle is created.

Users of supply chain software, for example, often focus on license purchase cost and business models that recognize multiyear license revenue mostly at initial purchase. But many manufacturing companies that own licenses to these powerful tools haven't implemented them because no one is consistently championing the benefits after the initial purchase event.

We have found that success is born from writing a business case and then sticking with the plan. Those CIOs who successfully deliver on ROI promises tend to be disciplined. Moreover, because the CIO is only part of the equation, and some of the potential areas for savings are owned by someone other than the CIO (for example, the COO, VP marketing, VP supply chain), ensuring a high ROI on software (however it is defined) comes down to the process rigor.

# What Is Software ROI, and How Is It Defined?

Return on investment (ROI) is a rather overloaded term that means different things to different people. In some cases it means the value of the software activity at the time it is undertaken. To others it is the value of the activity at a later date. In other cases it is just a catchword for the difference between the cost of software and the savings anticipated from the utility of that software. To still others there is a more complex meaning.

One traditional measure of ROI for any activity, whether software related or not, is given as

$$ROI = \text{Average Net Benefits/Initial Costs}$$

The problem with this model for ROI is the accurate representation of average net benefit and initial costs.

Commonly used models for valuation of some activity or investment include net present value (NPV), internal rate of return (IRR), average rate of return (ARR), and profitability index (PI). The section "Typical Financial Calculations of Software ROI" of this chapter reviews these and related calculations.

Other methodologies for valuation of software or related benefits include Six Sigma[4] and proprietary Balanced Scorecard models. These kinds of approaches seek to recognize that financial measures are not necessarily the most important component of performance. Further considerations for valuing software solutions might include customer satisfaction, employee satisfaction, and so forth, which are not usually modeled with traditional financial valuation instruments.

One way to resolve the paradoxical nature of software as both investment and expense, as well as to deal with allocation of a limited IT capital budget, is to use a portfolio management approach. Table 11.1 provides an example of such an approach.

---

4. A quality measure and improvement program developed by Motorola that focuses on the control of a process to ensure that outputs are within six standard deviations from the mean (or Six Sigma) of the specified goals.

**Table 11.1** Portfolio Model for Software and Related Activity Capital Allocation (figures are in millions of dollars).

|  | Value to Business | Capital Requirements | Total Cost of Ownership |
|---|---|---|---|
| Software option A | 4.5 | 1.2 | 2.3 |
| Software option B | 3.6 | 0.7 | 2.1 |
| Initiative C | 2,3 | 0.5 | 0.6 |
| Initiative D | 1.6 | 0.2 | 0.6 |
| Table entries are in estimated dollars. |

Using such an approach allows the CIO to balance the benefits of the software or initiative (such as increased productivity and increased revenue) with costs. Validating opportunities and costs in this manner requires a thorough and detailed workflow analysis, which often has the residual benefit of uncovering process inefficiencies.

# ▶ Alignment of ROI Analysis and Metrics

Whatever the approach to cost (or value) determination, there are numerous software packages to make the collection and analysis of data easier. Unfortunately, the widespread availability of this software means that anyone can use or misuse ROI type calculations. Some middle managers, for example, don't always understand the nuances of tracking software costs. These middle managers, particularly if they came up from the technical ranks, are unfamiliar with a balance sheet, income statement, and other basic financial instruments that are ultimately linked to the metrics used in these software packages.

Typically, the buyers of ROI calculation software are C-level managers who use this software to determine if projects are successful. But C-level executives usually don't know how to write queries, so there is a fundamental disconnect between the data and the decision-making processes. Balanced Scorecard tools address the problem by taking the business intelligence engine out of the loop and perform simple balanced scoring of the data for use by senior managers. While these tools are tunable, most managers can't measure more than one or two metrics effectively and never more than three.

Metric mismanagement problems and the eventual erosion of ROI occur when CEO-level metrics don't align at the project levels. (Figure 11.1).

Most nonsenior managers don't understand ROI because they are not close enough to the discussions at the high level to understand the impact of lower level discussions. Unfortunately, when people managing low-level projects are asked to cost-justify what they do, they don't know how to do it. So, what is happening to all the day-to-day process improvement decisions? How are they captured? How do they translate to the C-level metrics like IRR, ARR, payback, and so on? The answer is that they are not being properly filtered up the organizational hierarchy. Therefore, it is important that those at the lower levels are educated in the financial aspects of the business. This is where automated tools can be useful because they put everyone on the same page, and planning to use these tools has the effect of forcing metric alignment.

Furthermore, acculturation is important to ensure that each of the metrics along the line are not distorted or mismapped into the next level of metric. Moreover, understanding the nature of the metrics used and how they are applied is rather important.

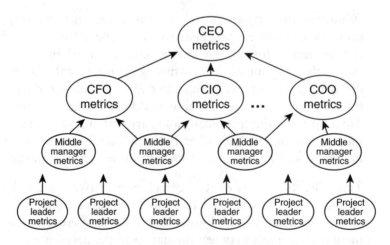

**Figure 11.1** Migration of various metrics from low-level project metrics to C-level metrics.

Finally, a word of caution about metrics. Remember that you get what you measure; that is, the measurements must align with the strategic goals. For example, consider one scenario of metric mismanagement involving a printed circuit board manufacturing company. The director of manufacturing says, "To get to the level of no-post delivery failure, I insist on 75 percent no-failure post-test." Production people determine that to achieve this, every board needs to be inspected, which leads to 95 percent no failure. But this practice leads to skyrocketing costs. This is because the metrics don't reflect the strategic goals.

The key, then, in using ROI measures and automated tools is to align the low-level metrics with processes. Then align the low-level metrics with the strategic metrics. This requires strategic planning and communications throughout the organization.

# ▶ Typical Financial Calculations of Software ROI

We conclude with a review of a number of traditional metrics used to compute software ROI. This discussion is a quick refresher only—it is not intended to be a comprehensive introduction to the subject. Much of the discussion was derived from Raffo and colleagues (1999) and Morgan (2005); their works can be consulted for a more detailed introduction.

## Activity-Based Costing (ABC)

Activity-based costing is an accounting strategy that considers the costs of people, facilities, computers, supplies, and other resources consumed. To the CIO, the goal is to show the rationale for investment in IT infrastructure by incorporating the costs of contribution from all parts of the organization that touch the IT function. Specially trained estimators are needed to determine the average work hours for a variety of tasks that are part of broader endeavor. For example, installation of a software package on a single desktop is one step in upgrading the operating system in preparation for the installation of a new ERP system. Tools are available that permit analysts to enter in the relevant data, relate that activity data, and perform forecasting simulations.

Unfortunately, activity costs are often difficult to quantify and capture; they require, in any case, reliable information based on honest reporting. The latter aspect is often overlooked. Moreover, there can be tremendous variation in factors affecting the estimation, such as compensation levels, burden rates for personnel (an accounting term that relates to the overhead structure), and individual performance levels. These variations collectively contribute to a great deal of uncertainty in the cost estimation equations (Jones 1996).

See Moskowitz (2003) for a broad-based discussion and a number of examples of activity-based cost analysis.

## Average Rate of Return (ARR)

An overloaded acronym, ARR can stand for average rate of return or accounting rate of return. Traditionally, it considers the traditional accounting and definition of net income rather than cash flows. It does this by including depreciation and amortization in the computation of the cash flow (meaning it treats depreciation as an out-of-pocket expense, reducing the cash flow). Its proponents argue that publicly traded organizations are ultimately evaluated on accounting measures of net income, so capital budgeting techniques should be based on this approach to determining cash flow.

There are a variety of different ARR measures based on some notion of benefits divided by some notion of investment.

Here are some example definitions; the first is the one commonly mentioned in textbooks.

- average projected after-tax profit/average investment
- average projected after-tax profit/initial investment
- average projected after-tax cash flow/average investment
- average projected after-cash flow/initial investment

Profit and investment can have varying definitions, so various accounting adjustments may or may not be made.

## Earned Value Analysis (EVA)

Earned value analysis (EVA) presumes that a project adds value and that this value is going to be measured through the life of the project. In this way, forecasted and actual costs are tracked to allow for mid-project adjustments or even scuttling.

A somewhat atypical approach to EVA involves the following calculations (Morgan 2005).

First, at key points in the project's evolution the schedule variance ($SV$) is computed as

$$SV = BCWP - BCWS$$

where $BCWS$ is the budgeted cost of work scheduled and $BCWP$ is the budgeted cost of work performed. The cost variance, $CV$, can then be computed. The $CV$ is the difference between the budgeted and actual cost of work performed ($ACWP$). That is,

$$CV = BCWP - ACWP$$

The cost performance index,[5] $CPI$, is based on the relationship between the cost variance and the schedule variance. That is,

$$CPI = \frac{BCWP}{ACWP}$$

The $CPI$ can then be used to forecast the cost to complete the project ($FCTC$) by multiplying by the original budgeted cost of the work:

$$FCTC = \text{original budget for work remaining}/CPI$$

Finally, the forecast cost at completion ($FCAC$) is just the actual cost of work already performed plus the forecast cost to complete the work:

$$FCAC = ACWP + FCTC$$

---

5. Not to be confused with Consumer Price Index, which is also usually denoted CPI.

These simple metrics can be used by the CIO to monitor and control a project.

## Net Present Value (NPV)

A very commonly used approach to cost determination for some projects is the net present value (NPV) determination.

Here is how to compute NPV. Suppose that $P$ is some future anticipated payoff either in real cash or in anticipated savings. If $r$ is the discount rate[6] and $Y$ is the number of years that the cash is expected to be realized, then we can determine what the present value of that payoff is. In other words, if you want to find the NPV, some future value of the cash (FV), the discount rate ($r$), and the number of years into the future that the cash will be obtained ($Y$), use the following equation:

$$NPV = FV/(1 + r)^Y$$

NPV is an indirect measure because you are required to specify the market opportunity cost (discount rate) of the capital involved.

As a simple example, suppose that a programming staff training initiative is expected to cost your company $50,000. The returns of this improvement are expected to total $100,000 of reduced rework 2 years in the future. If the discount rate is 3%, should the initiative be undertaken?

To answer this question, we calculate the NPV of the strategy, taking into account its cost

$$NPV = 100{,}000 / 1.03^2 - 50{,}000$$
$$= 44{,}259$$

Since the NPV is positive, yes, the project should be undertaken.

For a sequence of cash flows, $CF_n$, where $n = 0,...,k$ represents the number of years from initial investment, the net present value of that sequence is

---

6. The interest rate charged by the U.S. Federal Reserve. The cost of borrowing any capital will be higher than this base rate.

$$NPV = \sum_{n=0}^{k} \frac{CF_n}{(1+r)^n}$$

The $CF_n$ could represent, for example, a stream of related expenditures over a period of time, such as the ongoing maintenance costs or support fees for some software package.

## Internal Rate of Return (IRR)

IRR is defined as the discount rate in the *NPV* equation that causes the calculated *NPV* to be zero. *NPV* is not the ROI. But the IRR is useful for computing the "return" because it does not require knowledge of the cost of capital.

To decide if we should undertake this initiative, we compare the computed IRR to the return of another investment alternative. If the IRR is very low, then we might simply want to take this money and find an equivalent investment with lower risk (for example, to undertake a different corporate initiative or even to simply buy bonds). But if the IRR is sufficiently high, then the decision might be worth whatever risk is involved.

As an example, suppose the programming staff training initiative just discussed is expected to cost $50,000. The returns of this improvement are expected to be $100,000 of reduced rework 2 years in the future. We would like to know the IRR on this activity.

Here, $NPV = 100,000/(1 + r)^2 - 50,000$. We now wish to find the $r$ that makes the $NPV = 0$, that is, the "break even" value. Using our IRR equation,

$$r = [100,000/50,000)]^{1/2} - 1$$

Plugging this into a calculator gives $r = 0.414 = 41.4\%$. This rate of return is very high, and we would likely choose to undertake this programming staff training initiative.

## Profitability Index

The *PI* is defined as the *NPV* divided by the cost of the investment, *I*:

$$PI = NPV/I.$$

That is, we take the present value of an investment and divide it by the initial cash outlay, *I*. This yields a kind of "bang-for-the-buck" measure. The *PI* is appealing to managers who must decide between many competing investments with positive *NPV*s but who have limited investment resources (or to managers in government agencies with limited budgets and many opportunities). The idea is to take the investment options with the highest *PI* first, until the investment budget runs out. This approach is not bad but can suboptimize the investment portfolio. Rank ordering by *PI* may rule out a large project with a good *NPV* because it is just over the limit.

For example, the programming staff training initiative previously discussed is expected to cost the company $50,000. The returns of this improvement are expected to be $100,000 of reduced rework 2 years in the future.

The *NPV* for this initiative at a discount rate of 3 percent is

$$NPV = 100,000/1.03^2$$
$$= 94,259$$

for a *PI* of 94,259/50,000 or 1.88.

Overall, *PI* is recommended as a secondary measure used to augment *NPV* in optimizing the allocation of investment dollars.

## Payback

Payback is the time it takes to get the initial investment back out of the project. Projects with short paybacks are preferred, although the term "short" is completely arbitrary. The intuitive appeal is reasonably clear: the payback period is easy to calculate, communicate, and understand.

For example, if changing vendors for a particular application software package is expected to have a switching cost of $100,000 and result in a maintenance cost savings of $50,000 per year, then the payback period would be 2 years.

Because of its simplicity, it is the least likely to confuse managers. However, if payback period is the only criterion used, then there is no recognition of any cash flows, small or large, to arrive after the cutoff period. Furthermore, there is no recognition of the opportunity cost of tying up funds. Since discussions of payback tend to coincide with discussions of risk, a short payback period usually means a lower risk. However, all criteria used in the determination of payback are arbitrary

## Discounted Payback

The discounted payback is the payback period determined on discounted cash flows rather than undiscounted cash flows. This method takes into account the time (and risk) value of money invested. Effectively, it answers the questions, How long does it take to recover the investment? and What is the minimum required return? If the discounted payback period is finite in length, it means that the investment plus its capital costs are indeed recovered eventually, which means that the NPV is at least as great as zero. Consequently, a criterion that says to go ahead with the project if it has *any* finite discounted payback period is consistent with the NPV rule.

So, in the preceding example, with a switching cost of $100,000 and annual maintenance savings of $50,000 and assuming a discount rate of 3 percent, the discounted payback period would be longer than 2 years because the savings in year two would have an NPV of less than $50,000 (figure out the exact payback period for fun). But because we know that the there is a finite discounted payback period, we know that we should go ahead with the initiative.

## ▶ References

Jones, C., 1996. "Activity-Based Software Costing." *IEEE Computer*, May, pp. 103–104.

Morgan, J. N., 2005. "A Roadmap of Financial Measures for IT Project ROI." *IT Professional*, Jan./Feb., pp. 52–57.

Moskowitz, K., and H. Kern, 2003. *Managing IT as an Investment*. Prentice Hall PTR.

Raffo, D., J. Settle, and W. Harrison, 1999. Investigating Financial Measures for Planning of Software IV&V. Portland State University Research Report #TR-99-05.

# 12

# Starting with the Users

*Melissa Skelton and Gerard Gallucci*

## ▶ Introduction

It is no small achievement that the position of CIO has been added to the executive slate. That information management and technology have garnered such a position of respect in the corporate organization speaks both to the technological wizardry available to us in this day and age and to the concrete evidence amassed that empowering users with IT boosts the bottom line.

But in some cases, this upward movement has reached a plateau. Where it has, the problem has been the old disjuncture between the technology and the human beings it is intended to help. A growing rift between the organization that provides technology and the people who must use the technology to do their work is creating an ever more demanding set of challenges for the CIO. In the past, a good CIO was someone who understood technology, kept an eye on the horizon of potential new devices and software, and could create and implement a strategic plan for equipping the enterprise. Today, however, it is imperative that a

CIO also understand the business, the work that is being done to realize business objectives, the people doing that work, and how to talk to them about technology.

There was a time, not very long ago, when technology was an area of specialization viewed as something of a black box by outsiders. The CIO and his IT staff were viewed as the gurus, and they were entrusted with just making sure that the technology worked. However, time and experience have brought users into that previously closed world. They've been through software implementations. Their desktop PCs have been upgraded, and many of them have been handed PDAs. What's more, the Internet's ubiquitous presence and bottomless well of information have led these same users to start installing these devices and software applications at home, making them de facto technologists, if self-taught and limited in their expertise. As users become more familiar with technology implementations, more sophisticated and informed, and with greater direct access to personal technologies (PDAs, multipurpose phones, and high-powered personal computers), it will be increasingly difficult to leave them out of the IT planning, design, and development process.

The question that drives this chapter is whether users should conform to the technology put in front of them or technology should mold itself around the users. For a long time, and particularly in the context of enterprisewide solutions, the answer has been that users should adapt to the IT tools that the organization places in front of them. If transaction processing can be sped up by installing an ERP, then the onus is on the user to learn how to use the new system for the benefit of the organization. But in an age in which technology isn't such a mystery to users who've been burned and burdened by previous deployments, the CIO isn't going to be able to tune out the rising voice of the user population as so much armchair quarterbacking. In fact, the CIO who embraces the need to make technology suit the user, and who can master the art of eliciting the business requirements, user needs, and user desires and matching those with emerging technologies will be the successful CIO in the next generation.

## How the Disconnect Occurred

In the beginning, IT was the simple extension of the equipment and wiring used for communications, elaborating systems such as the telephone, radio, and telegraph. These were basic capabilities that created the possibility of moving information and therefore created "users" of such technologies. When the computer entered the picture, it was yet another form of hardware that would make the previous forms of communication more efficient. Eventually, computers became small enough to be used by individuals and merged with an even simpler form of machine, the typewriter, so that creating, moving, and capturing information became not only a corporate but an individual capability. Users were now required to develop a higher degree of sophistication with regard to the technology itself, and they in turn developed requirements of their own for what the technology needed to do for *them*.

Yet the field of corporate IT remained a process of merely inventing or improving essential hardware, as if it would continue to be used as transparently as the older forms of communication devices. IT shops purchased the latest equipment, installed it, and gave scarce thought to how the users might receive it. Newer products promised the ability to do more and faster, so users would certainly embrace them. The PC was introduced as just another piece of hardware. It would have been difficult for anyone to imagine the power of the PC and its ability to transform how we would do our jobs via the Internet and all manner of powerful new software. In any event, the PC was rolled out for users—as an improved typewriter—and the stage was set for continued technology-driven changes to the workplace. IT specialists continued to view technology as merely a product to put forth. Users began to rely on technology and to see technology as a fundamental tool for getting the work done, without having any role in its design or planning.

Initially, IT staff were analogous to plumbers who brought water to the townspeople through a largely hidden system of pipes and valves. Grateful to have easier and better access to water, the townspeople didn't need to know how the plumbing worked or whether there might be a better system than the one the plumbers employed. In modern terms, we were given typewriters that not only recorded but *remembered* what we typed; then we were networked with other computers so that we could see what others were doing; then we were given email so that we could communicate directly with those other people from the very same system on which we were typing. We had thought that we had been working fine without those technologies previously, but hey, who could argue that this new stuff wasn't helpful?

But as time went on and the role of the CIO evolved, the IT staff seemed to focus primarily on thinking up new ways to bring the townspeople water. Continuing the analogy, they had done a great thing in meeting the unrecognized requirement for indoor plumbing, and people were happy to have it, so surely better plumbing would be equally useful. However, as those people grew accustomed to the presence of water, they began to see new applications for water, and the needs grew, as did the desire for greater convenience in accessing that water. They began making requests of the plumbers to install another faucet, or to differentiate between the hot and cold water supply. Though eager themselves to install the latest "faucets" on the market, the plumbers came to hear the pleas of the villagers as distractions at best and as informed interference at worst. The townspeople were trying to tell the plumbers that more water moving faster wouldn't be beneficial if the temperature couldn't be controlled and fancier faucets wouldn't help if it still brought the water to just one room of the house; the plumbers were telling the townspeople that they should be grateful for the water and leave the rest to the experts. Neither side seemed to know how to talk to the other in terms the other understood. So has been the relationship between IT and users. A piece was missing, a framework for translating between what users needed and wanted and what IT could do. That is the way it now reads, eh?

Bridging the gap between user and IT expert requires a paradigm shift on both sides. The CIO needs to ensure that IT isn't just creating fancy plumbing, while the users need to learn how to articulate the business requirements in a way that allows both sides to succeed. But users don't usually know the right questions to ask; many of them think of technology as "magic." At the same time, the IT "wizards" don't always know how to elicit this information from users without becoming bogged down in the complaints and pipedreams (no pun intended) of the users.

## Why Do Users Matter So Much to a CIO?

IT's sole raison d'etre is to envelop, manage, and serve information for and to users. In the context of defining *knowledge management*, the American Productivity and Quality Center (APQC), a nonprofit organization specializing in benchmarking and best practices, particularly in knowledge management, defines information as data plus analysis. Furthermore, knowledge is information in action: people actually using the data plus analysis in the course of doing business. Knowledge management is then a systematic approach to getting the right information to the right people at the right time. So IT, in its role to process information and knowledge, is a vehicle not just for managing the capture and storage of data but for connecting people with the information and connecting people with other people who have the knowledge needed to get the job done.

So fundamentally, IT is about the people, because without them, IT would be unnecessary. Sure, in futuristic sci-fi scenarios, we have seen IT operating without humans, but in today's practical environment, IT is entirely reliant on people. Users are required to input the data or information, to approve or edit throughout the workflow, to do something with the output or with the information that has been stored. It is in fact hard to imagine a form of IT that would not be utterly pointless without users. Clearly, IT needs users, and increasingly, users need IT.

IT developed, installed, and institutionalized without user input, needs, requirements, desires, level of skill, and proficiency taken into account runs the risk of being "useless" in the very real sense of ending up without users who can or will use it. Too often, as technologists, we ignore that element of the equation because we are convinced of the intrinsic value of the techno-wizardry—the fact that the tool is exceptional *must* mean that it will be an improvement for users, that it will be welcomed, that it will help, that it will be a worthwhile investment for the organization. Every day, that theory is proven wrong as organizations search for the promised ROI on technology investments that never seem to materialize and as people grow progressively more frustrated by the technological environment that isn't meeting their needs.

More importantly, however, users must be included in the process because if the technology *doesn't* suit them, they will simply find their own way to do things, which is less than optimal both in that it wastes or duplicates effort and that it poses significant security risks. A recent survey that was responded to by more than 1,000 users within a large Ffederal agency revealed that *more than 85 percent* admitted to using personal email accounts such as Yahoo! or Hotmail to conduct official business, albeit unclassified, in direct violation of the department's security regulations and information sensitivity policies in existence at the time. Most justified their behavior by citing the inability of the agency to deliver remote access to their email accounts, whether through Web interfaces or via PDA devices, in spite of the overwhelming and inescapable need to do business off-site at all hours of the day. The business of getting the work done must go on, and human nature will find a way to achieve it, whether the technology permits it or not, with or without the CIO's permission or assistance. When dissatisfied customers take matters into their own hands, it deepens the divide between technology and users, between planning and reality, and between holistic organizational goals and that organization's ability to meet them.

Finally, seeking to identify, understand, and meet user business requirements can provide necessary focus for IT efforts. There is a particular danger for IT employees in taking a "let's stay at the cutting edge" approach, rather than a "let's see what would be useful to our users" approach. For IT professionals, it is increasingly difficult to stay abreast of the ever-expanding world of technological advancement. When IT professionals are expected, even as a collective staff, to be consistently up to date on the latest and greatest, across software, hardware, telecommunications, and more, they become overwhelmed, unfocused, and ultimately incapable of being effective at responding to the here-and-now requests of the company. At the current pace of growth and innovation, IT staff cannot reasonably be expected to both get the work done of managing the networks, installing the equipment, upgrading the software, and troubleshooting user issues and also be adequately educated about all the new and potential technology coming down the pipeline. Working through the available technologies and products and all the updates and emerging development, without a clear sense of direction gained by a global and detailed understanding of the organization's business requirements, makes this already difficult job even worse.

# ▶ Successes and Failures: Illustrations of "Why Bother?"

## The Underachievement of ERPs

In the mid-1990s, enterprise resource planning (ERP) implementations were all the rage. Vendors of these products convinced corporations and government institutions alike that the real value to be gleaned from IT was in implementing these advanced, comprehensive transaction systems that would integrate multiple functional areas along the supply chain. The potential for streamlining these processes, reducing duplication, speeding the time to results, and thereby lowering costs significantly was virtually assured. IT wouldn't be cheap to get there; deployments ranged from a few hundred thousand dollars for a single module to tens of millions for a complete system. Organizations barreled ahead, though, confident that the promised ROI would make the effort worthwhile.

Yet many of these companies found that once the ERP was installed, little had changed other than the process by which these transactions were completed. The jackpot of savings didn't materialize, and these organizations found themselves wondering where they went wrong and whether there was some way to get back on track toward these tremendous savings they were counting on to revolutionize the back office. Consulting firms large and small scrambled to shift their sales focus from implementing ERPs to showing clients how to maximize the value of their investment. A hard sell, they found, for customers who'd already spent millions of dollars to install the systems, but with the alternative being to see no ROI for the considerable sunk cost, these same organizations dropped a few more project dollars to see what they might have missed the first time around.

The answer? In spite of having chosen good products and, in most cases, having properly and thoroughly deployed them, budget-conscious companies running these efforts through the IT department frequently sacrificed the "soft" side of the program. Training budgets and change management programs were consistently trimmed or cut altogether, sometimes before the project even began. The assumption was that this technology was largely behind-the-scenes; most people in the organization wouldn't directly use software or would use it in only a limited capacity. The primary benefit was in how the systems would work together and would work with the systems of suppliers and customers, so the money was shifted to ensuring that these interfaces worked smoothly. Further, because these systems were "off the shelf" and intended for use across back-office functions that are considered fairly universal, it was also assumed that little business process analysis would be necessary. Billing is billing whether you sell food or trains, so although there would probably be some minor adjustments in learning to do invoicing through the new software, there shouldn't be a large customization component or a major learning curve. Right?

Unfortunately, most organizations—and many of the consultants and product vendors who installed the systems—just plain underestimated how unique these processes could prove to be from one company to the next. Moreover, they underestimated how unique the *people* using these systems would prove to be and how much of an impact that would have on the success—or failure—of the ERP. From an IT perspective, they did everything right; there was a value proposition, the technology was sound, the implementation team was usually large and well trained, and no expense was spared to get the thing up and running as soon as possible. From a *user* perspective, it was all wrong: "Somebody upstairs decided to change the way we do our jobs, they brought in a bunch of outsiders to install a system, nobody asked us how we actually get the work done and *why*, and they didn't figure we'd need much training to learn how to do our jobs completely differently via this new system." This major disconnect may have seemed to most executives like a simple matter of "they'll adjust," but in reality, it wasn't just about unhappy users. The missing link in the chain was the very fact that the approach was usually to implement this promising new technology rather than to solve an actual business problem or seek to understand how this technology might best serve the business at hand. Way back in *Reengineering the Corporation*, Hammer and Champy made the point (and we're paraphrasing here) that automating a bad process just returns bad results faster.[1] In the case of the ERPs, it just made the automated processes more expensive and complex.

Of course, this is something of a sweeping generalization about ERP implementations. Some did go well, and many were ultimately able to work through—although often after the fact and for many additional consulting dollars—to the results they first expected. It is, however, illustrative of the problem of approaching technology from the perspective of the promise it holds, the possibilities it exposes. How different might that entire decade of work have been if organizations had instead identified a problem with back-office functions (other than their sheer expense) and sought to find a technology that not only solved the problem but addressed the specific needs of the users who do the work?

---

1. "Automating existing processes with information technology is analogous to paving cow paths. Automation simply provides more efficient ways of doing the wrong kinds of things." *Reengineering the Corporation,* Hammer, Michael, and Champy, James, 1993, HarperCollins, New York, p.48.

# Paradigm Shift at the State Department

At the United States Department of State, the CIO and the IT staff have historically been very good plumbers. The CIO's organization, the Information Resource Management Bureau (IRM), focused on equipping the organization with baseline resources, managing the deployment of those resources, and conducting subsequent upgrades. Concerned primarily with securing sensitive and classified materials, the Department required IRM only to make sure that whatever technology it implemented would be invulnerable to intrusion or unwanted dissemination. In turn, IRM was less reactive to growing user requirements for technology than to the inescapable need to be able to manage a global network and rapidly increasing volume of electronic information and to communicate about it with other agencies. So, CIOs at State did well with a fairly minimalist approach to technology.

When Colin Powell became Secretary of State, however, a shift occurred in the overall approach to IT that rippled through the Department. Powell believed that it wasn't enough to simply keep up; in 2002 he asserted that "The success of U.S. diplomacy in this new century depends in no small measure on whether we exploit the promise of the technology revolution." In fact, he was surprised to discover shortly after his arrival that desktop Internet access was not a universal capability of all Department employees. In the age of the information superhighway, how can we get the job done without universal access to a resource that even a fifth-grader has at school, if not at home? He vowed to ensure such access to each and every employee, and by the end of fiscal 2003, the Department's IT staff had done it.

But beyond simply ensuring that basic technology needs were met, Secretary Powell had a vision for how to more effectively exploit that technology revolution. In early 2001, Undersecretary for Management Grant Green approached Ambassador James Holmes about heading up a new task force that would focus on the user aspect of IT, on issues of connectivity and managing knowledge effectively, and on the IT decision-making process. Holmes shrugged his shoulders and said, "But I don't understand why you want me. As far as IT is concerned, I'm nothing more than a disgruntled user." Green said, "*Exactly*. You're my man." Appointing a career foreign service officer as the first director of the Office of eDiplomacy represented a fundamental shift in the way technology would be approached in the future. eDiplomacy reported directly to Undersecretary Green, but it spent its days working hand in hand with the newly appointed CIO. Its mission was to help the Department improve interagency connectivity, develop a knowledge management strategy, and ensure that the user perspective was considered in every technology decision.

In 2003 eDiplomacy graduated from a task force to an official office, but what really illustrates the success of the model is that the new office was placed *within* the IRM organization. The new CIO embraced the idea of business practitioners helping to shape the technology environment. This did not occur, by the way, because users clamored for such a change; it occurred because the executive levels recognized the value of both the technological enablement and the voice of the user in identifying what technologies to adopt and how to implement them. Once established formally as a part of IRM, eDiplomacy's mission expanded to include direct participation—rather than occasional consultation— in a number of Department-wide IT efforts. They even took on the task of leading one themselves: deploying a new enterprise search engine.

It had become clear, as the Department's intranet Web content had exploded over the previous 2 or 3 years, that the existing search engine was no longer adequate to meet the demands of both increasingly sophisticated users and of exponentially expanding content. Choosing to make use of an existing product license, eDiplomacy began the task of installing a new and improved enterprise search engine tool. The approach was somewhat unique, however, because of eDiplomacy's own mission to serve as the voice of the user. But although the software decision was made largely internally to IRM, eDiplomacy's ownership of the search project allowed them to devise a development program that brought users into virtually every other aspect of the process. Business requirements for the software were drafted by a cross-functional knowledge management community of practice. An Executive Stakeholders Group was convened to permit pilot groups, large stakeholder organizations, and other technology initiatives to have some transparency into the project. User focus groups representing more than 75 users from more than seven different bureaus, both functional and regional, both civil service and foreign service, both domestic and overseas, were convened to talk about their use of search and how a new search tool might best address their needs, even before development of the product had begun. The tool went live, on time, in January 2005, and while the effort certainly was not without its share of glitches, users who have provided feedback have been overwhelmingly supportive. And as the feedback they provide goes into subsequent iterations of the tool, the tool becomes ever more effective and useful to the people who need it. As a result, the project is perceived as successful, the budget for ensuing releases of the product is funded, and an effective model for conducting technology implementations goes forward.

# ▶ What Should a CIO Do About It?

How does a CIO go about ensuring that technology is user-driven without crippling her/his own organization? How can a CIO make certain that users are meaningfully integrated into IT decision making without slowing down the process or adding unnecessary chefs in the kitchen? When and how is it appropriate to include individual users or end-user group representatives? Is it always necessary to include users explicitly, or is it enough to simply bear them in mind as IT strategic planning is taking place? To be effective in the endeavor to take a user- and business process–based approach to IT, the CIO needs more than a practical construct. The following discussion provides some guidelines for helping steer the CIO toward the user perspective without drowning her in user complaints.

## How to Accomplish It

One simple way to increase the chance of success is for organizations to select CIOs who were previously business practitioners, thereby making the user perspective endemic to the position. Since there are some practical limitations with that approach, including attracting business practitioners to a role typically viewed as a technical specialization, and because this book deals with how to help the CIO already in office, we focus on option two: institutionalizing user representation in the IT process from beginning to end.

### Acknowledgment and Understanding

The first and most important step is perhaps obvious but deceptively difficult: recognizing the problem. This may sound trite, but more than one organization has suffered from an executive's mistaken belief that he or she is already doing A when the reality is clearly B. Before professing the adoption of this framework, a CIO must fully understand what the "user perspective" really means. The following series of questions should help direct you to the user-based line of thinking:

1. What are the organization's key business objectives, as identified by the people who do the work (i.e., the potential users of enabling technologies)?

   (a) Does the answer vary by business unit? By geography?

   (b) Are there particular business problems or identified unmet business user needs, new developments, longstanding problems?

2. What technologies are involved in those business issues?

   (a) Are the current technologies perceived as helping or hindering the effort to alleviate these problems?

   (b) Have users identified any particular business issues as being a result of either the technology that exists or the lack of technology to enable or assist them?

3. Are users asking for any particular technologies?

   (a) If so, what drives those requests—media information about those technologies? competitors, suppliers, or customers with those technologies in place?

   (b) If not, why not? Does the organization have a culture that fears or resists new technology? Is the workforce largely untrained in computing technologies? Is there a history of poor performance of technologies or implementations gone awry?

Collecting the answers may be as simple as reflecting on information gleaned in staff meetings or executive conversations, or may require some research into one or more areas of the organization. The eDiplomacy Office in the State Department has made targeted use of user surveys and focus groups. In any case, the answers to these questions are the desired end result, but making the effort to engage with users in the first place is vital.

## What to Do with the Answers

This section talks a little bit more about what the answers to those questions might imply in terms of the approach the CIO would take. The essence of the task is to ensure user involvement (direct when necessary, through information gathering when not) in each phase of IT planning, design, development, testing, and implementation in an iterative fashion that allows user requirements and technology to remain in an active dialogue throughout the process.

### How to Involve Users at the Strategic/Capital Planning Level

1. Perhaps one of the most important steps a CIO can take that is simultaneously the easiest and the hardest is to **get out of the office once in awhile**. A 2003 *CIO Forum* newsletter article entitled "The Big 10 CIO Mistakes That Cost You" identifies as the first mistake, "Reign from your office." The majority of your time should be spent with your customers and the front line of the business, not in meeting after meeting with your direct reports and vendors.[2] How can you possibly develop a strategy that incorporates and satisfies users if you don't know any? Quit drinking the IT Kool Aid, step out into the user world, and make some new friends.

2. **Ask the organization to help you.** Your first step doesn't have to be as extensive as establishing an office (like that of eDiplomacy) to ensure user representation in the big decisions, but having the executive team structure the capital planning process in such a way that both permits and encourages greater participation can only strengthen your ability to do so. Too often, capital planning is done in a big rush and under a dark curtain; opening the process to greater preliminary discussion can help, provided the CIO ultimately retains autonomy and isn't penalized for the user-focused approach.

3. **Form a senior user group**—perhaps including top officials of the chief business operation groups of the organization—to discuss and approve major IT investments before they get underway. This can be mirrored by lower level groups that vet IT proposals before they go to the senior board and track implementation. In some

---

2. "The Big 10 CIO Mistakes That Cost You," *CIO Forum*, Issue 20, March 26, 2003, Richmond Events Ltd.

special circumstances, design and development of major IT projects might be overseen by a joint management/IT/user group acting through the project manager.

4. **Institute change management procedures** to bring users into the process of getting ready to use a new technology or system early. This also offers an opportunity to bring together all parts of the organization that need to work together to help ensure the rollout of the new program works smoothly. Although this may seem like a project-specific task, too often change management activities are the first sacrifices of already tight budgets. Instituting change management practices at the corporate level provides both the leverage and the consistency to ensure they are carried through on every IT endeavor.

### How to Involve Users at the Project Level

1. One of the first lessons in the change management track at business school was that if you want to successfully implement a change, **get some vocal objectors on your team**. It may seem counterintuitive, but it works: inviting the "enemy" to directly participate gives voice to the concerns of the other side, not only succeeding in making those people feel heard but also giving you the opportunity to address those issues as part of the development process rather than as an opposing force to success once development is complete. Making converts is a key strategy for success, but it only works if the person being converted (a) didn't start out as mostly in your camp to begin with; (b) really is heard by you and is sought to be accommodated; and (c) really does buy in to the final solution such that he will support it both inside the team and out.

2. Simply put, **user focus groups work**. They work not only for consumer product development, like identifying the next flavor of toothpaste or the right color for a soda can, but also for collecting and discussing business and technology requirements in a functional, concentrated environment where the IT staff can have some insight into the conversation. Users will talk about the IT project with or without a formal request from the IT folks; better to invite them in to have the conversations in your presence so that you can learn from them. Do more than one focus group. Select a handful of users from as many different

types of user groups as you can, because different functional or geographic areas will use information and technology differently. Ask the same set of open-ended questions (e.g., What do you search the Web for? What sources do you search? How do you want the results to be organized?) of every group, and be prepared to hear things you weren't expecting. Finally, listen to what those users tell you and factor that input into the structure of the project, the timeline, and of course, the product itself.

3. **Pilot the product**—hardware or software—as early as possible and with a limited but representative number of users, *and expect problems*. Too often, the pilot is set up as an eleventh-hour dress rehearsal, after which only a few minor adjustments can be made. In reality, pilots should be viewed as one of the best learning opportunities for the technical team. Users will often have difficulty articulating their needs, requirements, wants, and preferences in a vacuum; until they have something to see and react to, they can only be so descriptive and specific. Test the product with the same user focus groups who gave you input in step 2, which accomplishes several objectives: they will have a greater sense of involvement (and consequently, buy-in); you will be better able to compare apples to apples because the same people who said A last time can now see what A looks like; and the rapport you will have developed by establishing a longer-term relationship with those people will permit more candid, more meaningful feedback that will actually give developers and installers the information they need to succeed.

## What to Expect of the Users

Lest the CIO feel that the burden is entirely upon him to make technology work for the users, it's important to emphasize that users too have a responsibility in this process. Not all of the discord between users and IT has been the result of some IT myopia. Users, whether because of frustration borne of bad experience or feeling they have an inadequate vocabulary for making themselves understood, are often complacent about asking for what they need, or they assume that it is simply easier and of no particular harm to just find a workaround solution. Successful technological enablement of business processes is equally dependent upon the users' willingness and ability to contribute value to the process rather than be a roadblock. If the CIO and IT staff are going to ask the right questions and take the time to include users, what should users have to do in return?

Some users will never "get it," while others, probably a minority, will not only understand the issues but see the importance of participating. But few users, whatever their interest level, will have more than a layman's understanding of how technology really works or will know how—and with what vocabulary—to talk about it. Put differently, they may not know how to articulate what they need in technologically meaningful terms. They will, however, have plenty of thoughts to share, if only the IT staff can elicit them. Expect users to have something to say, and expect to have to work a little to understand what it is. The important mindset here is "Seek to understand, not to be understood."[3] We have found that a surprising number of users will participate gladly in surveys, focus groups, and other forms of outreach. The key is "outreach," an active effort to find users where they live—in their own habitat, so to speak—and learn in the manner easiest for them, what they do, what they need, and how they react to the technology you want to place in front of them.

Is it reasonable for the CIO to expect that users will participate directly in the IT decision-making and development process when invited? Inasmuch as the CIO needs to include the users, the users in turn may be thought to have a responsibility to play their role. But users typically feel pressure to focus on their own job responsibilities. This is the reality. In the final analysis it may be necessary to assign (and reward) a small group of users (on a rotational basis) to represent user interests in the IT process. If the organization also has an active knowledge management program—possibly including communities of practice and other elements of change management and knowledge sharing—then there may already be a body of tech-aware users to draw from.

The bottom line for the CIO interested in success—for the organization, for the IT shop, for himself or herself—is this: Working with users to meet business IT requirements helps maximize the chances of achieving positive results and avoiding outright failure. It helps ensure that users greet the latest rollout as something *they* asked for, that *they* helped develop, and that will make *their* jobs easier and more efficient.

---

3. "Hints to Help Succeed: A Perspective on Working with Others for 47 Years," Richard Skelton, 1997.

# Business Process Improvement

*Peter Kraynak*

## ▶ What a CIO Needs to Know About Business Process

It is unfortunately quite common for a company to buy information technology assets with merely the good intention of saving money, expanding sales, or to develop a competitive advantage in the marketplace. To make matters worse, it is unlikely for that same organization to have a full understanding of what value the investment has produced or will produce. Most IT professionals go about their daily working lives talking about how IT is an "enabler" and how important the latest IT platform is to the business. Most feel strongly that every IT investment should have tangible benefits and well-defined business objectives. But do people really mean it? Do IT leaders just say these things, or do they also *act* accordingly?

In the earlier days of IT, people were often paid to develop information systems without being held accountable for clear requirements or expected benefits, and so it seemed like such an accomplishment when IT shops eventually mandated a requirements definition for every initiative. Some years later the IT professionals became more involved with the business strategists and began to develop vision statements for systems in advance of systems design and development. Using vision to guide the effort certainly gave more context to the requirements-gathering process that was happening by IT policy and was a welcome advancement for strategy-conscious CIOs. However, requirements alone weren't really enough. Most organizations are only now realizing that the genesis of systems vision and related business requirements occurs deep within the business process. Therefore, business process is the first thing a CIO or an IT staff member should think of for each and every system concern. Knowledge of the business process in detail is the core of an IT organization's existence.

What is a business process, and what should a business process include? A process can be defined as "one or more bounded work activities or specific functions that convert inputs from suppliers into outputs of information, services, and/or products that are useful to consumers of those items." For a CIO, it is useful to have at the minimum a "low-flying" bird's-eye view of the organizational processes and functional interdependencies. This is a snapshot of how the business operates, and it shows all the elements of the supply chain from cradle to grave—suppliers, inputs, steps, outputs, decision points, and customers. It should be important enough for an IT leader to take the time to identify all relevant elements of a process before attempting to begin an improvement project—that includes all IT initiatives. To that end, a holistic picture of a business process must include, in one integrated view of the relevant software, data feeds, reports, databases, and procedures to show how these elements are both embedded and flow together, alongside manual activities, operational workflow, and other business functions.

Developing and maintaining a picture of business processes for a company is important because those diagrams describe the nature of the organization, how it operates or doesn't. They help identify the business drivers, can define the core strengths and weaknesses of the organization, and even show the competitive threats if done holistically. For example, a good business process picture would reveal how much time it takes for the products to reach customers, or how much time on the average it takes until the company's primary competitors get an opportunity to enter a customer account.

For better or for worse, the job of the CIO is to know *everything* about business process. That's not to say that the IT staff wouldn't be accountable for all the detail of a particular set of business process pictures, but it is to say that a CIO should be entirely competent in process analysis. Here is a short primer on some basics of business process analysis:

- A process map is a diagram, also known as a business process picture or a process model. Because this picture could be worth a thousand words, it provides a common understanding of how a process operates as well as a means for discussing that process so that the steps can be analyzed, hand-offs clarified, and improvement opportunities identified.

- There are generally two kinds of process maps: the "current" process and the "future" process—both reflective of the state of the company's operations at two very different points in time. Process targets are needed to guide the process during improvement efforts into the right direction toward the "future" state. There are two types of process targets: including Final Performance Standards and Interim Performance Targets. Care must be taken not to confuse industry benchmarks with existing metrics for the company.

- The main elements of a process picture include Activities, Decisions, Connectors, and Entities. The supporting elements might include Role, System, and Performance Measure. The role is a participant in the process, the system is any technology element that is part the process, and the performance measure is a metric that quantifies some aspect of the process. It is important to define the name, purpose, start, and endpoints (scope) of each process in question, as well as the inputs and outputs. The owner, customers, and suppliers of the process should be also identified.

- Performance measures in a business process enable control and visibility over the process status if the measurement responsibilities are clearly defined and assigned. The measures must effectively describe the critical issues and performance levels as opposed to defining only those that are easy to measure. Performance measures usually fall into three distinctive categories: Service Quality Characteristics (communication, reliability, responsiveness, access, competence); product quality characteristics (performance, features, timeliness, reliability, serviceability, durability); and process performance issues (cost, quality, cycle time, quantity, customer satisfaction).

- A business process should be examined to identify problems as well as opportunities for improvement, as viewed from three different perspectives: People, Technology, and Workflow. The People perspective considers resources, competencies, and suitability of the organization for the task. The Technology perspective considers the adequacy of the data, the interoperability of the IT platforms, and technical support. The Workflow perspective considers the bottlenecks, disconnects, non–value-adding steps, and potential problem areas in the process. Various formal analysis techniques should be used during examination.

A good business process analysis will reveal the deficiencies that can be categorized with severity and frequency, leading to a prioritized set of improvement needs. The requirements for such initiatives become increasingly obvious as you more clearly and deeply define the process. Approaching requirements in this way also increases the likelihood of identifying the correct requirements for a software development initiative. Process mapping provides the context for how and where IT fits into the organization and will secondly reveal where the IT team can have the highest impact in support of process and cost improvement.

In order to effectively capture a useful process model, the organization must rely on the specialized competency of facilitation. Whether a company uses its own internal resources or utilizes the services of a professional outsider, the skill level of the facilitation has the potential to make or break the success of a process mapping effort. Subsequent to the facilitation and modeling process, the next crucial step lies in the interpretation of the diagrams. With a qualified and competent interpretation, the company sets itself up to save valuable time and money by identifying gaps, bottlenecks, disconnects, and potential future challenges. These deficiencies form the key targets for the improved process picture, and it is upon this foundation that the CIO should compute estimates of cost savings, time efficiencies, new revenue opportunities, and other quantified benefits for the organization.

There is a real need for executive leaders and management team members to learn the competency of business case development. However, this can't happen at any meaningful level unless a good process analysis is completed first. Whether the business case is substantiated with a

CBA (cost-benefit analysis) or with an ROI (return-on-investment analysis), the business and IT leadership of a company should feel accountable for IT dollars being spent. That investment, or the proposal thereof, needs to be predicated upon a proper business process analysis.

# ▶ What Six Sigma Is and Why It's So Effective

Six Sigma is an industry accepted and proven methodology used for business process improvement. Six Sigma was first developed more than 15 years ago by Motorola in order to reduce the number of manufacturing defects and to thereby achieve a higher level of customer satisfaction. The primary driver of Six Sigma is to minimize "defects" in a process, an effort that may have the effect of retaining customers, creating new efficiencies, and even expanding sales. Throughout the years, many professionals have found that Six Sigma can offer as much promise for improving a service process as it does for a manufacturing process. A defect in a service process might be defined as too long a delay company response to a customer inquiry or the occurrence of a call center representative speaking in an unprofessional way to a customer.

The Six Sigma approach helps an organization achieve superior performance and improved profitability by applying several specialized skill sets to streamline operations. Those skill sets include process analysis, statistical measurement, and group facilitation. The success of Six Sigma also relies on a handful of key principles. With the introduction of Six Sigma into a company's approach to process improvement, the leader of a learning organization is more likely to achieve gains faster and more effectively because of the emphasis on those key principles—two of which are merely included in other process improvement methods but not with the intensity of Six Sigma: namely, metrics and control.

A focus on metrics, also known as measurements, is crucial to the success of a Six Sigma program. A process or activity cannot be improved if it has not been measured. In fact, that process cannot be completely understood or even properly discussed unless someone can explain to the group the latest measurements concerning the activities that make up the process. Metrics are sometimes known as *key measures* or *quantified parameters* within a department or division of a company. Metrics give an organization a framework for charting its course, the ability to plan how to get there, and a worthy cause for which the team can rally. The backbone of an effective business dialogue should be centered on a set of numeric goals and objectives, to make it known how close the organization is coming to achieving them. This provides context for a discussion about what the group is doing or not doing to fulfill the plan and offers very valuable insight and lessons for business success.

When a process or activity is measured in an organization, the leadership is then poised to realize savings or increased revenue because options are identified and quantified. Comparisons can then be made between the current process or activity and a similar one in another department, company, or industry. Such comparative benchmarking provides powerful results because it usually spurs the competitive nature of a workforce to strive to be "better" or perhaps even to be "the best" or sometimes motivates people to avoid being perceived as inferior or low-quality producers. It is also the measuring of an activity or process that allows realistic goals to be set and pursued.

An effective Six Sigma initiative can help an organization identify processes that truly add value and will move everyone and every activity closer to the customer and the customer's needs. Just like any commitment to improvement or change, the support for a Six Sigma program has to be solid at the top. Though the top leaders do not need to be experts in Six Sigma, they certainly must support those spear-heading process improvement as well as the troops who are making it happen.

Executives and business leaders have come to love the results produced by Six Sigma because this approach also enables them to make decisions that are fact-based and data-driven. For example, Jack Welch has claimed that General Electric saved billions of dollars by using Six Sigma.[1] Six Sigma helps an organization achieve superior results by removing the inconsistency in any process, and it ensures that the work being done meets requirements that are critical to quality. The discipline of Six Sigma enables management and the workforce to determine performance and quality standards in advance and then empowers people to achieve them. IT plays an important role in the Six Sigma approach but is limited to the improvement activities as an enabler to better business performance, which ensures that all IT investment is done wisely. Therefore, money will

---

1. "Revealed at Last: The Secret of Jack Welch's Success." Forbes Online. http://www.forbes.com/forbes/1998/0126/6102044a_print.html. 11/8/01

be spent on automation only if it results in business process improvement that is measurable and has organizational value.

Statistically speaking, the main purpose of Six Sigma is to reduce variation. Variation is considered to be the enemy. The goal of Six Sigma is to achieve a process that produces only very small variations to the extent that the organization is able to meet or exceed the expectations of the customer. The term *sigma* is the Greek letter used to represent in statistics how much variation there is in a set of data points known as *standard deviation*. Six Sigma focuses on standard variation because there is an inherent problem with the measurement of "average": it often masks problems that you would want to be aware of in a process.

By way of example in the process of a pizza delivery service, the goal of Six Sigma improvement for the delivery process would be to reduce the number of defects, defined as early or late arrivals at the customer's home, to be no more than 3.4 deliveries out of every million pizzas delivered. The terms commonly used in a Six Sigma initiative include the letter Y to represent the outcome of a process, in this case the pizza delivery time. The X's are the causes or contributing factors to the outcome Y. X's for the pizza delivery service might include staff size at the time of delivery, the number of ovens in the capacity, time of the day due to busy cycles, what the subprocess is to estimate the time it takes to drive to the destination, the factors affecting when the delivery person can leave for a delivery, and so forth.

Six Sigma is a very powerful approach because it listens to the two most important voices and avoids bias and subjectivity of politics, agendas, and assumptions of the past. Those voices include the "Voice of the Customer (VOC) and the "Voice of the Data." Secondly, Six Sigma is all about a proper investigation or exploration into what's really going on. A good Six Sigma consultant or project team will not be afraid to say that they don't yet know how to solve the problem at hand. The right approach is to just focus for now on figuring out exactly what the problems are and what is the root cause of those problems. People in corporate life are afraid to admit that they don't yet have a solution when discussing an issue. Because of that discomfort, we have a business culture that races to a solution prematurely or assume they know what the problem is. This is indeed a very dangerous alternative to the most significant benefit of Six Sigma, which is true process knowledge and permanent solutions, an investment of time well worth it because millions of dollars are at stake.

# ▶ An Overview of the DMAIC Framework

The process improvement framework of Six Sigma is called DMAIC (pronounced *duh-may-ick*) and is an acronym for define, measure, analyze, improve, and control. The DMAIC framework is a very simple yet effective roadmap to moving an organization or department within a company to higher levels of performance. The five steps of DMAIC should be worked in a circular fashion, with an underlying assumption that the project team will frequently compare the latest performance of a process against the original performance level on a numeric basis. The leaders of any organization can improve a business process within the scope of its supply chain by applying the DMAIC framework of Six Sigma with the other powerful tools offered by Six Sigma.

- **Define:** Six Sigma's DMAIC starts with clearly identifying the scope and goals of an initiative. It is quite amazing how many companies have not yet defined their core processes involving so many factors that directly impact customer satisfaction. A Voice of the Customer exercise often proves to be very powerful and tends to provide an early guideline to what the main gaps are in the current process. This step also provides insight into what the requirements will be for a delighted customer, and in certain circumstances, knowledge about your competitors comes to light. This can be accomplished with a simple journalistic approach, including some basic yet meaningful questions. A SIPOC diagram is a tool used in the Six Sigma methodology to identify all relevant elements of a process improvement project. It may also help define a complex project that may not be well scoped. SIPOC stands for supplier, inputs, process, outputs and customer. A "Current" Process Map is a hierarchical method for displaying processes to illustrate how things get done. It is a visual representation of the workflow either within a process or of the whole operation. A "stakeholder" is an individual who will be affected by the business process or can influence it. The "Voice of the Customer (VOC)" is a process used to capture the requirements/feedback from the customer (internally or externally) to determine what attributes are required of the process to provide the customers with the best-in-class service or product quality.

- **Measure:** Defining process steps is not sufficient to understand what is going on in the business. It is also necessary to quantify the key aspects within a framework of priorities that outlines the biggest impact to the customer. This is the opportunity to set performance benchmarks for the process under scrutiny. Most companies find out that the things they have been measuring are not the right things, and this is a common setback on Six Sigma projects. The corrective action would be to redefine the data measurement plan and then take time again to capture data for the relevant metrics. The "Critical to Quality (CTQ)" factors are the key measurable characteristics of a product or process whose performance standards or specification limits must be met in order to satisfy the customer. They align improvement or design efforts with customer requirements.

- **Analyze:** Most modern managers and executives think they know the answer to a process question in all cases; however, the discipline of Six Sigma pressures a project team to take a real look at the underlying facts and data. If the sponsorship of a Six Sigma program is sincere about its desire to reap the value of this approach, then the leadership must give the proper time, attention, and resources to the project team and not just to gathering data but also to analyzing it in full. This doesn't imply that the project has to become an overly quantitative exercise—it just has to be appropriately quantitative. A few basic statistical tools can go a long way, and this is the chance to be play detective. There is nothing wrong with allowing relevant parties (i.e., stakeholders) who are interested to inspect the data and have open discussions about what the data is saying, also known as "Voice of the Data." This is the sure-fire way to identify the root causes of problems for the business process in question. Once the parameters are identified and measured, then the current performance is documented and the process baseline gets marked with key metrics. Now the process investigator is in a good position to analyze the root causes in order to see opportunities for improvement. The key to success is to select the few factors for the improve step that will have the most significant impact.

- **Improve:** This step has three distinct activities—to contemplate solutions to root cause issues, to select the appropriate solution alternatives, and to implement the solution. This step incorporates the process development life cycle, with a special focus on managing the change to the process, especially the human aspects of it. Additionally, a review of best practices in the industry helps the company set benchmarks for the target improvement area (i.e., performance levels for the organization's process improvement). The immediate results of all improvement actions are also reviewed.

- **Control:** This is the part of the DMAIC framework that closes the loop and brings long-term sustainable value. This step is all about comparing the new process results to the original process results and then managing the organization to sustain the new process or make adjustments where necessary. Where the results of the entire cycle are reviewed, a process status is communicated to interest groups, and the cycle continues with a review of the process for additional improvement. This step, if done correctly, sets up an ongoing pressure for someone to continually monitor the key metrics that are now implemented within an improved process. This means that it is part of someone's regular job to review the data for measures identified as important to success and must include both outcome measures, Y, and the X's that drive the Y.

# ▶ Case Study of One Company's Six Sigma Success

In this discussion, we illustrate the DMAIC framework of Six Sigma by way of a business case involving a large commercial insurance brokerage house.

The insurance industry that serves commercial insurance to small and medium-sized businesses has become much more complex in the past 20 years. Each carrier in the marketplace has determined that the key to success is being able to offer a comprehensive set of product offerings with limits, deductibles, and coverages that can be adapted to each individual company's needs. Insurance brokerage companies are also offering an ever-widening range of financial products through constantly expanding distribution relationships and specialty offerings. This has caused the job of a commercial insurance broker to become quite complex and adds a much heavier burden of informational analysis and strategy to the broker's role than was the norm in previous years. While the strength of the relationship for the broker with the policyholder (i.e., the customer) is still crucial for brokerage success, the ability to recognize and implement value-add program alternatives on behalf of the customer has become equally as important.

Despite the improvements made recently in information systems, the typical steps of a commercial insurance broker have gotten quite unwieldy and cause time lags in meeting the customer requirement of being responsive. Keeping a broker's workload and staff support levels to an optimal amount is only one way that insurance brokerages attempt to improve customer satisfaction while simultaneously increasing their commission on a deal. Today's customers demand a positive service experience—accurate, thorough, and responsive—every time. If that doesn't happen, then commercial customers do not hesitate to switch to a different insurance broker.

As part of this case study, we examine the operations of a mid-sized insurance brokerage house. As with all Six-Sigma initiatives, our project team needed to first define the overall business goal of the project: to increase customer satisfaction by reducing the job response time, Y, for current-account renewals processing. We were on a quest to understand and reduce the variation in Y and would be considered successful if we identified the root causes of variation and slowness in response time and if we could provide solutions for those root causes.

First, our team of Six Sigma professionals defined the scope of the problem by developing the Problem/Opportunity worksheet on which we drew boundaries around the problem and any existing or latent opportunities. Then, we created a Project Charter to establish project parameters—time, budget, resource, and so on—and followed it by a stakeholder analysis to determine how key process owners would be impacted by the new solution. Next, we conducted a Voice of the Customer study that included key internal and external customers to determine the needs of the market and hunt for differentiation opportunities. This exercise helped reveal that reducing the job response time Y would lead to several tangible benefits, as follows:

- Enable the broker and the carrier to ward off competitors in their attempts to the steal the business.
- Delight the broker with an increased ability to service policyholders by being able to respond faster to their needs.

- Enable the broker to still pursue other ways to serve its policy-holders if the carrier decides to turn down a piece of business being proposed.
- Provide the broker with more time to ask questions and get more underwriting information, which in turn supports better decision making by the carrier in tough cases.
- Provide the broker with more time to pursue business on behalf of the carrier.
- Free up the broker's time to better leverage its strengths of marketing and selling to produce new business opportunities rather than spending time on tracking the status of approval requests.

Next, we conducted an in-depth current business process mapping to reveal clues in the process/operations (the way business is conducted on a day-to-day basis) about the higher-than-acceptable job response time (Figure 13.1). The triangles in the diagram identify the deficiencies, which get documented in a table to show the severity and an associated recommendation.

Finally, as part of the Define stage, our professionals created a set of key process requirements considered to be the CTQ factors to ensure that the solution improves the primary problem while maintaining or

**Current Process Diagram**

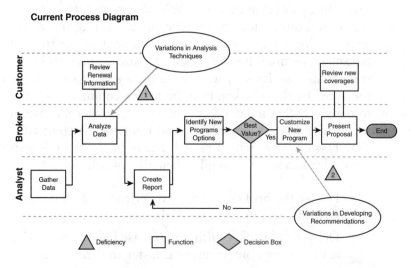

**Figure 13.1** Current business process map.

improving performance across the board. Even at such an early stage, our team began to suspect a positive correlation between the commercial brokers' ability to derive value-add programs custom made for the policyholder and the customer's degree of happiness.

As part of these activities, we identified the most important measures and drivers that will help us solve the business problem. Our professionals measured the response time Y from the current process to get a current snapshot with a corresponding sigma level for how things are operating at present. We described the current standard for response time and created the following data gathering plan:

- Stated performance (i.e., as advertised or claimed)
- Level of performance that underwriters perceive
- Actual performance using facts and data
- Targeted level of performance (i.e., goals at present)

This approach also helped us establish performance target levels as well as determine the difference between discrete (yes/no, groupings, etc.) and continuous data (dollars and time). Our team then used the CTQ Tree developed during the process-mapping exercise to determine and measure the possible causes(X's) that contribute to a higher-than-acceptable response time (Y). From a preliminary interview with the underwriting department, the following is a sample list of X's that seemed to have the strongest effect on Y:

- Renewal request as compared to broker experience—size of account (small: less than $10 million; medium: $10 to $25 million; high: more than $25 million); territory/location; type of work; and project size.
- Completeness of policy information on file for that account— salary survey, business liability narratives, self-audit results, 3-year financials, references, credit reports, pricing adjustments, risk mitigation factors.
- Broker work volume—business cycles, bid activity, travel, account maintenance, and so on.
- Carrier appetite for this business—experience, loss ratio, and so on.
- Brokerage capacity at present—management competency, number of resources, technology, and so on.

- Broker's urgency—competition, renewal due date, availability, and so on.

These data were collected using the "current" process as the source of facts, to shed light on the root-cause drivers. The specific goal of this phase was to search for root causes and then investigate them to verify what X's were suspected as guilty, which would set up the project team for success in determining possible improvements. In our project scope, the data for key process steps was collected for the eight commercial insurance brokers in the office. Some of the descriptive statistics for each process step are included in the Table 13.1.

**Table 13.1** Potential Cost Savings

|  | Data Gather | Data Analysis | Create Reports | Identify New Program | Customize Program | Total |
|---|---|---|---|---|---|---|
| **Current Process** | – | – | – | – | – | – |
| **Average Process** | 2.5 | 3.6 | 2.1 | 2 | 1.7 | 11.9 |
| **Median Process** | 2 | 3.5 | 2 | 1.5 | 1.5 | 10.5 |
| **Mode Process** | 2 | 1 | 2 | 1 | 1 | 7 |
| **Optimal Process** | 0 | 2 | 0.5 | 0.5 | 0.5 | 3.5 |

Our consultants used a combination of several tools and customized templates such as Pareto charts, more detailed process maps, deficiency analyses, and regression analyses to discover patterns and statistical contrasts in the data. Upon data verification of the suspected root causes for slow response time, the team performed some further analysis on the wide variations that exist in the "current" process time durations consumed for the steps of data analysis and customize program.

The team pursued improvement opportunities that would deliver the maximum value with the least cost. We concluded that the company could realize a tremendous savings if just the variation of the process times across brokers could be minimized. By all eight brokers conforming to merely the mode for each step (i.e., to follow what most of the group is doing for time duration at each step, not even improving the process overall!), the company could achieve an accumulated savings over a calendar year in the amount of 2,335 hours. This is illustrated in the chart in Figure 13.2.

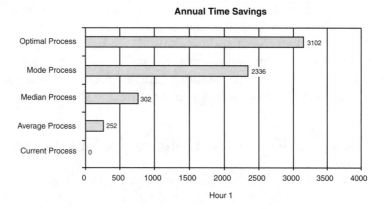

**Figure 13.2** Annual time savings.

This offered the company a clear and low-cost path to a positive ROI by simply creating standard procedures for these process steps and implementing training. With the conservative assumptions of an average hourly value for a broker's time at $50, then 2,335 × $50 will result in $116,750 of savings for the company.

The project team then conducted a technology solutions analysis, which identifies relevant solution alternatives in the marketplace as compared with automation opportunities to drive accuracy, faster turnaround, and lower costs for the company. These comparisons of the company's technology needs versus the marketplace will save management time in future RFP phases and will help the company to establish a baseline for a detailed business case on IT upgrades and implementation projects.

The project team used this information to propose other projects with a positive ROI that would involve implementing better IT tools and systems to support the broker and the analysts who assist the brokers. As part of this project, our consultants then determined how ongoing operations are to be monitored at all levels of the process and business, with appropriate control monitors defined for every level. During the control activities of DMAIC, it is important to measure the performance levels of the new business process for key metrics on a regular basis and to identify any additional ongoing metrics to monitor the continued effectiveness of the improved state.

Our team established a standard process improvement procedure in which we documented the lessons learned and the steps taken to improve the process and maintain the gains by standardizing processes. The management also planned to establish a strategy for controlling further improvements or solutions to this process and, together with the project team, they created recommended next steps and future plans.

## Why a CIO Should Utilize a Six Sigma Approach

So many leaders of America's biggest corporations have proven success in their process improvement programs through the adoption of Six Sigma, and so doesn't it follow that there is value contained within it for small and mid-sized companies? Six Sigma provides a company with a deliberate method to set out and find the root causes of waste, duplication of effort, or gaps. This positions a management team for success through making adjustments that will most likely eliminate those problems or take advantage of the newly discovered opportunities.

A Six Sigma approach always starts with the customer in mind—whether that's an internal or external customer—and with a proper look at the process, enables a leader to get his or her hands around the elements that have the most impact on customer satisfaction. It makes sense, of course, to set performance targets with an acceptable spectrum of parameters so that the organization can achieve a series of small successes that add up to a big win in the long run.

It's one thing to initiate a discipline of doing a business case on projects before a company division such as IT goes down the path of implementation. It is entirely another thing to assure that the other executives are brought into that path early on so that the organization demonstrates a full commitment to achieving success. Most companies don't even define the criteria for success along the way of a project, much less at the outset! It is this pattern that leads to wasted value of IT investment. To be in a position to define a criteria for success, also known as the definition of success for a particular project, a leader must ask this very question—early and often: How will we know we're done? In other words, what is the definition of what we'll agree on as having been successful? Partial failure is okay. Some failure is good because it is actually what allows an organization to learn. If there is no time made to do a lessons-learned session at the end of an initiative, then the organization cannot wholeheartedly learn from its mistakes and improve for the next go around. It also would not be able to repeat its successes, thereby missing out on the immense value of reuse. It would be like raising a small child without ever recognizing the learning opportunities. How many of us have a child who grows to full maturity without ever having any failures? Therefore, the absence of failures, a lack of admittance of mistakes, and the absence of at least a minimalist lessons-learned process demonstrates that something is truly deficient deep in the organization's core. And it is the understanding of a business process that is the key to defining your success criteria for making changes.

Although there are many different approaches and methodologies for process improvement, and most of them follow a similar pattern of problem definition, assessing the current, identifying gaps, designing improvements, and implementing them, it is rare to find an approach that is as powerful as Six Sigma. Some of the most valuable benefits for a CIO include the following:

- Positive return on IT investment for projects that are well-defined
- Organizational visibility
- High degree of executive comprehension
- IT investment agreement from senior management
- Clear method for defining a project's success
- Solid foundation for declaring an IT success along with metrics to prove it
- Buy-in of key stakeholders, including board members, customers, system users, vendors, and IT staff members

Adopting the discipline of Six Sigma for the purpose of improving business processes is one way to guarantee a better outcome for every dollar a CIO spends on IT. This approach ensures a better chance of success for IT projects and increases the likelihood of success for the systems developed and implemented. It ensures that both the executive team and the IT team truly understand the process for why IT exists. The artifacts created during the DMAIC life cycle formulate the foundation as well as the realization for the business case that can be communicated to any or all stakeholders. For those initiatives that involve vendor software packages, this approach sets the CIO up for success with the creation of a judicious system for package evaluation and selection.

A Six Sigma approach documents the current condition, identifies metrics to measure against, identifies the root causes of problems, and builds a shared understanding of what is possible. A CIO can now lead the stakeholders through discussions about future states and is now well-positioned to work together to select the best organizational choices, is able to manage the organizational change, and can easily monitor results. The Six Sigma approach lends an objective and normally independent view of the underlying process, and if changes are carried through organizationally, then the company and its CIO now have their fingers on the pulse of the organization's key vital life signs as well as measurable results.

If just one executive falls in love with the techniques and power of Six Sigma, then gaining some degree of value for the organization is inevitable. The DMAIC framework helps to rally the management team around a table with a common cause of mitigating or eliminating the enemies of success. It arms those managers with the tools to execute corrective actions that are based on real evidence instead of a "gut feeling," thus enabling fact-based decisions. All executives are under constant fire about how much they are spending, and it is demanded that they reveal how much benefit they were able to derive from those expenditures. Six Sigma, along with the DMAIC framework provides, a proven methodology for having that conversation, and not just once but on a continual basis.

## ▶ References

"Revealed at Last: The Secret of Jack Welch's Success." Forbes Online. http://www.forbes.com/forbes/1998/0126/6102044a_print.html. 11/8/01.

# The Five Ws of IT Outsourcing[1]

*Phillip A. Laplante, Pawan Singh, Sudi Bindiganavile,*
*Thomas Costello, and Mark Landon*

Outsourcing of IT functions has become so pervasive over the last several years that IT managers and CIOs cannot ignore it. For example, Gartner Dataquest has projected that the IT outsourcing market will reach $159.6 billion in revenues by 2005 (Sykes 2003). Yet in many cases outsourced IT projects have failed. For example, in one study, IT managers reported only a 33 percent satisfaction with outsourced IT services as compared with a satisfaction rate of 70 percent to 80 percent for non-IT services (King 2001).

To complicate the matter, outsourcing to other countries has become increasingly popular. There are a number of advantages to this type of outsourcing, including cost savings, 24/7 operations, and access to highly specialized skills. Yet a strategic alliance with a remote and foreign partner presents its own unique problems.

---

1. Reprinted with permission from Phillip A. Laplante, Pawan Singh, Sudi Bindiganavile, Tom Costello, and Mark Landon, "The Who, What, Where, Why, and When of IT Outsourcing," *IT Professional*, January/February, pp. 37–41, 2004.

Therefore, the strategic question of whether to outsource or not to outsource is one that is not to be undertaken lightly nor avoided. The strategic decision can be made, however, by analyzing your responses to the following five key questions—the five Ws:

1. What is outsourcing?
2. Why outsource?
3. Who should outsource?
4. Where should you outsource?
5. When should you outsource?

The remainder of this article is focused on the answers to these questions and a discussion of how to outsource once the decision is made to do it.


# ▶ What?

The first question to be answered is, What is outsourcing? "Outsourcing is the use of external agents to perform activities that were previously performed within the organization" (King 2001). Classic examples include electrical component manufacturing and perhaps the earliest form of information processing outsourcing—payroll processing.

For the IT organization, there are two kinds of outsourcing: IT outsourcing and business process outsourcing (Kobitzsch 2001). By IT outsourcing, we mean outsourcing the development of relatively large software development projects. For example, hiring a few consultants to serve as internal members of the IT organization is not really IT outsourcing.

Business process outsourcing, on the other hand, can include outsourcing of a call center or help desk function or even the computer security function. While the third possibility might raise some eyebrows, there are some justifications for this kind of outsourcing. Schneier (2002) notes that, in general, outsourced functions have one of three characteristics: they are complex, they are important, or they are distasteful. Computer security reflects all three characteristics. Moreover, computer security is the kind of domain in which only the most expert knowledge is really helpful—knowledge that is generally only available from very specialized companies or a few experts.

# ▶ Why?

Why should an organization outsource? IT outsourcing is generally done for cost savings, to achieve a better focus on the core business, or because the internal IT function is considered to be inefficient, ineffective, or incompetent (King 2001). From an economic standpoint, if an IT activity can be considered a commodity, then there is little justification for performing that activity internally. In these cases, a focused vendor should be able to provide the service at a higher level of quality, lower cost, or both (King 2001). In other words, outsourcing takes advantage of the economies of scale of another business that specializes in that domain.

One study proposed that firms choose to outsource as the costs and disadvantages of the traditional permanent employment arrangement become prohibitive because of increasing technological and environmental change (Slaughter 1996). The study further notes that outsourcing provides firms with increasing flexibility.

# ▶ Who?

Who should outsource? This question is actually a composite of two questions: What kind of organization (who) should outsource? and To whom should you outsource?

## Who Should Outsource?

So, who should outsource? It is perhaps easier to answer the question, Who should *not* outsource?

There is myth that outsourcing is cheap. It is not. Even in India, where the perceived difference in relative economy would suggest a lower labor cost, the cost of a skilled developer is $25 per hour.

In most cases, vendors will only take on large to very large projects—making outsourcing less accessible to smaller IT organizations.

Finally, in all cases, a strong communication infrastructure is needed to make it work. The infrastructure costs could include significant domestic and international travel, telecommunications costs, providing specialized equipment to the vendor, and so on.

Therefore, it is easy to conclude that outsourcing is generally not for very small organizations.

## To Whom Should You Outsource?

The next "who" question to be considered is, To whom should you outsource?

In answering this question, consider that you are transferring knowledge when you outsource. This knowledge can be valuable. It is possible that a vendor can cut-and-run after the outsourcing project is completed—and nondisclosure or noncompete agreements are more difficult to prosecute if the outsourced vendor is not based in the United States. Therefore, the vendor must be a trusted one.

In choosing a vendor, you also must be very careful about protecting your brand both through accountability for the actions of and by transference of the reputation of the vendor. One example of non-IT outsourcing gone wrong recounts the outsourcing of toll-free–call answering for a travel bureau for a particular eastern state. The call center was actually based at a women's prison within the state. While there is nothing wrong in providing work for the inmates, and they apparently provided excellent service, when word leaked that potential travelers to the state were consulting with convicts, it hurt tourism for a time, particularly because this state had a reputation for a high crime rate.

Outsourcing overseas is becoming increasingly popular. Australia, India, Ireland, New Zealand, and former Soviet Bloc countries like Bulgaria and Russia, to name just a few, have become favorite destinations for American IT projects. But in dealing with other vendors overseas, a number of issues have to be investigated. For example, is the vendor competent and reliable?

Attention must be paid to the legal organization of the potential of the vendor. For example, a vendor that is organized as a subsidiary of another company can be disconnected in the event of a lawsuit, making it difficult to obtain remedies in the case of malpractice. Similarly, disputes with an overseas vendor might be more difficult to resolve because of cultural differences and because legal remedies are more complicated and more costly to obtain.

Whether the outsourcing is domestic or foreign, the chemistry and culture of the vendor and client have to mix.

Remember that the vendors to whom you outsource should view your company as a partner, not as a client to be milked. Table 14.1 summarizes some differences between a vendor looking for a sale and a partner looking for a long-term, collaborative relationship.

**Table 14.1** Choosing a Partner

| Criteria | Vendor | Partner |
|---|---|---|
| Value added services | Hit and run | Only where in the interests of the partner (customer) |
| Executive involvement | When problems develop | Continuous |
| Project management | Command and control | Collaborative |
| Financial approach | Sees revenue | Sees opportunity |

*Source:* Adapted from Charles Gearhards, "Achieving Success Through Effective Public/Private Sector Partnerships," presentation to the CIO Institute, November 2002, Malvern, Pennsylvania.

# ▶ Where?

Where in the enterprise should outsourcing be used? A commonly held view on where to use outsourcing is one that is similar to the economic notion that the market does not pay a company for diversifying risk.

Analogously, the market does not pay a company for doing things outside its core business. A straightforward interpretation of this statement is that any IT function of a business that is not part of its core is a candidate for outsourcing.

For example, ERP systems may not be a company's specialty and therefore can likely be outsourced. On the other hand, a company such as Wal-Mart may require an ERP that can predict consumer behavior, which is therefore within its core business and hence not suitable for outsourcing (Figure 14.1). It is therefore incumbent on the IT manager to understand what part of the IT function lies within the core.

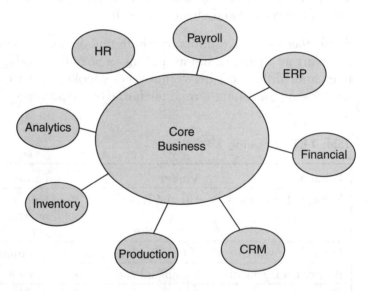

**Figure 14.1** Identification of core business as opposed to non-core business IT functions. IT functions that are outside of the core business might be considered for outsourcing.

Any IT function outside the core business might be considered for outsourcing. However, just because the function is outside of the core does not necessarily mean that the function should be outsourced (Figure 14.2).

For example, in cases where the benefit is low, there is no need to outsource. In cases where the benefit is high and the function is not within

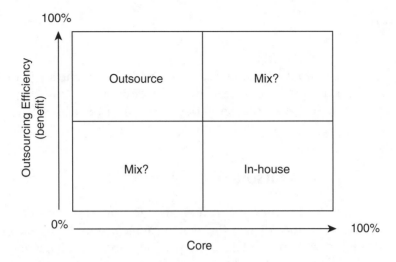

**Figure 14.2** The decision to outsource or not is based both on whether the IT function is within the core and whether there is a benefit to outsourcing (efficiency).

the core business, there is a strong incentive to outsource. However, when the function is outside of core but the potential outsourcing benefit is low or when the potential outsourcing benefit is high but the function is within the core business, there is some judgment to be made.

Furthermore, consider that today's core function might be tomorrow's auxiliary. The converse might also be true. Foresight, then, might suggest that a core IT function could potentially be outsourced if it is envisioned that it will not remain within the core. Nor would a non-core function be outsourced if there is some perceived benefit in performing that function in-house, gaining domain expertise, and then incorporating that function into the core business.

There is an opposing view on outsourcing, however. Some IT managers believe that they should only outsource those aspects of the IT operation that they know well so that they are not at a disadvantage in negotiating the contract and in managing the delivery process. Conversely, then, those who hold this viewpoint might not outsource something outside of their core—even if there is economic benefit to doing so.

# ▶ When?

When should outsourcing be done and at what stage of the process? You usually recognize you need to outsource, and then it is too late. Therefore, the decision to outsource must be made early, and you must analyze the cost-benefit ratio of waiting too long to decide.

## How to Outsource

Many companies fail in the execution of strategic outsourcing. There are a number of ways in which they can fail—for example, organization culture mismatches. In addition, morale damage may occur due to any layoffs that might be involved.

Another reason for failure is outsourcing for the wrong reasons. For example, outsourcing cannot absolve you of your responsibility. You can't outsource your problems.

There are several standard methodologies for outsourced software development. For example, consider the three-tier model (Figure 14.3). The figure depicts a recommended distribution of outsourced work in which 10 percent of the work is held closely and performed onsite by vendor's staff under close supervision. Twenty percent of the effort is also done onsite by a combination of vendor and in-house staff under normal supervision. The remaining 70 percent of the project is done entirely offsite by the vendor.

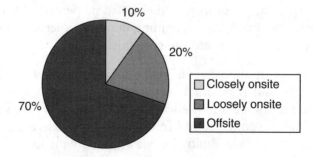

**Figure 14.3** A three-tier strategy for outsourcing.

When outsourced work is performed offsite, it is critical your own agent is at the site of the outsourcing. A good rule of thumb is to have one of your staff for every 20 staff working offsite. The rule of 20 is largely based on the incremental cost of housing an agent offshore to supervise the work.

One other consideration: outsourcing can be a learning endeavor. It might seem rather mercenary to bring in a vendor outsource to learn from, and then jettison a vendor, but this is a risk that the vendors understand and factor into their margins.

The following best practices and rules of thumb are suggested.

1. Whether the project is outsourced domestically or overseas, have your own agent at the vendor's site: one agent for every 20 persons outsourced.
2. For costing purposes, we have found that overseas projects cost about $25 per hour, U.S. projects $75 per hour.
3. When negotiating the contract and throughout the project life cycle, carefully set expectations.
4. Have a quality management infrastructure in place.
5. In the case of overseas outsourcing, take into account language, culture, and time differences.

For each successful project, there was a detailed process of project definition and specification development. This ensured that the project methodology, scope, schedule, and deliverables were unambiguously defined and understood by both parties. Contract negotiations served as a mechanism for building shared understanding (Heeks 2001).

# ▶ Conclusion

Outsourcing is not for the faint of heart and does not fit most situations. However, in those cases where outsourcing fits, with proper supervision and careful attention to expectations and details, it can provide a significant business advantage.

# References

Gearhards, C., 2002. "Achieving Success Through Effective Public/Private Sector Partnerships," presentation to the CIO Institute, November, Malvern, PA.

Gurbaxani, V., 1996. "The New World of Information Technology Outsourcing." *Communications of the ACM*, 39(7), 45–46, July.

Heeks, R., S. Krishna, B. Nicholsen, and S. Sahay, 2001. "Synching or Sinking: Global Software Outsourcing Relationships." *IEEE Software*, 18(2), 54–60, March–April.

King, W. R., 2001. "Developing a Sourcing Strategy for IS: A Behavioral Decision Process and Framework." *IEEE Transactions on Engineering Management*, 48(1), 15 –24, February.

Kobitzsch, W., D. Rombach, and R. L. Feldmann, 2001. "Outsourcing in India: Software Development." *IEEE Software*, 18(2), 78–86, March–April.

Lakenan, B., D. Boyd, and E. Frey, 2001. "Why Outsourcing and Its Perils." *Strategy & Competition*, 24, 54–65.

Schneier, B., 2002. "The Case for Outsourcing Security." *Computer*, 35(4), 20–21, 26, April.

Slaughter, S., and S. Ang, 1996. "Employment Outsourcing in Information Systems." *Communications of the ACM*, 39(7), 47–54, July.

Sykes.com, 2002. "North American IT Outsourcing Industry to Experience Continued Growth Through 2005." Available: http://www.sykes.com/english/news_it_growth.asp. Last accessed March 7, 2003.

# 15

# Outsourced Environments

*Raghvinder S. Sangwan*

## ▶ Introduction

Outsourcing software development has gathered pace in recent years with Gartner and Forrester Research predicting this trend to continue to rise(Reich 2003). Most of the software is being outsourced from the United States and Europe for development in India, China, and eastern European nations where labor rates are low. The distributed nature of such development, however, exacerbates the problem of clearly and unambiguously communicating information between collaborating teams, making it difficult to coordinate tasks and enforce common goals, policies, standards, and quality levels(Carmel & Agarwal 2001). It is therefore no surprise that many outsourced projects fail to deliver quality products within budget on time(Kharif 2003). This chapter examines some of the challenges faced by outsourced projects and suggests ways to manage software development in outsourced environments.

# ▶ Challenges of Outsourcing

Although cost reduction plays a big part in its business justification, a number of other important factors lead to outsourcing of software development. A corporation may acquire an offshore company to add to its suite of products within a product line or for local market presence. Under such circumstances, the expertise for the product lies with the acquired company and is not easily transferable to the acquiring company. A corporation may also seek partnership with an offshore company if it lacks experience with the new technologies or expertise in a given domain. Sometimes, it is simply the shortage of staff and the time-to-market pressures forcing a company to do more development in parallel.

While outsourcing can help reduce cost, shorten the time to market; take advantage of the global economy; and bring together the best minds for innovation, technical skills, local market, or domain know-how, it is not without risks.

Time zone differences and distance make it difficult to control and coordinate the work of collaborating teams. While technologies such as email, net meeting, and videoconferencing can help, research shows they are not as effective as face-to-face meetings(Carmel & Agarwal 2001). One way, therefore, to overcome this difficulty is to have teams work as independently as possible and minimize the communication and coordination required between them (Battin et al. 2001). This can be achieved by breaking up the system into loosely coupled subsystems with a shared underlying architecture akin to a product line (Ebert & De Neve 2001; Martin 1995).

There must, however, be a single organization that owns the requirements for the system under consideration, its underlying architecture, and the specification of its subsystems (Repenning et al. 2001). This organization is responsible for distributing the development of these subsystems, their continuous build, and testing to avoid integration headaches (Fowler 2003; Simons 2002). Without such an entity, there will be a lack of control on the schedule and quality of the product being developed.

Team building can also be challenging in a distributed environment. While it is true that technical communication is more likely to occur between team members if they are located within 10 meters of each other, beyond 100 meters, further separation becomes immaterial (Allen 1977); over larger distances, because individuals do not know each other, cultural and language barriers make it even harder for teams to communicate(Ebert & De Neve 2001). Therefore, considerable effort must be made to create a shared project vision, build cooperation. and establish trust. A way to achieve this is to require some individuals to straddle multiple teams. These individuals, if involved early in the development process, can become familiar with the architecture and domain of the system under consideration and act as liaisons or ambassadors, helping with team building, answering domain- or architecture-related questions, and bridging the communication gap (Battin et al. 2001; Fowler 2003). There is, however, a risk that if an organization is not careful with expertise it shares, it may potentially lose its core competencies to its outsourced partners.

Tool vendors for distributed projects must be asked to provide international support, which may require coordinating all support activities through the central organization that tracks and reports all team issues (Battin et al. 2001).

# ▶ Managing Outsourced Projects

There are many different models for outsourced development (Cockburn 2002). *Multisite* development occurs in a relatively few locations with complete teams at each site responsible for developing a well-defined subsystem. *Offshore* development involves designers in one location sending specifications and tests to programmers in another country. The offshore locations lack architects, subject matter experts, designers, and testers. *Distributed* development has many small teams spread across many locations around the world. Development continues around the clock with daily communication among collaborating team members. This type of development, therefore, has been characterized as the "sun never sets" development (Chidamber & Kemerer 1994).

No matter what the model, an outsourced project has to be carefully planned, organized and monitored in order to be successful. In the sections that follow, we look at the planning, organization, and monitoring aspects of such projects.

# Planning

The following questions and related concerns are significant during the planning effort(Lakos 1996; Strigel & Wolfgang 2004):

- **Who Should Outsource?** While cost reduction is a significant motivator, outsourcing is not cheap. Apart from the labor rates, significant cost can be incurred in travel and telecommunications. In addition, a strong communication infrastructure is required to achieve effective collaboration. It can therefore be challenging for small IT organizations to benefit from outsourcing.

- **To Whom Should They Outsource?** The supplier should be a reliable and competent partner looking for a long-term relationship. A partner is one whose executive involvement is continuous and not absent when problems develop, whose project management style is collaborative rather than command and control, and who sees the outsourcing relationship as an opportunity and not a source of revenue.

  Besides the skill set and knowledge, the supplier organization should be able to manage the size of the development operation. It should be fiscally sound so as to not cut corners due to its financial condition. It should provide a dedicated development team and possibly a shadow team for added protection against turnover of key personnel. The supplier should also have a defined development process with possible ISO or SEI-CMM accreditation.

- **What Projects Should Be Outsourced?** Innovative projects carry high risk due to unstable requirements. Highly iterative tasks such as user interface design require a lot of interaction, creating a significant communication overhead. Suitable projects for outsourcing, therefore, are those requiring little or no innovation and minimal collaboration, domain expertise, and dependencies on other projects. Such projects have stable requirements and clear acceptance criteria and performance expectations. Projects involving an organization's core competency must never be considered for outsourcing.

- **What Is the Right Phase of the Project to Outsource?** Earlier phases of a project involve requirements engineering, architecture description, and system design, activities requiring considerable creativity and domain expertise. The later phases dealing with coding, testing, and maintenance are relatively less creative. These are therefore more suitable for outsourcing and can also offer significant savings because they also happen to be more labor intensive.

Once these concerns have been addressed and a decision made to outsource, a process needs to be established for product development. A standard software product development process can be adapted to the needs of outsourced environments. Such a process has four significant stages in the development lifecycle (Royce 1998). The *inception phase* is the vision milestone phase wherein the problem under consideration and its potential solutions are investigated to determine feasibility of the project. Once considered feasible, the project enters into the *elaboration phase*. This is the core architecture milestone phase wherein requirements are prioritized and those deemed architecturally significant implemented first. At the end of the elaboration phase a fairly reliable software development plan is put into place, and the *construction phase* of the software begins. This phase is the operational capability milestone phase because at the end of this phase the software is deployed in the production environment of one or more beta costumers to demonstrate its operational capability. Once operational, the software moves to the *transition phase*. This is the product release milestone phase in which the software product is now generally available in the market.

These phases can span over multiple iterations, each iteration leading to an executable release of a fraction of the complete product. The inception phase typically lasts a single iteration. The number of iterations in the elaboration and construction phases will depend on the size of the project. The transition phase is primarily focused on the product release and therefore will have one or two iterations to deploy the product at a beta customer before it is generally available in the market. The length of an iteration is typically 2 to 4 weeks (biweekly or monthly release boundaries), although longer duration iterations have been suggested for larger projects.

As pointed out earlier, the inception and elaboration phases are unlikely candidates for outsourcing because they involve creative tasks requiring significant domain expertise. The construction and transition phases, however, are labor intensive, requiring development and deployment of the software system based on specifications from the earlier phases, and can achieve significant cost savings when outsourced. Using the following guidelines can increase the chances of a successful outcome should these phases be considered for outsourcing:

- **Model the Requirements:** Create a single electronically verifiable model of product requirements using, for example, a UML-based modeling tool that enables semiautomatic extraction of system requirements, test plans, and project tasks (Berenbach 2003). This will accelerate design by giving architects and designers something they can transform rather than several hundred pages of text they need to read (Berenbach 2004).

- **Use a Component-Based Architecture:** The architecture aims at breaking a complex system into components with well-defined interfaces making distributed development easier. Not doing so will lead to a much flatter structure with indeterminate interconnects requiring all team members on multiple development teams working at multiple sites to know many details on many pieces of the system and will require frequent coordination and synchronization. Componentization helps contain teams to discrete tasks on a geographic basis, minimizing interteam communication, an important goal of distributed development (Martin 1995; Turnlund 2004).

- **Adhere to Time-Boxed Iterations:** Once biweekly or monthly iteration cycles have been established, they should be followed strictly. It is better to sacrifice a piece of functionality than push the timeline for a release; otherwise, the benefits of incremental iterative development are lost (Larman 2002). These benefits include continuous feedback, validating the product under construction, and a gratifying sense of measurable progress toward the stipulated goal.

- **Follow Continuous Integration:** Ideally, integration should occur on a daily basis as product features and functions are implemented. Multisite version control and build tools are now available that can make this process largely automatic. Continuous integration exposes problems that result from disparate components interacting with each other on an ongoing basis rather than one big bang at the end (Fowler 2003; Simons 2002).

## Organizing

Development projects that are strategic in nature require a stronger alliance between the teams involved in the development effort (Kishore et al. 2003). These teams may be affiliated with each other in the following ways (Kobitzsch et al. 2001):

1. Separate teams in basically independent companies
2. Separate teams in legally related companies
3. One team distributed across multiple sites of legally related companies
4. One team distributed across multiple sites of several basically independent companies

While legal, development, project, and quality management issues are a concern in all four affiliation models, models 2 and 3 make them comparatively easier to manage because the teams are parts of legally related companies.

Regardless of the model chosen, there needs to be a central team that controls the activities of the early phases, such as requirements engineering and specification of architectural and application components, and also manages the schedule, quality, and integration of architectural and application components into a testable application (Repenning et al. 2001). A product manager can be assigned to head this team and be responsible for the entire product life cycle and commissioning of component teams worldwide. Each component team can be led by an R&D manager responsible for delivering components for the product to the central team.

## Monitoring and Control

Metrics must be established to determine if suppliers are meeting their performance goals. These metrics could include number of use cases implemented in each release, number of lines of code per programmer per day, and number of defects per 1,000 lines of code. The purpose of these numbers should be to provide early indications of problems to the development team and set them on the right course (Reifer 2004; Strigel & Wolfgang 2004).

Metrics can also be used to assess quality attributes such as maintainability and understandability of a software product, two attributes that have a significant impact on maintenance and support costs. A software visualization tool, Headway reView (http://www.headwaysoft.com) can be used for gathering such metrics. This tool uses hierarchical directed graphs (or higraphs) that show a system's components and their relationships. Users can drill down into each component to uncover details of the classes that make up a component and their interrelationships, ultimately visualizing the methods and attributes of each class. Headway reView therefore can be used to assess the quality of a software system using static software quality metrics as described in various works (Chidamber & Kemerer 1994; Lakos 1996; Martin 1995; McCabe & Butler 1989).

# ▶ Conclusions

Projects good for outsourcing are those that do not require significant innovation, collaboration, critical or strategic code, specialized domain know-how, or dependencies on other projects. The hardware and software platforms for these projects should be fairly stable; requirements, performance goals, and acceptance criteria clearly defined; and internal management and domain expertise available to aid the supplier. Reifer (2004) suggests outsourcing not be simply a cost reduction endeavor but to be undertaken only if it makes good business sense. He suggests a number of best practices described in the following paragraphs.

Suppliers must be chosen with establishment of long-term relationship in mind. You may look at the U.S. government, an organization that outsources a large number of projects, to gain this insight. Instead of establishing long-term relationships, it encourages competition among its suppliers and grants contract to the lowest bidder. Most of its projects, however, run over budget and time, and fail to meet the intended specifications. This is contrary to commercial organizations such as Boeing and General Electric that have had considerable success because forming strategic relationship with their suppliers was one of their significant criteria for outsourced projects.

These relationships have to be nurtured to create win-win situations with the suppliers. For instance, an organization may decide to fund new product initiatives for some of its smaller suppliers, creating an amicable partnership. The suppliers in return may consider offering deep discounts on the work they do for the organization.

A core competency must never be considered for outsourcing; this is what distinguishes an organization from its competition and gives it the ability to lead the market through innovation. Giving this knowledge away can take away an organization's edge and prove detrimental to its success in the long run. Outsourcing should instead be treated as a technology transfer opportunity where the outsourcing organization learns from its suppliers the work they were hired to do.

Performance of the suppliers should be measured as quantitatively as possible with the focus of the measurements being toward enabling teams to see early signs of problems. Exceptional performance should be rewarded through financial incentives.

# ▶ References

Allen, T., 1977. Managing the Flow of Technology. MIT Press, Cambridge

Battin, R., R. Crocker, , Kreidler, J. and Subramanian, K. 2001. "Leveraging Resources in Global Software Development." *IEEE Software*, 18(2), 60–77, March/April.

Berenbach, B., 2003. The Automated Extraction of Requirements from UML Models. *Proceedings of the 11th IEEE International Requirements Engineering Conference (RE 2003)*, Monterey Bay, CA, USA, pp. 287.

Berenbach, B., 2004. Comparison of UML and Text-Based Requirements Engineering. *OOPSLA 2004*, Vancouver, British Columbia, Canada, pp. 247–252.

Carmel, E., and A. Agarwal, 2001. "Tactical Approaches for Alleviating Distance in Global Software Development." *IEEE Software*, 18(2), 22–29, March/April.

Chidamber, S., C. Kemerer, 1994. "A Metrics Suite for Object Oriented Design." *IEEE Transactions on Software Engineering*, 20(6), 476–493, June.

Coar, K., 2004. "The Sun Never Sets on Distributed Development." *ACM Queue*, 1(9), 33–39, December/January.

Cockburn, A., 2002. *Agile Software Development*. Addison-Wesley.

Ebert, C., and P. De Neve, 2001. "Surviving Global Software Development." *IEEE Software*, 18(2), 62–69, March/April.

Fowler, M. 2003. Using an Agile Software Process with Offshore Development. Available: http://www.martinfowler.com/articles/agileOffshore.html, Last Referenced July 2005.

Headway reView, a software visualization tool. http://www.headwaysoft.com.

Heeks, R., S. Krishna, B. Nicholsen, and S. Sahay, 2001. "Synching or Sinking: Global Software Outsourcing Relationships." *IEEE Software*, 18(2), 54–60, March/April.

Kharif, O., 2003. "Hidden Costs of IT Outsourcing." *The Business Week*, October 27.

Kishore, R., H. Rao, K. Nam, S. Rajagopalan, and A. Chaudhury, 2003. "A Relationship Perspective on IT Outsourcing." *Communications of the ACM*, 46(12), 87–92, December.

Kobitzsch, W., D. Rombach, and R. Feldmann, 2001. "Outsourcing in India." *IEEE Software*, 18(2), 78–86, March/April.

Lakos, J., 1996. *Large-Scale C++ Software Design*. Addison-Wesley.

Laplante, P., T. Costello, P. Singh, S. Bindiganavile, and M. Landon, 2004. "The Who, What, Where, Why and When of IT Outsourcing." *IT Professional*, 37–41, January/February.

Larman, C., 2002. *Applying UML and Patterns*. Prentice Hall, 2002.

Martin, R., 1995. "OO Design Quality Metrics: An Analysis of Dependencies." *ROAD*. Available: http://www.objectmentor.com/resources/articles/oodmetrc.pdf.

McCabe, T., and C. Butler, 1989. "Design Complexity Measurement and Testing." *Communications of the ACM*, 32(12), 1415–1425.

Mockus, A., and D. Weiss, 2001. "Globalization by Chunking: A Quantitative Approach." *IEEE Software*, 18(2), 30–37, March/April.

Reich, R., 2003. "High-Tech Jobs are Going Abroad! But That's OK." *The Washington Post*, November 2.

Reifer, D., 2004. "Seven Hot Outsourcing Practices." *IEEE Software*, 21(1), 14–16, January/February.

Repenning, A., A. Ioannidou, M. Payton, W. Ye, and J. Roschelle, 2001. "Using Components for Rapid Distributed Software Development." *IEEE Software*, 18(2), 38–45, March/April.

Royce, W., 1998. *Software Project Management: A Unified Framework*, Addison-Wesley.

Simons, M., 2002. Internationally Agile, *InformIT*, March 15. Available: http://www. informit.com/articles/article.asp?p=25929.

Strigel, W., 2004. "Outsourcing: What Works." *Software Development*, January.

Turnlund, M., 2004. "Distributed Development Lessons Learned." *ACM Queue*, 1(9), 27–31, December/January.

# Enterprise Information Architecture

*Thomas Costello*

> *An immense and ever-increasing wealth of knowledge is scattered about the world today; knowledge that would probably suffice to solve all of the mighty difficulties of our age, but it is dispersed and unorganized. We need a sort of mental clearinghouse for the mind: a depot where knowledge and ideas are received, sorted, summarized, digested, clarified, and compared.*
>
> —H. G. Wells, *The World Brain*, 1938

> *The significant problems we face cannot be solved at the same level of thinking we were at when we created them.*
>
> —Albert Einstein

At any given moment, you will find an organization executing a series of projects targeted at optimizing several aspects of the company. These efforts will be spawned from nearly every corner of the firm in nearly every direction: from the functional teams, from operations, from IT, from the bottom-up, and from the top-down. The list of solutions can range from system implementations (ERP, CRM, SFA, etc.) to optimization processes (Six Sigma, Kaizen, etc.), to strategic alignment efforts (balanced scorecard, Project Office, communication plans, etc.), and more. Eventually, every one of these efforts will draw the same conclusion: that there are data problems in the organization, and the lack of information and knowledge sharing is holding back growth.

Many organizations can supply an array of perfectly rational-sounding reasons for having created a patchwork of systems and processes to solve business needs. Too many of these situations, however, have evolved simply due to the lack of a cohesive and comprehensive map of how operations, strategy, and technology should be linked together to grow the organization. As firms begin to seek an answer to this dilemma, they are discovering or being told they need an enterprise information architecture (EIA).

Sometimes, to best understand what something "is," it is easier to start with defining what it "is not." An EIA is not a methodology, though you will need an approach to handling your environment. An EIA is not a tool, though there are tools available to help you with specific aspects of your environment. An EIA is not a document that outlines your hardware or data, though documentation of these and other components are necessary for any organization.

EIA is the real-world execution of the connectivity between business functions, business processes, data, physical architecture, rules, strategy, time, and people that allows an organization to extract information and knowledge for competitive advantage. I would further argue that valuable EIAs should include the desired metrics and outcomes by which success will be measured.

At this very moment, you have an EIA. You probably have plenty of systems, redundant data, mixed platforms, and applications that don't talk to each other. You have multiple businesses solving the same problem with different applications. You have an intertwined environment so complex it has to be drawn from multiple perspectives (and they don't connect to each other). You are sure you don't even know everything that is out there. And it keeps changing! You leverage information where you can find and have very limited levels of real knowledge transfer. Welcome to your current EIA. Simply put, an EIA is a state. You're reading this because you sense a need to optimize your current information state through evolution or revolution. In that sense, EIA is a target outcome.

# ▶ Enterprise Information Nomenclature

For a moment, imagine that I've just helicoptered you deep into the woods in Alaska. I've informed you that you have 24 hours to make it to Kodiak. I have given you all of the equipment and supplies you'll need to make the trip. There are only two things that are missing in this equation: where you are and what lies between here and your destination.

In other parts of this book, you will find chapters and references relating to IT plans, portfolio management, gathering user requirements, balanced scorecard, and other tools to help you chart what you are doing, for whom, and how you'll measure it. All of these are useful tools in defining what you need and how you'll know success, but it doesn't tell you where you are or what lies between here and there. A valuable EIA will allow you to define your current position in great detail, and it should also allow you to understand and define the transitional needs as you move to your "target state."

---

**Key Point 1**

Definition and Purpose

The organization must have a definition of what an EIA is and must ensure the purpose becomes a part of the organization's dialog. Wider acceptance may be accomplished by seeding the term from the business side of the organization rather than as a technical term from IT.

---

# ▶ How Did We Actually Get Here?

If you were actually starting an organization from scratch, you would start by describing how all of the parts of the enterprise will be connected. Your plan would probably describe macrolevel functions and what you expect each of the different users to experience, as well as information they will have at their disposal. Your vision would be an environment with accurate information, available instantaneously to all parts of the organization, where knowledge is extracted to give you an edge.

As you start to select the actual packages for each of the functional areas, you'll begin to introduce wrinkles in your EIA. In order for a software vendor to create a successful package, the vendor must control its data environment. By doing so, it has to make assumptions that would be true for the broadest segment of the market (including multiple uses and industry verticals), which may or may not match your plan. These vendors are focusing on making their product work, not helping you make it work with every other system in your environment.

You suddenly find yourself considering all manner of middleware to regain the visibility you desire. While this is a step in the right direction, you'll find that this approach doesn't tap into the information and knowledge that should be available in your data. Organizations that can afford to do so begin a larger data warehouse effort to extract this information. In all cases, the issue of unreliable data and inconsistent definitions surface extremely quickly. The fact that there is an entire segment of software known as ETL (extract, transform, load) speaks to the enormity of the problem.

If you are part of a larger enterprise, this scenario probably describes the history of your organization for the past 10 to 15 years. Does that necessarily mean that you need a data warehouse and that having one provides you with a base for a high-performing EIA? The basic answer is, maybe, and probably not. Again, by definition, a solid EIA recognizes far more than data and systems. Having connectivity between business functions, business processes, data, physical architecture, rules, strategy, time, and people is just part of the EIA. Now you have to do something with it—extract and leverage the information and knowledge to competitive advantage.

## Vertical Versus Horizontal Views

Typical enterprises organize their functional areas or teams in such a way as to create "silos" of information and knowledge. Each enterprise IT department addresses the needs of these teams through some combination of "buy versus build" application solutions, the result of which is an array of vertical data stores. In many evolving organizations, the lack of dedicated systems results in a myriad of disparate applications and private data repositories. Where systems are in place, the vertically focused applications typically are not properly adapted to the business needs of the team, let alone the enterprise.

Regardless of the evolutionary progress of the organization and its related systems, there are some common process/workflow issues that each team must face. Look at any process in your enterprise, and you should see a series of steps interspersed with analytic events. At each of these events, the user is seeking some information or knowledge to make an accurate decision or take a correct action. When the user faces these analytic events, the most meaningful information may not be available. This could be the result of application limitations, errant or absent data collection processes, security or permission limitations, users' lack of knowledge that the needed information exists, or users' failure to understand the value of the information.

If you "bought" a solution to a given workflow or business process, the question becomes whether you modified your process to meet the application (the software development firm knows best because they captured best practices), or you modified the software to meet your business need (and accepted the risks associated with future upgrades, etc.). If you "built" your solution, did you really sit down and map out the business process in detail and capture the critical analytic points and information needed? The reality of most homegrown systems is that they were built to "capture and store" information and to present data that may have been captured in a prior event within the workflow *for that given functional team.*

These contained, vertical environments require a given amount of care and feeding to keep the business users satisfied and to remain adaptive to the changing business environment. Whether you are applying upgrades to purchased packages or modifying your homegrown code, you are probably not regularly reviewing the workflow and adapting the application to meet your users' environment.

Likewise, you would also not then be looking at how this vertical data could be useful to other functional areas. At each point where there is a horizontal hand-off or gateway opportunity between users or systems, there are additional risks and challenges. Many organizations may find that they have already gathered useful information or mapped these processes as part of localized application efforts.

However, these service mappings are rarely cataloged by the enterprise. If such a catalog is produced, the opportunity to unify, standardize, or share services as well as data between enterprise functions can be realized. As an example, a process or service to verify credit information may exist within one department, be useful to but missing in another department, and be present but different in yet a third department. By reviewing the business and information needs of each process, the determination can be made as to the best solution, and the outcome can be documented as part of the EIA.

## ▶ What Can a Company Hope to Accomplish with an EIA Effort?

Many organizations start describing the goals of an EIA as *all* of the items in the following list. While that would be the state of EIA nirvana, a more achievable approach might be to focus on only one or two of the following:

- Remove redundancy and complexity of the enterprise environment.
- Better address growth and competitive pressures.
- Assist IT and business in better understanding and leveraging the enterprise's information products and stores (horizontally and for rollup).
- Aid in the integration and consistency of information and services shared between businesses (through applications).

- Ensure the accuracy and consistency of data/information used for all executive monitoring systems (dashboards, metric systems, etc.).

---

**Key Point 2**

Goals

The organization must clearly articulate the primary goal and additional expected benefits. As with any effective goal, a macro timeline and metrics should be established.

---

# ▶ What Are the Typical Triggers for an EIA Project?

The rate at which organizations are now considering EIA efforts has risen in recent years in direct correlation with the complexity of the environments and the changing business missions. The most common triggers for consideration of an EIA effort are

- As a follow-on effort behind a CRM or ERP implementation resulting from massive data inconsistencies and multiple data sources.
- As part of a content management project for a Web or application effort where the collection of collateral was overwhelming and the opportunity to reuse the collected data is being squandered.
- As part of a data warehousing or data mining project where the effort required to respond to business needs cannot be met in a timely (and therefore valuable) manner.
- As part of a forward-looking strategic business or technology initiative where it is recognized that the lack of a cohesive plan will cause an exponential increase in business and IT costs as the problem further proliferates.

## Should These Teams Be Driving the EIA?

The triggers just listed are all legitimate origins for the EIA concept, but that does not necessarily make them the ideal candidates to drive an

EIA effort. Think back to the lessons learned from CRM, the Web, and the other more recent initiatives across the business horizon. The vast majority of organizations have typically started those efforts in a "bottom-up" manner—a business unit reacting to business pressure and addressing it with a system solution. Depending upon the size of the enterprise, it was not uncommon to have multiple ongoing efforts with differing approaches, tools, and timelines. These organizations suddenly found themselves in the midst of a proliferation of inconsistent, encapsulated solutions.

The balance that must be struck, however, is to ensure that each team drives an effort that solves its individual functional needs, yet is consistent with the overall needs and strategy of the organization.

---

**Key Point 3**

Principles

While the initiation of the EIA effort may reside within a given functional team, a corporatewide set of guidelines and principles that address the entire span of the enterprise must drive every EIA effort.

---

## ▶ How Do Companies Typically Get Started in Their EIA Efforts?

Though the conceptual views of EIA have been in existence for over 30 years, the complexity of today's corporate environment has challenged and stretched the founding theories.

Clive Finkelstein and John Zachman developed one of the earliest EIA data modeling approaches in the early 1970s. Their initial approach attempted to "blueprint" the connections between data, functions, platforms, and so on. Later iterations included rules, people, and strategies (initially focused on technology strategy). For the most part, this approach has evolved beyond the pure data perspective but still has a heavy technology tilt imbedded in the approach and deliverables.

Over the past 30 years, we've gone from a completely internal, controlled, mainframe environment to a world that includes PCs, the Internet, intranets, extranets, PDAs, wireless communications, and more. Along with these technologies have come a multitude of new users (both internal and external to the organization), new applications, and a host of security concerns. Couple that with the speed with which information is needed, and you can quickly see that the initial approaches to EIA cannot properly define today's enterprise.

As a result, the latest processes and tools to address any EIA effort are generally in their infancy, and as such, many of the methodologies that are available are ethereal, philosophical, or conversely, deeply complex.

---

**Key Point 4**

Accept That an EIA Is Complex

The process of actually documenting an existing or target EIA will involve a wide variety of complex variables, both business and technologic in nature. Prior to using a commercially available tool or methodology, the enterprise should perform a review to verify that the tool is current and that it properly spans the full breadth of information relationships.

---

# ▶ Can an EIA Really Be Implemented?

Make no mistake: mapping all of the information and connectors relevant to an enterprise is deeply complex. Many commercial tools and methodologies lack an implementation path, and those that even consider how to deliver the solution do so as a "big bang" project. Very few companies have the capability to solve this problem with a single effort, and attempting to do so may risk the operational stability of their organization.

One only needs to look at Hershey Foods in the third quarter of 1999 to find an example of the dangers of a "big bang" implementation. The company was experiencing shipping delays, was shipping incomplete orders, and found themselves sporadically unable to ship at all during its busiest season. The problem affected the back-to-school, Halloween, and Christmas sales windows. This was the result of an attempt to install and upgrade several systems simultaneously. The company reported that the system problems resulted in a 19 percent drop in sales for the third quarter alone.

The challenge facing any organization starting an EIA effort is knowing which path will lead the company to success and which will result in lots of effort yielding limited results.

---

**Key Point 5**

Incremental Business-Driven Delivery

The delivery of projects that lead an enterprise toward a well-defined EIA must be done in an incremental manner. To maximize the impact on the organization, the ordering of these individual efforts should be primarily driven by business need, with some percentage of the mix aimed at strategic movement toward the end goal.

---

# ▶ Possible Views of Approaches and Resulting Trade-Offs

There is an old saying that goes:

> To the person who only knows how to use a hammer, every problem looks like a nail.

With that in mind, great caution must be exercised in the construction of the leadership and team that will drive the EIA effort.

## When Approached by a Methodologist

EIA efforts directed by methodologists are typically marked by starts and restarts as the team tests a variety of methodologies to solving the problem. Some teams try the "shotgun" approach: collecting data from database administrators, process maps, interviews, and so on. These teams then go underground as they try to sift through all of the collected input. This approach has the greatest risk of spinning wildly with little output. It is very difficult to monitor or assess progress of the effort. If this team lacks tangible deliverables, the result can be disastrous. The risks of this approach can be exacerbated if the effort attempts to address the entire organization in a single pass.

## When Approached from a Data Perspective

A data-perspective approach involves the mapping of all data used across the enterprise. Given that this will typically be handled by database administrators, the process generally begins with the review of all known applications and all of the aspects relating to the use of that data (editing rules, etc.). This data-modeling approach doesn't recognize the business requirements (existing or required). The resulting effort can be extensive and distract operational resources. The deliverables typically have little value to the business.

## When Tackled by a Business Analysts

An analysis of the business may be among the better starting points to addressing an ultimate EIA view. In order to be effective, though, this approach must also be aware of two additional, critical components to the enterprise—the stated strategic goals and the timeline for the future target. In the absence of these two components, the exercise will, at best, create a view of "what is done" rather than "what should or will be done". In addition, being aware of how the landscape will be changed will allow the EIA team to best assess the volatility of specific areas and to differentiate between areas of bedrock and areas of quicksand.

---

### Key Point 6

Not All Authors Are Equal

Be deliberate in constructing a team that will produce useable documents. These documents must define an outcome that addresses the goals, can be understood by executives, and can be implemented by the enterprise. Do not let the team create "techno-babble" output.

---

# If an EIA Initiative Is This Complex, Why Would I Even Want to Start One?

There is little doubt that the efficient organizations of the future will require a complete understanding and optimized control of their information environment. There are current examples of early leaders in this space, and they are proving that this awareness, control, and ability to adapt their environment is giving them a great competitive edge.

Consider the case of Wal-Mart and its use of information. Wal-Mart has made a significant investment in a data warehousing effort. It is legendary among those in the data warehousing field. The investment in the tool is critical, but not the meaningful component. Without adding the appropriate analysis and use of that information, it would be nothing more than a massive collection of tools, servers, and data. Wal-Mart understands the power of the information. It has made the system the center of its arsenal and has culturally driven the use of the tools and information. Wal-Mart continuously explores new ways to leverage the power of this knowledge. Ask any of Wal-Mart's suppliers what it is like to walk into the room to negotiate a contract. Wal-Mart can typically tell the suppliers more about their own products and the consumers that purchase them than the suppliers could ever discover from their own systems and market research combined. Who do you believe has the upper hand in the negotiations?

Now consider the case of Kmart. This organization was not an early adopter of data mining. Nor did it understand the value of the information that could be extracted from the data on hand. In 1997, Kmart had approximately 6 terabytes of data in its data warehouse. At the same time, Wal-Mart was at approximately 7.5 (but arguably already doing a better job of analysis). By 2002, Kmart was at 92 terabytes, and Wal-Mart was up to nearly 500 terabytes. For comparison purposes, the IRS in 2003 had a data warehouse of approximately 40 terabytes.

More importantly, Kmart's revenue moved from just below $32 billion in 1997 to roughly $37 billion in 2002. Wal-Mart, on the other hand, moved from nearly $118 billion to $191 billion.

Does this mean that we need a data warehouse and that bigger is better? Not necessarily. Beyond showing that data warehouses can become quite large, these numbers actually show that Wal-Mart clearly extracted value from its data and began an expansion campaign that further rewarded the business.

The key takeaways are that all of Wal-Mart's operations focus on this centralized data repository. There is little redundancy of data within the organization. Data rules are consistently and uniformly applied. Data definitions are consistent. And the use of the tool has been institutionalized across the organization; it is culturally desired (though there probably was some force applied in the early stages).

Wal-Mart effectively eliminated what I refer to as the "cost of confusion." Like squeezing through that narrow opening in the hourglass, it was able to quickly expand into unleashing the power of the information at its disposal.

Current ROI techniques (when used) rarely account for the drag caused by the confusion aspect and certainly don't allocate the power, benefit, and value of knowledge. While there is far too little data to have benchmark statistics on EIA costs and benefits, any ROI justification should recognize the presence of confusion as a cost and impart the prospect that increased knowledge could result in a "steep positive slope" in value.

---

**Key Point 7**

ROI Justification

ROI justification for an EIA effort should note the cost of "confusion" and the value of knowledge. Case studies should be included in ROI justifications until benchmark data (either internally or externally collected) becomes available.

---

## ▶ How Do We Start an EIA Effort?

The first thing each organization must consider is its overarching governance model for IT. Governance, by definition, is how decisions are made. This aspect is more important than your organization structure.

If the business units in your organization are autonomous and typically can pursue their own approaches in an effort to foster innovation, you have to look for examples in your organization where centralization has successfully occurred—and mimic those models. The model may be as small as a centralized "center of excellence" that provides guidance and expertise to each of the subteams, or it can range all the way up to a centralized team that will drive, procure, develop, and grow a centralized solution. As you will probably glean from the successful models, this approach is as much about patience and politics as it is about the solution. The advantage is that while you may (or may not) have full control of all implementations, you certainly have visibility and can gain consistency. This advantage alone will serve your organization well as the implementation evolves.

If yours is an organization that is heavily centralized around IT (in theory and in action), then you will have all of the advantages named above, plus control, and you will more likely gravitate to a single solution. With these advantages, however, comes the responsibility of being a solid "service provider" to your internal business teams.

Technology teams, in all cases, must strive to raise the bar in their execution of an EIA effort. Technology cannot be purely reactive and create a solution that meets 80 percent of each business team's needs and together achieves little for the overall organization. My favorite analogy for this scenario is the original attempts at the combination of printer, fax, scanner, and copier—a multifunction machine that did all four jobs equally poorly. Likewise, technology cannot be driven by a purist mentality to the construction of an EIA effort. In the end, this approach typically results in a technologically sound solution that achieves no business purpose—and dies a horrible death from low buy-in and use.

Overall, every EIA team has the responsibility of being the "evangelist" for the cause: providing example outcomes and implementations (both good and bad). The team must become intimately familiar with the business outcomes that are possible from various EIA approaches and educate the internal business users. The business teams are busy with the day-to-day operations of their functional areas and typically will not have the time to invest in the deep research a centralized team can bring to bear on the problem.

Through this research and sharing, the combined technology and business teams can better describe the approaches necessary to satisfy the business needs. If well done, the benefits could include the following:

- A level of trust that only helps the downstream connectivity and integration of all solutions.
- If not complete consistency, this approach that ensures common needs and approaches can be leveraged within the organization.
- Better budget planning, procurement, and cost distribution between disparate teams.
- Better management of efforts and expectations
- Potential better information sharing between teams that typically haven't communicated on prior efforts (where the opportunity for savings and learnings have been missed).

This brief primer and overview of how to approach an EIA should dispel notions of network topologies and project checklists as substitutes for a true enterprise architecture. You can find multiple examples of models with varying degrees of complexity, and this chapter provides a guide for qualifying those examples against your organization's needs. In the end, the purpose of an EIA is not to end up with a pretty diagram; rather, it is imperative that it act as a blueprint to define your "present state" and to aid in the quantification of the effort required to move to a "target state" as your business evolves. With this knowledge, the next step is to invest your time in transferring this reading into a useful outcome.

# ▶ References

Wells, H. G.(1938), *World Brain*. London: Methuen. p. 69

Zachman, John A (1987), "A Framework for Information Systems Architecture." *IBM Systems Journal*, vol. 26, no. 3, 1987. IBM Publication G321-5298.

# Adaptive and Aware: Strategy, Architecture, and IT Leadership in an Age of Commoditization

*Robert T. Kelley*

## ▶ Introduction

As a way of eliciting comments on the most pressing issues facing CIOs, IT managers, and their business clients, I often ask them, "What keeps you up at night?" The range of the typical answers—from data security, to shrinking budgets, to technical complexity, to just keeping basic services running—reflect not strategic but survival-oriented concerns. Some responders indicate their anxiety quite directly, perhaps relieved to be able to tell someone that "I'm not sure where to invest our time and money" or "I don't know what IT's role is in the company" or "I can't quite tell where the industry is going and what my career path should be." Such stress about IT, especially when articulated by IT professionals, is why Nicholas Carr's 2003 *Harvard Business Review* article, "IT

Doesn't Matter," and 2004 book, *Does IT Matter?*, both enraged and delighted those who have invested in IT and information systems careers. Carr's basic assertion in both pieces, that IT is being commoditized, stung for its truth, but it also laid bare the growing realization that IT no longer has a privileged place in corporate spending. IT is no longer a cool innovation, no longer a differentiator; it has become part of the necessary framework of any corporation. At the same time, increased opportunities for outsourcing IT tasks have changed the contours of internal IT work, making it that much more important that IT professionals think about what their futures, the futures of their departments, and the future of IT in general may be.

Carr's argument should lead us to expect that the commoditization of IT will lead to repeatable, dependable returns on IT investments. But such returns have not yet materialized on the whole. Hardware has standardized, and we do get significant processing power for a fraction of what we used to pay. But information technology investments continue to rise in most organizations. And while we can do more, we don't seem to be able to do more with less. We don't even seem to be able to do more with the same amount; in most organizations, IT expenditures continue to rise. Much of the expense—often 80 percent or more of a company's IT budget—is for maintaining existing systems, leaving a small fraction of the budget for improving business capability or decreasing the cost of doing business.

At the same time, the strategic potential of IT is increasing, in every industry, globally. Carr also made this point, but it's been overshadowed by IT professionals and pundits who lament the loss of IT's privileged place as the skunk works, the innovation center, the place with little-to-no accountability. The truth we must face as IT professionals is that post-Y2K, post–dotcom boom and bust, the market has changed, and those changes are already having far-reaching implications for us. We are part of the business now, a necessary—and, at best, a strategic—part.

In this chapter I examine some of the ways these changes have reverberated throughout the IT organization and the business it supports. I examine the clear economic and technical trends that are driving these changes, identify the implications for IT professionals, and recommend specific approaches for IT best practices, those that provide the best chance of success for IT leaders.

# The IT Landscape

## Brand You

In 1999, with the dotcom boom making it cool to be in IT, Tom Peters's *The Brand You 50* appeared. Introducing themes he would articulate in subsequent books, Peters asserted that he believed that "90+ percent of white collar jobs will disappear or be reconfigured beyond recognition. Within 10 to 15 years" (Peters 1999:4). At the time, many of us thought "Cool! What a great time to be in IT!"

Things changed quickly. Y2K went okay. The dotcom market busted. September 11 happened. Outsourcing, Offshoring, and Globalization swept over us. Both the ubiquity of the Web and the staying power of legacy systems continue to surprise us. It may still be a great time to be in IT, but the contours of that world have changed considerably, and they continue to change. And while IT remains embedded deeply in even the most brick-and-mortar firms, its very ubiquity and invisibility have made it harder, rather than easier, for organizations to justify continued spending on information technology.

## Commoditization and Globalization, Leadership, and Creativity

What Carr calls the "industrialization" of IT is one of the forces that is changing that landscape, a process strikingly akin to the emergence of the factory model in the 19th century, when manufacturers adopted interchangeable parts and assembly line fabrication dominated manufacturing. Likewise, with standard hardware and software, IT promises out-of-the-box solutions, minimal assembly required. When global logistics allowed for economically feasible transfer of interchangeable parts, manufacturing went global. Essentially, when commoditization and good logistics are in place, the geographical range of a technology expands and economic forces guide its adoption, its pricing, and its production. Advances in standardization and economic forces have driven IT commoditization, and economic forces and logistical advances are encouraging globalization. Though we have not reached the end of IT, or a moment when IT doesn't matter, we have already arrived at "end of IT as we know it," as more than one reaction to Carr's original article was titled.

As if in clear confirmation of these challenges, two recent texts on the changing economic conditions of work, Daniel Pink's *A Whole New Mind: Moving from the Information Age to the Conceptual Age* and Thomas L. Friedman's *The World Is Flat: A Brief History of the Twenty-First Century*, lay out the dilemma facing modern "knowledge workers," with special implications for IT professionals.

Daniel Pink begins his book with a brief examination of the forces that seem to be transforming the world economy, namely, the three A's: Abundance, Asia, and Automation. *Abundance* relates to the fact that the basic needs (food, shelter, etc.) of the citizens of leading (and emerging) economies are met and exceeded, leading workers to ask, "Is what I'm offering in demand in an age of abundance?" *Asia* refers to the power of the emerging Asian economies, specifically India and China, and the impact they are already having on world production of both physical and intellectual capital, leading workers in U.S. and European economies to ask, "Can someone in another economy do it cheaper at the same quality?" *Automation* specifically addresses the impact software and computer automation has had on the role of workers, leading workers to query, "Can a computer do my job faster with reduced cost?" (Pink 2005:51). Pink argues that in this age of commoditization and globalization, the information worker is left with one clear value-add, one way to ensure that he or she does not answer those questions in a way that signals his or her obsolescence, namely creativity. "The MFA is the new MBA," he asserts (Pink 2005:54).

Thomas Friedman notes that two by-products of the dotcom crash were excess telecommunications capacity and nascent experience in global collaboration. With these capabilities in place, entrepreneurs now can identify intellectual property work that can be disaggregated (broken into component parts), delivered, and distributed to be reassembled into finished product, with no latency and little additional effort over past methods (Friedman 2005:7). This "flattening" of the world presages substantial opportunities for economies and nations, and it is happening quickly, driven by the ambitions and desires of professionals worldwide. Quoting L. Gary Boomer, Friedman asserts that the upshot of this fact is that globalization and commoditization make it so that "those who are caught in the past and resist change will be forced deeper into commoditization. Those who can create value through *leadership, relationships, and creativity* will transform the industry [emphasis added]" (Friedman 2005:14).

Leadership and creativity are the very characteristics we need to possess as IT professionals if we seek to grow and remain relevant in our organizations.

## Emerging Infrastructures

When electricity was first introduced in the United States and we had not yet settled on a standard, many small generating plants sprung up. When it became clear that alternating current could be transmitted further with less power loss, it won out over direct current. During the 1990s, a similar process occurred regarding IT. IT services became "infrastructural technologies," like electricity, widely available and readily understood, of no proprietary advantage. Ravi Kalakota and others in the late 1990s imagined the Web would offer "knowledge tone," a counterpart to dial tone, supporting all of our knowledge-based activities. And, quietly, in the bust after the boom, this hope has been realized. WiFi and WiMax tie devices together; car manufacturers add Bluetooth to the automobile's infrastructure, enabling your car to recognize your phone. Phones have become PDAs (and vice versa), and are now evolving into general personal communications devices. Grid computing is moving from a theoretical concept to an extended experiment, with the SETI screen saver and other parallel computing opportunities evolving into a serious topic of consideration in high computation need environments. And the evolution of Service Oriented Architectures (SOAs) and Web Services (as outlined in Min-Jung Yoo's chapter in this book) along with the growth of on-demand computing and the maturation of application service providers such as Salesforce.com competing seriously with SAP, Peoplesoft, and Seibel heralds even more substantial changes.

All of these trends were nascent in the 1990s; most of them promised amazing change and (like any kind of infrastructural technology) delivered subtle, pervasive change. What they provide for the computing professional today is the kind of increasingly stable, consistent platform on which to deliver solutions—as any kind of standardized technology does.

## Strategy Is Dead, Long Live Strategy

Commoditization and globalization have exposed IT, making the glass house transparent even outside the organization. "By erasing many traditional operating advantages and making companies' processes and prices more transparent to customers, IT threatens to become a kind of universal solvent of business strategy, speeding up the natural forces that over time push companies toward competitive parity," Carr asserts. The challenge is "how to defend their company's advantages...while at the same time allowing information to flow freely in and out of their organizations through the general IT infrastructure." So, while Wal-Mart may be able to keep its IT advantages somewhat proprietary by doing all its own custom development, this is a truly unique position, one undermined by the use of standards-based technologies like RFID that they need to work more effectively with their suppliers. So if the technology itself cannot be kept as a proprietary advantage, what can separate an organization from its competitors?

The competitive advantage must be found elsewhere. The logical place to look is in the human workforce, but as Levy and Murnane argue in *The New Division of Labor*, the nature of work itself is changing. Rules-based jobs, which are easy to outsource or automate, are disappearing. What remains are "expert thinking and complex communication as the domains of well-paid human work. What is true about today's rising skill requirements will be even more true tomorrow."

What do such jobs look like? What separates them from the rest of the current economy, makes them less vulnerable to automation? These jobs are focused on information processing, not usually on information availability (Brynjolfsson 2003). They demand great skill in facilitating interactions among people and between people and that information. The successful professional in this post-commoditized, post-globalized environment, then, understands what we do with information, how we enable good decision making. This may seem patently obvious until we recognize that it may be the *entirety* of future IT departments' missions, where IT's role is strategically focused on planning enablement and on information and knowledge facilitation rather than on information or data processing.

# ▶ The Current State of IT Strategy and Planning

As the ground moves beneath us, we must still work, honoring the charge of senior management to make real change based on our knowledge of the business and best practices while simultaneously recognizing the need for IT to support the business and to work as advertised. In fact, these two balanced desires frame the most basic facets of IT's corporate existence, as we can see through considering three well-understood challenges CIOs face.

## Three Challenges

### Operator, I've Been Disconnected

In a recent McKinsey study, CEOs noted that they want their CIOs to provide systems that support executive decision making and to invest in technologies that will garner scale advantages (Mark 2004). Contrast this to the 2004 top priorities of CIOs as reported by *Information Week*: streamline or optimize business processes, boost worker productivity, improve customer service, gain better return on IT capital investments, and keep up with change (Dunn 2004). CEOs want IT leadership, CIOs want to keep up. And yet, in that same McKinsey study, the CEOs said that the greatest CIO blind spot is "the assessment and monitoring of IT's benefits" (Mark 2004).

### Where Is the Money Going?

Estimates vary, but the consensus is that most organizations spend 80 percent or more of their budget on maintaining the status quo and 20 percent or less in developing new capabilities. The Gartner Group notes that, on average, IT spending is 70 percent on operations, 22 percent on capital expenditures (not new capabilities, e.g., desktop refresh), and 8 percent on hidden or business unit spending (which may actually be much higher, up to 25 percent). And much of our IT investment is underutilized. Bob Napier of Hewlett-Packard has asserted that given the server and capability proliferation that occurred in the dotcom boom, less than 50 percent of IT capacity is actually used (Waters

2003). Even if the waste is not that egregious, we intuitively recognize that we have not been spending as intelligently in IT as we might.

### Failure Is an Option (Unfortunately)

The classic—and all too familiar—Standish Group statistics bear repeating: only 16 percent of all projects are completed on budget, on time, with all features and functions as initially specified. Thirty-one percent are canceled during the development cycle (Standish 1994). While some organizations plan better than others, and certainly some incredibly disciplined organizations have beaten these statistics, they remain a dark truth of IT planning.

## Predicting the Weather

Together, these three elements sketch a dire state of affairs. An inability to plan effectively, an incomplete understanding of the environment, and a failure to support executive decision making (no way to visualize the organization's direction) all add up to no control. Recently, a client concisely described the systems environment in her organization: "It's chaos," she said. Less a judgment than an insight, she meant "chaos" in the complexity theory sense of the word, as the concatenation of intertwined forces that make the weather, for instance, impossible to predict. Such chaos is the evil twin to Metcalfe's law; as a network of connected systems grows, the number of connections grows with it, and its complexity grows too. If this complexity is ungoverned, unchecked, the ensuing mess hurts the organization so much that the effects are evident at every level. Ask a help desk professional, and he or she can readily tell you what doesn't work in the organization, what applications fail to meet business needs. Ask a CEO, and you're likely to hear that "CIOs are not up to speed on issues confronting the businesses and can't think through the implications of systems trade-offs, on a business level, for planned implementations or IT investments" (Mark 2004).

# ▶ The Future of IT Strategic Planning: Enterprise Architecture and the Adaptive Leader

All that said, we come to the heart of the matter: What's a pragmatic CIO do to survive and thrive? First, he or she needs to recognize that the paradigm of custom products, a monolithic system, one-off solutions to problems, and an accretive, complex manner of working and conjoining systems is becoming a thing of the past. The new paradigm capitalizes on commoditization, stressing modular elements, coupled resources, considered solutions, and an improved and improving environment in which as much as possible remains transparent (Figure 17.1).

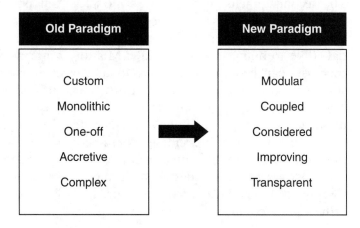

**Figure 17.1** Paradigm shift.

Second, the CIO needs to be cognizant of what this new model makes possible: reproducible and modular elements tantalize us with the notion that fast, cheap, simple solutions might really be possible. Traits of a familiar fantasy, these dream criteria are being realized in some organizations.

## The Future of Process

Geoffrey Moore outlines a two-axis model for evaluating the focus an organization should give to enterprise processes. He defines "core" business processes as those that create differentiation or enhance the staying power of an organization's differentiation. All other processes, those that don't contribute to differentiation, are "context." While organizations need context, knowing which processes are which is important from both a financial and an IT perspective. Ideally, Moore recommends, you want to *capitalize core* (including knowledge as well as people), and you want to *expense context*. In addition, systems developed in support of the core processes should be custom, because they will further your staying power of differentiation. Wal-Mart, as noted earlier, follows this custom development strategy closely. Problem arise if and when differentiation changes, when core processes become context processes. Differentiation in context is a liability because it precludes taking advantage of maturing standards and best practices (Moore, 2002:37).

The second dimension of Moore's model is "mission-critical" versus "supporting" processes. Mission critical processes keep the business running (like payroll); supporting processes enhance but are not essential (like running the cafeteria). Mission critical and supporting processes can be either core or context. Payroll, for example, is Mission-critical but for most organizations is a context task (Figure 17.2). Therefore, it would be appropriate to outsource it—as many, many organizations have done. But as already noted, it's the evolution of core to context that makes deciding whether or not to outsource certain functions tough. Should you outsource email? Hosting of Web servers? The answers to those questions are more organization-specific. (See Chapter 14, "The Five W's of Outsourcing," for a detailed description of best practices in making these evaluations.)

The practical implications of this model are manifold. First, learn not to fall in love with core systems that you own. Eventually, *all* differentiators fade away, so all core systems must be built with the understanding that they will move to context. Second, put in place evaluation and metrics-based systems that give you what Moore calls "visibility." As the CEOs in the McKinsey study noted, their evaluations of their CIOs lacked measurable elements. Given the speed at which business is changing and the nature of the technologies supporting them, that lack can be a critical failing. As both John Wollman and Thomas Costello note in chapters in this text, metrics and mechanisms that provide corporate visibility are key. The new IT leader will be a process- and measurement-oriented professional, with the CIO becoming, in many organizations, the *chief process officer*, the individual who

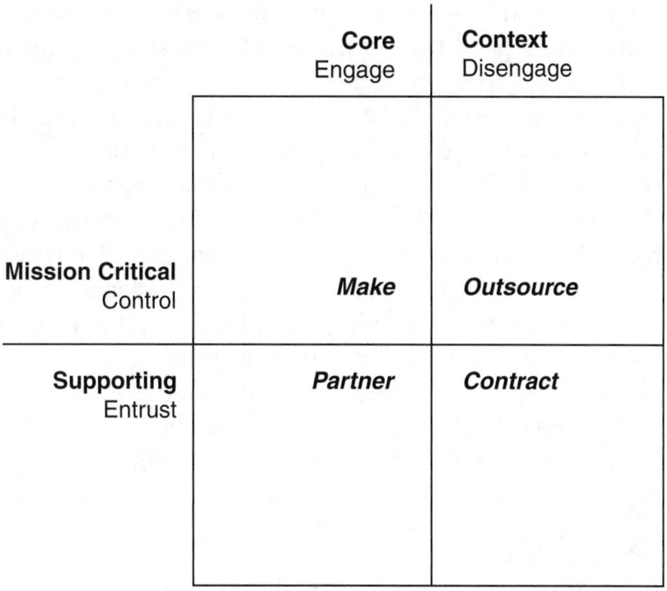

|  | Core<br>Engage | Context<br>Disengage |
|---|---|---|
| **Mission Critical**<br>Control | *Make* | *Outsource* |
| **Supporting**<br>Entrust | *Partner* | *Contract* |

**Figure 17.2** Resource allocation

*Source:* Geoffrey A. Moore, *Living on the Fault Line: Managing for Shareholder Value in Any Economy.* Revised Edition. New York, Harper Collins, 2002.

sees into the business processes that run the organization. In other words, the new IT leader must be *adaptive.*

The need for adaptivity today is evident in terms of recognizing which core processes are evolving into context processes, and identifying which of the remaining core processes are also mission critical. Those are the processes on which you should invest your budget. Being able to acknowledge that all core development will someday become context, CIOs can begin to "future-proof" technologies, leveraging commoditization by skillful outsourcing and partnering. Doing this well requires a sophisticated understanding of reusability. Being able to intuit which core processes are likely to become context soon is not the work of a savant. It's rooted in a clear understanding of the strategic nature of your suppliers (in this case, hardware, software, and services), and how they can support mission-critical but not core services. It is part of the new position of IT leader as the *demand manager.*

Thankfully, this is easier than it sounds, in part because advances in software have lagged behind those in hardware. Packaged software reliability continues to improve; nevertheless, custom software development and systems integration still go on at most organizations, because even those who recognize the core/context distinction cannot complete transitions overnight. Although vendor consolidation has driven some standardization, the continuous upgrade and feature expansion cycle of both desktop and business solution products means the enterprise technology environment never settles down. Thus, the challenge for many enterprises is to get the same level of plug-and-play capability from software as we get from hardware. A fresh technical approach, developing Web Services as wrappers around or extensions of existing systems, promises to make such standardization possible. Specifically (and perhaps most valuably). Web Services and SOAs demand that an enterprise adopt a "service orientation," looking at IT as a series of services that support specific business processes, "abstracting" them from the actual technologies.

What SOAs provide, in short, is the real possibility of commoditization. The sea change in IT that Carr imagined is truly possible, thanks to the creation of reusable components, what one analyst has called the "mechanization" of software products (Schmelzer 2004). While this has been presaged by changes in object-oriented development and the introduction of software design patterns, only with the introduction of SOA, and more specifically, of Web Services, has true, transparent reusability emerged. With SOA, the process of reusability begun in object-oriented programming is extended, with application logic exposed through well defined interface standards. This standardization allows for one of the hallmarks of SOA, "loose coupling"—the ability for the services to be assembled and disassembled easily, allowing for reuse. Web Services are then services developed in an SOA model that expose their interface via a Web URL and that adhere to standards for automatic discovery via a directory on a network (UDDI, Universal Description, Discovery, and Integration). Across an entire enterprise, an SOA implementation (sometimes referred to as Enterprise Services Architecture) enabling service reuse or application assembly as well as a federated control model for security, management, and deployment of the services, becomes the paradigm for "commoditized" development, and thereby supports the reusability required to support the core-to-context transition.

This kind of approach accrues other benefits to an organization as well. A successful SOA requires a business orientation in IT design, with services representing business processes rather than underlying systems or monolithic applications. In this model, the Vice President of Sales doesn't want CRM installed, she wants single-customer lookup enabled. Another opportunity is for the integration of systems beyond the enterprise boundary, extending to trading partners and other external service providers, easing the burden of supporting processes we do not want or need to own. SOA is not a bleeding-edge architectural approach but rather is the leading method for future application design, as well as packaged software implementations. We can expect major platform vendors to continue to push this direction (Microsoft and IBM have already been leaders in this space) and major ERP and package vendors to put major investment here as well (SAP's expressed commitment is to deliver an all–Web Services architecture by 2007). Clearly, strategies that support reusability and flexibility have gained credence, and the maturing software market is moving toward an on-demand model.

In some ways, the most important aspect of the advancement of SOA and related technologies is that they reveal, again, the need for the new IT leader to be vigilant about change in the business and in technology. The market will continue to change, new technologies will continue to find their way into the mix; therefore, the successful IT leader will need to be not only *adaptive* but also *aware*.

## The Future of Planning

The real issue in IT planning is not business focus, organizational structure, or financial issues; instead, the areas of greatest concern in the IT planning process are those aspects most in flux, particularly the core-to-context transition organizations face as their central technology infrastructure moves from a differentiated model to a commoditized model. Fortunately, this kind of agility is the focus of a form of architecture planning currently receiving increased attention. With the growing popularity of SOA, interest in the working models underlying Enterprise Architecture, and attention to portfolio management, many organizations are finally able to assemble a coherent, flexible model that afford them the agility they require. We call this integrated planning model the *Enterprise Service Approach* and find that it addresses organizations' current needs while helping them evolve toward more sophisticated, planned future states (Figure 17.3).

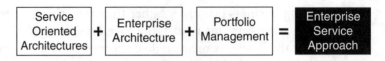

**Figure 17.3** Enterprise service approach.

Enterprise Architecture is a discipline and a framework documentation process that integrates Technology Architecture (including applications and infrastructure), Business Architecture (the processes and structures that define the business), and Governance and Management (the processes that ensure ongoing relevance and support of the Architectures). Specifically, enterprise architecture provides a process by which an organization can document its high-level business processes as well as its technical architectures, and then map the two together, identifying dependencies and gaps in the organization's enabling technologies. Zachman, TOGAF, and the Federal EA standard, among others, provide definitions for Enterprise Architecture; all indicate that, in its most basic form, Enterprise Architecture incorporates two views of the business, technology and governance of an organization. First, it is a reference model, a conceptual representation of business and technology components and their interdependencies, that offers an organized view of current IT resources, standards, assets, principles, and guidelines. I mean this quite literally: the majority of Enterprise Architecture models (including Figure 17.4, the reference example from my own organization) represent the organization's architecture visually. This is an important element of the discipline, for it allows organizations to use a common, shared mode for representing the interrelationships among elements of the business and the processes that govern them.

Second, enterprise architecture is a framework for managing the continuous synchronization of the organization's business and technology architectures. It is a vehicle for ongoing governance with principles, guidelines, rules, and standards that should govern ongoing management of IT resources and initiatives.

When Enterprise Architecture is complete and the framework is in place to assist in the development of ongoing technology and business architectures, a Project Portfolio can be constructed that outlines the transformational path for the organization. A multiyear plan with "snapshots," or views of the organization's architectures at future

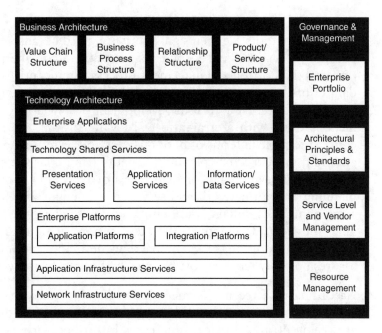

**Figure 17.4** LiquidHub enterprise architecture reference model.

points in time, can provide a clear, visual representation of the path of the organization, its goals and aspirations. The portfolio represents the projects that must be completed—business process documentation, reengineering, and implementation to technology initiatives, as well as transformations of the organization's business–technology linkages. The combination of Enterprise Architecture framework with Portfolio Management provides a dynamic or "living" model of the business, one which avoids the trap of some IT strategy approaches: becoming "shelfware." In the Enterprise Service Approach, reusability, disciplined planning, and ongoing management combine to allow for adaptive and aware management.

The business case for this approach is obvious, resting in its simplicity and potential impact. With organizations spending 80 percent or more of their budget on maintaining the status quo, a planning discipline that addresses specific economic pain points is a necessity. With the Enterprise Services Approach, the advantages accrued are substantial. First, the use of an SOA brings significant value in two ways. Through the reusability of existing services loosely coupled in other applications, the time to do new applications development is reduced. In addition, the maintenance tasks are then significantly reduced because work on existing services is simplified. Second, the introduction of enterprise architecture and the Portfolio Management process significantly reduces redundant effort because applications and their dependencies are understood and planned for. New custom development or new application procurement is done with a straightforward view toward the impact to the entire enterprise in terms of both business and technical architectures. In addition, infrastructure planning benefits from consistent implementation strategies, allowing for high levels of reuse and better investment planning in both network and server investments. Therefore, given the same number of dollars, an organization will have more funding available for new development because system maintenance costs are reduced. In addition, SOA's impact on new application development assures not only reduced cost but also higher productivity (Figure 17.5).

According to a recent Gartner report, organizations that combine an SOA development model with a rapid application development (RAD) are seeing 40 to 60 percent increases in productivity, as compared to

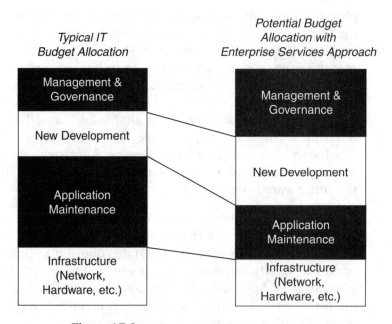

**Figure 17.5** Budget allocation with ESA.

traditional development models (Blechar 2004). And, with the use of an Enterprise Architecture/Portfolio Management planning model, the time that becomes available for deeper governance and management increases the likelihood of continuing to accrue new benefits year after year. In this model, the IT leader works like an "equity analyst," a portfolio manager sitting at the table with other business management, helping to qualify and quantify the long-term value and direction of IT investments (Varon 2003).

# ▶ 21st Century IT: A Roadmap

The commoditization of IT provides an opportunity for higher reliability and repeatability. The same forces that Carr identified, and that have been seen as negative by large portions of the IT community, represent a significant opportunity for IT as it evolves in the 21st century. With the migration of IT to a more reproducible model, organizations can begin to apply quality and availability standards to IT systems and processes, gaining flexibility and more appropriate levels of cost and support. I believe IT is being commoditized, but I also believe businesses need this reproducibility, that they are hungry for it.

## The Future of IT Leadership

Recently, one of my employees confided in her manager that she wanted to pursue opportunities in project management, particularly involving global delivery with our Delivery Center in India. This individual is an incredibly skilled programmer, with a firm understanding of the leading edge in the Java/J2EE programming space. When the manager asked about this desire, the programmer replied that it was obvious that there would only be two kinds of leadership jobs in the near future: architects who design solutions and project managers who coordinate the projects. She wanted opportunities to fill those roles. Is this professional displaying alarmism or foresight? Perhaps a bit of both, but she is certainly catching the drift of the market.

Even as the number of college graduates focused on science and technology continues to fall and our focus as a country turns away from IT leadership, the U.S. Bureau of Labor Statistics suggests the number of new U.S. Information Technologies jobs is expected to grow more than 34 percent between 2002 and 2012 (President's Council of Advisors on Science and Technology 2004). But the nature of that work has become uncertain. Therefore, like the concerned programmer, IT professionals must think hard about the kind of career paths available for skilled work in the applications development and systems integration space. Moreover, this is no longer primarily a U.S. issue (although it is, perhaps, voiced most loudly in the United States), but rather a global one; expertise in managing within a commoditized market is applicable to IT leaders anywhere.

## Agility

From a departmental and functional perspective, IT leaders need to consider how to begin to educate themselves and their teams in the evolving expectations for IT. Given the inevitable shift from core to context and the balance between mission critical and supporting processes, an IT organization must do its own planning, defining a model that will permit it to change direction quickly. A few basic operating principles that should become part of the charter for any IT organization become apparent. First, professionals should demand that any new system or system under revision evince high reusability. Retire or replace systems that have closed architectures; the business case for doing so is based upon the long-term maintenance costs and opportunity costs to the organization. Second, adopt standards that allow for high interoperability at both the applications development and infrastructure level. This does not (as some have asserted) demand an open source approach. Rather, this is a feature of a clearly understood enterprise architecture, one that identifies how all of the systems relevant to your business interrelate and how they will evolve over time. A manufacturing enterprise with computer-aided machining will have different needs than a pharmaceutical research organization that prizes knowledge sharing; each, however, will be subject to the same pressures to support interoperability. Third, make sure that all members of the IT organization are aware of the pressures of commoditization. Often, strategies are articulated only at the highest level of an IT organization, even though the implications of commoditization will affect the daily decisions each member of the IT team makes. Programmers and Architects decide on code design,

Business Analysts guide their business users to functionality in systems, Project Managers set and meet expectations about delivery quality and timeliness. The Enterprise Service Approach is a discipline that goes from the top to the bottom of an organization. While portfolio management is enacted at the planning level of an IT organization, SOA and Enterprise Architecture must be enacted at all levels. In fact, the great challenge of implementing SOA and integrating Enterprise Architecture into an organization's model is the inculcation of the principles underlying them into the daily practice of not only the IT department as a whole but also the business professionals outside of IT whom they support.

## Awareness

In becoming a service provider to the business and a strategic partner who enables business vision through technology, the IT organization must develop a new quality of awareness. First, the IT organization needs to develop insight into the direction of the business, to its drivers and the value chain, to direction and differentiators. This knowledge is critical in doing enterprise architecture planning, to acknowledging the external drivers as well as the business direction embraced by the organization as a whole. Second, the IT organization needs to facilitate visibility into its operations. The obfuscation traditionally attributed to IT, in which technical complexity was a smoke screen hiding rogue decision making, needs to be removed both in perception and in reality. With commoditization and increased requirements for repeatability, expectations of measurable performance have increased. If an organization holds external providers to a high service level, why not hold internal IT to similar standards?

IT remains an exciting and evolving field, and the opportunities for CIOs and IT management continue to expand as IT becomes more deeply embedded in the business processes of firms of every stripe. It is true that the field is changing, that the nature of IT leadership has moved from technical excellence to business acumen, but this should not be daunting. Since the origin of the field in the mid-20th century, those who succeeded were the innovative few who rode the wave of change, enjoying the challenge that IT, and its evolution, provided.

# References

Bernard, S., 2004. *An Introduction to Enterprise Architecture.* Author House.

Blechar, M. J., and M. Hotie, 2004. "SODA Return on Investment Model Productivity Factors." The Gartner Group. 13 October. Gartner G00123501.

Brown, J. S., and J. Hagel III, 2003. "Flexible IT, Better Strategy." *McKinsey Quarterly*, No. 4.

Brynjolfsson, E., 2003. "The IT Productivity Gap." *Optimize Magazine*, 22, July.

Carr, N. G., 2004. *Does IT Matter? Information Technology and the Corrosion of Competitive Advantage.* Harvard Business School Press.

Carr, N. G., 2003. "IT Doesn't Matter." *Harvard Business Review*, May.

Dunn, D., 2004. "Catch the Wind." *Information Week.* January 5.

Friedman, T. L., 2005. *The World is Flat: A Brief History of the Twenty-First Century*. Farrar, Straus and Giroux.

Jackson, S. A., 2002. *The Quiet Crisis: Falling Short in Producing American Scientific and Technical Talent.* BEST: Building Engineering & Science Talent.

Kalakota, R., 1999. *e-Business Roadmap for Success.* Addison-Wesley Longman.

Gomolski, B., 2003. "Management Update: Enterprises Should Assess How Their IT Spending Stacks Up." The Gartner Group. 13 August, Gartner IGG-08132003-01.

Hecker, D. E., 2004. "Occupational employment projections to 2012." *Monthly Labor Review*, 127(2), February.

Levy, F., and R. J. Murnane, 2004. *The New Division of Labor: How Computers are Creating the Next Job Market.* Princeton University Press.

Mark, D., and E. Monnoyer, 2004. "Next-generation CIOs." *The McKinsey Quarterly*, July.

McGovern, James, S. W. Ambler, M. E. Stevens, J. Linn, E. K. Jo, and V. Sharan, 2004. *A Practical Guide to Enterprise Architecture.* Prentice Hall.

Moore, G. A., 2004. "Mind Your Core Business." *Optimize*, November.

Moore, G. A., 2002. *Living on the Fault Line: Managing for Shareholder Value in Any Economy.* Harper Collins.

Perks, C., and T. Beveridge, 2003. *Guide to Enterprise IT Architecture.* Springer-Verlag.

Peters, T., 1999. *The Brand You 50: Fifty Ways to Transform Yourself from an "Employee" into a Brand that Shouts Distinction, Commitment, and Passion!* Knopf, 1999.

Pink, D. H., 2005. *A Whole New Mind: Moving from the Information Age to the Conceptual Age.* Penguin.

President's Council of Advisors on Science and Technology (PCAST), 2004. *Sustaining the Nation's Innovation Ecosystems: Report on Information Technology Manufacturing and Competitiveness.* January.

Rindlaub, J., 2004. "K-12 Public Education: Ignoring Good Management Practices and Risking America's Future." Washington Policy Institute, April 15.

Ross, J., and P. Weill, 2004. "Recipe for Good Governance." *CIO Magazine*, June 15.

Schmelzer, R., 2004. "Outsourcing, SOA, and the Industrialization of IT ZapFlash." Available: http://www.zapthink.com. Document ID: ZAPFLASH-10132004.

Spewak, S. H., 1992. *Enterprise Architecture Planning: Developing a Blueprint for Data, Applications and Technology.* John Wiley & Sons.

Standish Group International, 1995. The CHAOS Report. Available: http://www.standishgroup.com.

Standish Group International, 1999. CHAOS: A Recipe for Success. Available: http://www.standishgroup.com.

Varon, E., 2003. "2010: The Future of the CIO." *CIO*, 15 December.

Waters, R., 2003. "Corporate Computing Tries to Find a New Path." *Financial Times*, 4 June.

West, K., and N. Martin, 2004. "Services Take IT Back to Basics." *Optimize*, 22, June.

Woods, D., 2003. *Enterprise Services Architecture.* O'Reilly.

# 18

# Open Source: Time for a Plan

*Thomas Costello*

## ▶ It's Not Coming—It's Here

Do you know how much Open Source is currently in use in your organization? Notice I didn't ask "if" you have any. It is there, and no matter how closely you're watching, there's more than you think.

If you are running any variation of Linux, such as RedHat, SuSE, Mandrake, or BSD, you're using Open Source. If you have Apache in your Web environment, you're using Open Source. According to the April 2003 review by Netcraft,[1] which scanned 40 million public-facing Web sites, 63 percent of those sites were using Apache. A survey by that same organization run in April 2005 showed the market share now at 69 percent—of over 62 million servers.

---

1. Netcraft Web Survey, April 1, 2005, http://news.netcraft.com/archives/web_server_survey.html

For the most part, American firms that are using Open Source tools are doing so at the infrastructure level. Head to South America, Europe, or Asia and it is a much bigger story, with Open Source in use for devices, desktop, and mission-critical business applications.

Whether you are an expert, novice, or are uninformed on Open Source, you need to start preparing an Open Source strategy for your enterprise. If you're a CFO or a CEO of your firm, you should be asking for one. If you are a nonprofit organization, government, a cash-lean organization, about to start a company from scratch, or investing in a seed startup, you must consider Open Source as a path for your technology strategy.

## Motivation and Justification

The reasons for initiating Open Source fall into a couple of key categories:

- Cost savings on licensing
- Reduction of support costs
- Alternative to proprietary solutions
- Better functionality
- Better security
- Performance improvement
- Higher quality
- Pressure from overseas locations
- Open standards
- Strategic readiness

As you're reading this, there are a few technologists (and others) steaming over the wording of many of these bullets. They are already grabbing their pens or typing email replies about why Open Source tools aren't better than their current solution at one of many of the items listed. There isn't enough space in this entire chapter to wage that war on a tool-by-tool basis. Suffice to say that many organizations are finding Open Source tools to be enterprise ready, and they need to be considered, not discounted.

# Prove It?

In much the same way our nightly "world news" is very U.S.-centric (myopic), information in U.S.-based periodicals relating to Open Source is thin at best when it comes to telling us about technology in the rest of the world.

Here are some quick details:

- In Peru one local government official calculated the cost of properly licensing their desktops with Microsoft tools was nearly four times their annual IT budget—and promptly initiated a switch to Open Source. In 2004 a Peruvian national legislator initiated efforts to mandate the exclusive use of Open Source tools across the country.

- In Brazil 2003 legislation mandated that 80 percent of all computers in state institutions and business be moved to Open Source, going so far as to establish a Chamber of the Implementation of Software Libre.

- IDG reported that over 500 different agencies within the German government are working with the Federal Ministry to implement Open Source software. The city of Munich recently agreed to convert over 14,000 desktops to Linux.

- Diane Unger, the CIO of DaimlerChrysler, announced that the company's conversion to Linux provided it with both a 40 percent reduction in cost and a 20 percent boost in performance.

- In 2000 IBM announced a strategy to push Open Source in Europe. Hewlett-Packard followed suit shortly thereafter. By 2003, if you purchased an IBM server in Europe, it came with Linux. As of November 2004, IBM leads the world in overall server sales and growth. Hewlett-Packard, IBM, and Dell accounted for over $1 billion in Linux server sales in the third quarter of 2004 alone.

- At LinuxWorld 2004, Jack Messman, CEO of Novell, predicted that 2004 would be the year Linux would become mainstream in the enterprise—with major software vendors making their applications Linux ready.

- The transition is occurring across a wide spectrum of industries, including Wall Street and beyond. Merrill Lynch and Verizon released studies in 2003 showing savings in hardware, software, and administrative costs—Verizon reporting a savings of over $6 million in hardware alone. In March 2005 Merrill Lynch reported that it has seen a price-performance improvement by a factor of four.

- According to CSIS (Center for Strategic and International Studies) 24 countries have now mandated the use of Open Source for some or all government operations or are actively creating alternatives based on existing Open Source products (e.g., Brazil, Portugal, France, Spain, China, Red Flag initiative, Peru). With global government software procurement at over $17 billion in 2004 and increasing by approximately 10 percent per year, the direct and downstream impacts of Open Source on software and service providers is clear—adapt, compete, or be prepared for a shrinking market.

## Open Source Defined

While the United States is still discovering and exploring the use of Open Source tools for infrastructure (and predominately Web-based, at that), the rest of the world is moving forward with Open Source implementation of tools and applications for back office, front office, devices, peripherals, desktop, and more. Yes, Open Source is way more than Linux. Likewise, Open Source is way more than just code. A clean definition of Open Source has to be carved into three key categories: methodology, tools and applications, and licensing. We tackle these subtopics in that order as we move through this chapter.

## Open Source: The Methodology

In the early 1990s, Eric Raymond (at that time an accomplished developer and UNIX evangelist) was shocked by the manner in which the Linux operating system had been developed and evolved. Linux was not evolving using the traditional methodology of a structured team with a choreographed and controlled development approach. Eric wanted to understand, define, and adapt/enhance what he learned about the growth of Linux to redefine how software development could be most effective. His book *The Cathedral and the Bazaar* outlines his personal observations and findings running a successful 1996 Open Source initiative. This text has become the source for key differences in Open Source development methodology.

Among the more obvious challenges is the virtual nature of the development team, typically constructed of volunteers scattered about the globe working on various components of the application. Contributions and ideas for enhancements or new functionality can come from anyone at any time. Open Source development initiatives have a leader who acts as a combination product manager and negotiator, resolving all issues related to what should be included and how it should be done. Unlike more structured and proprietary development efforts, the Open Source application (and the source code) are assembled and made available to anyone on a very frequent basis for review and improvement.

## After the Installation

When the end product is finished, purchasers of proprietary applications turn to the vendor for implementation and development support. In the proprietary model, this connection is clear and has distinct economic ramifications to the vendor. However, given that an Open Source "project team" is a virtual collection of developers, the end user is faced with a new paradigm: there isn't a "company" on the other side, and the old rules and approaches don't quite apply.

While this scenario has its obvious problems, there are also distinct advantages for the end user. In the proprietary world, there is only one source to which the buyer can turn for true modification to the application engine: the vendor. This isn't to be confused with consultancies who can implement and or configure an application. True modification and extension to the core engine can only be accomplished by the vendor given the closed nature of the source code. Changes or enhancements to the core engine require the vendor product manager to approve, define, fund, and schedule requests. Remember the last time you were waiting for that key bug fix to be rolled out from your vendor? There are quite a few CIOs who completely understand this process and quite a few vendor salesmen who do not.

In the Open Source world, when an end user requires support, the search starts with both the development project team and boutique support organizations (typically aimed at particular applications). Each option normally consists of developers who contributed to the original coding effort. Given that the team will not charge for code, support is the predominant manner in which money can be made in the Open

Source model. Many have complained that there aren't enough (and in some cases, there aren't any) support organizations capable or local enough to provide reasonable support. As is true with any application, the more successful and widespread the installation base, the more support organizations will appear.

The mere ability to support and construct extension is the underlying tenet that causes the application to improve and grow for the entire user base. As a result, most projects have a very positive and self-preserving reason to provide quality support.

## Dilution of Resource Effort

Neither the Open Source community nor proprietary vendors have cornered the market on good or innovative ideas. Each still faces the challenges of features and functions as well as time to market. Neither approach restricts the number of teams or companies attempting to build the next great application. In the case of the proprietary teams, developers are funded with the pace and scope directly related to the funding of that team. Open Source initiatives, however, are heavily dependent on volunteer developers. The Open Source community presently faces a challenge of too many efforts producing many variations of similar applications, all competing for a limited pool of developers. At times, this causes a dilution of resources interested or competent to work on the given application type.

Though the Open Source methodology may allow the teams to move at a brisk pace with a wide array of input, the real-world practicalities have resulted in a vast number of efforts ranging from great to poor and any number of efforts that just stop and go on the shelf. Either the available quantity of resources must be applied to a narrower set of efforts where more robust Open Source applications would be produced more quickly, or more resources must become available.

## Development Tools

Many people confuse the creation of an Open Source product with the Open Source tools used to produce software. As an example, the LAMP architecture (Linux, Apache, MySQL, and PERL) is a common toolset used to produce code. Each of these tools is an Open Source product. There are many other Open Source tools available to aid in the development of software beyond this list, including development environments and testing tools. The use of these tools can decrease both the cost of development and the end-user environment required to run the resulting end product. Software created using Open Source tools is not necessarily Open Source software. There is no restriction or obligation to make the final application Open Source as a result of using these tools.

## Market Acceptance

The array of desktop applications for business, recreation, hobbyists, and beyond is staggering. Again, in the United States, little attention or press is given to Open Source applications available and/or under development. Market share is garnered through word-of-mouth or the serendipity of a review by a technical magazine.

In 2004 many people began to discover a then little-known browser called FireFox (known as Phoenix in its earliest stages). After years with little to no change in market share for browsers, FireFox moved from virtually unknown to just over 6 percent of the browser market in roughly 6 months.

While this isn't as earth shattering as some new revolutionary package or "the next big thing," it is a sign of the evolution of Open Source to more mainstream thinking beyond Linux—and a sign of acceptance of Open Source desktop applications. But how do you measure the impact of a free Open Source product when the traditional measure of market share has been based on "sales"? Various organizations are tackling this in different ways: measuring quantity of downloads, surveys, output from professional organizations, and data from Open Source providers themselves. As the market continues to mature, more reliable means of measuring will continue to evolve the very broad array of Open Source products and the impact on both consumers and enterprise.

## Beyond Servers: Applications and the Desktop

While Linux is most often thought of as a server operating system, it is not just for servers anymore. Product vendors roll out a wide variety of distributions (called "distros") of Linux. Each distro comes with the current version of the Linux kernel along with the vendor's recommended/preferred set of supporting tools and applications. Some of these distributions include an extremely wide array of applications and utilities not found on your current desktop, along with development tools and other applications that may not be of interest to a typical end user.

Most distributions include two different flavors of a desktop environment: KDE and GNOME (or some variations of these). Anyone who has seen these desktop environments will quickly verify that these are not primitive tools. For those of you who lived through the WordPerfect-to-Word transition, you'll find your first experience with these tools quite similar. You'll mentally be thinking of the menu option by name and looking for the similar option in the new tool. Almost immediately, you'll find that these tools are so similar that the learning curve is quite low. Many of the latest variations of Linux desktops have begun to sculpt their menu structures to be more similar to Windows, thus easing the transition and learning curve.

Included with these desktops are a set of office suite tools. The most popular of these is Open Office, which includes a word processor, spreadsheet, presentation and math/calculation (for complex math) applications, a drawing tool, and more. These applications can both create and open files in Microsoft formats as well as produce PDF output. Again, a quick review of these tools will show that they are not primitive.

In 2003 these desktop environments did not appear to be ready for "prime time." Coupled with the low availability of IT expertise in the arena, it was hard to recommend their use for enterprises or for common consumer use. At that time, only the tech savvy needed apply. Installation on both desktops and laptops required a fair amount of technical skill to ensure all drivers and devices would properly function. Once running, however, these environments were the model of stability. Today, these distros and desktop environments have made huge progress—faster than could have been envisioned even a year ago. While not perfect, the progress on both the applications themselves and the resource skill sets available is such that many organizations have found the environments to be "enterprise ready."

While Open Source desktops may not be perfect for all parts of the organization, most enterprises should be running lab experiments on various flavors and mapping against departmental needs. For those of us old enough to remember the transition from mixed desktop environments running various word processors and spreadsheet applications to a unified, standard desktop, a Linux desktop lab should conform to many of the best practices learned from that conversion. Your lab should simulate and re-create the needs of each department with sample data (clones of real-world materials) and undergo the kind of testing you would utilize for software development, including acceptance criteria.

So now that I have you seriously thinking about getting your feet wet, we need to discuss the most important yet least understood aspect of Open Source: licensing.

## Licensing

The most important yet confusing aspect of the Open Source debate is licensing. If you are like most other software users, you have never read the End User License Agreement (EULA) for any of the software you are currently using, proprietary or otherwise. One study noted numbers that ranged from 31 percent to as many as 96 percent of the users of given applications had not read any of the licensing terms.

Though there are countless variations of proprietary licenses, there are some basic elements that you should consistently find in those agreements. For proprietary software, the creator retains ownership and is granting you a license to use the software under a set of described conditions, possibly including the number of machines that the code may be installed upon, servers or processors, and so on. Typically, you are not granted access to the underlying source code and therefore cannot change or extend the software. Likewise, proprietary licenses typically prohibit you from reverse engineering the software to understand or re-create how it runs. In the cases where you are able to extend vendor software, you are normally granted access to APIs or modules that exist outside of the vendor's core engine.

In the Open Source world, there are numerous variations to five core license types: GPL (General Public License), LGPL ("Lesser" General Public License), the New BSD License (Berkeley Software Distribution), MIT, and the MPL (Mozilla Public License). The GPL and MPL tend to be the predominant standards for Open Source licenses. The Open

Source Initiative site (www.opensource.org) provides detailed sample text for these license types and more. Some of the primary tenets of Open Source licensing are the restriction from charging for the code itself, that the source code must be made available and allow for modification (with restrictions and obligations), and the obligation to ensure that the Open Source licensing persists to variations and derivatives of the original work.

While a lively discussion could ensue regarding the merits or failings of any of these licensing types, rather zealous arguments often erupt over the corporate economics of Open Source. Some have accused Open Source licensing as being "communist" or at least "anti-capitalist" and others have even filed legal action attempting to invalidate the GPL licenses and its variations. When reviewed from the perspective of the creator of the code, however, it is clear that the Open Source licenses enable the individual developer or team to release their work to the world at large without the expectation of direct profit.

## The Cultural Implications

And this brings us to the stickiest part of the Open Source debate: culture shock. All indications are that Open Source has evolved way beyond a pure techie phenomenon—evidenced by the transformation of most Open Source conferences from the "t-shirt crowd" to the "suits." Now the debate is raging well beyond base questions of speed, algorithms, and methodologies. Like nearly all other technology questions (but especially when asked of a technologist), Open Source is a word that immediately sparks emotional, zealous reactions.

For some, Open Source appears to be a socialist threat to overthrow the intellectual property, free market–driven economy in which we live. To others, it is the best hope (or threat) to halt the real or perceived Redmond juggernaut. To others, it is a software equivalent to the credo of the scientific world that believes that experiments must be documented, shared, repeated, improved, and eventually lead to the improvement and advancement of mankind.

If you can get past these stances and get to the core value of using Open Source solutions, you'll recognize that most major vendors and the rest of the world are moving down the Open Source path to varying degrees. Open Source isn't just about "free" software. As many in the Open Source world point out, it is "free as in freedom, not as in free beer" (a quote most often credited to Richard Stallman).

## Who Must Change?

While the "anti-capitalist" remarks and intellectual property lawsuit are somewhere between entertaining and annoying, they are smoke screens of a greater issue: that proprietary vendors are unprepared (if not unable) to come up with a business model to compete with "free software."

Only time will tell whether those vendors who are embracing the change potential of Open Source are leading their organizations to greatness or walking the plank.

The Open Source community, fragmented by its very definition, must find a way to address its shortcomings and needs that are becoming more evident from the growth into the enterprise market. There will be those within the Open Source community who are uncomfortable with the maturity curve transition from the great experiment to enterprise readiness. The entire Open Source model will require evolution but will create a vast array of new businesses to support the increased demand as part of the maturity process.

CIOs and enterprises at large must learn how to work with the new models presented by the Open Source community to leverage the opportunity to the benefit of their organizations. They must become versed in the new models to find and engage the right vendors. They will be tasked to change some of their bureaucratic processes and axioms in order to even connect with these vendors in a timely and efficient way. They will need to adapt their own delivery organizations to absorb the new technologies, tools, and approaches.

## What Next?

The IT workforce has changed and will continue to change. The economic landscape in which enterprises function has also changed. CIOs must find the balance between economic prudence and growth for their organizations at a time when they are being tasked to do more with less. Open Source presents new challenges and opportunities for organizations of every size and type.

While this chapter has barely scratched the surface of just a few Open Source issues, you have a few topics as starting points. If you have the resources, I highly recommend that you take an average machine from your environment and pull down one of the Linux variations. Select one of the desktops and just take a look at the tools. I recommend that you work with your CFO to closely review and compare the prospect of using Open Source tools in your environment. You should consult your legal team (internal or external) to advise them of your interest in Open Source to ensure they're prepared to assist you. You should work with any professional organizations to which you belong to start probing about their experiences with Open Source. You should identify Open Source resources in your organization and have them capture research on potential opportunities and alternatives. But most importantly, you need to start asking how your organization can leverage Open Source—and discover how it can become part of your strategy and tactical plans.

# IT Governance: Toward a Unified Framework Linked to and Driven by Corporate Governance

*David Pultorak*

## ▶ Introduction

At the time of this writing, the industry has yet to sort out the precise nature of IT governance. IT governance remains an evolving concept within an evolving concept: that of corporate governance. The old adage, "What you see depends on where you sit," describes precisely where we are in the discourse around the nature of IT governance. Existing perspectives on the nature of IT governance include the following:

1. IT managers and specialized IT staff tend to see IT governance as a mechanism for aligning business and IT at the level of the program office, projects, and significant IT investments and architectural decisions.

2. IT Auditors tend to see IT governance as a control mechanism to ensure compliance with relevant authorities and to manage risk to the business.

3. IT service management professionals tend to see IT governance as ensuring IT services are aligned to current and future business needs, meet quality objectives as perceived by the customers, and are managed for efficiency and effectiveness.

4. Corporate board members and top managers sometimes do not know what to make of IT governance (just as they are sometimes at a loss for what to make of IT in general) and have in some cases abdicated responsibility for IT governance.

Except in the last instance, there is nothing inherently wrong with any of these perspectives. What is wrong and dangerous is an over-focus on one perspective or the persistence in the organization of multiple, unaligned perspectives. For example, many organizations coping with Sarbanes-Oxley start to see corporate governance solely as control around financial reporting and pay little regard to other aspects of governance. The operational reality in many of today's organizations is that IT governance is conducted as an unaligned set of activities based on a mix of competing micro-theories, the unintended consequence of which is the creation of the very inefficiencies and risk exposures that governance mechanisms are intended to address.

This chapter looks at IT governance from a perspective and scope that is different from what is common today. It takes the position that IT governance, properly construed, is a *discipline* within corporate governance, and as such, the board's perspective should be primary and the board should be the ultimate driver of IT governance. As a discipline within corporate governance, IT governance activity should be directed in the dimensions important to corporate governance: Conformance, Performance, and Relating Responsibly (CPR), where

- Conformance is ensuring that the corporation meets relevant regulatory requirements.

- Performance is ensuring that the corporation achieves its performance objectives.
- Relating responsibly is paying appropriate attention to relevant stakeholders.

We start by briefly recounting the evolution of the concept of corporate governance. We then outline a three-part CPR framework for board-directed governance and provide guidance on how to implement the CPR framework for IT governance.

# ▶ Corporate Governance: An Evolving Concept

In the wake of the previously unthinkable business debacles that marred the early days of this century, everyone seems to acknowledge the need for corporate governance. But what *is* corporate governance, precisely? Specifically, *who performs it, to what end, and by what means?* At times there seem to be as many answers to these questions on the nature of corporate governance as there are people talking about it. As shown in Table 19.1 and outlined in the paragraphs that follow, while the end game of corporate governance has not changed, who performs it and by what means has evolved considerably from traditional concepts.

## Corporate Governance: Unchanging End, Changing Means

Historically, the end game of corporate governance has been sustained financial results *by means of a focus on financial management*, so much so that in the recent past, corporate governance was virtually synonymous with the measuring, monitoring, and reporting of the financial condition of the enterprise. While focus on sustained financial results is an appropriate and timeless end, the landscape upon which business is conducted has changed such that the *means* to achieving that aim must change in a number of important ways. The paragraphs that follow outline how the business landscape has changed and how the means of governance must change to fit that landscape.

**Table 19.1** Toward a New Concept of Corporate Governance:
The CPR Framework

| Corporate Governance | Performer | End | Means |
|---|---|---|---|
| The traditional concept | The board, top management, financial auditors | Sustainable financial results | Avoidance of realization of risks to financial results through control |
| The CPR framework | The board, all management, a variety of auditors, all staff, external entities | Sustainable financial results | Managing and leading for results in three dimensions: CPR for the four assets any business must govern: infrastructure, clients and external stakeholders, internal people and process, value creation |

Today's organizations are complex, distributed, networked entities in a complex, distributed, networked marketplace. In the past, it might have been possible for a single person or small group of people to "get the whole system in mind" and exercise governance. This is less and less feasible and is impossible in some cases. The impact is that *who performs corporate governance must change.* In the traditional view, corporate governance was the responsibility of the board and its immediate delegates (top management and financial auditors), and the focus was financial. In today's complex organizations, where the corporation's "value constellation" is made up of a constantly changing set of entities (some outside of the corporation's direct control), governance activity must be extended both down into and outside of the organization to include an expanded role for internal staff and external entities. In addition, as IT and security have emerged as significant risk areas to the business in addition to financial practices, IT and security auditors must be added to the mix.

The networked nature of today's businesses and marketplace means aspects beyond financial ones can have an immediate and lasting impact on the organization. The result is that *the scope of key performance indicators (KPIs) that must be managed to achieve sustained financial results must be expanded beyond the financials.* About a decade ago, Kaplan and Norton (1996) highlighted the fact that focusing on financial performance alone was not enough to ensure sustainable results. Kaplan and Norton dramatically extended the factors to be considered in corporate governance, recommending a balanced scorecard of governance dimensions: financial performance, business process, customer fulfillment, and learning and growth (Figure 19.1).

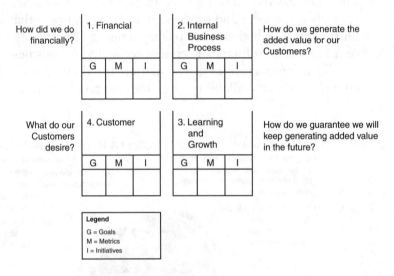

**Figure 19.1** The Balanced Scorecard.

Weill and Ross (2004) highlight the object of governance as six key assets to be managed:

- Human
- Financial
- Physical
- IP
- Information and IT
- Relationship

Both the Balanced Scorecard and Weill and Ross's work are certainly contributions to the industry and useful tools to be included in any governance framework. These frameworks are working to answer the question, What are the principal assets of a firm that any business must mind in order to thrive? Pultorak (2001) attempts to update the answer to this question in the form of the Technical and Operational Architecture (TOA) dashboard, which is shown in Figure 19.2. The TOA dashboard is a technical and organizational architecture dashboard because it encompasses both the technical (infrastructure) and the organizational (clients and external stakeholders, internal people and process, value creation) architecture that all firms must have to succeed.

The TOA dashboard is intended to capture the four assets—infrastructure, clients, people and process, and value creation—that any business must manage, whether it is a bakery, a mid-market manufacturing firm, or a Fortune 500 financial services company. All businesses must have a solid infrastructure as a foundation for doing business, with high enough levels of availability given the cost required for further levels of

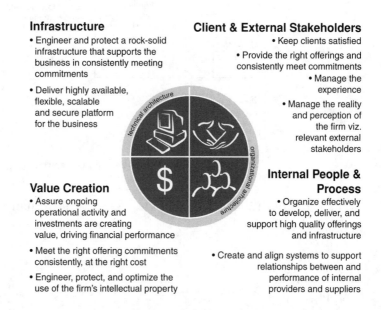

**Infrastructure**
• Engineer and protect a rock-solid infrastructure that supports the business in consistently meeting commitments

• Deliver highly available, flexible, scalable and secure platform for the business

**Client & External Stakeholders**
• Keep clients satisfied

• Provide the right offerings and consistently meet commitments

• Manage the experience

• Manage the reality and perception of the firm viz. relevant external stakeholders

**Value Creation**
• Assure ongoing operational activity and investments are creating value, driving financial performance

• Meet the right offering commitments consistently, at the right cost

• Engineer, protect, and optimize the use of the firm's intellectual property

**Internal People & Process**
• Organize effectively to develop, deliver, and support high quality offerings and infrastructure

• Create and align systems to support relationships between and performance of internal providers and suppliers

**Figure 19.2** TOA: Technical and organizational architecture. The four assets any business must govern.

*Source:* Adapted from Pultorak, D., "Yes We Can Do It—And This Is What It Will Cost." *Presentation to the itSMF Annual Conference,* 2001, Brighton, UK.

availability. They must serve their customers in ways that make customers want to come back. They must ensure relationships with external stakeholders are maintained in a manner that enables rather than disables the business, because the organization's reputation is often its most valuable asset, the most easily lost and the most difficult to regain. They must take care of the people who serve the customer, including suppliers, and ensure that business processes are optimized. Lastly, they must ensure the value creation capability of the firm is maintained and enhanced so that the firm has the basis for driving toward business value and financial performance. The TOA dashboard in combination with the CPR framework, outlined later in the chapter, are intended to form the bones of a sound governance framework that can be used across the corporation.

In the current business landscape of highly networked enterprises in a highly networked marketplace, normal operating conditions include a relative frequency and variability of demands (opportunities and threats) that are high and increasing. In this climate, *the scope of mechanisms for achieving sustained financial results must be extended beyond merely controlling for business risk to driving toward business opportunity.* While some see risk management as including understanding and managing both negative and positive risks (positive risks being opportunities), many do not. Controlling risk is an appropriate focus, and the need for such focus is clearly increasing, but today's complex organizations may not be able to achieve sustainable results if driven solely by the avoidance of risk. Achieving sustainable results requires more than just "avoiding pain" (e.g., controlling, directing, and managing to avoid breakdowns, risks, and negative consequences); it requires "moving toward gain" (e.g., supporting and enabling positive performance, and appropriate risk-taking.) As such, a governance framework must provide a mechanism for both seeking gain (maximizing value) and avoiding pain (managing risk). Control is but one of many means to the end of sustainable results.

The business landscape of highly networked firms in a highly networked market means the number of stakeholders relevant to a firm's sustained success might be an order of magnitude greater than in a landscape that is not networked. As a result, *the scope of stakeholders relevant to sustained financial results must be expanded, and along with it, the scope of effort required to manage both the reality and perception of the corporation's functioning.* Many corporations have stumbled as they worked toward achieving sustainable financial results for two reasons: first, they overlooked important, relevant stakeholders, and second, the way they conducted themselves "turned off" rather than "turned on" relevant stakeholders. Proper governance requires attention to both *what* you do and *how* you do it in the eyes of relevant stakeholders.

Any useful operational definition of corporate governance must address these issues. The TOA scorecard forms part of such an operational definition, identifying the four assets any business must manage in order to thrive. What is missing is the specification of the dimensions along which these assets must be managed. The CPR framework, first introduced in Pultorak (2003) and presented below, is just such a framework. The CPR framework, used in combination with the TOA dashboard, is intended as a governance framework applicable across the enterprise.

# ▶ The CPR Framework for Corporate Governance

The CPR framework defines corporate governance as follows:

> Corporate governance is the systematic pattern of behavior of the board, management, and staff of a corporation that is directed toward the corporation achieving sustainable financial results. The behavior that is corporate governance must be directed toward the four primary assets of the business:

> 1. Infrastructure
> 2. Clients and external stakeholders
> 3. Internal people and process
> 4. Value creation

> by managing the current and creating the future state of the corporation by expending effort in three dimensions:

> 1. Conformance—to legal and regulatory requirements
> 2. Performance—financial and otherwise
> 3. Relating Responsibly—maintaining rapport with relevant stakeholders

To ensure success, the behavior that constitutes corporate governance must be ordered within a framework established by the board that aligns and informs day-to-day decision making, objective setting, achievement monitoring, and communication.

There are a number of important distinctions made in this operational definition of corporate governance:

1. The aim of corporate governance is clear and singular: sustainable financial results. However, sustainable financial results cannot be achieved solely by directing the management of the current state of the organization; it also requires directing the organization toward its future state. The ancient Greek philosopher Heraclitus considered "becoming" as preceding "being," To him, if "becoming" should cease, then all things, including "being," would cease. Therefore, it goes with corporate governance: a governance framework that focuses on regulating the "being"—the current, steady state of an organization is not sustainable. What is required is a governance framework that propels it toward what it is to be, a governance framework that focuses on "becoming." Danny Maco (2003) echoes this sentiment by stating that ". . . what a company is now is less important than what a company plans to be."

2. Governance is primarily *behavior* that constitutes a relationship between the corporation and its relevant stakeholders. Stewardship is perhaps the best word that captures the nature of such behavior. While artifacts like systems, policies, and controls may enable (and in some cases disable) governance, they do not constitute governance itself. Governance is constituted by behavior, and it is that behavior which constitutes the relationship among relevant stakeholders, including owners/shareholders, the board, and top management. This view stands in sharp contrast to other positions on what constitutes governance, including those that see governance primarily as decision making (as behavior includes action as well as decision) or those that equate governance with its mechanisms and artifacts.

3. Effort expended on governance should be driven efficiently from the right source. The right source is the corporate board, hence the requirement in the CPR definition of corporate governance that "corporate governance must be ordered within a framework established

by the board that aligns and informs day-to-day decision making, objective setting, achievement monitoring, and communication."

The corporate governance framework set out by the board must constitute a compelling vision and a simple set of policies and procedures that serves four purposes:

- Clarifies the direction of the corporation
- Motivates people to take action in the right direction
- Prioritizes, informs, guides, and aligns the many decisions, actions, and communications made each day
- Provides a basis for monitoring progress

4. The object of governance is the four primary assets of the business: infrastructure, clients and external stakeholders, internal people and process, and value creation. Without effort along the right dimensions toward managing these assets, no business can survive or thrive.

5. Governance requires effort in the three dimensions of CPR mentioned earlier. *Conformance* means ensuring that the corporation meets relevant legislative requirements. *Performance* means ensuring that the corporation achieves its performance objectives. *Relating responsibly* means paying appropriate attention to relevant stakeholders. Effort within each dimension is necessary, but each alone is not sufficient for sustainable results. Sustainable results require more than just driving toward financial performance and more than controlling, directing, and managing to avoid breakdowns, risks, and negative consequences. Sustainable results require the supporting and enabling of positive performance, appropriate risk taking, and "moving toward gain." As such, a governance framework must provide a mechanism for both seeking gain (maximizing value) and avoiding pain (managing risk). Just managing risk is not enough. While it is certainly necessary to prevent and mitigate situations and conditions that are, or could potentially, affect performance negatively, considerable effort and focus must be directed toward creating and driving situations and conditions that would positively affect performance. How one gets there also matters a great deal, which means that building and managing the relating-responsibly aspect

with relevant stakeholders is also essential. The sections that follow describe the three dimensions more thoroughly.

The CPR framework for governance is depicted in Figure 19.3. The CPR framework includes the vital task of managing risk through controlled compliance to relevant regulatory authorities (Conformance). However, effort in two additional dimensions (Performance and Relating Responsibly) is a necessary part of good governance because governance, properly construed, cannot be just about mitigating risks, about avoiding the pain of lack of compliance with regulatory authorities (Conformance). Managing negative risks is not enough. No business would survive that had as its sole governance focus the avoidance of risk and pain. What every business must do is move toward gain (Performance) in financial and other relevant dimensions, while conducting itself in such a way that good relations (Relating Responsibly) with relevant stakeholders are maintained.

The sections that follow further outline the three dimensions of the CPR framework.

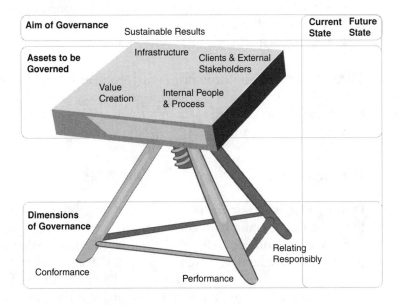

**Figure 19.3** The CPR governance framework: conformance, performance, relating responsibly.

# Conformance

Conformance is about ensuring compliance with relevant authorities as a means of minimizing risk to the business. It is about meeting the corporation's financial and other legal, contractual, and regulatory obligations. It is establishing and managing the control objectives. Conformance activities consist of documenting what you plan to do, doing it, and accumulating evidence to demonstrate that you are indeed doing it. The goal of conformance is compliance with relevant authorities. The instruments for measuring conformance results are the KPI dashboard (continuous) and the audit (periodic).

All business must conform to relevant laws, regulations, guidelines, and expectations, including:

- Financial requirements such as those put forth by the SEC and IRS
- Legal requirements, such as the Sarbanes-Oxley Act
- Health and safety regulations such as HIPAA and the Clean Air Protection Act
- Market expectations of customers and professional associations, such as quality certifications and hotel ratings
- Professional codes of behavior and ethics

Theoretically, all conformance areas are mandatory, but enforcement varies. While government enforcement springs to mind when the topic of conformance is raised, the market will enforce conformance to areas relating to quality and ethics.

# Performance

Performance is about ensuring efficiency and effectiveness. It is doing the right things right. The goal of performance is efficiency and effectiveness in maximizing shareholder and customer value and creating predictable, sustainable value, profit, and wealth, ensuring the long-term financial viability of the business. The instruments for measuring performance results are the KPI dashboard (continuous) and the assessment review (periodic).

All businesses must measure, monitor, and manage to performance indicators from the perspective of all relevant key stakeholders, in areas such as

- Infrastructure
- Client satisfaction, including customer fulfillment
- Product capabilities
- Employee productivity, including learning and growth
- Internal business process
- Agility in all the aforementioned areas
- Business value, including the all-important financials

As you can see, these areas extend further the balanced scorecard idea of governing beyond financial performance indicators as a means to sustainable results.

## Relating Responsibly

Relating Responsibly is about ensuring that the business relates to relevant stakeholders in a consistent and responsible way. It covers social values and standards, providing transparent performance statistics, demonstrating integrity, and balancing the interests of stakeholders, including

- Meeting professional, social, and ethical responsibility
- Delivering on commitment to values
- Providing transparent, timely, accurate disclosure of information regarding financial situation, performance, ownership and governance of the company; it is important to note that this aspect is not intended to duplicate the Conformance dimension—the focus here is on *how* conformance is done, rather than *what* is done, and whether or not the "how" enables or disables key relationships
- Demonstrating integrity, accountability, and fairness to, and balancing the interests of, owners, shareholders, and relevant stakeholders, including regulatory authorities
- Managing perception as well as the reality

It is about ensuring that how you do things (the means) is welcomed, rather than rejected, by relevant stakeholders. The goal of relating responsibly is stakeholder satisficing (where *satisficing* is defined as "good enough and just a little bit better"), meaning that good relations exist with relevant stakeholders. The instruments for measuring relating responsibly results are the KPI dashboard (continuous) and the survey (periodic), which entails asking key stakeholders about their perceptions of the firm and its offerings.

All businesses must relate responsibly with relevant stakeholders such as those in Table 19.2.

**Table 19.2** Typical Stakeholders of a Corporation

| Stock owners | Partners |
|---|---|
| The board | Contract staff |
| Executive management | Customers |
| Management | Industry bodies |
| Employees | Consumers |
| Suppliers | Interest groups |
| Partners | Industry analysts |
| The press | Industry associations |

Ensuring a focus on relating responsibly also acknowledges that, as pointed out in the CIMA Discussion Paper on Enterprise Governance, "…with strategic alliances, joint ventures, etc., the single-company view of corporate governance is too narrow." In other words, while it is vital to do so, it is not enough to relate responsibly with clients and shareholders, those stakeholders "internal" to the company. Relationships throughout the firm's "value constellation" must be governed.

Maintaining rapport with key stakeholders is as vital as how you get results and ultimately affects the results you get. Unidentified stakeholders and unmanaged stakeholder relationships represent a significant risk to the business. In the words of Guy Kawasaki, author and columnist for *Forbes* magazine, "good reality" is necessary. However good reality—the actual, objective situation and performance—while necessary, is not sufficient for sustainable results: good perception by key stakeholders is also necessary. Ensuring good perception requires the systems and shrewdness of the politician, not just the technician. As Danny Maco (2003) states in *CIO Wisdom*,

> politics by definition is the art or science of governance.... Politicians, if nothing else, understand the importance of relationships as the means of getting things done within an organization.

## CPR: Toward a Common Communications Channel and Protocol for Governance

The three governance dimensions—conformance, performance, and relating responsibly—are like two-way radio channels. The board and each corporate department simultaneously monitor, transmit, and receive on all three channels. For example, the board might

- Request a report from manufacturing to monitor status on environmental compliance.
- Transmit a request to engineering to map projected product development in a context of fiscal performance against the corporate business plan.
- Receive a description from IT describing the value it brings to the corporation in terms of the services it provides to corporate departments.

The point of this illustration is that no department should have a private communications link with the board with its own protocol, terminology, and timing. All departments must communicate along a standard interface with a standard protocol using standard terminology to avoid the creation of unnecessary risk and inefficiencies. All departments must strive to describe their activities with the same business-oriented, goal-based vocabulary. In all cases, the board should reasonably expect to receive timely, descriptive, and jargon-free replies.

## ▶ Applying the CPR Framework to IT Governance

As stated in the introduction to the chapter, IT governance, properly construed, is a discipline within corporate governance; as such, the board's perspective should be primary, and the board should be the ultimate driver of IT governance. As a discipline within corporate governance, IT governance activity should be directed in the dimensions important to corporate governance: CPR. This section provides guidance on how to implement the CPR framework for IT governance.

Applying the CPR framework to IT governance has a number of important implications, many of which flow down from the overarching discipline of corporate governance:

1. The board, not the IT function, must be the prime driver for IT governance and must provide a framework for governance to provide a standardized communication interface and channel for governance along with simple rules to align and inform everyday decisions and actions toward sustainable financial results.

2. As with the corporation as a whole, sustained financial results must be the objective and prime driver for IT decisions and actions.

3. Govern four assets with the purview of IT governance (infrastructure, clients and external stakeholders, internal people and process (including suppliers and partners), and value creation) in the three dimensions of CPR, and governance must include managing the current and propelling toward the future state of the enterprise.

4. Since governance is behavior, emphasis in implementing this framework must be on changing behavior rather than introducing or changing work artifacts; roles must be set out, including expected behavior changes, not just for the board and top management, but for auditors (IT, security, financial), internal staff, and external entities (such as suppliers).

5. Other IT governance activities (such as IT service continuity management) and frameworks (such as the IT Infrastructure Library) must be aligned within the CPR framework, including program office, project, financial/investment processes, service-level management, business/IT alignment, security and IT audit/conformance, and IT service management processes.

These implications lead to a set of five imperatives for governance, shown in Table 19.3.

**Table 19.3** Five Imperatives for Implementing IT Governance

| |
|---|
| Ensure the board drives governance and provides the governance framework. |
| Focus on sustained financial results. |
| Govern four assets—infrastructure, clients and external stakeholders, internal people and process, value creation—in three dimensions—conformance, performance, and relating responsibly—and include within governance managing the current and directing toward the future state of the firm. |
| Organize around governance as behavior involving key stakeholders. |
| Align sources of guidance for all IT governance within the CPR framework. |

The sections that follow highlight how to go about applying the CPR framework to the IT function by suggesting how to implement governance measures to meet each of the five imperatives. The five imperatives are addressed in turn.

## Ensure the Board Drives Governance and Provides the Governance Framework

Governance is an activity performed jointly by the board and corporate departments. The board sets direction and policy, and departments execute and contribute their best advice and judgment. The IT function cannot be an exception. Where IT really matters to the corporation's future, it makes sense to involve corporate directors in infrastructure concerns. The following statements, from a recent article by Thomas Hoffman (2004) attest to this fact.

> A small number of companies, including Novell, Inc., and FedEx Corp., have elevated responsibility for IT governance to their boards of directors in an attempt to ensure that they have high-level oversight of technology investments.

> Novell's oversight committee, which also includes four other directors from outside the company, monitors major projects and decisions about Novell's technology architecture.

FedEx created an IT oversight committee four years ago that includes board members. Like Novell's committee, the one at FedEx oversees major IT-related projects and architecture decisions and advises both the senior IT management team and other board members on technology issues, according to a spokeswoman for the Memphis-based company.

While the board should rightly drive IT governance, this does not mean that you, the CIO, cannot or should not work to influence how they go about it. In fact, you must ensure that you have what you need to be successful in your role. This starts with understanding your board's current posture, that is, the role they play in the corporation. Typical board postures include

- Window dressing (provide image enhancement)
- Strategic (address long-term and policy issues)
- Operational (direct day-to-day activities)
- Networking (create and enhance relationships)
- All-purpose (work at all levels to some extent)

Understanding your board's current posture is essential because you may need to take steps to make the integration of corporate and IT governance a "real and present" concern for your board.

Reckoning your board's current posture or raison d' être is a vital first step to understanding what you can do to influence their perception. This is essential to getting the m to drive IT governance, as they must see it as a real and present concern in order to do so.

Once you have taken into account the current posture of the board, you must decide where responsibility for IT governance should reside. You will need to define the roles and relationships relative to IT governance of key stakeholders, including owners/shareholders, the board, and top management. The following is intended as a helpful guideline for dividing these responsibilities in a large enterprise:

- Performance aspect: the board
- Conformance aspect: corporate governance committee, compliance committee, audit committee
- Relate responsibly: the board and committees

It is important to map these roles specifically to the IT function to ensure clarity of purpose and completeness of coverage.

You may also have to adjust the board's tasks, roles, and education to ensure that the integration of corporate and IT governance "takes." Ask, Do you have someone on board who has

- primary responsibility for IT governance, including in their role and responsibilities?
- the requisite specialized knowledge and expertise to do the job?
- the interest to invest the appropriate time and energy required to make a difference?

If not, consider including an outside director for this role.

Also, ask yourself the following questions:

- Do you have an independent audit, corporate governance, or compliance committee?
- Are members clear on their role in crisis management for major IT incidents, including how they should liaison with operational IT crisis teams? Have they been trained to do so?
- Is the intersection of IT and corporate governance part of your ongoing education program plan for your directors and part of your orientation program for new directors
- Is IT governance information part of the package prepared for new board members?

So far, the tactics mentioned for getting the board to drive IT governance have been largely influence, education, and role specification. Another key tactic is to leverage Service Level Management as the "communications interface" between corporate and IT governance. This tactic is outlined in the paragraphs that follow.

### Leverage Service-Level Management as Nexus between IT and Corporate Governance

Properly construed, IT organizations are service providers within the corporation. Ideally, they provide a defined set of IT-based services to business customers (those who shape and fund the services) and users (those who rely on the services to perform their work). The notion of IT as a service provider is the essence of the concept of IT service management (ITSM). ITSM is a model for managing IT as a business, where the quality of service, as perceived by the customer, is the number one driving and aligning force in the organization.

ITSM guidance includes the Service Level Management (SLM) process, which consists of the following activities:

- Defining and agreeing to the services provided (quality, service levels, cost)
- Aligning IT infrastructure provider activities to deliver on commitments
- Managing the service experience
- Managing customer–provider (and provider–provider) relationships
- Improving service levels and value within cost constraints
- Delivering as agreed, consistently maintaining commitments

The benefits of SLM include:

- Enhanced understanding by the business and IT of each others' requirements and constraints
- Better information for IT and business decision making
- Better alignment between the business and IT
- More focused and accountable providers and suppliers
- Clearly defined services, cost, and value
- Continuous improvement of services and lower costs
- Enhanced customer and provider satisfaction
- More effective business use of IT

Service-level management is the primary mechanism for managing the IT function as a services business. As shown in Figure 19.4, a good deal of effort goes into ensuring that the services IT provides meet business needs, are delivered in a way that creates and maintains customers' satisfaction, and ultimately help the corporation create value and drive profit.

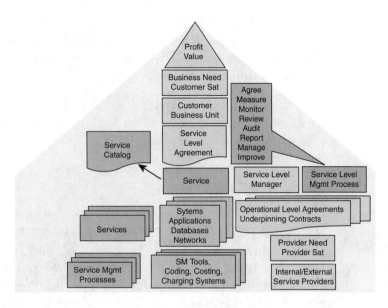

**Figure 19.4** The service-level management pyramid.

*Source:* Pultorak, David. Exploring the Intersection of Service Level Management and Corporate Governance. BetterManagement.com Web Seminar, Thursday, December 4, 2003.

As you can see, in managing IT as a services business, services are at the center of all activity. To ensure services are delivered and supported according to commitments, the underlying technical infrastructure and systems must be up to the task. The boxes on the left-hand side of the diagram depict services as part of a larger catalog of services and may depend on other services as well as on service support and delivery processes for proper functioning. The boxes on the right-hand side illustrate that services need tending—a service manager of some sort—and rely on internal agreements between organizational units (operational level agreements) as well as contractual agreements with suppliers (underpinning contracts) to function properly. The relationship with providers needs tending, including both internal and external service providers.

The right-hand upper boxes show that a service-level management process—a process that ensures services are designed, developed, delivered, and supported as they should be through agreeing, measuring, monitoring, reviewing, auditing, reporting, managing, and improving—

must be in place to ensure consistent results and value. Lastly, the boxes at the top of the diagram show that the service-level agreement (SLA) is the primary interface to the customer, existing only to meet business needs that drive value and financial results.

Service-level management provides an ideal basis for the interface between IT and corporate governance because it and corporate governance have much in common; both service-level management and corporate governance

- Are governance mechanisms.
- Have the aspect of agency/representation; that is, a small group of individuals represents the interests of a larger group.
- Have a "down and in" management aspect and an "up and out" leadership aspect—in other words, both SLM and corporate governance require managing infrastructure and internal people and process as well as managing clients and external stakeholders.
- Focus on performance, conformance, and relating responsibly to stakeholders.
- Focus on maximizing value and minimizing risk.
- Have stakeholders in common.
- Are evolving areas after many years without change.
- Feature widespread agreement on "why" and "what" and just as widespread lack of agreement on the "how" of implementation.

### How to Integrate Service-Level Management and Corporate Governance

To leverage SLM as the nexus for IT and corporate governance, it helps to start by adopting and adapting internationally recognized standards that are understood by IT. The de facto international standard for IT service management is the IT Infrastructure Library (ITIL), an open standard developed by a consortium of industry experts. ITIL includes the service-level management process and is an excellent place to start. While ITIL guidance is strong in the areas of performance and relating responsibly, it is weak in conformance aspects. To cover these, one should look to the internationally recognized guidance contained in

CobiT, which is also internationally recognized guidance, in this case focusing on control and compliance. A standards-based approach leveraging ITIL and CobiT helps ensure a defensible compliance position and accelerates compliance. A word of warning: while CobiT and ITIL can and should be used in conjunction, one should not expect them to fit together like so many jigsaw puzzle pieces; for example, a key difference is that CobiT tends to focus on describing where you should be, whereas ITIL has more coverage of how you might get there.

## Focus on Sustained Financial Results

To drive governance down into the IT organization, all day-to-day decisions and actions must include a focus on and consideration of sustained financial results as a goal. For example, a "go/no-go" decision on an IT change should not be made just on technical merits; the business impact of the change must be considered as well.

Maintaining focus on financial results is another area where utilizing industry-standard ITIL guidance is extremely useful. ITIL includes process guidance for Service Level Management, as previously mentioned, which ensures a focus on the business value of services, as well as guidance for Financial Management for IT Services, which covers aspects of investment appraisal, budgeting and accounting, and charging.

Govern four assets—infrastructure, clients & external stakeholders, internal people & process, value creation—in three dimensions—conformance, performance, and relating responsibly, and include within governance managing the current and directing toward the future state of the firm

Table 19.4 outlines the dashboard of metrics required to manage the current state of the IT function and its future state along the dimensions of CPR and in the four key areas all businesses must pay attention to: infrastructure, clients and external stakeholders, internal people and process, and value creation. The idea is that a short list of the most relevant metrics for the organization be represented in each of the boxes and measured and managed to, ensuring that the IT function is driving toward sustainable financial results.

**Table 19.4** CPR Key Performance Indicator Dashboard

| Asset Areas _ | | Infrastructure | | Clients & External Stakeholders | | Internal People & Process | | Value Creation | |
|---|---|---|---|---|---|---|---|---|---|
| Governance Dimensions_ | State_ | Current | Future | Current | Future | Current | Future | Current | Future |
| Conformance | | | | | | | | | |
| Performance | | | | | | | | | |
| Relating Responsibly | | | | | | | | | |

## Organize Around Governance as Behavior Involving Key Stakeholders

Each internal key stakeholder must have his or her activities relative to IT governance stated as a set of job parts and standards (completing the statement "performance is effective when..."). Figure 19.5 is adapted

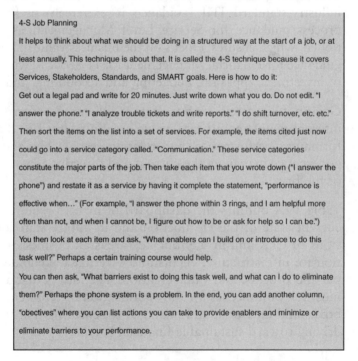

4-S Job Planning

It helps to think about what we should be doing in a structured way at the start of a job, or at

least annually. This technique is about that. It is called the 4-S technique because it covers

Services, Stakeholders, Standards, and SMART goals. Here is how to do it:

Get out a legal pad and write for 20 minutes. Just write down what you do. Do not edit. "I

answer the phone." "I analyze trouble tickets and write reports." "I do shift turnover, etc. etc."

Then sort the items on the list into a set of services. For example, the items cited just now

could go into a service category called. "Communication." These service categories

constitute the major parts of the job. Then take each item that you wrote down ("I answer the

phone") and restate it as a service by having it complete the statement, "performance is

effective when..." (For example, "I answer the phone within 3 rings, and I am helpful more

often than not, and when I cannot be, I figure out how to be or ask for help so I can be.")

You then look at each item and ask, "What enablers can I build on or introduce to do this

task well?" Perhaps a certain training course would help.

You can then ask, "What barriers exist to doing this task well, and what can I do to eliminate

them?" Perhaps the phone system is a problem. In the end, you can add another column,

"obectives" where you can list actions you can take to provide enablers and minimize or

eliminate barriers to your performance.

**Figure 19.5** 4-S job planning.
*Source:* Kern, Pultorak et al., *IT People: Doing More with Less*, 2005.

from the author's chapters in *IT People: Doing More with Less* (2005), which you can refer to for a worksheet and more information about how to go about it.

A similar exercise is recommended to describe the roles of clients and external stakeholders in order to capture their roles and responsibilities, although of course such documentation would not constitute job parts and standards.

## Align Sources of Guidance for IT Governance with the CPR Framework

In this section, a number of common IT governance frameworks are mentioned in turn, with guidance on how each can be aligned within the CPR framework.

### ISO/IEC 17799 and BS7799-2

ISO/IEC 17799 is an international standard code of practice that constitutes best practices in information security. Security guidelines are provided in the ten areas shown in Table 19.5.

**Table 19.5** The Ten Guidelines Areas of ISO/IEC 17799

| Business continuity planning | Personnel security |
|---|---|
| System access control | Security organization |
| System development and maintenance | Computer and network management |
| Physical and environmental security | Asset classification and control |
| Compliance | Security policy |

BS7799-2 is a complementary standard to ISO/IEC 17799, providing a model for managing and improving compliance with BS7799-2 standards. BS7799-2 is the standard that one can be certified against, while ISO/IEC 17799 is a code of practice providing guidance on the identification and implementation of controls to meet the standard.

ISO/IEC 17799 and BS7799-2 can be integrated into the CPR governance framework primarily within the conformance dimension. Tracking of improvements falls under the performance dimension, and managing perceptions around security issues falls under the relating responsibly dimension. Infrastructure and internal people and process are the two primary asset areas within which ISO/IEC 17799 and BS7799-2 fit.

### CMM/CMMI and ISO/IEC 15504 (SPICE)

The original Capability Maturity Model (CMM), and subsequent integrated versions (CMMI), were created by the Software Engineering Institute (SEI) to optimize software development through a framework of continuous process improvement. CMM defines five levels of maturity of software processes: initial, repeatable, defined, managed, and optimizing. ISO/IEC 15504 (also known as SPICE) is a framework for assessment methods compatible with CMMI, the first elements of which were published in 1995.

CMM/CMMI and ISO/IEC 15504 can be integrated into the CPR governance framework primarily within the Performance dimension. Tracking of compliance to specified policies and procedures falls under the Conformance dimension. Managing perceptions around capability achievement falls under the "Relating Responsibly" dimension. The primary asset area that these maturity models fall under is Internal People and Process.

### Deming, EFQM, BNQP, ISO/IEC 9000, TQM, Six Sigma

Deming, EFQM, BNQP, ISO/IEC 9000, TQM, and Six Sigma are quality management systems and methods. The management aspects of these frameworks fall primarily under the Conformance dimension. The improvement aspects fall largely under the Performance dimension. The primary asset area governed by these frameworks is Internal People & Process, although Infrastructure is also important here.

### IT Governance: Weill and Ross

Weill and Ross's recent book (2004) is widely quoted as a reliable source of research on IT governance. It is research-based, describing how real practitioners view IT governance. In it, Weill and Ross conceptualize IT governance as decision making within a decision-making framework; their consequent focus is on decision rights and accountability. The book comes from an IT perspective: your perspective, that of CIO.

Weill and Ross's work spans all asset areas to be governed, and the authors provide their own take on what those assets should be: human, financial, physical, IP, information and IT, and relationship. While the book spans all dimensions of governance as well, the focus is on a subset of governance behavior—decision making. Weill and Ross's contribution is an excellent source of guidance for realizing many, but not all, aspects of the CPR framework.

## CobiT

The Control Objectives for Information and Related Technology (CobiT) framework focuses on compliance and control. The guidance comes from an IT perspective, this time from the perspective of IT auditors. CobiT (ISACA 2000) substantially strengthens the EDP audit function. It is detailed, prescriptive, and complete, and provides a standardized approach to IT accountability.

As Table 19.6 shows, CobiT provides guidance in four key areas: Planning & Organization, Acquisition & Implementation, Delivery & Support, and Monitoring.

Because CobiT focuses on control and comes from the perspective of IT audit professionals, CobiT is ideal for approaching the Conformance dimension of IT governance. While the focus is on control, CobiT is applicable beyond the Conformance dimension, with guidance in seven criteria areas:

- Effectiveness
- Efficiency
- Availability
- Integrity
- Confidentiality
- Reliability
- Compliance

**Table 19.6** CobiT Provides Guidance on 34 Processes in Four Key Groups

| PLANNING & ORGANIZATION | ACQUISITION & IMPLEMENTATION |
|---|---|
| Define a strategic IT plan | Identify automated solutions |
| Define the information architecture | Acquire and maintain application software |
| Determine the technology direction | Acquire and maintain technology infrastructure |
| Define the IT organization and relationships | Develop and maintain IT procedures |
| Manage the investment in IT | Install and accredit systems |
| Communicate management aims and direction | Managing changes |
| Manage human resources | |
| Ensure compliance with external requirements | |
| Assess and manage risks | |
| Manage projects | |
| Manage quality | |

| DELIVERY & SUPPORT | MONITORING |
|---|---|
| Define and manage service levels | Monitor the processes |
| Manage third-party services | Assess internal control adequacy |
| Manage performance and capacity | Obtain independent assurance |
| Ensure continuous service | Provide for independent audit |
| Ensure systems security | |
| Identify and allocate costs | |
| Educate and train users | |
| Assist and advise IT customers | |
| Manage the configuration | |
| Manage problems and incidents | |
| Manage data | |
| Manage facilities | |
| Manage operations | |

The primary asset area aligning with CobiT is Internal People & Process, with emphasis also in the Infrastructure asset area.

## ITIL

ITIL (the Information Technology Infrastructure Library) is a collection of best practices for IT service management. ITIL's guidance is written from the perspective of the IT professional and is aimed at alignment with the business and focused on efficient and effective IT services. ITIL has been developed and widely implemented globally over the last 20 years. ITIL is appropriate for all corporations because it is vendor-neutral, nonpropriety, and scalable. That is, no matter how large or small your corporation, national or international in scope, ITIL "fits" with whatever technology you have put in place. Over 10,000 companies are using ITIL, and over 100,000 IT professionals worldwide are certified in ITIL practices.

The focus in ITIL is on effective and efficient IT processes (such as Change Management and Capacity Management) in support of the delivery of IT services. The objective is to position IT as a service provider, a partner with the business, and an enabler of business goals rather than as a mere operator of increasingly complex technology.

ITIL provides guidance and mechanisms that are ideal for realizing the performance and relating responsibly dimensions of IT governance. While the primary asset area that aligns with ITIL is internal people and process, ITIL guidance spans all four asset areas. In addition, while ITIL guidance is not focused on conformance, it enables conformance by specifying the process domains required to carry out the business of IT, which is a necessary basis for ensuring compliance with codes produced by relevant authorities (for example, a particular conformance area such as Sarbanes-Oxley compliance may require that change management processes be in place; ITIL provides the general outlines of such processes, into which controls can be inserted to ensure compliance). As such, it provides an ideal complement to CobiT as the basis for realizing full coverage in all three dimensions of governance: conformance, performance, and relating responsibly.

As such, IT must broadcast its contribution to the corporation in service terms. Who, what, where, why, and when has IT applied the resources at its command to support the business? Running an infrastructure, no matter how complex, does not add value to customers and profit to the corporation. Aligning that infrastructure engine so that it drives toward understandable business results is the goal, and this alignment can only come about through ongoing, specific dialogue between IT and the business on the subject of service.

The focus in ITIL is on effective and efficient IT processes (change management and capacity management, etc.) and tools (service-level agreements and configuration management databases) in support of the delivery of IT services.

ITIL is very clear on what needs to be done for IT to support a business service. In focusing on business and IT alignment, it drives home the performance and relating responsibly tenets of governance through close definition of a set of processes. These processes are directed at IT customers (i.e., corporate departments that define and commission IT services) as well as users (i.e., employees that use IT day-in and day-out). The ITIL service management processes and their aims are listed and described in Table 19.7.

These ten disciplines work in concert to present the power of the underlying IT infrastructure in ways understandable to the business. Principal among its tools are the service catalog and corresponding service-level agreements (SLA) that document the mutual expectations of IT and the business. According to Weill and Ross (2004), the service catalog and SLAs...

> list available services, alternative quality levels, and related costs. Through negotiations between the IT services unit and the business units, an SLA leads to articulation of the services IT offers and the costs of the services. These negotiations clarify the requirements of the business units, thereby informing governance decisions on infrastructure, architecture, and business application needs. (p. 101)

The service catalog and SLAs drive all of the other ITIL processes. The service catalog acts a menu, and the SLA as an agreed "order" from that menu, forming the basis for common ground between corporate departments and IT. It establishes the boundaries of conformance because it has the business and IT work together to plan what to do, to do it, and to accumulate evidence that it has been done. It records the

**Table 19.7** Information Technology Infrastructure Library

| Corporate Departments as IT Customers (Service Delivery) | | Fellow Employees as IT Users (Service Support) | |
|---|---|---|---|
| Process | Aim | Process | Aim |
| Service-Level Management | Agree, maintain, and where necessary improve IT service in line with business need | Incident Management | Restore normal service operation as quickly as possible or agreed |
| Financial Management for IT Services | Provide cost-effective stewardship of the IT investments and the financial resources used in providing IT services | Problem Management | Minimize the adverse business impact of incidents and problems |
| Capacity Management | Ensure that all current and future business capacity and performance aspects are supported by appropriate and cost-effective IT resources | Configuration Management | Maintain a logical picture of the IT infrastructure, including relationships among the components that constitute the infrastructure |
| IT Service Continuity Management | Support overall business continuity management by planning recovery of the required IT technical and services facilities | Change Management | Ensure standardized methods and procedures are used for efficient and prompt handling of all changes |
| Availability Management | Optimize the availability of the IT infrastructure and supporting organization | Release Management | Release new or revised IT services where both technical and nontechnical aspects are considered together |
| *Source:* Process definitions abridged from van Bon, Pieper, and van der Veen (2004) | | | |

mutual understanding of quality whose measurement brings performance characteristics to the fore. Lastly, it sets the cost parameters—what the business can afford and what IT can spend—reflecting the balance of supply and demand that underscores relating responsibly.

IT service management is not a one-step approach for infusing IT with the three-part framework of governance, but it takes the first step by elevating the dialogue where business goals and objectives are the nouns, service is the verb, and the innumerable details that constitute the technical infrastructure are secondary.

In short, the service focus proposed here allows the board to expect more, to demand more, and to require greater transparency in reporting on the business value of IT services. Microsoft adopted and adapted ITIL, transforming it into the Microsoft Operations Framework (MOF) to secure even stronger benefits for the corporation and its goals. As Ron Markezich, CIO for Microsoft Corporation says, "Our goal in IT at Microsoft is to use technology as a competitive advantage for Microsoft. Our focus on Microsoft Operations Framework and service management helps us ensure a foundation of reliable, effective and trustworthy IT services that are required for our users to get the most out of the services IT provides."

## *Other Mechanisms Associated with IT Governance*

Some professionals equate IT governance in whole or in part with a variety of management mechanisms in use in organizations. Chief among them are program, project, and portfolio management, enterprise architecture, business and IT alignment, and the strategy, policy-setting, and planning functions performed by the board, executive management, and specialized staff. A variety of guidance exists for these mechanisms, such as the PMBOK for project management. While it is beyond the scope of this chapter to review all such guidance, it is important to note that many consider such mechanisms an important part, and in some cases, the primary part of IT governance, sometimes going so far as equating these mechanisms with governance. While each has a role in governance, the general guidance given here is to apply such mechanisms within an overarching framework that aligns them.

# ▶ Call to Action

Governance requires action. In fact, governance *is* action, equivalent to the sum of the behaviors that guide relationships between and among corporations and their constitute parts. While governance can sometimes be viewed as formal rules and procedures, there are things you as CIO can do tomorrow to shape your board's view of IT governance. Some ideas for how to proceed follow:

- Suggest a discussion on governance be placed on the board agenda to gain concurrence on your board's thinking on the matter.
- Have the wider definition of governance broadcast throughout the corporation.
- Suggest that the wider definition of governance filter out to key customers and suppliers.
- Arrange joint IT–company management discussions on vital business drivers to further business and IT alignment.
- Start working with selected corporate departments (finance, manufacturing, sales, etc.) to start the process of ascertaining the business value of IT services, conducting a business impact analysis and initial service-level agreement discussions.
- Secure an invitation to a meeting of the board of directors to report on the effectiveness of service-level agreements already in place within the corporation.
- Join in discussions with fellow CIOs on the contribution governance makes to customer value and company profit.

In the end, governance is strongly oriented toward sustainability: ensuring that the corporation is successful today and positioned for tomorrow. Corporate governance, including IT governance, is simultaneously the scout and sentry on the frontier of company growth.

# ▶ IT Governance Checklist

## Conformance

1. Do you have and follow a formal risk management process to evaluate the technical and business advantages and disadvantages accompanying infrastructure projects?

2. What listening posts have you established to understand the nature of new regulatory or legal requirements that are being considered applicable to your industry?

3. Have you charted the IT infrastructure implications of the result of the three recent major marketing initiatives your corporation has launched? Are there ways you should "tie in" to such initiatives to anticipate the IT impact?

4. Which industry-specific codes of behavior and ethics influence the operation of the IT functions within your corporation? How are you accumulating evidence that you support such codes?

5. Have recent EDP audit findings and recommendations been addressed as part of the day-to-day practice in your area?

## Performance

1. Are you satisfied with the mechanisms you have in place for measuring and reporting the cost of IT services to the business? Have you analyzed those costs in comparison to the value the business derives from these services?

2. What productivity metrics have you identified for IT staff roles and positions? Have you seen improvement in the measurements over the last quarter?

3. Since IT services support business processes, how have you and the business collaborated in continuous process improvement programs to drive additional effectiveness and efficiency?

## Relating Responsibly

1. Have you identified the key internal and external stakeholders in the quality delivery of IT service? Do you have a periodic means to communicate with such stakeholders?

2. How does your IT organization "give back" to the community surrounding your installations?

3. Are your suppliers aware of your goals and objectives? Have you invited them to participate in key IT service management initiatives?

4. Does your corporate board or owners see IT acting in a leadership role in shaping governance procedures and execution?

## Infrastructure

1. Has the infrastructure been engineered such that it consistently supports meeting the requirements and commitments of the business?

2. Is this infrastructure robust enough to maintain acceptable service levels to the business?

3. Has the infrastructure been designed, developed, and implemented to provide for high enough levels of availability, flexibility, scalability, and performance?

4. Is the infrastructure internally and externally secure?

## Clients and External Stakeholders

1. Is there an appropriate level of customer satisfaction with the level of service?

2. Are the services provided appropriate and fit-for-purpose?

3. Is the customer experience and feedback being gathered and used in a continuous service improvement process

4. How well are the organizational culture and perception of the services provided being monitored and compared against the value proposition to the customer?

## Internal People and Process

1. Are the ongoing operational activities and the investments being made to provide the necessary services being monitored?

2. Are these activities and investments being compared to the results and valued-added benefits being provided?

3. Is the offering determined as fit-to-purpose based on the value provided and the cost effectiveness?

4. Does the service provided leverage and maximize the use of the organization's intellectual property?

## *Value Creation*

1. Are there effective quality processes in place to ensure the development, delivery, and ongoing support of the IT services and infrastructure?

2. Are there processes in place to support the internal and external relationships between service providers and suppliers and their interactive performance?

# ▶ References

Literary Sources: Linking Corporate and IT governance

Pultorak, D., and J. Kerrigan, 2005. "CPR: A Framework for Corporate and IT Governance." *Directors Monthly*, 29(2). February.

Pultorak, D., 2003. Exploring the Intersection of Service Level Management and Corporate Governance. *BetterManagement.com Web Seminar*, Thursday, December 4, 2003.

Pultorak, D., 2001. Yes we can do it—and this is what it will cost. *Presentation to the itSMF Annual Conference*, Brighton, UK.

Literary Sources: Corporate Governance

COSO, 1994. *IT Internal Control—Integrated Framework (COSO report)*. Committee of Sponsoring Organizations of the Treadway Commission. 151 pages. Zaltbommel, The Netherlands.

Kaplan, R. S., and D. P. Norton, 1996. *The Balanced Scorecard: Translating Strategy Into Action*. Harvard Business School Press.

Literary Sources: IT governance

Brand, K., and H. Boonen, 2004. *IT Governance: A Pocket Guide Based on COBIT®*. Van Haren Publishing.

Hoffman, T., 2004. "IT Oversight Gets Attention at Board Level." *Computerworld*. May 17.

IT Governance Institute, 2003. *Board Briefing on IT Governance* (2nd ed.). IT Governance Institute.

Information Systems Audit and Control Association (ISACA), 2000. *CoBiT Framework*. ISACA and IT Governance Institute.

Maco, D., 2003. "Governance." In Dean Lane (Editor), *CIO Wisdom*. Prentice Hall PTR, pp. 123–149.

van Bon, J., M. Pieper, and A. van der Veen, 2004. *IT Service Management: An Introduction Based on ITIL®*. Van Haren Publishing.

van Grembergen, W., 2004. *Strategies for Information Technology Governance*. Idea Group Publishing.

Weill, P., and J. W. Ross, 2004. *IT Governance: How Top Performers Manage IT Decision Rights for Superior Results*. Harvard Business School Press.

Weston, H. (Editor), 2001. *Service Delivery*. The Stationary Office. London, England.

Web Sources: Corporate and IT Governance

Balanced Scorecard: http://www.balancedscorecard.org

Bettermanagement.com (Exploring the Intersection of IT Service Level Management and Corporate Governance, Archived Web Seminar): http://www.bettermanagement.com/Seminars/Seminar.aspx?LibraryID=8341

CIMA Enterprise Governance: a CIMA Discussion Paper: http://www.cimaglobal.com/cps/xbcr/SID-0AAAC564-00E392AB/live/entgov_execrpt_0204.pdf

The Conference Board Inc.: http://www.conference-board.org/

EZCOBIT: http://audit.byu.edu/website/tools/COBIT/cobit.cfm

Fox IT, LLC: http://us.foxit.net/

IT Governance Institute: http://www.itgi.org/

Information Systems Audit and Control Association (ISACA): http://www.isaca.org/

Information Technology Infrastructure Library (ITIL):
http://www.ogc.gov.uk/index.asp?id=2261

Information Technology Service Management Forum (itSMF):
http://www.itsmf.com/

Institute of Chartered Accountants in England and Wales (ICAEW),
information on corporate governance:
http://www.icaew.co.uk/index.cfm?AUB=tb2i_47496,MNXI_47496

KPMG Audit Committee Institute:
http://www.kpmg.com/aci/home.html

National Association of Corporate Directors: http://www.nacgonline.org/

Organization for Economic Co-operation and Development, on Corporate Governance:
http://www.oecd.org/topic/0,2686,en_2649_37439_1_1_1_1_374
39,00.html

Pultorak & Associates, Ltd.: http://www.pultorak.com/

# E-Government

*Dianah Neff*

## ▶ Introduction

In the United States, federal, state, and local governments are facing a challenge. How do they continue to deliver government services while keeping taxes down? Citizens' expectations of their governments have never been higher. They expect to interact with government in the same manner that they interact with local banks or retailers—via online self-service capabilities and with the ability to do what they want, when they want, and however they want. The challenge does not end there. In addition to meeting citizen service expectations, governments must find a way to do this in a cost-effective manner. Government budgets are strained comparatively to past years, and scrutiny has never been higher surrounding the concept of raising taxes as opposed to cutting costs and driving organizational efficiencies to deal with budget deficits. So, the question facing governments is, How do we provide greater care for our constituents in a cost-effective and efficient manner? More simply stated, How do we do more with less?

# E- Government Is Government

Governments have allocated a tremendous amount of time and resources to develop their e-government capabilities. In the majority of cases, e-government focus was intended to provide better access to existing services by providing them online. This sometimes met citizen needs to interact with government on their own time as well as reduced the cost for executing that transaction. In some cases, e-government initiatives were undertaken as a "me too" project: everyone else was doing it, and the lack of a Web site, portal, search engines, and self-service transactions online meant that that government was a "technology laggard." What has evolved and has become apparent is that e-government—providing self-service capabilities that include online capabilities, self-service kiosks, and interactive voice response (IVR) solutions—*is* government and is not just another way "to do government." It has become the primary method that governments use to deliver value-add services at lower costs.

For all of its benefits to the constituent and to the government, self-service and e-government also created a new challenge. Too often, e-government became simply an exercise in creating a virtual copy of existing government services. Multiple systems were created, multiple architectures were supported, and new and more resources were required to support both the traditional and the new "virtual" or self-service transactions. This was certainly not the intention of e-government. To solve this problem, governments realized they needed an approach allowing them to leverage both channels—legacy and self-service, with one architecture, standardized processes, one copy of the "single-source of data truth," and one standardized presentation layer to the citizen—regardless of how the citizen was interacting with the government (Figure 20.1).

However, there remained one additional challenge. Now that the self-service channel was in place, the government needed to ensure the adoption and use of the self-service model. The key was to be able to provide a consistent process with a consistent presentation layer to the customer, regardless of the channel being used. Whether a citizen decided to conduct a transaction online, at a kiosk, over the phone, or in person, her experience with the government must be the same. This ability to provide ubiquitous and consistent delivery of services to the citizen with just one infrastructure to support has been instrumental in

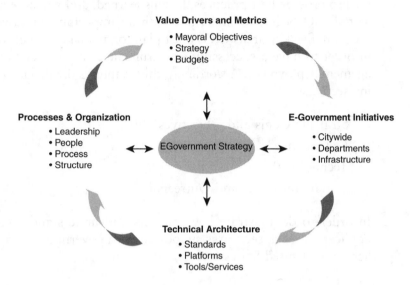

**Elements for Success**

**Value Drivers and Metrics**
- Mayoral Objectives
- Strategy
- Budgets

**Processes & Organization**
- Leadership
- People
- Process
- Structure

EGovernment Strategy

**E-Government Initiatives**
- Citywide
- Departments
- Infrastructure

**Technical Architecture**
- Standards
- Platforms
- Tools/Services

**Figure 20.1** A holistic approach to e-government.

increasing the adoption of meeting the citizen expectation while lowering the cost of service delivery.

### *Four Key E-Government Outcomes*

1. Provide new information and services to their citizens not previously available or easily accessible.

2. Further increase the capabilities and adoption of self-service solutions.

3. Further reduce the per-transaction cost of information and service delivery.

4. Adopt creative models such as public–private partnerships, shared services, and core-context for cost avoidance and investment into new and innovative government solutions.

# ▶ Chapter Overview

This chapter is written for the CIO, government or nongovernment, who is considering an initiative to deploy customer-centric e-government or customer relationship management (CRM) applications. It is the author's goal to provide best practices, lessons learned, and valuable information as the CIO begins to undertake such an important initiative. I believe there are five key areas CIOs must plan for, manage, and execute against in order to have a successful e-government–customer relationship management deployment. Accordingly, this chapter is divided into the following sections:

"Strategic Goals and Objectives"

"Governance"

"Technology"

"Communications and Outreach"

In order to demonstrate key concepts and understand their potential application, each section is supported with government examples from across the United States.

# ▶ Strategic Goals and Objectives

This is a story about the ability of citizens to readily access a customer-centric government. Many governments realize that citizen expectations have increased in a time of economic uncertainty. Budgets are under increased strain as they seek to meet unmet citizen needs in a time of deficit spending. These same governments now realize that becoming an easily accessible customer-centric government is in their self-interest and have made progress to improve service delivery via a single, easily recognizable format. This section presents three goals that any future deployment should provide.

## Improving Customer Delivery

Governments in the recent past seldom delivered citizen services as a single city, county, or state enterprise. They have been fragmented and composed of partially autonomous agencies and semi-independent departmental units. Each organization brought with it virtues of its own culture and often did not have shared values or sense of purpose with other departments within that government. Citizens were left with service delivery that was hard to access, slow, expensive, and most often was conflicted in its execution. Often, those citizens who most needed the government's assistance were those who were least able to access it, such as citizens who were destitute, in poor health, didn't speak English, or otherwise had limited access to government assistance. The state of Texas, with a population roughly equivalent to Canada or Australia, has both highly populated urban areas (three of the top 10 U.S. metro areas) and expansive rural areas with their own unique challenges in delivery of health and human services. In addition, there is a huge socio-economic gap between the haves and have-nots.

A series of nonprofit organizations across the state provided assistance to the poor, but awareness of how to access the help was low, the hours of operations were inconsistent, and the ability to access services outside the immediate areas was limited. The Texas customer-centric service project linked the services of the various nonprofits, the capabilities of the Texas Health and Human Services commission, and local caregivers in a statewide system with a single access number. Now citizens across the state know that a single number or Web site can provide them access to critical services no matter where they live or when they are calling or using the Web site.

In the area of economic development, many city and county governments have required business developers to own the burden of getting a building or business permit without city/county assistance. However, this is despite that it is in the government's best interest for the business to be successful in obtaining the permit. Placing the burden solely on a small business owner, developer, or the citizen to manage the permitting process can increase the cost of business and increase the potential that the customer will take a business or development to another jurisdiction.

In an increasingly global economy, cities compete with each other internationally. When it has become apparent that a city is not easy to work with, another city that is more readily accessible will be more competitive with others for the business. This is not, as some might think, a matter of acquiescing to all business demands at the expense of other government objectives. It is a matter of providing equal and consistent access to business and regulatory services and co-owning the issue with the developer. The combination of a single-enterprise economic development center accessible through the Web site, phone, or counter is a competitive advantage to this city and any jurisdiction that adopts this approach and mindset of ready access and customer-centric service delivery.

In one California city there was no single place, in an inwardly focused government service delivery process, where a citizen could go to start a new business or get a permit or a license, without stepping through a maze of disparate agencies. In this example it used to take up to 9 months for a developer to work through a process of engaging with nine different city agencies and then repeating these efforts with similar agencies in the county and state before a building and business permit could be approved.

The delay had an immediate impact of delaying the collection of property and income taxes the new business could otherwise be paying and also delayed the employment of new workers who would otherwise pay sales and property taxes. The delay made this city less competitive with cities in Asia, Europe, and North America, where other similar industries were being attracted.

Now that city has started a unique (enterprisewide) economic development center, accessible through either the city's 3-1-1 single-access number, a parallel single Web site, or a single physical location in city hall. How to access these services is up to the citizen, but whether the access is via phone, the Web, or in person, the city government's customers have a single point of access for all the services needed to start a business, enhance a neighborhood, or open a new center for the arts.

This government realized that in order to meet customers' previously unsatisfied expectations  and to concurrently manage its budget, an enterprisewide refocus of resources on customer need was required. The ability to address customer needs first required that this city government reduce or eliminate the impact of inwardly focused silo-ed agencies and departments, while minimizing the negative impact change can have on employee morale and organizational culture.

There was realization that by serving citizens, businesses, nonprofit organizations, and the educational community, government can achieve—by partnership—more than it can do alone. The city's customer single point of access enables any citizen or business to start a process that will accelerate economic and neighborhood redevelopment and improve the lives of its citizens while improving the tax base and consistency of tax collections in the city.

A new culture and new approach to conducting government business are leading the way with seamless communications and operations, clear roles and responsibilities, and improved organizational accountability. These actions foster cross-departmental and cross-agency work groups to improve service delivery and further the government goals of economic and neighborhood development.

Government employees, once acclimated to customer-centric values and objectives, will now ask themselves, when approached by a constituent, How can we, the government help? rather than, To whom do I need to divert or refer this person? Government employees will not require the constituent to engage with multiple agencies to achieve an economic or neighborhood objective when it is the government's responsibility and in its best interest to collaborate within its own sub-organizations to solve customer issues.

## Improving Organizational Productivity

The concept of creating a customer-centric virtual government has replaced the concept of a bricks-and-mortar physical reorganization. In a virtual government, the capabilities of disparate, siloed departments and agencies can become aggregated without negative employment and/or agency prerogatives serving as an obstacle. This is truly one time when government can "have its cake and eat it too." A new enterprise view of government seeks to share resources to improve citizen services.

The partnership begins internally, within government, with the realization that the government needs to share with itself. That is, each department and agency must be willing to eliminate duplicative functions and resources by viewing itself within the context of a larger enterprise or team. This process starts with examination of "core versus content" functional concepts in agency and departmental operations.

One government, for example, had determined that the secretary of state was the single agency that would collect money, specifically taxes and other revenues, for all other departments and agencies in the state. Over time, 13 different compartmentalized agencies/departments developed redundant revenue collection capabilities that employed over 3,300 persons, housed in state office buildings with duplicative cash-collection infrastructures.

Now, with the creation of an enterprisewide perspective, these resources can be refocused on the customer by creating a virtual government cash-collection capability that can be lined by the use of the state's intranet network and to the customer via the Internet and integrated call center to create a networked virtual organization, or NVO. The human resources, physical office locations, and cash-collection infrastructure can be shared without forcing the individual agencies/department to re-assign or reduce headcount.

Participants in the NVO determine what represents a core business function and what is context. In other words, mission-critical and "differentiating" functions are defined as core operational requirements. These are essential capabilities that must be owned or retained by each organization participating in the NVO.

Mission-critical functions are those activities that, if performed poorly or not at all, would pose an immediate risk to the organization. Likewise, functions that are differentiating capabilities that contribute to uniqueness of the organization are to be considered core. Differentiating functions are those capabilities that constituents, citizens, employees, and management believe are unique and distinguish one jurisdiction or government unit from another.

Context capabilities are those functions that are neither mission critical nor considered to be differentiating to a particular agency or department. A context function would be for most agencies nonessential but otherwise needed to fulfill customer needs. These capabilities would be shared by agencies for which this function is core, thereby reducing the redundancy, operational overhead, and cost.

Participant cooperation is expected and supported by mutual wins. The organization has a shared mission, values, and purpose. Policies and procedures are well defined and less formal. Common vocabulary and definitions are specified. The basic NVO business model provides for mandatory services by sharing core functions. Organizational units are responsible for resource allocation. The virtual organization is not vertically integrated; the NVO doesn't own all competencies required to produce a product or deliver a service. Information is shared by all of the virtual organization's participants.

# Reducing Government Costs

In a society where cost reduction and doing more with less have become the norm, governments every day are looking for new and innovative approaches to enable hard dollar cost takeout while increasing operating efficiencies and enhancing employee productivity—all while sustaining even higher standards of constituent satisfaction. This can be a significant task, but one made easier with the right tools, products, services, best practices, and methodologies all working in combination.

Over the past 10 years, a number of leading Global 500 companies and governments have undertaken significant and innovative efforts to drive cost out of day-to-day operations. Three initiatives have come to the forefront in achieving the cost takeout: the migration from disparate data, video, and voice networks to a converged network; the deployment of collaboration applications; and Web-enabling key business functions. In a recent study sponsored by Cisco Systems (Net Impact Study, available at http://business.cisco.com), it was found that these capabilities have helped the 2,000 U.S. organizations surveyed to reduce costs by $155 billion in the past 3 years. This astonishing discovery was attributed to improvements in customer care, back-office Web-enabled solutions, and collaboration tools and applications that introduced production and distribution efficiencies, reducing both logistical and labor costs.

While e-government initiatives and CRM are critical for governments to continue to remain relevant to their constituents and drive a higher level of customer information and service delivery, it has also proven to be a catalyst in enabling governments to either avoid new costs or remove costs from existing operations. If an initiative is designed and deployed to be able to take advantage of key technologies such as converged networks and applications such as collaborations tools and Web Services, the ongoing operational costs of the solution can prove to be significantly less than if legacy-based approaches to technology (e.g., separate data and voice networks, PBX solutions) are utilized (Figure 20.2).

Across the United States, a phenomenon is emerging: governments are realizing that their investment in e-government and CRM can be leveraged for other capabilities and shared with other jurisdictions. Although clearly not the case with all deployments, governments that decide to leverage emerging technologies and applications are finding new opportunities to leverage their investment, including:

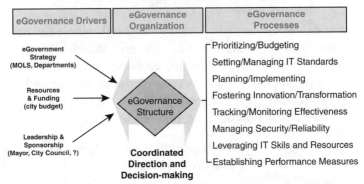

**Figure 20.2** Critical success factors.

- Leveraging the converged infrastructure and collaboration applications to reengineer legacy business processes or enterprise functions. Examples of these functionalities are being demonstrated in states and counties where existing infrastructures are being considered as a backbone for additional health and human services functions outside of government.

- Taking advantage of the converged infrastructure as a vehicle for local and statewide VoIP and toll bypass communication, reducing ongoing telecommunications costs.

- Leveraging the communications platform and endpoint communication devices, such as Internet Protocol (IP) telephony and softphones, as a vehicle for homeland security and disaster preparedness, providing the ability to offer citywide information dissemination via IP phones and emergency broadcasting.

# ▶ Governance

Among the first questions to ask in the planning of any project are, Who are the stakeholders? Who will lead the project? and Who will be responsible for the completed product? These questions take on new significance in enterprise e-government projects.

The impetus for the adoption of an e-government/CRM system is likely to play the largest role in determining the leadership and composition of your governance team. A mayor or city manager recognizing constituent benefit for a centralized customer relationship system, a human services agency with a legislative mandate or initiative to provide an integrated service, or a department of transportation seeking to consolidate information from various transit and roadway infrastructure agencies into a regional project can and will require different leadership models, given their inherent differences in business drivers and programmatic requirements.

When an e-government project is publicly called for or launched by a senior elected or appointed official, those responsible for carrying out that mandate operate in an environment with perhaps more public scrutiny than one initiated by an agency seeking efficiencies. They must be careful to include broad representation from both the internal stakeholders and the external community in order to mitigate the risk of criticism from those who may inadvertently be left out of the process.

Legislation instituting any system, whether from a state, county, or city, commonly fixes the responsibility for establishing the system and also often identifies the community of interest to include in the process. Even when interested parties are not named explicitly in the requirement, the legislative history may be sufficient: who testified in favor of or who opposed the measure.

An organizational recognition of the need for a new service, which derives from regular strategic planning, will more easily lend itself to identification of stakeholders and leadership. These projects have no less complexity or risk but tend to be less controversial and volatile than those initiated by external stakeholders.

Beyond the first champion for instituting the service, are their other executive sponsors required or whose support would enhance your success? This may include department or agency heads whose organizations will be impacted by the service or relevant community leaders. An executive steering committee may also be formed to provide senior leadership and ensure appropriate cooperation from staff across the enterprise. A project management approach that is appropriate to the host organization's culture and any internal standards should be adopted.

The revenue source for your project may have a significant impact on the governance and funding model chosen. For example, funds may be set aside for all capital and operational costs, or new revenue generation capabilities may need to be identified in order to cover operational expenses. In addition, there may be relative freedom when the funds are the result of a new appropriation or new revenue source. Where project funds are the result of redirection or diversion of existing budget allocations, it may be advisable to clearly delineate the return on investment, in dollars, resources, or enhanced service delivery, that will be generated as a result of the new service.

The type of initiative being deployed can make a difference in available resources and funding. A CRM system may rely on local general fund revenues or fees/taxes imposed on telephone users; however, this can vary depending on state law. Human services systems may rely on state or federal funds, redirection of local dollars from community-based information resource centers, and/or other sources. Transportation agencies are considering charging a fee for premium services such as having personalized traffic or transit information pushed to mobile devices.

For some projects, grant funding may be available for startup and even operational expenses. It is recommended that you research association and foundation Web sites (http://www.capwiz.com/unitedway/home/) as well as review case studies of other e-government/CRM/3-1-1 systems (http://www.centerdigitalgov.com/cdg/?pg=search). In any case, it is important to be creative and open to a variety of potential funding sources. For example, homeland security funds may be available if the initiative provides a central source to quickly and fully disseminate emergency information.

If there is a legislative mandate or initiative for the system, there is likely to be a funding source identified. This certainly simplifies the life of the project sponsors and leadership team considerably, although it is still critical to assemble a coalition to support the project. By building a broad-based supporting team whose job is to ensure buy-in of the initiative, there is a decreased risk of disruption in progress from disenfranchised parties.

In many e-government projects, there is a tension in balancing the needs of program and technical staff. While there are no simple answers to this common dilemma, it is important to note in developing the project team that appropriate representation needs to come from each area. Individuals with experience working successfully on cross-organizational teams are ideal because there is less need to acculturate them.

One of the most significant elements of an e-government initiative is recognition of the key content requirements from throughout the enterprise. It is in this area that a project manager be chosen for his or her ability to lead a cross section of personnel and have a good understanding of all of the services provided by the jurisdiction. Like portals before them, ERM systems are only as valuable as their ability to provide accurate and reliable information; yet there is a similar tendency to design the project with an emphasis on the technology and the service delivery model over the content requirements.

Early in the project, it must be clearly decided what kind of ongoing role the governance team should have during production, if any. A formal governance structure is critical in the initiation and project phases. There must be a clear decision-making body that can be the final arbiter in the many issues arising during planning and deployment of the new system.

After the development phase of the project ends and the new system moves into its operational phase, the organization structure can evolve in a number of ways. An advisory committee of stakeholders may meet or receive communications on a regular basis; program/agency clients may be convened to establish service-level agreements with the operations team; ad hoc groups could be convened to address specific issues; or the program manager may simple report to his or her executive management.

Regardless of who operates the system, clear methods for feedback and input from affected agencies are necessary. Building relationships with other agencies or departments is critical in the continued success of a service that crosses departmental boundaries and agencies.

Overall, once the executive sponsorship has been established, the governance body has been determined, and a project manager has been selected, it is important to develop a clear understanding of three overarching elements:

1. What is the business case? Specifically, the stakeholders need to be convinced that there is a clear business challenge, problem, or opportunity that should be addressed.
2. The solution has been articulated in business terms and appears credible and realistic. A list of important criteria to the governance

committee has been established in order to guide the selection of the solution.

3. There are initial metrics established that will show the governance committee and stakeholders that the solution has been successful in addressing the agreed-upon business challenge, problem, or opportunity.

## City of Hampton 3-1-1

A review of the Hampton, Virginia, case study demonstrates a good example of how to incorporate the issues of both internal and external stakeholders. Hampton, Virginia's model of 3-1-1 was strategically placed under the city manager's office. Operating directly under upper management continues to give the call center visibility and political influence with other departments and agencies. Executive support and sponsorship for the project and for operations is critical to its success. This support and sponsorship can help overcome obstacles as needed. The case study is available at http://www.hampton.gove/311/.

# ▶ Technology

In this new age of computers and information technology, customer service expectations have risen. The new customer service expectation ties back not only to consumers in the marketplace but to citizens, businesses, tourists, and other agencies across the different levels of government. Though improvements have been made in both Web access and in-person interaction, governments are increasingly looking to portals, call centers, and CRM to handle all types of issues, problems, services, and transactions. A "one-stop shop" for citizens, businesses, tourists, and other agencies would provide Internet-based self-service capability for the computer savvy to conduct transactions, such as pay bills. Customers would be able to search on frequently asked questions to find a solution instead of, or before, talking to a live operator. With these types of requests now expected, a government executive should consider topics such as the following when developing a technology strategy to accommodate future e-government or CRM call center deployment.

- **Key Technology Requirements:** What type of technology is most cost effective and practical in deploying a CRM call center that ties to an e-government portal? Functional requirements, existing equipment that may be available with extra capacity or low-cost enhancement capability, type of middleware software that is used, and budget requirements will help define key technology requirements.

- **Application Components:** What specific functional requirements are needed with the software application?

- **Call Center Telephony Components:** When moving to a CRM call center approach for problem resolution, what types of telephony requirements are needed to provide both good service and options to the customer as well as work most effectively given the various locations of the call center operators? Or do you centralize them?

- **Back-end Integration:** If this is a one-stop shop for customer service, what other systems or applications should be considered for integration with the call center application? What should the architecture look like given the locations of the data as well as the different platforms on which the various applications reside?

- **Business case:** What is the correct information to collect in order to demonstrate a reasonable return on investment for your jurisdiction?

- **Call Center Technical Operations:** Because your call center will be the life line for your citizens, businesses, and other agencies, what is the correct internal support needed for your systems to be operational 24/7? Should they be operational 24/7? How does this requirement conflict with the operational hours of the various systems and applications that hold the data that will be accessed in the knowledge database?

Figure 20.3 shows how the City of Denver envisioned its 3-1-1 CRM system.

## How To

How do you get started in implementing the technological solution at the heart of the CRM system? Numerous steps must be taken to ensure a complete, robust, and secure system that not only provides the level of customer service expected from government but also reduces the ongoing transactional costs for these services.

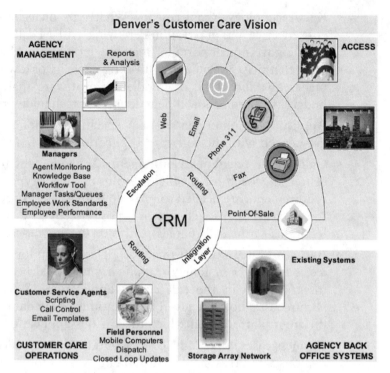

Figure 20.3 Denver's customer care vision.

## Understanding As-Is Systems

One of the first steps in this process is to identify and inventory the existing installed tools and technologies of all systems that are likely to be included and interfaced with the system. This activity should include identifying the type of technologies utilized (operating system, software, database, etc.), the architecture and infrastructure these systems reside within, the data models and data types within each system, and the approach to ensure effective exchange of information across the applications. Figure 20.4 shows a diagram illustrating the City of Denver's current approach on those technology components.

Denver's 3-1-1 CRM initiative is the signature project of the city's mayor and one that Denver leadership believes will go a long way toward achieving their customer service goal. Denver is taking a phased approach to implementing CRM. This approach includes the gathering of requirements through a facilitated process, analyzing call volumes and Web

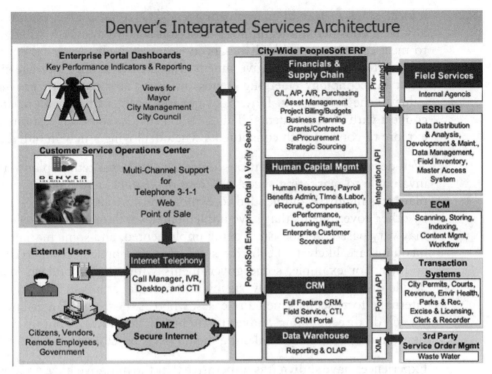

**Figure 20.4** The City of Denver's current approach on those technology components

Image used with permission.

questions that different agencies are receiving, modeling an as-is technology environment, and piloting the project through the Wastewater division because that division has an existing call center and its needs may cross all modules of the future application. The phase-in of additional services is expected to take 1 to 2 years for the high-volume services.

# ▶ Communications and Outreach

In society today, the attention span of constituents is continually decreasing. Between cell phones, traffic signals, signs, TV commercials, junk mail. and Internet pop-up windows, citizens are becoming immune to many of the ways organizations are attempting to communicate and connect with them. This is even more difficult when that organization is a local, state. or federal government agency. Government has traditionally been considered a technology-adoption laggard and slow to adapt to meet constituent needs. It has become increasingly clear that enterprise initiatives such as e-government and CRM not only leverage the latest in technology emerging trends but offer new means to provide value to the constituent. How does government get the word out and connect with its constituents? This section provides some suggestions to explore to connect with constituents when deploying a new initiative.

Well-developed communication, outreach, and marketing plans are invaluable to marketing success. Before developing a communications plan, it is highly recommended to explore the various plans developed by other governments that have implemented similar systems. Specifics may vary based on the system being implemented, and some marketing mediums are likely to be better suited for one budget compared to another. For example, some governments with smaller budgets may decide only to use radio advertising and newspaper ads in addition to internal efforts such as media releases, whereas those with larger budgets will do direct mailings, advertise on buses and subways, put up road signs, and use as many marketing mediums as possible.

Experiences have shown it is imperative that the initiative have an identity, one that can and should include an effective communication strategy, remindful logo, and a mission statement that concisely describes the value of the system and its intent. The communication strategy is explained as *the right people delivering the right message to the right audience at the right time*. This strategy should spell out who your audience is and how you intend to share this valuable information with them. The mission statement (one to two sentences) should be communicated on all marketing materials with the chosen logo.

Examples are shown in Figure 20.5.

As can be seen in Figure 20.5, San Antonio includes additional text beneath its logo to explain the number's purpose; Iowa includes the explanation with the logo.

Examples of mission statements follow:

- To enhance the quality of life in our Village and provide a safe environment by raising the level of public safety and reducing the fear and incidence of crime.

Chapter **20** | E-Government

Dial 311 for Non-Emergencies

**Figure 20.5** Successful identity communication campaigns.

- To provide a customer service assisting with information and human services referrals that is accessible and usable by all people in California.
- In response to diverse information needs, X County is committed to a supportive lifelong learning environment empowering individuals, professionally and culturally to contribute to a global community.

Once a concise mission statement, logo, and service message are established, the actual population to be communicated with must be identified. Should it be communicated only to road travelers? To people with medical conditions? To people in crisis situations? To everyone possible? These questions are critical when determining the marketing mediums to leverage in communicating the message.

Some organizations have found different mediums more or less valuable depending on the individual city or state or system being implemented. In large cities with a formalized bus or subway system, banner advertisements are very effective, especially for human services hotlines. Ideally, the message needs to reach the people at the time they need it. For instance, 5-1-1 transportation systems are effectively advertised using billboards, flyers at rest stops, and department of transportation signage along major interstates. The Minnesota Department of Transportation, for example, uses billboards and radio advertisement.

Following is a list of marketing mediums that governments have utilized to communicate their marketing messages for their e-government initiatives. Internal approaches are those which were executed internally; external are those where government outsourced the delivery of the message.

## Internal Approaches

- Media release with information packets
- Regional conferences
- Political figure endorsement through ad campaign
- Utility/tax bill insertions
- Brochures distributed by direct mail
- E-mail distribution list (citizens must sign up)
- Internet/Web site, with recorded news conferences and other supporting information
- Government and public access cable TV announcements
- DOT roadway electronic signs
- Road signs
- Rest stop signage and brochures
- Travel kits with other information

## External (Outsourced) Approaches

- Billboards
- Radio advertisement/public service announcements
- Newspaper/newsletter advertisement
- Television advertisement
- Bus/subway banner advertisements
- Partnerships with organizations
- Bumper stickers

# Compliance

*John Supplee*

## ▶ Introduction

It is nearly impossible to put a value on corporate data. Some would say it is invaluable. Compliance, at least in the realm of information technology, has much to do with how that data is stored and accessed. The amount of data an organization holds and the role of this information has only increased the complexity of IT within the organization. How do you ensure that only those who are supposed to use that data see it while at the same time make it easier for those with permission to get their jobs done? You must intelligently manage this data in order to comply with the thousands of regulations that control how companies store and access their data. In this sense the CIO's job has become more complicated with every new scandal and subsequent regulation.

This chapter was written mostly for CIOs of small to mid-sized companies looking for some suggestions on how to handle compliance. Most large companies have a compliance team and often in-house lawyers who keep on top of all the regulations. This team can also consist of someone from IT where that is their main job. This person ensures that the CIO doesn't have to spend much time thinking about whether the company is compliant. In smaller companies it often falls upon a team of professionals from all the different business units, each having their regular job to do also. In this setting it is imperative the CIO be involved because the company most likely does not have the expertise or manpower in-house to handle compliance. According to *Wall Street and Technology* (2004), "With an unending wave of scandals being revealed in financial services, no one can argue that the focus on compliance will increase. As a matter of fact, a recent *Information Week* Research survey found that 65 percent of senior executives on Wall Street plan to spend more on compliance this year." It won't be just financial firms bogged down with regulations either. Health care has to figure out HIPPA, and public companies have Sarbanes-Oxley.

Why should you have a compliance program, and why should a CIO care?

The most pressing reason to have a compliance program is to comply with the rules and regulations that govern your industry. It is impossible to ensure compliance with the laws and rules without a strong compliance program and culture. Up-to-date compliance policies and procedures are essential for an effective program. Falling behind could mean more visits from regulators to ensure you are doing everything to keep up. Everyone at the company affected by these rules must buy in to the procedures and follow them. Employees must be aware that compliance is the law and there are real consequences with not abiding by the rules and regulations. This type of culture is ultimately what will save you in an audit.

All of this talk about the law and rules ignores the fact that most regulations make good business sense. Often, these rules govern practices that any good operation should have in place, such as disaster recovery or security policies. Violations of any of the laws could ultimately harm your company's reputation, not to mention the bottom line, but a disaster could put you out of business for good. According to Michael Dortch, "Beyond lost revenues and productivity, sufficiently disastrous disruptions can threaten an enterprise's very existence. According to some industry-watchers, as many as 20 percent of companies that experience serious, sustained disasters go out of business completely within 24 months of such events"(2003). A compliance program is often a proactive way to head off any problems before they come about. You need a method for identifying and controlling risks before they become a violation. A good compliance program should encompass all business lines and operations.

The IT department of any company has the control to be the key in every process within every function. These days nothing gets done without touching some type of technology, and that includes compliance. As CIO your job is both strategic and tactical. It is your job to keep your department running smoothly while supporting a whole array of diverse business units. You must also focus strategically on the long-term vision of your business in order to find the best payoff between business objectives and technology.

When something goes wrong in compliance, it can suck your staff into an endless cycle of emergencies and fixes. No other group within your organization has this draining affect. By being proactive, you can ensure that everything runs on time and on budget. The basis of this chapter is to give you the tools to navigate through the maze of regulations. There is no one-size-fits-all with regard to regulations, but I have tried to put together some helpful hints from my experiences.

# ▶ Know Who Is Involved

It is important when you work as a CIO to fully understand everyone involved in the compliance process. From the agency regulating your business, there could be many, to the internal staff charged with keeping you compliant, to the auditors you hire to find the problems before the government does you should know them well. Quarterly conversations, meetings or updates can help you grasp regulations, and their impact on your business, before the regulators are asking why you are not complying.

## Regulators

Regulators often offer newsletters on a regular basis, usually via postal or electronic mail. The newsletters are packed full of information about upcoming regulations and what the hot buttons of that regulatory body currently are. You may not have time to read them in depth, but look them over for important new or revised items. These are the items you should concentrate on because they are what the regulators will be looking for the next time they are in. Usually, the newer subjects are the ones you have spent the least amount of time addressing.

Understand the goals of the regulations in order to understand what the auditors will be looking for. Regulations are often very vague. This is done on purpose because not every company is exactly the same and regulators do not like to tell you how to solve issues. They rarely tell you what types of technology to use or if any is needed at all. Figuring out the goal of a new regulation is a great way to build a relationship with a governing body. When a new rule comes out, call your regulator for clarity, even if you feel you have a good grasp on it. A 20-minute talk between audits lets regulators know you take their jobs seriously and often makes the next audit a little more comfortable (if an audit can be comfortable). It may also increase the time you have between audits. If you are always known for running a tight ship and being up on all the new regulations, the regulators may push your next audit off when their time schedules are squeezed with more egregious companies.

The FFIEC offers a great series of books that explain exactly what they will be looking for and how they will determine whether you are compliant. I have made binders of these manuals and reference them when needed. If you do not work for a financial institution, then check with your governing bodies to see what they have to offer on guidance.

## Internal Staff

Internal compliance staff can be invaluable when the regulators are about to come in. If your staff is seasoned, allow them to do what they are trained to. They have been through audits before, and if they are worth their salt, they know what is coming. They will have alerted you in plenty of time when a new regulation has been approved. It is up to you to work with the compliance staff to determine how a new regulation will affect IT and to have a solution worked out. Many regulations have nothing to do with technology, but as business processes and technology become more pervasive, these regulations often get pulled into the technology mix.

If you are starting a compliance staff from scratch or you are the compliance staff, then you need to take a step back and assess strengths and weaknesses. Following is a list of steps that will come in handy when organizing for compliance.

1. Determine how often the regulators will be reviewing your company.

2. Create a map of all the different regulations. Identify all of the different areas that overlap; this goes for both departments and regulations. Determine what common tasks can be done to minimize the amount of work needed to be compliant.

3. Lay out what actions the compliance function will take to ensure compliance. Compliance, with the approval of upper management, should have the ability to take disciplinary steps toward employees who blatantly break regulations.

4. Policies and procedures for the compliance function must be updated regularly. New regulations seem to be coming out every day. You must have someone responsible for knowing what those regulations are and updating the company.

5. Internal audit, or external if your company does not have an internal audit function, should review the compliance program on a regular basis.

6. Publish, maybe on your intranet, procedures for employees to report compliance issues. Be sure these procedures do not inhibit reporting; for example, establish alternative means, other than to their supervisor, for employees to address issues. Departmental heads may want to bypass compliance and resolve issues themselves.

7. Review every business unit's compliance procedures and their effectiveness. Take corrective action if required to keep each function on track.

8. Regular training sessions must be held with all staff in order for a compliance program to remain effective.

9. Report all findings and actions taken to executive management and the board of directors. First, you must determine within your structure who reports to whom, how difficult issues get resolved, who makes the call.

10. I believe the most important thing you can do to help stay compliant is to get upper management buy-in on the importance of compliance and then convey that commitment to the staff. Have the CEO speak about compliance regularly. When a new regulation comes out, have someone high up sign the memo that goes out to update the staff. The staff needs to know that compliance is supported from the top.

# ▶ Compliance Staff Structure

The structure of your compliance staff can also have a big impact on its ability to meet new challenges and get you through an audit.

## Head of Compliance

If at all possible, the head of compliance should have no other duties. This person should report directly to upper management and not be affiliated in any way with another department. This person must work closely with department heads to ensure they take compliance seriously. They also must have free reign to be able to talk to any employees at any time. Training is essential not only for the compliance personnel but also for the other staff members.

If your company is too small to dedicate someone as a compliance officer, then you should choose someone to head up the position. It is vital to fill this role and not to depend on a committee to handle compliance. In some instances, a committee may work fine, but having someone responsible is most desirable. Regulations are usually not clear, so ideally this employee should be able to think creatively. Often, it is hard to get upper management at a small company to understand, but this employee must also be able to report to a high-ranking officer of the company on compliance issues. He or she also must be able to go straight to the board of directors with any issues that cannot be worked out with upper management. See Figure 21.1 for a sample organization chart.

# Compliance Staff

Ideally, it would be great to have a staff to support the head of compliance, but if you are in a smaller company, that is not always possible. I believe the next best way to handle support staff for compliance is to assign one person from every department to compliance. Have this person report to two people: department head and compliance head (Figure 21.1). This helps bring many issues to the forefront of compliance long before they become larger issues and also helps create the sense that compliance isn't someone else's problem. Never put the department head or second-in-command on the compliance team because department heads don't like anyone scrutinizing their departments, and this could inadvertently cause things to be hidden from the compliance team's view.

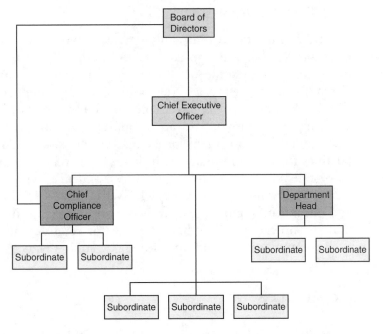

**Figure 21.1** Compliance organizational chart.

# ▶ Institutionalize Compliance (Make It Everyone's Job)

## Formalize Procedures

By formalizing and publishing your compliance procedures, you eliminate the plea of ignorance of the law. No longer can you tell regulators that you were unaware of a specific regulation or their interpretation of it. At your level, CIO, you should never use this excuse anyway. Getting your procedures in a manual and training staff on them is a very important step in overall compliance. Sometimes, training prompts employees to bring up compliance issues of which you may not have been aware. Such early discoveries allow you to adjust procedures before they becomes an issue with regulators. Task your employees with learning regulations that affect their functions. Make everyone head of compliance by conveying the importance upper management has put on staying compliant.

Always be mindful of old regulations when you have a new technology or process being proposed. Sometimes the regulators will assign an old regulation to some new technology your firm may be utilizing. Often, these are the types of regulations that can catch you by surprise. The books and records requirements set forth by the Securities and Exchange Commission are an example. These rules may have been written in 1934, but many brokerage firms received multimillion-dollar fines for not complying with them. On a very simplified basis, the rules state that you must keep all correspondences with clients and personnel concerning business as such. With the advent of electronic mail and instant messaging, some firms did not realize, until it was too late, that the procedures they had in place for retaining and reproducing such communications did not meet SEC requirements.

## Governance

"Nothing gets a board of directors' attention like the word *liability*. In a corporate compliance environment where new privacy and security regulations like Sarbanes-Oxley and the USA Patriot Act hold board members to a high degree of responsibility for lax corporate governance, board members are turning to the CIO and IT department for updates, answers and assessments on how tight security measures are operating." said Brian O'Connell of Bank Technology News (2004).

Investor confidence in corporate governance has dipped to an all-time low. This has prompted an attempt by politicians and regulators to reform corporate governance. Regulations in this area will only increase, and it is imperative that management and the boards of directors keep current with the latest developments and implement necessary changes to handle the ever-changing rules. Because every company is different, there is no standard way to handle governance, although a formal corporate governance structure is a key way to ensure you meet any standards that are put in place.

Corporate governance is a system of checks and balances between the board of directors and management to produce an efficient company that allows investors to feel comfortable with the ethics of that company. Recently, the boards of directors at every company have had to take their responsibilities much more seriously. Audit committees that used to be a rubber stamp for accounting are now scrutinizing every detail in hopes of heading off any minor issues before they become major problems. The CIO should strive to create a board of directors committee to help oversee IT. This helps increase awareness of the inherent risks technology introduces to businesses and allows the CIO a forum to identify risk and manage appropriately.

Following are some keys to successful corporate governance:

1. Training the board of directors on what is expected of the member. Many colleges offer courses on corporate governance that are geared toward directors.

2. Identification of potential conflicts of interest and the board's responsibility.

3. Strategy and planning for the company—for the company overall and for individual departments, such as IT and HR.

4. A robust risk management and compliance process.

5. Understanding financial statements and critical policies in financial reporting. This touches on Sarbanes-Oxley for which financial transparency and disclosure are critical. The CIO is instrumental in helping to facilitate this transparency.

Some ways to help you improve the structure already in place follow:

1. Understand any existing changes in regulations.
2. Determine what resources are available to the company and whether you need to look outside the company to fill any needs.
3. Review and, if necessary, change any existing governance programs to create a program that meets the company's needs and circumstances.
4. Ensure that regulators are kept up to date with any changes made.

## Risk Management

Every company should ensure an adequate risk management structure exists. Some companies can afford to have a separate department dedicated to risk management that review such areas as audit, compliance, information security, and disaster recovery. Edward Hurley of CIO News (2003) stated, "Many federal regulations require a risk assessment. A thorough risk assessment may show holes that the company didn't know existed. A risk assessment may also help identify programs to cut." An overall risk assessment is the first step in comprehensive risk management.

1. Determine which functions/departments within your company need to have a risk assessment done. A key determinate is whether you need that department to keep functioning in a disaster situation. Some examples are:
   (a) Operations
   (b) IT
   (c) Marketing
   (d) Trading
   (e) Banking

2. Determine what the risks are that could occur in each area. Perform a risk matrix for the department as a whole and then on each risk within the departments. See the Modified Risk Assessment form for an example risk matrix for the IT department as a whole. This matrix is a modified version of what the Federal Reserve Bank of Philadelphia recommends.

3. Determine how each risk impacts the company as a whole. Some examples of categories are:

(a) *Credit risk* arises from the potential that a borrower, other counterparty, or vendor will fail to perform on an obligation.

(a) *Market risk* is the risk to the company or to an external vendor resulting from adverse movements in market rates or prices, such as interest rates or capital market prices.

(b) *Liquidity risk* is the potential that the company or an external vendor will be unable to meet its obligations as they come due because of an inability to liquidate assets or obtain adequate funding.

(c) *Operational risk* arises from the potential that inadequate information systems, operational problems, breaches in internal controls, fraud, or unforeseen catastrophes will result in unexpected loss to the company.

(d) *Legal risk* arises from the potential that unenforceable contracts, lawsuits, or adverse judgments can disrupt or otherwise negatively affect the operations or condition of the company.

(e) *Reputational risk* is the potential that negative publicity regarding the company's business practices, whether true or not, will cause a decline in the customer base, costly litigation, or revenue reductions.

4. Upon identification and analysis of risks, each product/business line must be assessed as high, moderate, or low depending upon the risk associated:

(a) *High inherent risk* exists when the activity is significant or positions are large in relation to company resources, when the number of transactions is substantial, or when the nature of the activity is inherently more complex than normal. Thus, the activity potentially could result in a significant and harmful loss to the company.

(b) *Moderate inherent risk* exists when positions are average in relation to company resources, when the volume of transactions is average, and when the activity is more typical or traditional. Thus, while the activity potentially could result in a loss to the company, the company in the normal course of business could absorb the loss.

(c) *Low inherent risk* exists when the volume, size, or nature of the activity is such that even if the internal controls have weaknesses, the risk of loss is remote, or, if a loss were to occur, it would have little negative impact on the company's overall financial condition.

5. Within the risk matrix, assign what direction each risk is moving.

(a) *Decreasing* exists when the type of risk has been addressed and the risk is no longer stable or increasing.

(b) *Stable* exists when the risk has remained the same over a previous assessment.

(c) *Increasing* exists when a risk has increased because of new regulations or lack of compliance.

# ▶ Get Involved

There cannot be enough said about knowing what is going on around you. Recently, I had to deal with a large financial firm whose employees were not following their email and Internet policies. My well-trained and knowledgeable employees alerted my compliance officer to the situation, who in turn alerted me. Together we approached the other company about its employees' behavior. No one in compliance or upper management was aware of the problem until I brought it to their attention. Regular meetings with department heads along with training sessions would have resolved this issue long before it became a problem with us.

As CIO, you'll want to meet with compliance personnel on a regular basis. As do all department heads, I view compliance as a partner in keeping the business running as efficiently as possible. I have a formal quarterly meeting and informal meetings on compliance as needed. Find out how you can help before compliance asks for help. Often, by the time they get around to asking, it is already an emergency and you must pull staff from important projects to handle regulations that have most likely been out for over a year.

Modified Risk Assessment
Information Technology Risk Assessment
Risk Assessment Matrix
As of Date _____

| Type of Risk | Quantity of Risk | Quality of Risk Management | Overall Risk | Direction of Risk |
|---|---|---|---|---|
| Credit | N/A | N/A | N/A | N/A |
| Market | N/A | N/A | N/A | N/A |
| Liquidity | N/A | N/A | N/A | N/A |
| Operational | Moderate | Moderate | Moderate | Stable |
| Legal | Low | High | Low | Stable |
| Reputational | Moderate | Moderate | Moderate | Stable |
| Overall Risk | Moderate | Moderate | Moderate | Stable |

**Definition of Terms**

*Quantity of Risk:* Assesses the nature, complexity, and volume risk within each component and is expressed as low, moderate, or high.

*Quality of Risk Management:* Assesses the strength of risk management processes and controls for each risk and is expressed as strong, acceptable, or weak.

*Overall Risk:* Balances the level of quantity of risk with the quality of risk management for each risk and is expressed as low, moderate, or high.

*Direction of Risk:* Indicates the likely change of the risk profile over the next twelve months and is expressed as increasing, stable, or decreasing.

Acknowledged By:

_____

Board of Directors, Chairperson

_____

President, Chief Executive Officer

(Form adapted from Federal Reserve Board "Framework For Risk-Focused Supervision of Large Complex Institutions," August 8, 1997.)

Have the head of compliance alert you immediately when a new regulation comes out. Even if the deadline is far into the future, sit down with compliance and do the following:

1. Figure out what new capabilities are required to address the issue.
2. If no new capabilities are required, assess the impact on current procedures.
3. Determine how you will implement and support these capabilities.
4. Assess who—what departments—will be impacted.

This is a good time to bring into the discussion any department that is impacted. Often, the department heads already know what is going on with new regulations and have thought of some solutions on their own. This is where you can start to discuss how to get some value out of the regulation. Upper management sometimes perceives regulatory requirements as generating no value. You should strive to consistently show value each time a new rule comes out. This way, any time a new rule is instituted that doesn't generate value, upper management won't feel so overwhelmed by useless regulations.

## ▶ Communicate Often with Upper Management

There are many books and magazines out there to help you in communicating with your boss, whether that is the CEO or CFO, so I will not go into great detail on this subject. Within the realm of compliance it is very important that you do indeed have an open line of communication with your superiors and the board of directors. When your compliance team has a new regulation or existing issue to deal with, it is best that you present the information pertaining to technology to the CEO. Ultimately, the CEO is responsible to the board, and you are responsible to the CEO, so the information has to be correct and timely. When communicating compliance to upper management, you need to focus on all possibilities. Is it clear to the BOD, CEO, CFO, and so on? Did you cover what each of these positions might be concerned with? If you are communicating to the group as a whole, it is often a challenge to be concise and yet thorough. If I have to present to a committee consisting of upper management, I often do the following:

1. Take the time to write up what I think each of the members will want to hear about. This means thinking of how the CFO, CEO, and BOD, will react to any given topic and tailoring a response.

2. Find any commonality in the response and make it more concise.

3. Take all of the responses and build a case for how to handle the compliance matter.

## Talk to Vendors about Solutions

Vendors can be your best friend and worst enemy all in one package. When Sarbanes-Oxley came out, I had an army of consultants and vendors in and out of the CFO's office. Each vendor had the silver bullet product or method on handling Sarbanes-Oxley. Just install its dashboard or tracking system or methodology and you'll be compliant with minimal cost, effort and time.

I give vendors a hard time, usually deservedly, but they do come in handy. Though it was time consuming, the process of talking to many vendors made us realize there were no silver bullets, and in fact there were no specific ways to handle Sarbanes-Oxley. Sarbanes-Oxley is mostly about controls and documentation. If your business is relatively orderly and you haven't had a crazy number of recent mergers, you'll probably find that you can document and create these controls without a million dollars in software and fees.

Have a list of trusted vendors that are involved with and know your company and industry. You can then call them when a new regulation comes out and see how they are telling their other clients to handle it. By having multiple vendors to contact, you cut down on the misinformation you can often get from vendors. Many opinions are better than one.

## ▶ Talk to Your Outside Auditors

Talking to outside auditors is, in a way, a lot like talking to the vendors. The difference is that the relationship with an auditor is much more trusted. Whether financial or IT, your auditor knows your company inside and out and often tailors a response to fit your situation better than a vendor could. Auditors usually are also independent of any product or consulting relationship, so they don't give you specific ways to solve a problem but can help in guiding you to a solution. You are not the auditors' only client, so they see how many different companies are tackling the same issue. They can offer insight to what others are doing in your industry and have often been in contact with the same regulators that will be visiting your office. In this way, they can tell you exactly what that regulator looked for in their last examination so you can be prepared.

## ▶ Use Regulations to Produce Value, Competitiveness, and Productivity

This is one of those phrases that gets a little worn out. As CIO, you are always looking to produce value, competitiveness, and productivity. You cannot always achieve each of these items when new regulations come about, but that should be your goal.

1. Look at all regulations and how they can fit together.
2. Spend ample time in the planning stage to understand all aspects of the issues so as to help produce the value.
3. Take this chance reevaluate any manual processes and either change or automate them.

## ▶ Conclusion

A CIO's job is one of the toughest in business. You must understand both the business your company is in and how the technology handles that business. You must always be wary of rogue employees and hackers while still trying to accommodate an ever-growing list of wants and needs from your employees. Each new gadget or technology suddenly becomes a must-have even though the employee who must have it was able to productively do his or her job for decades without it.

Whether you are responsible for setting up compliance or are just one voice in many, there are certain things you should always do. Structure the compliance staff in such a way that it will not inhibit the discovery and correction of issues. Know each of the individuals involved in the compliance process. Make compliance everyone's job, including the CEO and board. Create a comprehensive risk assessment for the organization and each function. Talk about the issues with upper management and the board, and train employees so as to create a culture of compliance. Talk to outside vendors and auditors when looking for solutions. And last but certainly not least, try to use each new regulation as an opportunity to create business value.

Compliance with federal and state regulations just adds to the complexity involved with the CIO position. You now have to worry about what every department is doing and the inherent risks with those activities. You must ask yourself such questions as, Is it safe for accounting to send that information through email? How well is the operations department trained on technology compliance? Each new regulation brings with it a new challenge. The key is to put your company in a position where everyone knows and understands what it is to be compliant and can assist in helping you stay compliant.

# ▶ References

Dortch, M., 2003. "Disaster Recovery and Business Continuance: Best Practices." *CIO News*, January 6.

Federal Reserve Board, 19973 "Framework for Risk-Focused Supervision of Large Complex Institutions." August 8.

Hurley, E., 2003. "A Holistic Approach to Compliance." *CIO News*, December 12.

O'Connell, B., 2004. "Good Question: Bank Directors Want Answers from CIOs on IT Issues." *Bank Technology News*, September.

"Outlook 2004: Compliance Tops the Charts." *Wall Street & Technology*, February 12, 2004. Available: http://www.wallstreet-andtech.com/showArticle.jhtml?articleID=17603335.

# 22

# Navigating the IT Procurement and Outsourcing Process

*Francis X. Taney, Jr.*

## ▶ Introduction

In my role as a litigator and trial lawyer, I have performed autopsies on the carcasses of scores of failed IT procurement and outsourcing relationships. In my role as a legal counselor and contract negotiator, I have helped numerous clients identify and avoid or minimize problems that could have otherwise arisen in the course of their IT procurement or outsourcing relationships. Each of these relationships had unique features. However, a number of key areas consistently arose as potential failure points, which the successful companies were able to avoid. In the following discussion I offer the benefit of my experience as to what can go wrong and how to avoid these failure points.

First, I define a few key concepts. For purposes of this discussion I define information technology (IT) as any technology that allows automation of critical business processes that involve the processing, storage, and manipulation of information. By IT procurement, I mean the process by which a vendor and a customer agree that the vendor will provide an IT-related product or service. By IT outsourcing, I mean any situation in which a customer engages a third-party vendor to perform all or any portion of the customer's IT functions.

The IT procurement and outsourcing process deserves much more focus than it currently receives. As an initial matter, most IT experts agree that a significant percentage of complex IT procurement and outsourcing projects end in failure. In this context, "failure" means that the relationship experienced cost overruns, the work was not completed on time or at all, the customer was dissatisfied with the products or services, or the relationship ended with disputes or litigation. Clearly, these relationships are difficult to execute successfully. I believe that this high failure rate alone is reason enough to work at becoming adept at this process.

There are other reasons to work at these relationships. Because IT affects your company's critical business functions, the consequences of a failed relationship can be catastrophic. In addition, IT is increasingly a source of potential competitive advantage or disadvantage. Therefore, the companies that master the IT procurement and outsourcing process put themselves in a better position to benefit from IT and thereby gain a competitive advantage. Thus, these are high-stakes relationships for your company

Moreover, even if your company does not compete in an IT-intensive industry, your company will have continuing potential IT procurement and outsourcing needs over time. This is because your company will have to continue to assess whether to adopt the latest advances in technology or entirely new technologies as they emerge or as your company experiences changes in its business requirements, such as in the event of acquisitions, divestitures, and reorganizations. Thus, your company will likely engage in this process on a periodic, if not regular, basis over time.

Why are these relationships difficult to execute? They usually require the parties involved to simultaneously accommodate several often conflicting sets of considerations. There are business considerations, which are often expressed in terms of cost and time pressures. There are technical considerations, which are often expressed in terms of the complexity and performance limits of the technology involved. There are legal considerations, which are typically expressed in terms of allocation of risk and responsibility and the corresponding exposure that results. Finally, there are interpersonal considerations, which means the "human" factors and dynamics that can interfere with a business relationship.

As will be apparent from the following discussion, written mostly from the customer's perspective, conflicts among these competing considerations can rupture relationships. The companies who are successful at these relationships do three things: they thoughtfully consider in advance the key areas that are likely to create risk and generate disputes in their relationship, they draft a clear set of contract provisions to address the key areas they have identified, and they use the contractual provisions they have drafted to proactively manage the relationship.

# ▶ Scope Documents and Statements of Work

Every contract should contain a statement or description of the work that the vendor must perform in order to be entitled to payment. However, for numerous reasons, parties often don't create a clear description of the work. The resulting lack of clarity gives rise to disputes when the parties disagree over whether the vendor has performed all of the items of the required work or whether a customer is requesting a vendor to perform work outside the original project scope. While it is usually impossible to eliminate all ambiguity in describing the scope for a complex project, there are techniques you can use to head off disputes and protect yourself in the event that a dispute arises.

## *Know Your Audience*

The first step toward addressing this problem is drafting the statement of work with your audience in mind. Who is this audience? In the event of dispute, your audience will be a judge, jury, or one or more arbitrators. Litigators refer to these people as the "fact finder." During a trial or arbitration hearing, the fact finder will have to read the statement of work and determine whether your vendor has performed the required work or whether your company has requested the vendor to perform extra work.

The fact finder, whether a judge, jury, or arbitrator, will usually have two key disabilities that will affect how you have to draft the scope of work (and the other contract provisions, for that matter). First, the fact finder will typically know nothing about the dispute or the parties at the outset of the trial or hearing. Second, he or she will typically lack the technical expertise to understand the technology at issue without substantial assistance from the parties, lawyers, and expert witnesses.

This requires a particular focus and attention to detail in contract drafting. Clearly, you would explain a concept differently to a person whom you just met and who was unfamiliar with the issues than you would to a person whom you knew well and who was familiar with the issues. Your audience in litigation is the former person rather than the latter. You must draft your statement of work (and the rest of the contract) so that it is clear to that audience.

## Use a Multidisciplinary Approach for Drafting

One technique that will help eliminate or reduce unnecessary ambiguity is to apply appropriate business, technical, and legal resources to drafting the scope document. All too often, organizations fail to apply resources from one or more of these areas, with disastrous results.

For example, if you do not involve personnel with requisite technical expertise, your drafters may not include sufficient detail to ensure that your company receives the key functionality or technical value from the project. If you do not involve the businesspeople sufficiently, the end users or other stakeholders may be dissatisfied with the results of the project, or you may find that the project lacks buy-in or commitment from key constituencies. If you do not apply sufficient legal expertise, the scope may have otherwise unnecessary ambiguities and subject your company to unanticipated exposure in the event of a dispute.

On the other hand, those organizations that do apply expertise from all three of these areas find that each set of expertise adds value to the process. Indeed, the experts from each of these areas usually need input from the others to function most effectively. In the course of drafting, the technical people should be able to obtain guidance on the relevant business issues and legal risks affecting the project, the business people should be aware of the technical issues and legal risks involved, and the lawyers certainly should determine the business issues and technical risks inherent in a project in the course of giving legal advice.

In most organizations, these legal, business, and technical skills won't be resident in one person, so you will likely have to involve more than one person in drafting. Further, if your company lacks expertise in one or more of these areas, you should retain outside consultants who have these skills. Making the investment in appropriate expertise at the outset of a relationship can help you avoid much larger expenditures over disputes later in the relationship.

## Some Do's and Don'ts for Drafting Statements of Work

Your ultimate goal in drafting a scope document or statement of work is to create a set of instructions or descriptions that sets forth each item or aspect of the work in clear language, without ambiguity. In this context, an ambiguity means that a paragraph or sentence is susceptible to more than one interpretation.

The easiest way to test for ambiguity is to ask one or more people for their understanding of a provision you have written. If their understanding differs from yours, the provision is potentially ambiguous. When you encounter ambiguities, you should determine what caused this difference in understanding, and change the language to address the problem. Unfortunately, many companies do not use this basic drafting technique.

Beyond using this basic technique, avoid undefined jargon. IT relationships are technical in nature, so scope documents will necessarily include technical terms. However, if you must use jargon or industry-speak, define these terms somewhere in your contract. I have found that in IT, even industry experts can differ on the meaning of technical terms. Your judge, juror, or arbitrator is therefore very unlikely to have a clear understanding of industry terminology. You should address this by defining the technical terms and industry terminology.

You should also avoid the use or inclusion of marketing phrases. In the sales, bidding, or negotiation process, your vendor may use imprecise language like "best-in-breed," "customer-centric," "cutting edge," and "state of the art." These adjectives can mean different things to different people, and you should avoid them.

It is also helpful to depict concepts and requirements graphically where possible. The phrase "a picture is worth a thousand words" did not become a cliché by accident. For example, on software development projects it is often possible to show how the completed software should look with sample screenshots. In other instances it may be possible to depict complicated processes or work flows graphically. As a trial lawyer I know that that these diagrams and pictures can have a powerful effect at trial and can help foreclose arguments over whether a vendor has fulfilled its obligations. This is because you can't cross-examine a document, and it is difficult to argue that a party has complied with its obligations when, for example, its work product does not look anything like the screen shots contained in the scope of work.

Avoid commingling documents. On large projects, the customer may produce a several hundred–page request for proposal, or RFP. The vendor may respond with an equally lengthy bid document. Then the parties create another document with some commercial terms and legal boilerplate and agree that that contract will consist of this boilerplate document, the RFP, and the bid. There is little chance that a thousand-page contract comprised of different sections written by different people for different purposes will be free of ambiguities. Further, sometimes provisions from the various documents will directly contradict one another. It is almost always better to create an independent document, based on the various precontract communications between the parties, that clearly states the scope of the vendor's undertaking.

You should also pay attention to clearly defining divisions of responsibility. Often a complex project or relationship will require your company to perform tasks to assist your vendor, or may require your vendor to perform some IT functions but not others. This area requires just as much attention as does defining what the vendor will do. Again, if two people could come to different conclusions about the limits of your company's obligations to assist or work with your vendor, you have an ambiguity and a potential problem.

## ▶ Warranties and Performance Standards

This area is related to but conceptually distinct from scope descriptions. While scope descriptions and statements of work set forth what the vendor must do to earn its money, warranties and performance standards set forth how well the vendor must perform to earn its money. As is the case with scope descriptions and statements of work, you must take care to clearly define warranties and performance standards. Otherwise, you risk litigation in the event that the contract is less than clear about the standard to which the vendor must perform. Further, you may put your company at risk of not receiving the technical and business benefit for which it was bargaining.

### Tie the Standards to the Underlying Business or Technical Need

Usually, the easiest way to attack the drafting of performance standards is to use the underlying business or technical needs giving rise to the contract as the framework. For example, if your company needs software that will allow it to process a certain number of transactions or orders per second or per hour, then you should focus on that need in drafting the performance standards. You must make sure that the performance standard entitles your company to receive that level of performance from your vendor.

Once you have your standard in sight, you must describe that standard using language that is as clear and nonsubjective as possible under the circumstances. Ambiguity is your enemy in this area in the same way as it is in drafting the statement of work. You should therefore use the same techniques to eliminate or reduce ambiguity that I described in the preceding section. As with scope documents, this is not a place to use undefined jargon or vague adjectives. Your vendor will often help you in this regard in the course of differentiating its offerings from those of its competitors, because your vendor will usually at some point describe the differences in objective, technical terms or "metrics."

Your drafting in this area will benefit from the same multidisciplinary team approach that I advocate for drafting scope documents and statements of work, because your company's business requirements are usually tightly tied to the technical performance that the vendor or technology can achieve. Further, you have the same business and legal need to eliminate ambiguity and reduce your company's exposure in the event of a problem. The drafting of performance standards and warranties will therefore benefit from close communication among your company's business, technical, and legal personnel.

## Some Examples of Appropriate Metrics for Performance Standards

It would be impossible to give a comprehensive list of examples of effective metrics for all IT projects. However, I have set forth below some examples of metrics that companies have used effectively to bring clarity to the area of performance standards or warranties.

One easy metric to require, where applicable, is a requirement that the software, hardware, or other item of technology at issue have at a minimum the functionality described in the scope document or specifications. For example, your scope of work might provide that the vendor will provide an item of software with five essential features with certain screens appearing to the users in a particular order. In that case, you should require your vendor to warrant that the software, when completed, will function as described in the scope of work. This is a simple way to assure yourself of a minimum of protection insofar as major aspects of functionality are concerned.

Beyond using this general requirement, it is often possible to use other technical or numerical measures to define performance. Examples of this include requiring the technology to handle a certain number of transactions per second, to maintain a certain processing speed, or to accommodate a certain number of concurrent users. Where the vendor is going to be maintaining a network, Web site, or system over a period of time, then it is often appropriate to specify a performance standard in terms of percentages of uptime and unplanned downtime.

In the service contract context, if your vendor's response time to requests for assistance or problems is important, you should specify the maximum amount of time the vendor has to respond. Depending on the level of severity of the problem, you could provide for different response times and impose different levels of effort to be applied to correcting the problems. For example, you could provide that certain situations that threaten your company's ability to operate will require an immediate response and that the vendor must work around the clock until the problem is resolved. For other less serious problems, you might allow your vendor to respond within one or two business days and to work during normal business hours to resolve the problem.

Many other typical areas of concern in the IT context lend themselves to hard performance metrics. If you need your vendor to devote a particular number of personnel to certain tasks, or personnel from or in a certain location, or personnel with certain minimum levels of training or experience, you should address this in the warranty provisions and performance standards. If your company is in a highly regulated industry or subject to particular regulations, and your vendor's failure to comply with these regulations could subject your company to penalties, you should require your vendor to be familiar and comply with those regulations as part of its standard of performance. In sum, you should define and quantify the required effort in each important area of your vendor's work.

### Plan for What Happens in the Event Your Vendor Fails to Meet Its Warranty.

Your work is not finished when you define the warranties or performance standards. You must also consider and address what happens if the vendor fails to adhere to the required standard.

Often you can afford and will want to provide for consequences short of termination, at least at first. What is appropriate will vary from project to project. Some applications or services are so mission critical that you may need the immediate right to replace vendors or to take over functions from the vendor. In other instances you may be content with assessing a monetary penalty, or simply giving the vendor notice of the problem and an opportunity to cure the problem within a reasonable period of time.

Your vendor will likely want to have some period of time after learning of a problem to address the problem. There is nothing wrong with agreeing to give your vendor a reasonable amount of time to cure its default. However, you should tailor any notice period to your particular situation so that you don't have to wait an excessive amount of time before being free to take remedial action. Also, make sure that the contract sets forth to whom you must give notice and in what form. This will avoid disputes over whether you provided appropriate notice to your vendor.

# ▶ Documenting Key Assumptions

Vendors and customers almost always enter into contracts with assumptions about factors that impact the cost, difficulty, or inconvenience of performing under the contract, such as access to the work environment, coordination with other vendors, and cooperation between your company and vendors. You must make sure that the contract sets forth the assumptions that will apply. If not, you run the risk of litigation if the parties had different assumptions on key points or if the contract does not clearly set forth the operative assumptions.

## *Identify Your Company's Key Assumptions Regarding Contract Performance*

The best way to identify the key assumptions for your company is to examine the factors that will affect your company's cost or difficulty of performance and determine what conditions are must-haves for your organization. You should use a multidisciplinary team because cost, difficulty, and inconvenience issues often have technical, business, and legal aspects. Once your team has identified the assumptions that are important to your company, you should ensure that the contract clearly and unambiguously sets forth these assumptions.

Sometimes you will identify the need for additional conditions or assumptions in the course of negotiations and precontract discussions with your vendor. This is because your vendor may ask for accommodations or undertakings from your company that have the potential to disrupt your company's operations, increase your company's internal cost of performing under the contract, or even may be impossible for your company to provide. These requests require your company to confirm in the contract with equal clarity that it will or will not accommodate these requests, and on what terms, as the case may be.

Too many negotiators assume that avoiding discussion or clear resolution of a sensitive or sticky topic in the contract will give them an advantage in the event of a dispute. This is not the case. You risk trouble when you discuss important issues or assumptions with your vendor during precontract discussions but fail to address them in the written contract. Sometimes the vendor will use the contract's failure to address a subject one way or another to argue that the parties had a particular understanding on an issue where your company either had no understanding or had the opposite understanding. The key to foreclosing these arguments is to affirmatively address the issue in the contract.

## Examples of Areas Requiring Attention

The assumptions that customers and vendors bring into negotiations will vary from company to company and project to project. However, I've listed some of the areas that are likely to rise to assumptions on either or both sides of the contract.

One area giving rise to assumptions is access to the physical environment in which the vendor will perform its work, test its work-in-progress, and install its completed work product. If your vendor needs to have access to your facilities or to shut down or disrupt your normal operations to progress its work, test its work, or install its work product, you should ensure that the contract is clear on the terms on which you are obligated to provide access, as well as the vendor's obligation to avoid unnecessary disruption to your company's operations. If you fail to address these issues, your vendor may claim that it is entitled to additional compensation because it assumed that it would have more unfettered access and that by failing to give the vendor its requested access, your company delayed the vendor or caused the vendor to experience increased costs.

During contract negotiations, your vendor may mention to you that it is making assumptions about the quality or condition of your company's data or operating systems in agreeing upon a particular price. If you are unwilling to warrant that your company's data, operating systems, or other attributes are of a certain quality, you should make sure the contract reflects this. Otherwise your vendor may claim additional compensation for increased costs or difficulties it experienced as a result of problems in these areas.

Similar considerations apply to the compatibility of items such as operating systems, software, network components, and hardware. You should state in the contract who will assume the risk of extra costs arising from problems in these areas.

If your vendor must work with other vendors, or must rely on the work product of other vendors to complete its work for your company, your vendor will likely assume that your company will be responsible for problems that the vendor experiences if the work product of the other vendors is faulty or delayed. You may be willing to assume this responsibility, but you should address the limits and parameters of that responsibility in the contract.

If the contract will require a significant period of time to perform, the relative cost or availability of labor, equipment, and materials may change over the life of the contract, especially if the contract runs longer than expected or if the vendor otherwise experiences delays. The parties may have assumptions as to who will bear the risk of fluctuations in the cost of these items, and the resolution of these issues will depend on the particular commercial realities affecting each project. However, you should not leave these assumptions unaddressed.

Your vendor may require information or other cooperation from key individuals within your company to perform its work. Similarly, either or both parties may have relied upon assumptions as to the skill and experience levels of the other's employees in entering into the contract. You should ensure that the contract clearly sets forth the assumptions in these areas as well.

Further, the parties may assume that in the event of certain catastrophic events one or both parties' obligations will be excused or suspended. Parties sometimes refer to these events as *force majeure* events or "Acts of God." While by their nature these events may be difficult to plan for in advance, you should consider setting forth at least general assumptions governing these issues as well.

### Confine and Contain the Parties' Assumptions

As noted earlier, your vendor may have its own assumptions that it will want to include in the contract. Indeed, most IT relationships require both sides to cooperate to some degree to facilitate the vendor's performance. However, you must guard against overextending to accommodate your vendor's assumptions by agreeing to vague, potentially open-ended obligations. Therefore, you should work hard to remove ambiguities in this area.

A good technique to avoid this overextension is to use disclaimers to state what you will not do. In other words, if your vendor needs to be able to take your operating system off-line during your business hours, and you are willing to do this, but you need to keep this to a minimum, say something like "during the three week testing period, customer will allow vendor to take customer's operating system off-line to allow testing of the software from 3:30 p.m. to 7:30 p.m. but shall have no other obligation to take its operating system off-line during normal business hours." If used correctly, this technique will make it clear where your company's responsibilities begin and end.

Further, once you and your vendor have agreed upon the assumptions that will be part of the contract, and limited these assumptions appropriately, use an integration clause to confine the assumptions. An integration clause is a provision that states that all of the promises and representations upon which the parties relied in entering into the contract are contained in the contract document and that there are no unwritten side-deals, pre-contract promises, or pre-contract discussions between the parties that are enforceable. In many jurisdictions using an integration clause will prevent parties from raising claims or avoiding obligations based upon alleged pre-contract discussions.

# ▶ Compensation Structure

The compensation structure is the mechanism by which you will pay the vendor. The most common types of compensation structures are lump sum and time and materials, but there are others. Compensation structures allocate risk between the parties, and different structures allocate risk in different ways. There is nothing harmful with this in and of itself. However, because your compensation structure allocates risk, it will create incentives and disincentives for you and your vendor. You should give some thought to whether the compensation structure is putting unnecessary strain on your relationship and whether a different structure would more closely align your interests with those of your vendor.

### *Typical Assumptions About Common Compensation Structures*

With a lump sum arrangement, the vendor agrees to complete a given scope of work for a flat fee. With a time and materials arrangement, the vendor agrees to perform work for a fixed rate (such as hourly or per diem), often with no absolute contractual limit on the vendor's fee.

The common wisdom is that lump sum arrangements place the risk of problems (slow or inefficient progress) on vendors and that the purchaser is therefore always better off with a lump sum arrangement. Conversely, most assume that time and materials arrangements place the risk of problems on customers and that the purchaser is therefore worse off with a time and materials arrangement.

### Rethinking Some Common Assumptions

There is certainly merit to this common wisdom, and I don't mean to suggest that the common wisdom is wrong in all cases. However, you cannot afford to assume that in all cases, you as the customer will be better off with a lump sum arrangement.

When forced to bid for work on a lump sum basis, experienced vendors will include a premium in their bid to account for any perceived risk or uncertainty. Therefore, where a vendor views the project as high risk, you may not save money by using a lump sum mechanism. In other cases, you may fare better with time and materials arrangements where the scope or nature of the work is sufficiently definite that you can easily control and monitor the vendor's work and progress. In still other cases, if your vendor seeks to establish a longer term relationship with your company, this desire can provide discipline to maintain time and materials fees at a low level to earn more business. In such a situation you may do better with a time and materials arrangement.

Conversely, lump sum arrangements in the service context can tempt your vendor to skimp on service. If your vendor perceives that it can increase its margin by performing the services with minimal resources, your lump sum arrangement will motivate your vendor to short you. Time and materials arrangements can remove that improper incentive. On the other hand, in the appropriate circumstances, lump sum arrangements do impose discipline on your vendor that some vendors may not feel in the context of a time and materials context.

### Some Potential Alternative Arrangements

Beyond choosing carefully between lump sum and time and materials arrangements, you may also have the opportunity to choose alternative arrangements that more closely align your interests with your vendor's interests. One commonly employed alternative arrangement involves the use of so-called success fees. A good example of this is an arrangement whereby you agree that a vendor will receive a base fee for completing the work on time but an additional fee for early completion. With this arrangement the vendor's incentive will presumably be to progress the work more quickly than scheduled, which is presumably the customer's goal as well.

It may sometimes be possible to share license fees or revenue opportunities from the products at issue to bring the parties' interests into closer alignment. This is more likely to be a possible option in a situation where the vendor is creating a product that has potential utility for other companies in your industry or for companies in other industries. Certainly not all customers would be willing to allow other companies to purchase technology that they have had developed in all cases, but in some circumstances the vendor and customer will perceive added value in this arrangement.

Another example of a potential alternative arrangement is a hybrid lump sum/time and materials arrangement. This simply means an arrangement in which your company pays for a portion of the vendor's services on a lump sum basis and for a portion of the vendor's services on a time and materials basis, depending on which portions of the work are more suited to each arrangement.

Use- or volume-based fees may also help align parties' interests or at least avoid conflicts of interest. These fees are often calculated on the basis of a transaction or on a use basis and provide something in the way of residual income to a vendor. These fees sometimes allow a vendor to accept a lower up-front fee because the vendor perceives that it will realize greater income as the customer's business or use grows. In this arrangement both parties' incentives are clearly to see the project succeed, which is a perfect alignment of interests.

# ▶ Monitoring and Demonstrating Work and Progress

Most contracts of any significant length or size provide for a schedule of payments to the vendor over the life of the relationship. However, if you fail to properly link compensation to vendor progress or the delivery of value, the contract may create counterproductive incentives for the vendor and unnecessarily increase your company's exposure in the event that problems arise on the project. In addition, if the criteria for demonstrating that progress or delivery of value is unclear, you and your vendor may experience disputes if you disagree as to whether your vendor has achieved a milestone.

### Link Payment to True Progress and True Delivery of Value

Your chief concern in setting this schedule of payments is to maintain a proper balance between the compensation and ascertainable progress or the delivery of meaningful value. In this context, requiring your vendor to simply demonstrate the expenditure of man-hours, the passage of time, or some arbitrary measure of progress does not necessarily protect you. Rather, you must require your vendor to demonstrate meaningful progress or the delivery of valuable services.

You should not assume, as too many customers do, that you don't need to pay attention to linking value and progress to payment in a lump sum project. This is because if your vendor runs into problems relative to its own internal budget, it may look to avoid responsibility for its problems by blaming you or your personnel. Worse, your vendor may demand additional compensation to complete the work and threaten to cease work if you do not provide additional money. If the vendor does not perceive early on in the project that it must provide value or demonstrate true progress, the vendor may not feel sufficient incentive to progress the work adequately or provide the required value.

### Compartmentalize

One key technique to properly link payment to value is to break down or compartmentalize the vendor's work into discrete parts. One example of an area where compartmentalization is possible is levels of design detail. You could condition entitlement to successive milestone payments on completion of a conceptual design, a preliminary design, and a detailed design. Or, if an item of software is to have multiple modules or features, you could tie particular payments to the completion of individual modules.

You can also compartmentalize by tying payments to robustness of functionality. If, for example, your vendor is going to produce successive versions of software that are usable under successively rigorous conditions or with increasing numbers of concurrent users, these successive levels of functionality can serve as payment milestones. To give another example, if your vendor is providing a suite of services to your company, you can and should segment the overall fee into components corresponding to each individual service. These examples are by no means exclusive, and you should carefully analyze the products and services your vendor will provide to determine the extent to which compartmentalization is possible.

## Establish Clear Testing and Approval Criteria

Beyond compartmentalizing and linking payment to value, you must work to establish clear approval criteria. This not only requires clarity in defining the required result but often requires clarity in defining who will test the work, the rigor with which the work will be tested, and the testing methodology to be used. As is the case with areas such as scope documents and performance standards, ambiguity in these areas will give rise to disputes. Fortunately, you will often be able to remove ambiguity in these areas in the process of compartmentalizing the work, because that exercise will usually require you to focus on what constitutes success and the best method for testing whether the vendor has achieved that success.

Finally, your contract should encourage prompt resolution of disputes by escalating the level of decision makers involved in the discussions in the event that the parties cannot agree as to whether the vendor has met the milestone. For example, you might provide that the project managers will attempt to resolve any disputed claim, and that if they cannot resolve the claim within a set amount of days, the parties' respective chief financial officers will attempt to resolve the claim, and so on up the chain of authority.

The purpose of this escalation is to prevent disputes from persisting without resolution. Claims or disputes that persist without resolution have the potential to grow if the vendor continues to devote resources to the project. Moreover, many vendors may stop work if a dispute exists as to whether they met a milestone, so prompt dispute resolution will increase the likelihood that your vendor completes the work on time.

# ▶ Change Orders and Claims for Extra Work and Delay

For various reasons, your vendor may claim that it is entitled to additional compensation because your company caused or required it to perform work outside of the original contract scope. Alternatively, your vendor may claim that your company has delayed or hindered its work. If not managed properly, disputes over these types of claims can cause your relationship to rupture spectacularly. You may not be able to avoid these claims completely. However, with careful contract drafting and proactive contract administration you can contain the damage and prevent disputes over these claims from enveloping the project.

## Create a Workable Set of Contact Provisions to Address Claim Procedures

The first step toward managing these claims is to include a workable set of contractual provisions to address claims procedure. In doing so, you should realize that these claims arise in a number of contexts. Sometimes you and your vendor may agree that the vendor is entitled to a particular amount of additional compensation for extra work or for some other reason. On other occasions you and your vendor may not agree that the vendor is entitled to any extra compensation, let alone agree upon the amount. These different situations require different treatment.

For those situations in which you and your vendor agree that the vendor is entitled to some additional compensation, you should include a simple set of provisions that specify how the vendor must document the fact that your company has authorized or directed the extra work (often referred to as a "change order") and agreed to the additional compensation. At a minimum you should require that the change order be in writing and that only specified people have authority to approve change orders. You should require that the change order document identify the additional work in reasonable detail and clearly specify the additional amount of compensation associated with the work.

Disputed situations require more attention. You should still provide for a straightforward procedure for the vendor to provide a written claim to a specified person, with sufficient detail to enable your company to evaluate the claim. In addition, you should insist on provisions requiring the parties to escalate responsibility for resolving the dispute to decision makers with appropriate authority in the event that the first level of representatives for the two sides cannot come to an agreement, in the same manner applicable to disputes over progress. As with disputes over progress, prompt resolution will prevent your vendor from proceeding down the wrong path and increasing its costs (or damages).

It is also possible and in your interest to negotiate items of damages in advance, where possible. If you and your vendor can agree upon labor, equipment, and materials rates in advance, you should provide that in the event that the vendor performs extra work, your company will compensate the vendor at those agreed-upon rates. If the contract will be in effect for a period of years and escalations in rates are appropriate, this is something you and your vendor may be able to agree upon in advance as well. You are usually better off negotiating these items in advance than leaving the door open for disputes over these rates.

Regardless of whether your company disputes the vendor's claim, you should require the vendor to raise any claim for extra work relatively promptly after it arises. If you do not, you run the risk of relevant documents being lost or destroyed, of witnesses leaving your company (or leaving the vendor), or memories fading or changing over time. Disputed claims can become much more difficult to defend against if you allow your vendor to unduly delay raising its claim. Further, as noted above, claims tend to increase in size as the project progresses and the vendor continues working.

You may also be able to negotiate the recoverability and amounts of various categories of damages, such as overhead, administrative costs, and other "soft" costs. For example, you may be able to agree with your vendor that in the event your company delays the vendor or requires the vendor to perform extra work, the vendor will be entitled to an administrative and overhead markup of a certain percentage over the direct labor and materials costs. In the absence of an agreement on these items, you may become involved in a costly dispute over the "true cost" of a delay or item of extra work to the vendor.

### Require Periodic Review

Apart from basic provisions governing claim procedure, you should provide a forum for periodic reviews of project progress and status and require discussion of issues such as potential or perceived claims. This will force early discussion of problematic issues and increase the chances that the parties do not allow problems to fester for extended periods of time.

In addition, you should require the production of minutes or other written records reflecting the events of these progress meetings and insist that the minutes and records be generated shortly after the meetings and that the parties to sign off on the minutes or records. This requirement serves the same purpose as requiring your vendor to register claims promptly: it protects against fading or changed memories, destruction of documents, and departing witnesses.

### Take Advantage of the Contractual Provisions You Have Negotiated

Once you have an effective set of contract provisions to handle change order and delay claims, you must use them. The contract should not gather dust in someone's office. Rather, you must educate the personnel dealing with your vendor and administrating the contract as to the contents of your contract in general and the key provisions governing claim procedures in particular.

Apart from this, it is vital to document problems and communicate problems promptly and clearly. If you fail to communicate your intentions promptly and clearly, you may unintentionally mislead your vendor. Worse, your vendor may accuse you of intentionally misleading it. In either event your actions will look suspicious to a jury or judge reviewing the project after the fact.

# ▶ Disaster Planning and Recovery

Disasters, which I define as any event that materially impairs an organization's ability to operate, can affect both vendors and customers.

Disasters can arise from either natural or man-made causes, and from intentional and unintentional conduct. Inherent in the concept of a disaster is that it is unexpected and not always preventable. However, if you do not engage in sufficient planning for catastrophic events, your company may experience a second disaster in the form of unnecessary continuing disruption after the event.

### Consider Appropriate Physical and Technical Redundancy and Security

Measures such as firewalls, antivirus software, data encryption, passwords, physical security, and remote backup systems and/or system components (where appropriate) have become part of the general standard of care for IT practitioners. Indeed, there are an increasing number of statutes, laws, and regulations imposing information security responsibilities and potential liability on companies who fail to implement appropriate information security, both in the normal course of business and in the event of a disaster.

Therefore, at a minimum, you should consider the effect that your vendor relationship will have on your company's information security and ability to operate in the event of a catastrophe, including the related physical facilities and systems, and incorporate requirements along those lines into the contract. Further, you should ensure and require that your vendor incorporate appropriate security procedures and measures in providing its services.

What is appropriate will vary from situation to situation and with the sensitivity of the data involved and/or the nature of your business. For example, if your company's information security personnel have determined that certain measures and procedures are necessary for your company, you should at a minimum require your vendor to adhere to or refrain from disrupting those measures in providing its services. If your vendor will be providing a product, you should require that the vendor include appropriate security measures in the design of the product. If your vendor will be in charge of overseeing or implementing information security for your company and you have no in-house expertise to draw upon in negotiating security requirements with your vendor, you should consider engaging a consultant for that purpose.

## Establish Rights and Responsibilities in the Event of a Disaster

Especially if your vendor is providing critical services on an ongoing basis, you should also set forth in the contract the vendor's responsibilities in the event of a disaster. If your vendor has possession of key items of information, equipment, or other assets of your company due to the nature of its work, you should require your vendor to marshal these assets to the extent necessary to allow your company to respond to the emergency and continue operating.

Beyond this, include specific disaster or emergency response times for your vendor in the contract. Tailor the response time requirements to the particular technologies or operations involved, and specify the nature of the assistance that the vendor must provide. It is also wise to require the vendor to identify the contact people in emergency situations. Your company should know who at the vendor will be available to respond and assist in an emergency situation.

In the same vein, if you and your vendor agree that your company's personnel will have certain obligations in emergency situations, make sure that the contract delineates these responsibilities clearly. This will enable you to avoid disputes over whether your company's employees contributed to the adverse effects of a disaster by failing to assist your vendor as required.

## Consider Appropriate Source Code and Intellectual Property Escrows

Your vendor may often be providing a mission-critical product or service. If the vendor is the only person or entity that possesses the source code, technology, or know-how to operate the product or provide the service, your company is at risk if a catastrophic event impacts your vendor's ability to function. In that event, your vendor's disaster may become your company's disaster.

Requiring your vendor to provide an appropriate source code or technology escrow agreement can be a potential solution to this problem. With an escrow agreement, the vendor agrees to give a copy of its source code or other proprietary data or materials to a third party to hold. The escrow agreement typically provides that in the event that the vendor becomes unable to continue operating or functioning, your company will have access to the source code or other material to the extent necessary to allow your company to continue functioning and/or obtain a replacement vendor.

With escrow agreements, you should be sure that you clearly define the triggering events that will entitle you to access the escrowed material. Otherwise you may become involved in a dispute with your vendor or the third party over whether you are justified in requesting access. In addition, the agreement should provide for a streamlined procedure for giving notice to the vendor that you will request the release of the escrowed material, as well as for resolving disputes over these issues. Because these disputes will often arise in an emergency, your agreement should give you prompt recourse to court if necessary. You should also take care that the escrow agreement does not unreasonably restrict your company's ability to use the material in the event of an emergency.

# ▶ Exit Strategies and Transition Plans

Your current commercial relationships will all end at some point. Further, these relationships may end for a variety of reasons, and you and your vendors may or may not be on speaking terms when they do. Although this is a fact of business life, businesspeople usually don't focus on that fact at the outset of their relationships. Moreover, even the most amicable partings will almost always cause some disruption to your operations. However, if you do not clearly define your rights and responsibilities upon the termination of your relationship, you may experience otherwise unnecessary disruption if you and your vendor disagree about the terms of your separation.

### Define Rights and Responsibilities in the Event of a Material Breach

Your relationship may end because either your vendor or your company breached its obligations in a material way. You must clearly define the parties' respective rights and obligations in such an event. Specifying the measure and amount of monetary damages is one important consideration. Where possible, you should agree upon with your vendor and specify the elements of damages that are recoverable in the event of a breach by either side. As is the case with claims for extra work, it will often be possible to agree upon categories of damages that are recoverable and/or formula for calculating those damages. (Specific provisions limiting or liquidating damages are discussed in a subsequent section.) To the extent that you can reach agreement with your vendor in advance on these items, you should do so, because you can thereby avoid expensive disputes over the calculation of damages in the event of a breach.

You should also consider whether to provide for a notice and opportunity to cure procedure applicable to both you and your vendor. Here, as I discussed previously, you must tailor the length of any notice period to your operational needs and take care not to give your vendor so long to cure a material breach that your operations are materially impaired in the interim. Do not agree to a longer notice period than you can afford. You may also consider shortening the notice period for particular emergency situations.

Both sides may come into possession of information, materials, and equipment belonging to the other over the course of the relationship. In many cases, one or both parties will want the other to return these materials. To avoid disputes, you should set forth in the contract the particular items that each party must return to the other, and provide for a reasonable amount of time for the exchange to occur. If either or both sides will be retaining any materials belonging to the other, you should also specify any appropriate restrictions or limits on the parties' rights to use the materials.

## Other Terminations

It is important to consider whether to allow one or both parties to terminate the contract early in the absence of a material breach. This is sometimes referred to as a termination for convenience provision. Because the unexpected early termination of a contract can cause disruption, you should carefully consider whether to allow your vendor to have this right. For the same reason, your vendor may be reluctant to give your company that right or may insist on an early termination fee in that event because of the financial impact of any early termination. Nevertheless, if this flexibility is important to your company and you can agree with your vendor as to the monetary consequences, this is an option you can and should negotiate.

As with terminations for breach, there is the same need to plan for an appropriate notice and cure period in the termination for convenience situation. Also, you must plan for the handling, return, and use of materials and information, as is the case with terminations for breach.

Apart from terminations for convenience or for breach, you may face a transition when the contract expires of its own terms because the vendor delivered the agreed-upon products or services. Planning for this eventuality is usually less complicated because the parties have presumably negotiated the vendor's compensation for the products or services as part of the fundamental terms of the contract. However, in a situation where the contract is for a term of years and either or both parties have the option to renew the contract term or provide notice of their intent not to do so, you should include an appropriate notice period to avoid unnecessary disruption. Further, you must still plan for the handling, return, and use of proprietary materials and information.

### Planning for and Requiring Additional Aspects of Cooperation in Transitions

Beyond this, in all three types of circumstances you should consider planning and providing for additional aspects of cooperation. Some of these include, in appropriate cases, requiring your vendor to assist you with any necessary technical aspects of the transition; requiring your vendor to marshal or gather equipment, materials, and information belonging to your company that your vendor may have in its possession; and requiring your vendor to provide access to key personnel during the transition period. The overall key is to make sure that your vendor understands that it must disengage in a way that does not damage your operations.

# ▶ Trade Secrets and Other Intellectual Property

Vendors and customers will often have or gain access to the other's proprietary information and technology over the course of a relationship. The parties must of course take care to perfect their ownership rights and protect their trade secrets and other technology. Beyond simply protecting your technology, you must plan for the creation and use of intellectual property during and after the duration of the relationship. If you don't, you may find yourself hamstrung when your relationship ends.

## Plan for the Creation and Ownership of Intellectual Property

There are four main varieties of intellectual property protection that may be applicable to the information and material created in the course of an IT project or relationship: patents, copyrights, trademarks, and trade secrets. You should be aware of their potential applicability.

In general terms, patents protect the right to make or use inventions. Inventors can obtain protection for processes, manufactured articles, machines, or composition of matter, and any useful improvements thereof, provided that the invention is, among other things, useful, novel, and non-obvious. Inventors can also obtain design patents, which protect new, original, and ornamental designs for a manufactured article.

Generally, copyrights protect the right to display, copy, or show works of authorship. To be copyrightable, the work must be, among other things, original to the author and fixed in a tangible medium.

Trademarks generally protect words, phrases, symbols, or designs, or combinations thereof, that companies use to identify their products and services and/or to differentiate these products and services from those of competitors. To be eligible for trademark protection, the mark or phrase must do more than describe the product in general terms: it must also serve to identify and distinguish your company's product or service from those of your competitors.

Trade secrets are techniques, processes, skills, methods, or other know-how that give your company a competitive advantage in conducting its business. To qualify for trade secret protection, the "secret" must not be generally known outside your industry.

It is not at all uncommon for an IT procurement or outsourcing arrangement to generate protectable material or allow parties access to preexisting protectable material. Therefore, before you embark upon such a relationship, you should consider whether you and/or your vendor will be creating any materials, objects, or processes that are eligible for some kind of intellectual property protection. patent, copyright, trademark, or trade secret protection. If this is the case, you should make clear which party will own the intellectual property rights, and on what terms. I will discuss some applicable considerations in this area in the following section.

On some projects, your own employees may be participating in the creation of protectable material during the course of the relationship. In this situation, you should take care to require your employees to agree in writing that your company, and not the employee, shall ultimately own the intellectual property rights in the material. Otherwise employees may attempt to hold your company hostage when they leave or become disgruntled, and your vendor may as well.

## Match the Rights You Retain to the Commercial Situation

Not infrequently, customers engage in a tug-of-war with their vendors in precontract negotiations over ownership of the intellectual property that the vendor creates over the course of the relationship. Your options will typically be outright ownership or some kind of license to use the technology, with the vendor owning the intellectual property rights. In some situations, even though your company may retain ownership, you may decide to grant a license back to the vendor. Licenses can be for a fixed term of years or can be perpetual. They can also be exclusive or nonexclusive, revocable or irrevocable, and can vary in the nature of the use that they permit. Payment arrangements can vary as well, from one-time up-front payments to a series of payments over time.

The intellectual property ownership arrangements that are appropriate will vary from situation to situation. However, your goal in all cases should be to ensure that your company retains the control it needs over the right to use or profit from the technology in the most cost-effective way.

All other things being equal, you can expect your vendor to demand more compensation to give you ownership of intellectual property that it creates than it will for a mere license. The key factor here is the technology's suitability for use by customers other than your company. If the vendor perceives that it can make money by selling the technology to other companies, it will be reluctant to foreclose itself from that market unless you compensate it for that lost opportunity. In other situations, if your company is paying the vendor a substantial amount of money for a custom product that will have little use or applicability outside of your company, this issue may be less of a problem.

Often, you may be able to use the prospect of the potential revenue to be gained from selling the technology to other customers as a way to reduce your out-of-pocket price for the technology. As noted previously in the discussion of compensation arrangements, the vendor may be willing to reduce its fee in exchange for the right to market the product to other potential buyers, and this arrangement may also more closely align your interests with those of your vendor. However, if you seek to gain a unique competitive advantage from a customized product or service, you may be more reluctant to allow the vendor to sell or license the technology to other companies.

Regardless of what financial arrangement you choose, make sure that the intellectual property ownership structure is consistent with your company's business and technical needs. If you anticipate needing to use a product or technology for an extended period of time that will last beyond the vendor's involvement with your company, and you cannot obtain outright ownership, make sure that the license is long enough for your company's needs. Otherwise the vendor will be in a position to hold you hostage and demand higher license fees to renew the license. This is especially so if the technology will be difficult to replace without disruption to your company's core operations. On the other hand, if the technology is easily replaced, this will be less of an issue.

If you intend to incorporate the technology at issue into the products and services your company provides to its customers, make sure that you have the express contractual right to do so, either by license or by outright ownership of the technology. Similarly, if you know that you will need to make particular use of the technology in your business, or eventually modify or alter the technology, make sure that the contract specifically recites those permitted uses. You should pay particular attention to the possibility that your business may grow or change over time, and attempt to gain the broadest possible rights to use the technology in the event of mergers, acquisitions, or other reorganizations your company may undergo.

*Protecting What You Own or Create*

The procedures for perfecting and protecting your company's ownership interests in intellectual property vary depending on the particular form of property involved. To protect your rights in an invention, you must submit a patent application to the United States Patent and Trademark Office in Washington, D.C. In most cases, a patent will be effective for 20 years from the date the application is filed.

To protect your rights in an artistic or literary work, you must submit a copyright application to the Register of Copyrights in Washington, D.C. In most cases, for works created after 1975, the copyright will be effective for the duration of the author's life and an additional 70 years after the author's death.

To obtain federal protection of your rights in a trademark, you must submit a trademark application to United States Patent and Trademark Office in Washington, D.C. In connection with the application process you must demonstrate that you are using or intend to use the mark in commerce. While the federal government is the exclusive granter of patents and copyrights, the individual states allow trademark holders to register their marks and obtain state law protection. Most trademark holders view federal trademark protection as sufficient, however.

Protection of trade secrets is conceptually different because to protect trade secrets you must keep them secret. It is therefore important for the preservation of trade secret status to require your vendors and employees to restrict dissemination and disclosure of trade secrets during the course of a project to only that which is necessary. Further, except in very rare circumstances, you cannot register trade secrets as copyrightable or patentable material and maintain their status as trade secrets. It bears mention that depending on the nature of the technology, it may be more or less advisable to forgo applying for copyright or patent protection for technology that would otherwise be a trade secret, although this is a subject that is well beyond the scope of this discussion. Regardless, this is an area that you should carefully consider before engaging vendors who will create or have access to your company's trade secrets.

# Key Employees, Restrictive Covenants, and Nondisclosure Agreements

IT relationships often require your vendors and employees to interact with and to come into possession of your company's proprietary information. Unfortunately, from time to time vendors or employees may decide to use your company's information for their own benefit, or even for the purpose of competing with your company. While any attempt to misappropriate your company's information in this way will be disruptive, there are some relatively simple techniques that you can use to protect your company and minimize the harm and disruption if an attempted theft occurs. In addition, even in the absence of misappropriation or theft, you may want to control and limit the extent to which your vendor may hire and recruit key employees to avoid unnecessary disruption to your company. There are some relatively simple techniques to accomplish this as well.

## Retain Control Over Access to Your Key Employees and Proprietary Information

For various reasons, in the course of working with your company and your employees, your vendor may identify employees whom the vendor would like to hire. The vendor may be impressed with your employee's general technical ability, may view your employee's industry expertise as particularly useful, or may be interested for other reasons. Similarly, your employee may become interested in working for your vendor for numerous reasons as well.

There is nothing wrong with this in and of itself. However, from your company's perspective, it is necessary to retain control over the leeway that the vendor has to recruit and hire your employees. This is because the sudden departure of a key employee may be disruptive to your company. In addition, your employee may possess proprietary information that would harm your company in the event your employee used or disclosed the information to compete against your company.

For this reason, you should insist on including a contract provision giving your company the right to approve of or object to your vendor's hiring your current employees during the term of the contract for some reasonable period of time after the conclusion of the vendor's work for your company. You should also ensure that the provision covers indirect hiring as well, such as engaging the employee as an independent contractor or consultant or retaining the employee's services through a company that the employee or some third party operates. You do not have to withhold permission unreasonably, and often it is better business not to force an employee to continue working for your company if that employee wants to leave. However, it is more preferable to retain the express right to object to your vendor's hiring away your employee than to leave this matter to chance.

You should take similar care to include contract provisions prohibiting improper use or disclosure of your company's proprietary information. Your contract should identify the items or categories of information that your company considers proprietary and provide that the vendor shall only use proprietary information which it obtains or learns to perform its obligations under the contract. Further, the contract should require the vendor to restrict access to your company's information to only those people who need to have the information for the vendor to do its work. Your goal should be to keep the circle of outsiders who have access to your company's proprietary information as small as possible.

### Use Reasonably Tailored Restrictive Covenants to Protect Against Unfair Competition

In addition to protecting against improper use of your company's information and disruptive recruiting of your employees, you may also need to include provisions expressly preventing your vendors and employees from competing against your company for a certain period of time, in a specific geographical area, or in a certain field of commerce. This is usually because you believe your vendors or employees have gained access to proprietary information in the course of working with or for your company that they could use to compete against you. These provisions are known as restrictive covenants.

While restrictive covenants can be very useful, courts are sometimes reluctant to enforce these provisions. For public policy reasons, courts are suspicious of provisions that prevent employees from working in their chosen field and tend to construe these provisions narrowly. Also, courts do not like potential or actual competitors to agree not to compete with each other, out of concerns that consumers will suffer because of the reduced competition. For this reason, in drafting restrictive covenants you should strike a balance between providing the protection that you need, but do so in a way that is no more burdensome upon the other party than necessary.

To ensure that you protect yourself appropriately, specifically call out what you want to protect against. If you are concerned that your vendors or employees would be able to damage your company by pursuing your company's customers in a particular market segment or in a particular geographic area, then name that segment, geographic area, or customers specifically. Do not leave the matter open to interpretation.

On the other hand, be reasonable in specifying the geographic scope, temporal scope, and field of competition involved in the restrictive covenant. Courts are skeptical of restrictive covenants that are far greater in scope than the scope of your company's current geographic customer base. Courts are also reluctant to prevent competition for types of customers that appear unrelated to the kinds of customers your company is currently pursuing. Courts are also skeptical about covenants that prevent competition for an excessively long period of time, if your company's information will become less valuable as time passes. If you draft your restrictive covenants too broadly, you run the risk that a court will determine that it is wholly or partially unenforceable. Instead, you should tailor any restrictive covenants to protect against the true commercial and competitive threat.

### Put Yourself in Position to Enforce Your Rights

Often, money damages will not be a satisfactory remedy for unfair competition, improper hiring, or improper use or disclosure of your company's information. This is partly because it will sometimes be difficult or impossible to calculate the damages with precision. On other occasions money damages may never be able to undo the harm caused by unfair competition or other improper conduct. In these situations, to obtain a meaningful remedy you will need to stop improper disclosures and competition before the offending parties are able to make significant use of your information.

For these situations, your company's most meaningful remedy will often be injunctive relief. Injunctive relief means a court order that tells a party to stop doing something, or affirmatively to do so something, other than paying money. In some situations, you may need to obtain injunctive relief on an emergency basis to protect against the imminent threat that your vendor or employee will use or disclose your company's information improperly.

This relief is not easy to obtain, because courts are reluctant to issue orders against a party on an emergency basis before that party has had an opportunity to the usual pretrial discovery proceedings and a full trial on the merits of the dispute. Courts will usually require you to show that you have a clear right to relief and that your company is about to suffer immediate, irreparable harm such that your company cannot afford to wait until trial to obtain the requested relief.

Because of this heightened standard for obtaining relief, it will aid your company if you obtain your vendor's agreement in advance that certain types of improper disclosures or improper conduct will entitle your company to injunctive relief. You will still have to prove that the vendor or employee actually acted improperly, but obtaining this agreement will help remove the judge's doubts over whether the alleged improper conduct, if proven, is the sort of conduct that warrants immediate injunctive relief.

Beyond including this language in your contract where appropriate, you should demonstrate to the judge that you moved to seek injunctive relief as quickly as possible under the circumstances. Judges will be reluctant to find that an emergency exists when your own delay suggests that you did not view the situation as urgent. Therefore, you must be willing and able to devote the time and resources to apply for the relief as soon as possible when the situation arises.

# ▶ Liquidated Damages Provisions and Limitations on Liability

Your vendor may request that you agree to a provision limiting the vendor's liability for damages in the event of a breach. A vendor typically justifies this request on the grounds that its potential exposure in the event that the vendor's products or services affect your business may dwarf the amount of the vendor's fee, and that the vendor cannot afford to take that risk. You should take care in considering such a request that you do not leave your company without an adequate remedy. Also, in a situation in which it would be difficult or expensive to prove your own damages in the event of a breach, you should consider using a liquidated damages provision as an approximation of your damages.

### Ensure That You Have an Adequate Remedy in the Event of a Breach

Without a limitation on damages, typically a vendor will be liable for all reasonably foreseeable damages that result from the vendor's breach. Depending on the size of a vendor's fee and the nature of the work the vendor is performing for your company, the vendor may perceive that it is unreasonable for it to have this exposure. In many cases the vendor may have a point, and you may have to agree upon some cap or limitation on your vendor's liability in order to obtain a vendor willing to perform the work for an affordable fee.

Nevertheless, you have to strike some balance between accommodating the vendor's concerns and ensuring that your company has an adequate remedy in the event that the vendor breaches the contract and causes your company damages. The good news is that you will often be able to obtain concessions in exchange for agreeing to limit damages that may afford your company that remedy.

The place to start in negotiations is determining the potential severity of the harm that would result from a vendor's breach. Usually a vendor will agree to some out-of-pocket exposure equal to part or all of the vendor's fee. If the potential harm from a vendor breach bears some relation to the amount of the fee, then you will have an easier time providing for an adequate remedy, even with a cap on damages. Sometimes you may even be able to convince your vendor to agree to accept liability for damages in some amount in excess of its fees or in some multiple the amount of its fees, as long as this amount is capped.

You may also be able to obtain other concessions from your vendor besides an agreement to take responsibility for some out-of-pocket losses. Many vendors will agree to give a "repair or replace" remedy, either standing alone or in conjunction with some exposure for money damages. This remedy simply means that in the event of problems with the vendor's products, the vendor will repair or replace the product at its expense.

Sometimes problems may arise with the repair or replace remedy if the vendor fails to repair the defective product or replace it with a properly functioning product. After a certain point, waiting for a vendor who cannot deliver will cease to be a meaningful remedy for your company. You may therefore want to provide for the additional remedy of having the option of bringing in another vendor to repair or replace the work at the vendor's expense.

Obviously, whether all or any of these concessions are acceptable to you will vary from situation to situation. However, you must specifically consider the value of the remedy to your company in the context of the project at issue.

### Consider Carving Certain Kinds of Damages from Limitations on Liability

As is apparent from the previous discussion, I believe there are many instances in which vendor requests for limitations on their liability are commercially reasonable. However, I also believe that there are certain kinds of damages that you should usually insist be excluded from the scope of any limitation on your vendor's liability.

One key area of damages that you should carve out is damages you incur because a third party claims that it owned the intellectual property rights to the technology your vendor used or provided to you during the course of your relationship, and that you are therefore liable to the third party for infringement. You will usually not be in a position to know whether your vendor owns the intellectual property rights to the technology involved, while your vendor will know or should know whether this is the case. You should not let your vendor avoid liability for damages in this context.

Another area to consider removing from the scope of a limitation on liability is damages you may suffer from other claims asserted by third parties with whom you have contact, such as your customers or clients. Depending on the potential exposure, your vendor may be unwilling to be liable for these damages when they result from a simple failure to perform services according to the contractual standards and are more in the nature of normal consequential damages from the vendor's breach. However, there may be situations in which your vendor's employees are in direct contact with clients or customers and commit negligent, reckless, or intentional wrongful acts that cause your customers damages, for which your customers may be able to assert claims against your company. Depending on the circumstances (which will of course vary from contract to contract), your vendor may be willing to accept liability for these damages. Another potentially appropriate carve-out relates to damages or fines imposed by regulators or governmental entities that your vendor's misconduct may cause you to incur.

Damages you suffer from your vendor's intentional, illegal misconduct are another category of damages appropriately excluded from a damages limitation. Some examples of misconduct falling in this category include unfair competition, misappropriation of trade secrets, and raiding of employees subject to restrictive covenants. These acts go beyond simple failure to perform contractual obligations, and you should not agree to limit your vendor's liability for those acts.

### Use Liquidated Damages Provisions to Remove Uncertainty in Calculating Damages

Liquidated damages provisions set an artificial measure or formula for damages. These provisions make sense where it would be difficult, expensive, and/or speculative to calculate the actual damages arising from a breach. You can avoid this expense and uncertainty by using a mutually acceptable measure of liquidated damages. For example, you and your vendor could agree that the vendor will pay a specified per-diem penalty for late completion of its work, or that the vendor will pay a set penalty if your company experiences a certain level of unsatisfactory service.

Courts are usually receptive to enforcing these provisions, but you should take care to establish or at least recite in the contract that the parties believe that the measure of damages bears some reasonable approximation to the actual amount of damages arising from the breach. Further, if your vendor contests the enforceability of the liquidated damages provision, you must demonstrate that the provision is merely compensatory instead of punitive (i.e., a penalty). Reciting this fact in the liquidated damages provision will assist you in making this showing, but the fact remains that if the provision provides for damages grossly in excess of the likely actual damages, you will be at risk that a court will decline to enforce the provision.

# Dispute Resolution, Choice of Law and Choice of Forum

I've been discussing methods to avoid litigation. However, despite everyone's best efforts, disputes do arise. Parties often don't focus on the fact that they can choose the method of dispute resolution, the law that governs the dispute, and the place in which they resolve their disputes. All three of these factors can greatly impact your litigation experience. Parties who fail to plan for the impact of these three factors can experience unpleasant surprises in resolving their disputes.

### Choosing a Dispute Resolution Mechanism

The three main choices for dispute resolution are traditional "courtroom" litigation, arbitration, and mediation. With courtroom litigation, which is most familiar to the public, the parties use the public courts to resolve their disputes and submit their dispute to a judge or a jury that renders a verdict. With arbitration, the parties submit their dispute to a private decision maker who issues a decision that is binding on the parties. With mediation, the parties submit their dispute to a mediator who attempts to broker a settlement between the parties, although he or she has no authority to issue a binding decision.

You should not assume that one mechanism will be superior or inferior to the others in all cases. All three of these choices have distinct advantages and drawbacks in some important areas that vary with the individual situation.

Having a choice of the fact finder or dispute resolver is one consideration. With courtroom litigation you will usually have little or no control over your fact finder, especially if a jury trial is involved. Usually you will have a greater ability to select your fact finder with arbitration or mediation, which may make arbitration or mediation more attractive in some cases. However, you may or may not be able to find someone with specific expertise in the exact technology involved in your dispute.

Discovery rights, procedural protections, and appellate review are other important considerations. Discovery refers to the process of obtaining documents, written answers to questions, and sworn testimony from the other side before the trial or hearing. By procedural protections, I mean rules that ensure that each side has access to discovery, that each side has appropriate advance notice of the documents and evidence that the other will rely upon at trial, and that each side has a fair opportunity to participate in the dispute resolution process. Appellate review refers to the level of scrutiny that higher courts will apply to the fact finder's decision.

Courtroom litigation offers the most discovery rights, procedural protections, and appellate review, and is therefore advisable if you are concerned about obtaining information from the other side before trial, the fairness of the proceedings, and having an opportunity to appeal from a bad decision. In arbitration your discovery rights will often be limited and there will be fewer procedural protections. In addition, in most cases, unless you can prove that the arbitrator acted in collusion with your adversary or made a clear mathematical or typographical error in rendering his award, you will usually not be able to overturn an arbitrator's decision. Thus, from this perspective, arbitration can be a riskier venture than courtroom litigation. (There is typically no discovery with mediation, and because the mediator will not render a binding decision, procedural rights and appellate review are frequently non-issues.)

One potential advantage arbitration and mediation have over courtroom litigation is that arbitrations and mediations are private and courtroom litigation is typically public. Therefore, parties can use arbitration and mediation to handle potentially embarrassing disputes in private. Vendors in particular may want to use mediation and arbitration to avoid publicity over disputes with their clients. Therefore, you should consider carefully any request to submit your dispute to arbitration, because you may be relinquishing leverage by agreeing to keep your dispute out of a public courtroom.

The relative speed and expense of the dispute resolution mechanisms are two other important variables. Mediation is almost always cheaper and faster than arbitration and courtroom litigation. However, because it is a nonbinding process, you have no assurance that you will be able to resolve the dispute through mediation. Indeed, parties sometimes use mediation tactically for delay purposes or to obtain free discovery. In this sense mediation will only be as useful as the parties' willingness to resolve their dispute allows.

Many people assume that arbitration will be cheaper and faster than courtroom litigation, but this is not always the case. Especially in cases where the parties provide for significant pre-hearing discovery, arbitrations can be every bit as expensive and time consuming as courtroom litigation. Indeed, there are a number of "rocket docket" courts in various jurisdictions that will force the parties to try their cases faster than they usually would in an arbitration. On the other hand, if the parties restrict pre-hearing proceedings and provide for strict time limits for the arbitration hearing itself, it may be possible to have a quicker and cheaper proceeding with an arbitration.

You may also want to consider the impact that the dispute resolution mechanism will have on your relationship with your vendor. Mediation is usually the least disruptive procedure for your relationships. Because they are inherently adversarial in nature, both arbitration and courtroom litigation are usually very disruptive to your relationship. Parties often find it difficult to do business with each other once they have taken the arbitration or courtroom litigation process through a trial or hearing. Whether this matters to you will obviously vary from situation to situation, but you should think about this before you enter into the relationship.

## Choosing the Applicable Law

The law is different from state to state and country to country, in numerous material ways. Therefore, the parties' choice as to which law will govern in the event of a dispute has significant potential to impact the resolution of the dispute. Because you won't know in advance what disputes may arise in the course of a relationship, it is impossible to anticipate in advance whether the law of a particular jurisdiction will favor your position. In addition, on many occasions the parties will fare the same or similarly regardless of the choice of law. However, in at least several areas, it is possible to anticipate legal issues and negotiate the choice of law to achieve a particular result.

One area susceptible to planning in this regard is limitations periods. Each jurisdiction has different rules as to how long parties have to bring claims before those claims expire. You can use the choice of law provision to set the limitations period applicable to your contract.

The jurisdiction's treatment of parol evidence is another area for which planning can be appropriate. Parol evidence refers to evidence of representations and statements occurring before the parties sign the contract. As discussed previously, integration clauses can preclude parol evidence to varying degrees depending on the jurisdiction. Depending on the jurisdiction and on the language you include in your contract, it can be more or less difficult to introduce parol evidence. You may be able to pair the law of a particular jurisdiction with language that has been held by courts in that jurisdiction to severely limit the admissibility of parol evidence.

Similar considerations apply to fraudulent inducement claims, which arise when one party alleges that the other made intentionally false statements to induce them into entering into a contract. Some jurisdictions are very permissive in allowing parties to claim to bring these claims. Other jurisdictions hold that integration clauses are a complete bar to such claims.

Particular jurisdictions may take different approaches to the recoverability of damages. For example, in some jurisdictions, contract provisions limiting damages are unenforceable if you can prove that the breaching party acted dishonestly, recklessly, or with gross negligence. In other situations, jurisdictions may be more or less friendly toward claims for particular types of damages, such as punitive damages. This allows for advance planning as well.

These are some of the more common examples. However, if you know that your company has particular interests that are especially important to protect, you may be able to do some advance planning by negotiating for application of particular law in these and in other areas that will give your company the advantage or protection it needs.

### Choosing the Forum

You and your vendor are free to choose a jurisdiction as the exclusive place where you and your vendor may bring a claim. This is an important point to consider, because the location where you resolve your dispute can impact your litigation experience in many ways.

As an initial matter, you should consider the effect litigating a dispute in a particular location will have on the cost or difficulty of transporting lawyers, witnesses, documents, or other evidence to the courtroom. These kinds of expenses and difficulties can make litigating small disputes cost prohibitive or impractical for the disadvantaged party.

Beyond this, the choice of forum can make it more difficult to use your counsel of choice, especially if your lawyer is not admitted in a particular jurisdiction. Also, rules of procedure differ from location to location, as do the practices of individual judges. Given a choice lawyers, will always prefer working with familiar rules and judges.

Depending on the nature of the dispute, your company may or may not want to litigate the dispute in its home county or state. For example, if your company is a well regarded corporate citizen and a significant local employer, you may perceive an advantage in having a jury composed of people from your company's home county, or in having a local judge decide the case. If you believe that a jury from your vendor's home county would perceive your company as an unwelcome outsider, this is another reason to negotiate for the right to litigate in your back yard.

It is important to keep in mind that there is no requirement to agree upon a particular forum as the exclusive forum for bringing a claim. If you do not reach agreement on this issue, the parties are free to attempt to bring suit wherever they like, although you may or may not be able to force your vendor to litigate in a faraway forum if the vendor has had little or no contacts with the forum. In this sense, failing to agree on a forum constitutes a choice to a certain degree. The point is that you should carefully consider this issue, regardless of whether you reach agreement on a particular location.

## ▸ Conclusion

I sincerely hope that you will find the preceding discussion to be a useful reference when you approach your next project. I will leave you with six admonitions that I believe sum up the discussion and detail on the various particular points:

1. Each project or relationship requires individualized consideration, planning, and management.

2. You should employ an interdisciplinary team for contract drafting.

3. Put in the effort on the front end to avoid costly problems on the back end.

4. Being right isn't always enough if you haven't been clear.

5. Address problems sooner rather than later to keep them small.

6. Finally, be prompt and straightforward in your communications with your contractual partner.

If you remember and apply these admonitions in connection with your next project, I believe you will have a much greater chance of success. Good luck, and happy contracting.

# Index

## A

abundance, 252
access cards, and security, 54
access control, 56, 58–60
    card-access badge, standard
      technologies of, 58
    smart cards, 58–59
      biometrics with, 59
    software, 59–60
    testing of, 62
actionable intelligence, 147
activity-based costing (ABC), and
    software ROI, 169–170
adaptivity, 259
additive increase, 80
advertising, importance, 33
Agarwal, A., 222
Alexander, K., 129, 133

Allen, T., 223
Alliance Consulting, 95, 100
Ambler, S. W., 269
American Productivity and Quality
    Center (APQC), 180
Ang, S., 212
ANSI X12, 111
Apache, 271
appellate review, 395–396
application-level integration,
    110–111
application programming interface
    (API)–level integration, 110–111
approved portfolio, 22–25
arbitration, 395–397
Asia, 252
auditors, and IT governance, 284
auto-ID technology, 133–134
automation, 184, 252

401

# c

data and integration platform,
102–104

data management process focus,
104

executive sponsorship with
proactive leadership, 102

critical thinking, 16

Crocker, R., 222, 223

cultural changes, 16

current process maps, 195, 200

customer delivery, improving,
324–327

CxO, use of term, 13

# D

Daconta, M. C., 113, 123

DaimlerChrysler, 273

data gathering panel, 59

data marts, 147

data structure evolution, 95

data warehousing, 92–93, 96, 112,
145

database federating, 109–110

database technologies, 98

database-to-database integration,
109

data-level integration, 109–110

DCOM, *See* Distributed Component
Object Model (DCOM)

decreasing risk, 352

deming system, 308

denormalization, 95

Denver, Colorado, 3-1-1 CRM initiative, 335–337

destination, 19–20

development tools, Open Source,
276–277

digital sign, 62

disaster planning and recovery,
378–381

physical and technical redundancy and security, considering,
379

rights and responsibilities in a
disaster, establishing, 380

source code and intellectual
property escrows, considering,
380–381

discounted payback, and software
ROI, 175

discovery rights, 395–396

dispute resolution, 395–399

Distributed Component Object
Model (DCOM), 115–116, 125

distributed development, 223

distributed environment, team building in, 222–223

DMAIC framework, Six Sigma,
200–202

*Does IT Matter?* (Carr), 10

Dortch, Michael, 342

dotcom crash, xx

by-products of, 252

Dunn, D., 255

# E

EAN International, 133

earned value analysis (EVA), and
software ROI, 171–172

Eastern Technology Council, 36
CTO of, 44
Enterprise Awards, 42
*Technology Times* (newspaper),
36

Ebert, C., 222, 223
ebXML, 113–114, 123, 125
EDI (electronic data interchange), 111–112, 125
EDIFACT, 111
eDiplomacy model, 185–186
EFQM, 308
E-government, 321–340
  communications and outreach, 337–340
  customer delivery, improving, 324–327
  defined, 322–323
  governance, 330–334
  government co, reducing, 329–330
  Hampton, Virginia's model of 3-1-1, 334
  holistic approach to, 323
  key outcomes, 323
  organizational productivity, improving, 327–328
  strategic goals and objectives, 324–325
  technology, 334–337
Einstein, Albert, 233
electronic data interchange, *See* EDI (electronic data interchange)
Electronic Product Code (EPC), 133
End User License Agreement (EULA), 279
e-newsletter, CIO Institute, 40
Enron Corporation, 15
enterprise application integration (EAI), 149
enterprise architecture, 262–263
enterprise data models, evolution of, 96–97
enterprise information architecture, 233–247
  approaches, 242–243

business analysts, 243
  data perspective, 243
  methodologist, 242–243
complex initiatives, 244–245
defined, 234
getting started with EIA efforts, 240–241, 245–247
goals/purpose of, 235, 238–239
implementation, 241–242
incremental business-driven delivery, 242
nomenclature, 235
tradeoffs, 242–243
typical triggers for EIA projects, 239–240
vertical versus horizontal views, 237–238
enterprise information architecture (EIA), xxvi, 25
enterprise information systems (EIS), 118
enterprise integration, 107–126
  and agility, 108
  application-level integration, 110–111
  business processes integration, emerging technologies for, 119–124
  and complexity, 108
  data-level integration, 109–110
  defined, 107
  and diversity, 108
  enabling technologies, 111–119
    component-based computing technologies, 115–116
    data warehousing, 112
    EDI (electronic data interchange), 111–112
    Java Connector Architecture (JCA), 118–119

## J

## K

Nicholsen, B., 219
nondisclosure agreements, 388, 391
Norton, D. P., 287
Novell, 273, 299–300
Nowak, Paul, xxii, xl, 53

# O

OASIS, 114
object-level integration, 110
object naming service (ONS), 134
Obrst, L. J., 113, 123
O'Connell, Brian, 349
Office of eDiplomacy, 185–189
offshore development, 223
online analytical processing (OLAP)
   database, 112
online transaction processing
   (OLTP), 112
ontology tools, 94
Open Office, 278
Open Source, xxvii, 271–282
   applications and the desktop,
      277–278
   cultural implications, 280–281
   defined, 274
   development tools, 276–277
   dilution of resource effort, 276
   information in U.S.-based peri-
      odicals relating to, 273–274
   Initiative site, 280
   licensing, 279–280
   market acceptance, 277
   methodology, 274–275
   motivation/justification,
      272–273
   post-installation, 275–276
operational risk, 351
organization

and the chief information officer
   (CIO), 14–16
security issues, 54–55
outsourced environments, 221–231
outsourcing, 16, 17–18
   best practices/rules of thumb,
      219
   business process outsourcing,
      212–213
   challenges of, 222–223
   choosing the phase of the project
      to outsource, 224–225
   classic examples of, 212
   collaborating teams, control-
      ling/coordinating the work of,
      222
   computer security, 212–213
   contracts, error of, 18
   core competency, 228–229
   cost of, 214
   and cost reduction, 222, 224
   defined, 212–213
   ERP systems, 216
   of IT functions, 211–220
   legal organization of the poten-
      tial vendor, 215
   managing outsourced projects,
      223–227
      monitoring and control,
         227–228
      organizing, 226–227
      planning for, 224–226
   methodologies for, 218–219
   need for, 218
   overseas, 214–215
   purpose of, 213
   software development, 221
   suitable projects for, 224
   suppliers, 224
      performance of, 228

and transfer of business knowledge, 214–215
where to use, 215–216

# P

packaged software reliability, 260
Packet Internet Groper, *See* PING
packet loss, 73, 85
patents, 384–385
path diversity, 76–77
payback, and software ROI,
174–175
Payton, M., 227
Pearlson, K. E., 2, 3
people perspective, business process,
196
performance, defined, 285, 292
periodic review, 378
Perks, C., 259
personnel succession, planning for,
160
Peters, T., 251
Petri, C., 120, 122
Peuser, S., 122, 123, 124
Pham, H., 142
Philadelphia Information Technology Exposition & Conference
(ITEC) show, 42
Phoenix, 277
photoelectric detector, 61
physical security, 62
Pieper, M., 313
piggy-back rules, for access, 62
pilots, 191
PING, 73–75
Pink, Daniel, 252
platform and process maturity, 101
platform transparency, 115

PMBOK, 314
Powell, Colin, 185
problem solving, 16
procedural protections, 395–396
process maps, 195
product debates, 49–50
product-tracking technologies,
132–133
profitability index (PI), 166
and software ROI, 174
project level, involving users at,
190–191
project management office (PMO),
22
project planner, chief information
officer (CIO) as, 6
Project Portfolio, 262–263
Pultorak, David, xxviii, xl, 283,
288, 290, 306
push technologies, 98–99
pyramid of needs, 23–24

# Q

Qiu, Robin G., xxiii, xli, 107, 127,
132, 136, 137, 138, 140, 141
quantified parameters, 197–198

# R

radio frequency identification
(RFID) technology, xxiii, 127,
254
global identification codes
(GIC), 138–139
inventory-tracking and warehouse management solution,
129

just-in-time information retrieval
(JITIR), 139–140
real-time visibility of product
movement on supply chains,
135–141
responsive information server,
design for, 141
RFID transponder or tag, 133,
136–137
and semiconductor technologies,
133
toward collaborative supply
chains using, 127–144
user least-effort system, design
for, 139–140
Raffo, D., 169
Rahlff,, 135
Rajagopalan , S., 226
Rao, H., 226
Rappold, J., 128, 130, 131, 142
Rauscher, Karl, 76
Raymond, Eric, 274
real-time, mission-critical business
intelligence, 145–162
architectures, 147–148
collaboration, 157–158
correlation, 154–155
definitions, 146–147
definitive conclusions, 156–157
events and event management,
152–153
failsafe functionality replication,
158–159
hypothesis formulation, 153–154
interdiction, 155–156
key principles, 152–159
outbound information flows,
158
personnel succession, planning
for, 160

well-defined roles and responsibilities, 159–160
recoverability of damages, and jurisdictions, 398
RedHat, 271
*Reengineering the Corporation*
(Hammer/Champy), 184
Register of Copyrights, 387
regulators, compliance, 343–344
Reifer, D., 227, 228
relating responsibly, 290
defined, 285, 292
reliability, 76
Remote Method Invocation (RMI),
115–116
Repenning, A., 222, 227
reporting relationships, chief information officer (CIO), 7
reputational risk, 351
resource manager, chief information
officer (CIO) as, 6
resourcing plan, 25
responsive information server, design
for, 141
restrictive covenants, 389–390
return on investment (ROI), formula
for, 166
RFID transponder or tag, 133,
136–137
Rhodes, B., 137, 139
Richman, Joel, Jr., xxii, xxxiii, xli, 53
Rindlaub, J., 269
risk analysis, 25–26
risk, controlling, 289
risk management, compliance,
350–352
Rolfsen, R., 135
Rombach, D., 212, 226
Roschelle, J., 227
RosettaNet, 114

Ross, J. W., 269, 287, 288, 308, 309, 312
roundtables, CIO Institute, 38–39, 41–42
Royce, W., 225
rules-based jobs, 254

# S

Sahay, S., 219
Salesforce.com, 253
Sangwan, Raghvinder S., xxiii, xxvi, xli–xlii, 107, 127, 221
Sarbanes-Oxley, xviii, 13, 15–16, 96, 163, 284, 342, 348, 355
Sarma, S., 129
Schmandt, C., 135
Schmelzer, R., 269
Schneier, B., 212
Schultz, M., 129, 133
scoping documents/statements of work, 361–364
search technologies, and unstructured data, 95
security, 53–63
    access control, 56, 58–60
    building controls, 56, 61–62
    closed-circuit television (CCTV), 56–57
    convergence of IT and, 55
    data gathering panel, 59
    digital sign, 62
    fire alarm, 56, 60–61
    hardware, 55–61
    heating, venting, and air conditioning (HVAC), 56, 61–62
    implementation, 63
    incipient fire detection (IFD) device, 61
    ionization detector, 61
    network, 53
    organizational issues, 54–55
    photoelectric detector, 61
    physical security, 62
    procedures and policies, 62–63
    resolution, 63
    security systems
        complexity, 55
        installation, 54–55
    software, 55–61
    sprinkler systems, 61
self-service kiosks, 322
self-service "pull" models, 98
senior user group, formation of, 189–190
Service Level Management (SLM) process, 302–304
    integrating corporate governance and, 304–305
service management professionals, and IT governance, 284
Service Oriented Architectures (SOAs), 253, 260–265
service-level agreements (SLAs), 75, 304
service-level management pyramid, 303
service-oriented integration, 120–124
Settle, J., 169
Sharan, V., 269
signage messaging, 62
Silicon Valley's CIO group, 35
Simon, Alan R., xxiv, xlii, 145
Simons, M., 222, 226
Singh, Pawan, xlii, 211
SIPOC diagram, 200
Six Sigma, xxv, xxviii, 166, 197–199, 308

Traver, C. G., 111, 112
Turnlund, M., 226

# U

UML-based modeling tool, 226
Unger, Diane, 273
Uniform Code Council, 133
United States Department of State, paradigm shift at, 185–187
United States Patent and Trademark Office, 387
Universal Description, Discovery and Integration (UDDI), 122–123, 260
Universal Product Code (UPC), 132–134
unstructured data
    latency, 94
    structured data vs., 92–94
USA Patriot Act, 348
user focus groups, 190–191
user least-effort system, design for, 139–140
users, expectations, 191–192

# V

value chain, information management, 91–92
Van Bon, J., 313
Van der Veen, A., 313
Van Grembergen, W., 319
Varon, E., 265
vehicle identification number (VIN), 132
vendor misconduct, 394
Verizon, 273–274

"Voice of the Customer" (VOC), 199–200

# W

Wal-Mart, 244–245, 254, 258
warranties, 364–367
Waters, R., 255
Web Service Description Language (WSDL), 122–123
Web services, 120–124, 253, 260
    coarse granularity, 124
    components enabling, 122
    defined, 121–122
    features offered by, 124–125
    infrastructure, 124
    loose coupling, 124
    self-describing, 124
    standards, 124–125
Web Services Architecture (WSA), 123–124
Web Services Inspection Language (WSIL), 122
WebSphere MQ, 116
Weill, P., 269, 287, 288, 308, 309, 312
Weiss, D., 228
Welch, Jack, 198
Wells, H. G., 233
Wenger, Etienne, 47–49
West, K., 270
Weston, H., 319
Whole New Mind, A: Moving from the Information Age to the Conceptual Age (Pink), 252
WiFi, 253
WiMax, 253
Wollman, John, xxiii, xliv, 89, 258
Woods, D., 270

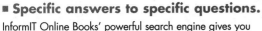

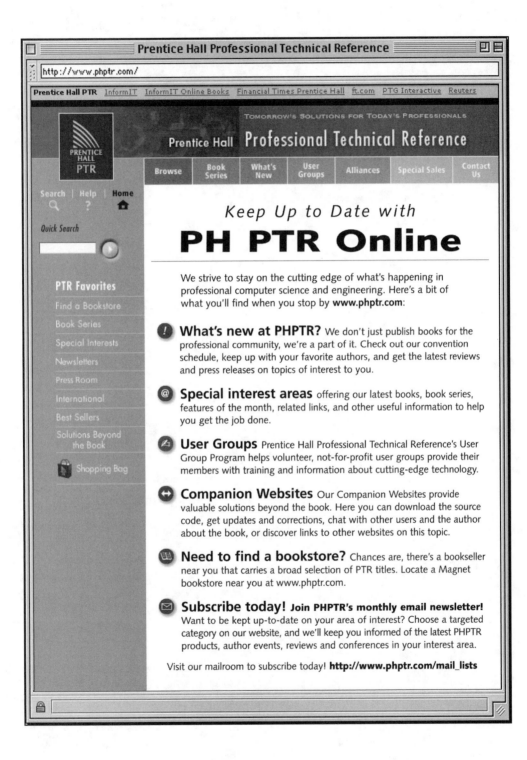